Economic Commission for Europe

Geneva

ECONOMIC SURVEY
OF EUROPE

1999 No. 1

DÉPÔT
DEPOSIT

Prepared by the

SECRETARIAT OF THE

ECONOMIC COMMISSION FOR EUROPE

GENEVA

UNITED NATIONS
New York and Geneva, 1999

NOTE

The designations employed and the presentation of the material in this publication do not imply the expression of any opinion whatsoever on the part of the Secretariat of the United Nations concerning the legal status of any country, territory, city or area, or of its authorities, or concerning the delimitation of its frontiers or boundaries.

Any data provided under the heading "Yugoslavia" relate to the Federal Republic of Yugoslavia which, in accordance with General Assembly Resolutions 47/1 and 47/229, cannot continue automatically the membership of the former Socialist Federal Republic of Yugoslavia.

UNITED NATIONS PUBLICATION
Sales No. E.99.II.E.2
ISBN 92-1-116703-5   ISSN 0070-8712

Copyright © United Nations, 1999
All rights reserved
Printed at United Nations, Geneva (Switzerland)

CONTENTS

CORRIGENDUM
Economic Survey of Europe, 1998 No. 3
page 46, table 2.3.3,
for January-September *read* January-June

LIST OF TABLES

LIST OF CHARTS

LIST OF BOXES

EXPLANATORY NOTES

The following symbols have been used throughout this *Survey*:

     .. = not available or not pertinent

     – = nil or negligible

     * = estimate by the secretariat of the Economic Commission for Europe

     | = break in series

In referring to a combination of years, the use of an oblique stroke (e.g. 1997/98) signifies a 12-month period (say, from 1 July 1997 to 30 June 1998). The use of a hyphen (e.g. 1995-1997) normally signifies either an average of, or a total for, the full period of calendar years covered (including the end-years indicated).

Unless the contrary is stated, the standard unit of weight used throughout is the metric ton. The definition of "billion" used throughout is a thousand million. The definition of "trillion" used throughout is a thousand billion. Minor discrepancies in totals and percentages are due to rounding.

References to dollars ($) are to United States dollars unless otherwise specified.

The membership of the United Nations Economic Commission for Europe (UN/ECE) consists of all the states of western Europe, eastern Europe and the territory of the former Soviet Union, North America and Israel.

The term *transition economies*, as used in the text and tables of this publication, refers to the formerly centrally planned economies of the ECE regions. *Eastern Europe* refers to the economies of Albania, Bosnia and Herzegovina, Bulgaria, Croatia, the Czech Republic, Hungary, Poland, Romania, Slovakia, Slovenia, The former Yugoslav Republic of Macedonia and Yugoslavia. The *Baltic states* refers to Estonia, Latvia and Lithuania and the *CIS countries* refers to Armenia, Azerbaijan, Belarus, Georgia, Kazakhstan, Kyrgyzstan, Republic of Moldova, Russian Federation, Tajikistan, Turkmenistan, Ukraine and Uzbekistan.

ABBREVIATIONS

BAFTA	Baltic Free Trade Agreement
BBC	British Broadcasting Corporation
BIS	Bank for International Settlements
CCFF	Compensatory and Contingency Financing Facility (of IMF)
CEFTA	Central European Free Trade Agreement
CETE	central European transition economies
c.i.f.	cost, insurance and freight
CIS	Commonwealth of Independent States
CMEA	Council for Mutual Economic Assistance
CPI	consumer price index
EBRD	European Bank for Reconstruction and Development
ECB	European Central Bank
ECU	European currency unit
EFF	Extended Fund Facility (of IMF)
EFTA	European Free Trade Association
EMS	European Monetary System
EMU	economic and monetary union
ERM	exchange rate mechanism
ESCB	European System of Central Banks
EU	European Union
EURIBOR	Euro Interbank Offered Rate
FDI	foreign direct investment
FOMC	Federal Open Market Committee (of the Federal Reserve Board)
G-3	Group of Three
G-7	Group of Seven
GDP	gross domestic product
GDR	German Democratic Republic
HICP	Harmonized Index of Consumer Prices
HWWA	Hamburg Institute for Economic Research

IFI	international financial institution
IIF	Institute of International Finance, Inc.
ILO	International Labour Office
IMF	International Monetary Fund
IPO	initial public offering
ITIC	International Trust and Investment Corporation
LFS	labour force survey
LIBOR	London Interbank Offered Rate
NACE	Nomenclature générale des activités économiques dans les Communautés européennes (General Industrial Classification of Economic Activities within the European Communities)
NAIRU	non-accelerating inflation rate of unemployment
NBER	National Bureau of Economic Research, Inc.
NIEs	newly industrializing economies
NMP	net material product
OECD	Organisation for Economic Co-operation and Development
OPEC	Organization of the Petroleum Exporting Countries
OPT	outward processing trade
PPI	producer price index
SDR	special drawing right
SETE	south European transition economies
SITC	Standard International Trade Classification
TFR	total fertility rate
UNCTAD	United Nations Conference on Trade and Development
UN/ECE	United Nations Economic Commission for Europe
USSR	Union of Soviet Socialist Republics
VAT	value added tax
WTO	World Trade Organization

PREFACE

The present *Survey* is the fifty-second in a series of annual reports prepared by the secretariat of the United Nations Economic Commission for Europe to serve the needs of the Commission and of the United Nations in reporting on and analysing world economic conditions.

Until 1997 the *Economic Survey of Europe* was issued once a year as was the *Economic Bulletin for Europe*, the secretariat's second publication which focused on trade and payments issues. At its 52nd Session, in April 1997, the Commission decided to replace these two publications with an annual *Survey* of three issues, starting in 1998. The issues will appear in April, July and November, respectively.

The Survey will continue to be published on the sole responsibility of the Executive Secretary of ECE and the views expressed in it should not be attributed to the Commission or to its participating governments.

The analysis in this issue is based on data and information available to the secretariat in mid-March 1999.

Economic Analysis Division
United Nations Economic Commission for Europe
Geneva

CHAPTER 1

OVERVIEW AND SELECTED POLICY ISSUES

1.1 The current economic situation in the ECE region

The crisis that hit the world economy in 1997 with the devaluation of the Thai baht persisted through 1998 with powerful boosts from the Russian devaluation and debt moratorium in August and the Brazilian crisis in the second half of 1998. Although the particular circumstances of each incident are different they have been linked by financial contagion and its subsequent effects on real activity and international trade. In early 1999 the crisis is by no means over: despite a large emergency support package from the IMF, Brazil was forced to let its currency float and, by the end of February, it had depreciated by about 40 per cent against the dollar, which in turn is likely to have ripple effects on other countries in the region. The collapse in commodity prices, especially of crude oil, is creating serious stability problems for oil producers, not least in the Middle East, and there is still much uncertainty over the economic outlook in China and the possible implications this might have for policy in that country, especially with regard to the exchange rate.

Although its weight in the world economy is relatively small, Russia's currency and debt crisis last August had a much greater destabilizing effect on the international financial markets than the Asian crisis of 1997 and its repercussions for other countries in the ECE region, especially the transition economies, were generally more serious. Some of the financial effects – such as the drop in stock market prices, including in some of the central European economies – were due to portfolio adjustments as investors liquidated positions in healthier markets to offset their losses in Russia. But the key element was a fundamental re-assessment by investors of the risks and attractiveness of investing in emerging market economies. Much of the foreign investment in Russia had entered when an IMF supported programme was being followed and no doubt investors assumed that if anything went wrong any losses would be avoided with the help of a bail-out organized by the IMF, as was the case in South-East Asia. That assumption was proved false in the Russian case and consequently there were considerable fears in September-October of a global recession being triggered by the falls in stock prices and the threat of a "credit crunch" as credit conditions were tightened significantly, not only for borrowers in emerging markets but also in developed market economies such as the United States where the spreads over United States Treasury Bills for corporate borrowing rose significantly. There were also large fluctuations in the value of the dollar against the European currencies, especially when there were exaggerated fears for a short while for the stability of the German banking sector because of its exposure to Russian borrowers. These tensions were eased by the series of cuts in United States interest rates between the end of September and mid-November, and by the coordinated cut in interest rates in early December by the 11 future members of the EMU. Stock prices have recovered, especially in the United States, from their levels of last autumn and a measure of calm has returned to the financial markets. But this may well be deceptive. The financial turbulence of the last 18 months or so has plunged large areas of the developing world into recession and the deflationary consequences for trade in goods and services, and investment income, has led to a steady lowering of growth forecasts for 1999 both in western Europe, where the steady deterioration in net export growth has not been offset by stronger domestic demand, and in many of the transition economies, where the slowdown in the growth of import demand in western Europe, together with the increased costs of international borrowing (for those who still have access to it), imply a tighter balance of payments constraint on their growth rates in 1999.

Throughout 1998 the adjustments to the crisis continued to be supported by strong growth in the United States where GDP grew by just under 4 per cent for the second year running. This was underpinned by the continued willingness of United States consumers to spend virtually all their disposable income and by the buoyancy of business investment especially in information technology. But it becomes increasingly uncertain as to how long this benign process can continue. Although inflation has not picked up, one consequence of the consumer boom is a record trade deficit which is increasing rapidly and depends on the willingness of foreign investors to continue financing it. In the short run this may not be a problem since the increased aversion to risk means that for investors there are few other safe havens capable of providing liquid assets on a large enough scale – but this cannot last indefinitely if the deficit continues to widen. Similarly, private expenditure has been supported by the fall in oil prices, equivalent to a large tax cut[1] and which is unlikely

---

[1] One estimate is that the fall in oil prices by over one third between the fourth quarters of 1997 and 1998 added a full percentage point to the increase in consumer spending. WEFA, *US Financial Markets Outlook*, 11 January 1999.

to be repeated in 1999, and by very high levels of borrowing against stock market gains. The growth in the latter cannot continue indefinitely and when the correction eventually comes there is likely to be a swift return to positive savings rates. The question is not whether this will occur but when and whether the adjustment will be mild or impose a sharp shock on the economy. In fact, the projected further widening of the United States current account deficit to quite a high level in 1999 requires, in principle, a change in domestic policies to bring about an increase in net exports. This will have to rely on both a reduction in domestic absorption and a depreciation of the dollar. Given the tight labour market, a weakening of the dollar alone would lead to mounting inflationary pressures. The ensuing tightening of monetary policy would then risk pushing the economy into recession (the "hard landing" scenario). The extent of domestic policy and exchange rate changes, however, will depend on the strength of domestic demand in Asia and western Europe. Given the well-known problems in Japan and the Asian emerging economies, this explains why the United States authorities are keen to see a faster rate of growth in western Europe.

Like the United States, western Europe initially benefited from the hardship suffered by the rest of the world: the large fall in the prices of commodities and, to a lesser extent of a range of Asian manufactured goods, led to a substantial improvement in their terms of trade which, in turn, kept down the already small rates of increase in consumer prices and boosted real disposable income. In addition, the "flight to quality" in the financial markets made it easier to reduce interest rates in a number of countries. However, in sharp contrast to the United States, growth in western Europe was well under 3 per cent in 1998 and was slowing down throughout the year, particularly in the third and fourth quarters. The failure of domestic demand to offset the weakening of net exports largely reflects the tighter stance of macroeconomic policies over the last few years. Fiscal policy was for the most part broadly neutral in 1998, but this follows two years of severe fiscal retrenchment in the run-up to the introduction of the euro and the present stance of policy makes no allowance for the weakening cyclical position in the region. Moreover, the rules of the Stability and Growth Pact for EMU members leave virtually no room for fiscal manoeuvre should the cyclical slowdown become more severe. In order to prepare for a fiscal response to a future downturn in the next millennium, the authorities appear to be prepared to tighten fiscal policy to reduce structural budget deficits during a possible slowdown now. Monetary policy also appears to be too tight in the euro area: although nominal interest rates are at historically low levels, real rates are still relatively high. A cut in interest rates and a postponement of the target dates for reducing structural budget deficits would improve the prospects for economic growth in western Europe. If this is achieved progress in reducing the budget deficits would be greatly eased, as the United States experience has shown, and it

would also strengthen investment and lower unemployment. The unemployment rate averaged 10.9 per cent in the euro area last year and was starting to rise again towards the end of the year. The situation is especially worrying in Germany where economic growth slowed sharply in the second half of last year and where the unemployment rate was 9.1 per cent in January 1999. Given the importance of the German economy both for western Europe as a whole and for many central European economies, the concerns of the German authorities about the current stance of economic policies should be seen as a European, not simply a national issue. Expectations for growth in western Europe in 1999 were still being lowered in the closing months of last year and the average forecast has now slipped below 2 per cent. On past experience, this implies no further reductions in unemployment and in all likelihood it will start to rise again.

The global economic crisis and the associated financial instability have begun to have a severe impact on the transition economies. At first, the principal direct effect of the Asian crisis was on the primary commodity producers of the Commonwealth of Independent States (CIS) and notably on Russia where the falling oil price has had a significant impact on export earnings and contributed to the crisis last August. For most of eastern Europe the direct impact was small because their predominant trade links are with western Europe. But the subsequent collapse of Russian imports was nevertheless significant for a number of east European exporters in 1998, and especially for the Baltic states which still have relatively large trade shares with Russia. With the weakening of west European import demand in the course of the year, there has been a rapid deterioration in the economic performance of the transition economies since the Russian crisis of last summer, a process which appears to have accelerated in the closing months of 1998 and in early 1999. The financial contagion from the Asian and Russian crises was relatively limited, even for the few countries which are relatively more integrated with the international financial markets but the real threat, as was pointed out in this *Survey* last year, lay in the real economy and the possibility of a sharper than expected slowdown in western Europe. Unfortunately this is what has occurred and the highly export-dependent economies of central and eastern Europe are being subject to a severe external demand shock.

The slowdown in economic growth in 1998 occurred in virtually all the east European and Baltic economies and, generally, was more severe than was expected earlier in the year. (Hungary is the principal exception, so far, to the general recessionary trend.) Instead of improving on the relatively weak performance in 1997, GDP in eastern Europe rose on average by just 2 per cent, less than half the rate implied by the official forecasts and nearly a percentage point lower than in 1997. The Baltic economies did rather better for the year as a whole (just over 4 per cent) but the deceleration from the 1997 rate was considerable.

For the leading reform economies and the Baltic states the relatively strong growth of the last few years was broken in mid-1998, largely by the deterioration in external conditions; but weak domestic factors also played a role, especially in south eastern Europe. Some slowdown had been expected in some of the faster growing countries because of measures taken to check a too rapid growth of consumer spending and rising current account deficits, but the deceleration was much more than anticipated. The full extent of the slowdown is still not fully reflected in the statistics, partly because many of the data are not yet available and partly because of lags, for example, between the inflow of export orders and actual deliveries. But the industrial production figures point to a rapid deceleration through the year, from a year-on-year average growth in eastern Europe of just over 6 per cent in the first quarter to 1.4 per cent for the year as a whole. These aggregate figures conceal a wide variation in national economic performance but, broadly speaking, in most of the faster-reforming and faster-growing economies of central Europe and the Baltic states the growth rates of industrial production have fallen considerably, while in south eastern Europe the recession in industry worsened in the second half of the year.

The deterioration in economic performance is also reflected in the labour markets where the modest improvements in the levels of employment slowed down or were reversed in most of the transition economies during 1998 and unemployment rates rose sharply from mid-year. In December the unemployment rate averaged 12.6 per cent in eastern Europe, up from 11.6 per cent in June; in the Baltic states it ended the year at 7.3 per cent, a full percentage point higher than 12 months earlier. Unemployment has also continued to rise sharply in January and February 1999, although this partly reflects the seasonal effects of a hard winter.

In the CIS, the picture is also one of sharply deteriorating economic performance. Particularly hard-hit by both the Asian and Russian crises, output has fallen (or at best growth has been severely weakened) and the slender gains of 1997 more than offset.

One of the crucial elements in the situation now facing the transition economies is the deterioration in their current accounts, all of which are in deficit. These deficits averaged about 4.5 per cent of GDP in eastern Europe in 1998 but the range was considerable from 1.5 per cent in the Czech Republic, which is now in a deepening recession, to some 7 per cent in Croatia and Romania and to around 11 per cent in Slovakia; in the Baltic states the proportions range from nearly 10 to 13 per cent. The majority of these deficits were deteriorating throughout the year and towards the end of 1998 most of them were much larger than even the more pessimistic forecasts made at the start of the year. For most of the east European and Baltic economies imports were still rising faster than exports last year and given the deterioration in their export prospects, the question arises as to how long the present deficits can be sustained.

The more rapidly growing economies of the last few years – Croatia, Hungary, Poland and Slovakia, for example – have all had large increases in their current account deficits, underlining the dependence of the transformation process on imports and foreign borrowing. But this import-dependent growth could be increasingly constrained in 1999 by at least three factors: the risk of a tightening of policy in some of the transition economies, shortfalls in capital inflows and the increased cost of foreign borrowing, and the slowdown in west European growth. The official forecasts for the transition economies (table 3.1.1 below) still point to an average rate of growth of just under 3 per cent in eastern Europe in 1999 and some 4.5 per cent in the Baltic states. But these are now looking very optimistic and it is increasingly likely that the actual outcomes will be much lower.[2] In the CIS, a fall in the average level of output appears unavoidable, but how large it will be is greatly dependent on what happens in Russia.

Given the sharp slowdown that now appears to be underway, this is not the moment to tighten fiscal policy in the transition economies, although the discussions in some of them suggest that this may be the intention. Such action, combined with an external demand shock, would intensify the downturn and ultimately be self-defeating by creating larger rather than smaller budget deficits. If anything, there is room for a loosening of monetary policy, as in a number of countries real interest rates rose sharply last year and were one of the domestic factors that contributed to the slowdown.

A faster rate of growth (and of import demand) in western Europe is highly desirable as the best way of supporting growth in the transition economies and also heading off the increasing pressures for protection from eastern imports, pressures which have already led to anti-dumping actions being started for a number of products. Western Europe is not only running a large current account surplus with the world but also with the transition economies. In the first nine months of 1998 the EU alone had a trade surplus of about $16.5 billion in its trade with eastern Europe and the Baltic states. If a faster growth rate in the EU cannot be achieved, ways should be found of recycling part of the EU current account surplus to the transition economies, especially to those which face increasing difficulties in raising funds on the international capital markets. This could involve official transfers or loans, but however it is implemented, the key point is to recognize that the west European current account surplus is having a deflationary impact on the countries of eastern Europe and the Baltic states. If the EU, as the major economic power in the region, acts with a broader sense of responsibility towards all the countries in the area, such measures would not only help to sustain growth and structural change in the transition economies but they would also provide positive feed-back to the EU

_____

[2]   The possible effects of the armed conflict in Kosovo are, of course, not reflected in this assessment of the outlook in 1999.

itself: in 1998 eastern Europe and the Baltic states imported about $100 billion worth of goods from the EU – that would seem to be large enough to be worth preserving and expanding.

1.2 Strong policies and weak foundations

Apart from their deleterious effects on the world's economies, the Asian and Russian crises have led to increased questioning of the economic policies which have been pursued for the last two decades or so, principally under the aegis of the G-7 leading market economies and the Bretton Woods Institutions. What became known as the "Washington Consensus" was a set of policies that were developed in response to the inflation crises in the developed market economies in the 1970s and 1980s and to the Latin American debt crisis in the 1980s. The "consensus" comprised two major elements, one concentrating on macroeconomic stability and the other on so-called supply-side reforms which would underpin both macro-stability and create the basis for spontaneous and sustained economic growth. Macroeconomic stability, reflecting the experience noted above, focused essentially on lowering inflation and then pre-empting any further outbreak with strict and attentive monetary policies. At the same time not only were general government budget deficits to be lowered in order to support the objectives of monetary policy but the level of government spending was also to be reduced as much as possible, the assumption being that the smaller the role of the state, whether in the actual production of goods and services or in its attempts to intervene in the workings of the economy, the better would be the economic performance of the private sector and of the economy as a whole. The programme of supply-side policies followed from the latter point: product and factor markets should be deregulated as far as possible, state owned assets and supply of services should be privatized, and international trade and capital markets liberalized. More recently, a proposal to change the IMF's Articles of Agreement to include capital account convertibility as an ultimate objective for all members was made by the Fund's Interim Committee in September 1997 – this would enable the Fund to insist on a country liberalizing its capital account as one of the conditions for receiving IMF assistance.

This "mainstream" policy framework was firmly in place when the communist regimes of eastern Europe and the Soviet Union collapsed between 1989 and 1991. Confronted with economies dominated by state owned enterprises and widespread government intervention and characterized by high levels of economic inefficiency and extensive restrictions on private initiative, the advice from most western governments and the international financial institutions was derived directly from the Washington Consensus: the transition to a market economy could best be made by liberalizing and privatizing the economy as quickly as possible while macroeconomic policy should establish and maintain low

rates of inflation and balance in the general government and current accounts. Previous issues of this *Survey*[3] judged that this approach greatly underestimated the task of *creating* a market economy: it focused on too narrow a set of exclusively economic variables and ignored the risk that liberalization without the appropriate institutional infrastructure was unlikely to establish a functioning and "efficient" market economy. Macroeconomic stabilization was unlikely to lead to sustainable development unless accompanied by a carefully sequenced programme of structural reforms. Moreover, in many transition economies, and Russia was a prominent but not unique example, it was difficult to see how the standard macroeconomic policy package could easily be applied when the banking and financial sector was so underdeveloped that the links between the real and financial sectors of the economy were too weak to support the use of traditional monetary instruments or when governments were unable to control their expenditure and revenue because there was no functioning fiscal system.

In several respects many of the policies recommended by the "mainstream" consensus have come dangerously close to being dogmas based on oversimplified models and incomplete evidence. The certainty with which they are proposed and pursued is not reflected in the available empirical evidence. This tendency to simplification is not confined to the policy recommendations for transition and developing economies.

(i) Unemployment

Unemployment in the European Union is by all accounts its major political and social problem and its major economic failure. The standard analysis from most of the international economic institutions and from western Europe's central banks is that the problem is essentially structural and that it must be tackled by measures to make labour markets more flexible rather than by policies to boost demand and output. However, comparisons with the United States, the usual exemplar in matters of labour market flexibility and lowering unemployment, do not suggest an unequivocal difference between Europe and America. Real wages in Europe appear to have been flexible in the 1980s and do not appear to have been more rigid than in the United States;[4] and, more recently, one leading labour economist has concluded that the assertion that "European unemployment is high because European labour markets are "rigid" is too vague and probably misleading. Many labour market institutions that conventionally come under the heading of rigidities have no observable impact on

---

[3]   For example, UN/ECE, *Economic Survey of Europe in 1989-1990*, chap. 1.

[4]   UN/ECE, "Wage rigidity in western Europe and North America", *Economic Survey of Europe in 1987-1988*, pp. 99-113.

employment".[5] There is little evidence that reducing employment protection is a solution to high unemployment although active labour market policies may help people to find work. Virtually every fall in unemployment in western Europe in the last two decades or so has been accompanied by an easing of macroeconomic policy (either fiscal expansion, or lower interest rates, or devaluation, etc.). Thus without demand, increased flexibility can have no effect. Restrictive macroeconomic policies over a long period,[6] linked more recently to the objectives of the Maastricht Treaty, have kept growth well below the 3 per cent annual average forecast when the Single Market was completed and, in turn, have led to an adjustment in productive capacities consistent with a lower expected rate of growth and an unemployment rate of around 10 per cent.[7] Lowering unemployment will therefore need stronger demand, but to be sustained there will also need to be more investment. Profit shares are now higher than they were in the 1970s and the 1980s, but real long-term interest rates, which were very high for a long time, have fallen only slightly below those in the United States (which is at a very different stage in the cycle) and need to fall further if investment is to rise and capacities to expand sufficiently to absorb the unemployed. In sum, a significant cut in unemployment in the EMU area requires a period of above-average rates of investment and of output growth.[8] This goes against the grain of the ruling policy prescription but, as one leading macroeconomist has observed, "it is necessary to underline that the international policy makers' "story" about the rise in unemployment and the way to cure it might be badly flawed. The confidence with which the prescription is administered does not yet correspond to a convincing mass of evidence".[9]

(ii) Inflation

The reduction and control of inflation occupies a prominent position in the "Washington Consensus" and has clearly been given high priority in western Europe and in the transition economies. This was a reaction to a general acceleration of wage pressures in Europe in the late 1960s and the cost-push effects of the two major oil shocks of the 1970s. The key argument for focusing on inflation as a principal objective of macroeconomic policy is that it distorts the information content of the price mechanism and by disrupting the basic coordination system of the market economy reduces the propensity to invest and hence economic growth. Also high rates of inflation are often accompanied by high rates in its variability and this also has a negative effect on expectations. The justification for continuing to give priority to inflation control, even when it has virtually disappeared in western Europe, is that without an attentive monetary policy it can quickly accelerate and veer out of control again. But both the costs of inflation and the dangers of acceleration once any slippage is allowed may be exaggerated.

The evidence suggests that inflation is costly in terms of lost output only when annual rates exceed 40 per cent – then there is a danger that high inflation will lead to low growth rates.[10] Below this rate, growth and investment can recover even though inflation is still in double digits: the important element is that there are expectations that it will remain on a downward trend. In most of the transition economies annual inflation rates are now below 20 per cent, with many in single digits, but, paradoxically, there appears to be a positive relationship between output growth and the average inflation rate between 1993 and 1998.[11] However, this reflects differences not so much in the rate of inflation but in its rate of deceleration over the period: where a more gradual approach has been adopted, conspicuously among the leading reformers, output growth has been rapid and investment encouraged. In contrast, the excessive emphasis on rapid price stabilization in Russia, for example, involving increasingly tight monetary policy, has had highly negative effects on the real economy and has contributed to the growth of payments arrears and other perverse outcomes.[12] Moreover, the persistence of moderate rates of inflation in much of central Europe reflects a continuing adjustment of relative prices as administrative controls are gradually lifted, adjustments which actually represent improvements in the market system. It would not be sensible to react to such price increases with tighter monetary policy. Nor is it necessarily desirable to accelerate the process of freeing controlled prices. (It is well known and accepted that public and semi-public housing rents are heavily subsidized in the transition economies and that a move to more economic levels is necessary for an improvement in the housing stock.[13] But this cannot be done abruptly as the subsidies are an important part of the social safety net in these countries.)

In western Europe inflation rates are practically zero at the present time yet policy is still deeply concerned

---

[5]   S. Nickell, "Unemployment and labour market rigidities: Europe versus North America", *Journal of Economic Perspectives*, Vol. 11, No. 3, Summer 1997, pp. 55-74.

[6]   G. Worswick, "The scope for macroeconomic policy to alleviate unemployment in western Europe", *UN/ECE Discussion Papers*, Vol. 2 (1992), No. 3 (United Nations publication, Sales No. GV.E.92-0-27).

[7]   J. Michie, "Unemployment and economic policy", *Development and International Cooperation*, Vol. XII, No. 22, June 1996, pp. 57-69.

[8]   R. Rowthorn, "Globalization and employment", *Employment Institute Economic Report*, Vol. 11, No. 10, January 1998.

[9]   M. Artis, "The unemployment problem", *Oxford Review of Economic Policy*, Vol. 14, No. 3, Autumn 1998, pp. 98-109.

[10]   M. Bruno and W. Easterly, "Inflation crises and long-run growth", *NBER Working Paper,* No. 5209 (Cambridge, MA), 1995.

[11]   Chap. 3.4 below. Although it is not suggested that high inflation leads to higher output growth.

[12]   UN/ECE, *Economic Survey of Europe, 1998 No. 3*, pp. 31-40.

[13]   Chap. 3.4 below.

that small monthly increases could set off another inflationary surge. But the evidence suggests this concern is misplaced: there appears to be no grounds for believing that inflation is related to previous rates of increase[14] and therefore little risk of an acceleration getting out of control. Moreover, this pre-emptive stance of monetary policy, at insignificant rates of inflation, appears to make no acknowledgement of the fact that inflationary expectations have changed significantly since the 1970s and 1980s, and that the structural and technical changes that have occurred in the developed economies since then have reduced the likelihood of present wage and price setting behaviour being quickly reversed. However, the belief that monetary policy will be tightened in response to minor upward deviations from set targets has a depressing effect on expectations of output growth and the propensity to invest. The view that close to zero inflation is a necessary, and even a sufficient, condition for strong, sustained growth and falling unemployment is not based on historical evidence. But continuing to focus on such an objective is likely to have deleterious effects on the prospects for reducing the currently high rates of unemployment in western Europe.

(iii) Trade liberalization

The weak links between strong policy recommendations and the supporting empirical analysis are not confined to the labour market and domestic prices. The transition economies were advised in 1989 that price and trade liberalization could not be introduced gradually despite the experience of western Europe which phased out its wartime price controls in line with supply-side improvements to avoid boosting inflation and which, together with North America, started to liberalize its foreign trade gradually over a long period starting in the 1940s and which is still not complete.[15] The recommendation for rapid trade liberalization was supported by an influential World Bank study of 17 countries which concluded that a bold liberalization tends to be more sustainable than one which is staged. But in a careful review of this seven-volume study it was pointed out that the great diversity of experience of the individual countries did not support the extravagant claims made for the generality of the study's conclusions.[16] A similar degree of uncertainty surrounds the relationship between trade liberalization and faster economic growth, a crucial issue since liberalization is essentially an instrumental

policy, not an end in itself. Some economists[17] find a close and positive relationship, emphasizing the benefits of removing the static and dynamic costs of import substitution; others[18] contend that the presumed relationship depends on the validity of specific microeconomic assumptions which rarely appear in reality and that once increasing returns to scale and productivity-boosting investment are brought into the picture the standard case for liberalizing trade to boost growth breaks down and a plausible case for interventionist policies can be made. Again, a careful review of the empirical evidence underlines its inconclusiveness – it is possible that trade liberalization may in fact favour output growth but not in a straightforward manner and that in the short run the adjustment costs may predominate over the benefits.[19]

The argument for trade liberalization is that exposure to increased competition will force domestic enterprises to be more efficient, and the more quickly this is achieved the better. However, there are two points to emphasize here. First, the scale of the adjustment shock of liberalizing trade will depend on how far the domestic output, employment and relative price structures have to change in response to the new competitive pressures. For many transition economies the scale of restructuring required by the shift from central planning to competitive markets is so large that the domestic economic, political and social institutions, which are also in a state of transition, are unable to cope with the adjustment costs, which in turn may generate large-scale resistance to reform. (The study of Romania in this *Survey* provides a telling example of this.)

Secondly, economic growth and development is a highly complex process, the causes of which are still poorly understood; but economic historians, and economists outside the neo-classical persuasion, have always emphasized the crucial role of institutions in stimulating and facilitating the process of change and of mobilizing and expanding the resources available for development. In the presence of a heavily distorted output structure, weak corporate governance and the absence of appropriate institutions – the situation in many transition economies – rapid trade liberalization may be more likely to lead to unemployment and stagnation rather than economic growth and positive structural adjustment. But generalizations are difficult. Poland, Hungary and, to a lesser extent, the Czech Republic appear to have gained from opening their economies to international trade, but there is little sign of similar

---

[14] J. Stiglitz, "Reflections on the natural rate hypothesis", *Journal of Economic Perspectives*, Vol. 11, No. 1, 1997, pp. 3-10. Despite popular beliefs to the contrary there was no persistent acceleration in the rate of inflation in the market economies between 1945 and the late 1960s.

[15] Israel also demonstrated in the 1960s that unilateral trade liberalization could be introduced gradually.

[16] D. Greenaway, "Liberalizing foreign trade through rose tinted glasses", *The Economic Journal*, 103(416), January 1993, pp. 208-222. See also, D. Rodrik, "Closing the productivity gap: does trade liberalization really help?", in G. Helleiner (ed.), *Trade Policy, Liberalization and Development* (Oxford, Clarendon Press, 1992).

[17] A. Krueger, "Why trade liberalization is good for growth", *The Economic Journal*, Vol. 108(450), 1998, pp. 1513-1522.

[18] L. Taylor and J. Ocampo, "Trade liberalization in developing economies: modest benefits but problems with productivity growth, macro prices, and income distribution", *The Economic Journal*, Vol. 108(450), 1998, pp. 1523-1546.

[19] D. Greenaway, W. Morgan and P. Wright, "Trade reform, adjustment and growth: what does the evidence tell us?", *The Economic Journal*, Vol. 108(450), 1998, pp. 1547-1561.

responses in Romania or Russia or many of the other countries that are lagging behind in the process of reform.

It is sometimes argued that the transition economies where GDP growth has been most rapid are those where liberalized trade and current accounts emerged quickly, where structural reform was rapid, and where inflation was falling. "It is very clear today that the countries that are succeeding the best are the countries that followed the [IMF] policy closest, and the countries that are lagging behind – Romania is an example – are the countries that were least able to stick to the strategy."[20] But such cross-country comparisons do little to establish the direction of causation. An alternative view is that the most successful reformers appear to be those where the initial conditions – in terms of both the required scale of restructuring and the institutional capacity to handle it – were more favourable to a faster rate of transition. In other words, governments were able to implement – and their electorates were willing to tolerate – a faster rate of change than in other transition economies. But this means that the pace of reform is largely determined by the historical legacy and not only by the choice, or the "political will", of governments.

(iv) Liberalization of international capital flows

The liberalization of the international capital markets is perhaps one of the most controversial elements in the ruling orthodoxy, especially since the Asian crisis broke in August 1997. The official case for free capital movements is that it is merely an extension of the argument for free trade in goods – countries with insufficient domestic savings to finance their own investment can draw on the surplus savings of others,[21] and by searching out the most profitable projects foreign capital will lead to a more optimal allocation of world resources and a convergence of per capita incomes. However, although the estimated benefits from free trade may also be controversial, there is no doubt that serious efforts have been made to quantify them and there is a body of evidence which points to significant gains even if these range considerably in size. In the case of capital account convertibility attempts to quantify the benefits, as Professor Bhagwati has pointed out,[22] are virtually non-existent and are more a matter of repeated assertion than careful analysis. In fact the available evidence casts doubt on many of the presumed major benefits of free capital movements. Contrary to expectation, domestic

investment and domestic savings rates tend to be closely correlated across countries: different rates of return on capital persist and are not equalized by foreign capital flows.[23] This is not so surprising if it is recalled that different rates of return will affect the flows of foreign capital, *other things being equal*. But "other things" are not equal in most of the transition and developing countries: legal and institutional structures are often inadequate to attract foreign investment, while economies of scale and conglomeration in the highly integrated economies of western Europe and North America still provide the major attraction for investors. Some 80 per cent of OECD FDI still flows to other OECD countries[24] and despite the large absolute flows to the rest of the world in the 1990s most portfolio investment in the United States and western Europe still goes into United States and west European shares respectively. Despite popular claims to the contrary, both capital flows and international trade are still more regionally concentrated than truly global.[25] This helps to explain – but only helps since there are many complex factors involved – why there is little evidence in favour of income convergence in the world economy.[26]

Nor do the great benefits claimed for free international capital markets appear to be reflected in better economic performance, irrespective of its distribution. Growth rates of GDP in the last two decades have generally been much lower than in the 1960s, in both the developed and developing countries, and investment ratios (to GDP) have generally fallen. Although there are many factors involved in this deterioration, and it should not be denied that some countries have benefited from increased liberalization, the proponents of unfettered international capital movements cannot claim that they have been generally associated with higher growth rates, more efficient resource allocation, or a more equitable distribution of incomes per head.

What is clear, however, is that the liberation of international capital flows, particularly by the developed market economies, has been accompanied in the 1980s and 1990s by a considerable increase in financial market volatility – interest rates, exchange rates and capital flows themselves all exhibit very much larger fluctuations than

[20] M. Deppler, remarks made at a Symposium organized by the IMF and the Bundesbank, 2 July 1998, reported in *IMF Survey*, 27(14), 20 July 1998, pp. 225-226. See also, P. Desai, *Going Global. Transition from Plan to Market in the World Economy* (Cambridge, MA, MIT Press, 1998).

[21] S. Anjaria, "The capital truth. What works for commodities should work for cash", *Foreign Affairs*, November/December 1998, pp. 142-143. (The author is Director of the External Relations Department of the IMF.)

[22] J. Bhagwati, "The capital myth", *Foreign Affairs*, May/June 1998, pp. 7-12.

[23] M. Feldstein, and C. Horioka, "Domestic saving and international investment", *The Economic Journal*, Vol. 90(358), 1980, pp. 314-329.

[24] OECD, *International Direct Investment Statistics Yearbook* (Paris), annual.

[25] UN/ECE, "Structural changes in North-South trade, with emphasis on the trade of the ECE region, 1965-1983", *Economic Bulletin for Europe*, Vol. 46 (1994); R. Kozul-Wright and R. Rowthorn, "Spoilt for choice? Multinational corporations and the geography of international production", *Oxford Review of Economic Policy*, Vol. 14(2), Summer 1998, pp. 74-92.

[26] UNCTAD, *Trade and Development Report 1997* (United Nations publication, Sales No. E.97.II.D.8), chap. II; R. Kozul-Wright and R. Rowthorn, "Globalization and economic convergence: an assessment", *UNCTAD Discussion Papers*, No. 131, February 1998.

in the 1960s and early 1970s. Sudden inflows, and equally sudden outflows, of foreign capital create considerable difficulties for the management of domestic monetary policy;[27] the resulting uncertainty and higher risks implied by financial volatility lead to caution on the part of governments (which tend to set interest rates higher than they might otherwise have been) and of private business (faced with increased costs of capital and increased uncertainty over future demand). The net result is a tendency for growth rates to fall below what is feasible,[28] a particularly serious consequence for the transition economies intent on closing the considerable income gap between themselves and the members of the EU.

The other aspect of financial volatility is its propensity for contagion, the tendency for a financial crisis in one country or region to spread to others largely irrespective of the state of the economic fundamentals in the latter. Contrary to the textbook model of large numbers of investors making careful, independent judgements as to profitable opportunities, the capital markets are subject to bouts of "herd behaviour" – that is, investors follow one another without forming their own judgements or expectations about individual economies. Contagion is reinforced by the adjustment of portfolios whereby losses or margin calls in one market are balanced by the liquidation of assets in other markets which may very well show no weakness at all in the real economy – indeed, in this context, the stronger and more liquid markets may be the more vulnerable. "Herd" behaviour turns into a classical financial panic when foreign investors rush for the exit when their expectations change, for whatever reason. This can trigger a run on the currency, a collapse in the domestic bond market and a liquidity squeeze on the domestic banks, as happened in Asia in 1997 and in Russia last summer. Although the origins of the crisis may be due to faults in the domestic economy where it began – clearly the case in Russia[29] – the "panic" tends to amplify the crisis beyond anything that might be justified by the original causes.

In the immediate aftermath of the Asian crisis there was a tendency to put the blame for it, not on the instability of the capital markets, but on the countries themselves: internal weaknesses such as weak regulatory frameworks, poor systems of corporate governance, a general lack of transparency in the financial and banking sectors, "crony" capitalism, and so on. The question is not whether such deficiencies exist but whether they played a significant role in causing and propagating the

crisis. The argument that lack of transparency etc. somehow deceived foreign investors into placing their funds in these countries is difficult to accept since these weaknesses have long been known to be part and parcel of the definition of economies as "developing" or "in transition". Weak financial and banking sectors may make the crisis worse, but capital flow reversals appear to be the main culprit in amplifying the initial crisis and transmitting it to other countries.[30] What countries are affected, and how badly, will depend on the extent of their integration into the international trade and financial structures. On the whole the transition economies of central and eastern Europe were less severely hit by financial contagion from the Asian and Russian crises than by the increased cost of borrowing on the international markets and the subsequent real economy effects on their exports, a reflection of the fact that their integration in world trade has proceeded much further than in the financial markets.[31]

The policy question that arises from the above is whether it is possible to reduce the instability of the international capital markets and, if not, whether countries can protect themselves against surges in capital inflows and their sudden reversal. Proposals to improve regulatory systems, improve transparency and generally improve the flow of accurate information in – and between – national economies are desirable in themselves as means to more effective market systems but, as suggested already, it is unlikely that deficiencies in these areas in the transition and developing countries played a major role in causing the crisis. The more serious weaknesses of governance and regulation would instead appear to be located in the developed market economies of North America and western Europe. The collapse of the LTCM "hedge" fund in September 1998, for example, focused attention on the excessive leverage available to such funds under the available regulations and the fact that at the same time such funds were able to escape from all regulation by the United States Federal Reserve. Also, there appear to have been "cosy" relationships between hedge funds, on the one hand, and the investment and commercial banks on the other. This is another area where there have been frequent and justified calls for more effective monitoring and regulation by central banks; and questions have been raised about western banks' credit evaluation procedures that allow excessively large exposures to hedge funds and other institutions to develop without proper monitoring. Swift action to repair some of these deficiencies in the developed market economies could make an important

---

[27]   See below, chap. 3.2(ii), and UN/ECE, "Surges in capital flows into eastern Europe, 1990-1996", *Economic Bulletin for Europe*, Vol. 49 (1997), pp. 99-147.

[28]   UN/ECE, *Economic Survey of Europe, 1998 No. 1*, pp. 9-10.

[29]   See, UNCTAD-UN/ECE, "The Russian crisis", paper prepared by the secretariats of UNCTAD and ECE for the UNCTAD Trade and Development Board (Geneva), October 1998, available as *Press Release, ECE/GEN/98/2* (16 October 1998), and UN/ECE *Economic Survey of Europe, 1998 No. 3*, pp. 31-40.

[30]   M. Fratzscher, "Why are currency crises contagious? A comparison of the Latin American crisis of 1994-1995 and the Asian crisis of 1997-1998", *Weltwirtschaftliches Archiv*, Vol. 134(4), 1998, pp. 666-691.

[31]   This is not to deny, however, that some transition economies are more integrated than others in the international financial markets (as shown, for example, by the large shares of domestic securities held by foreigners). In these cases, high levels of reserves and high real interest rates helped to reduce the contagion effects.

contribution to reducing instability: not only are these the principal sources of international capital flows but they are also the countries where both the urgency and the capacity for reform are greatest. There does not seem to be any reason why such reforms should have to wait for the more comprehensive proposals for reforming the international financial system.[32]

Another reaction to the consequences of the Asian crisis has been for greater stress to be placed on the need for a more gradual approach to the liberalization of capital accounts and for effective financial institutions to be in place before capital account convertibility is introduced. Since the Russian crisis the impression is often given that this has always been the approach but, in his resignation letter in mid-1998, the Chairman of the Interim Committee of the IMF's Board of Governors felt it necessary to warn that it was important "to proceed cautiously and with good advice. No country should be forced to liberalize immediately, or to remove controls when they are justified by legitimate reasons".[33] There is also increased acceptance of direct capital controls of the type applied by Chile, for example, but only as a temporary and emergency measure.[34]

In most of the reactions to the Asian crisis and the proposals for reform, only some of which were mentioned above, the underlying assumption is that capital market instability can be tamed by better institutional frameworks, better supervision, greater transparency, and a more careful preparation of transition and developing economies before they enter the liberalized international environment. Although all these steps may help, a more fundamental question is whether instability is inherent to the international capital markets or whether it arises from inappropriate institutions and unwarranted interference in the market mechanism. This is in fact a variation on one of the basic issues over which economists have divided for most of this century, namely, the origins of uncertainty and the source of dislocation in the system of market coordination. One view, exemplified by von Hayek, is that uncertainty is created by the distortion or suppression of information by interfering governments and central banks; left alone,

individuals will show a natural tendency to coordinate their various plans in an orderly and predictable manner. The other view, exemplified by Keynes, located uncertainty and coordination failures not in exogenous sources but in the system itself. Contrary to Hayek, Keynes thought government could play a role in reducing uncertainty and raising expectations. The influence of these two very different points of view about how a market economy works has dominated the postwar period in roughly equal halves, the Keynesian for some 28 years from 1945 and the Hayekian from roughly 1973.

The Keynesian view of the inherent instability of capital markets was reflected in the original design of the IMF and the postwar international monetary system. Both Keynes and White[35] saw the new institution's primary function as promoting growth via an open international trading system and the preservation of financial stability. International capital flows, which of course were considerably smaller than now, had to be subject to controls because, otherwise, it was feared they would develop an independent existence of their own and disrupt rather than support international trade. From the perspective of 1999, when international monetary transactions massively exceed the value of international trade, those fears seem exceptionally prescient.[36]

If the view that instability or volatility is inherent in international capital markets is accepted, although it may be reduced by better regulation, etc., it may be desirable to accept capital controls as a permanent instrument in the national policy tool-kit and to abandon attempts to include capital account convertibility as an ultimate objective for all IMF members. Under present arrangements legitimate attempts to control foreign capital flows are in fact made, by changing interest rates, but these are clumsy tools for this purpose as they may conflict sharply with other national objectives such as growth or macroeconomic stability.[37] More direct controls, such as those employed in Chile, would help to contain the disruptive effects of surges in short-term capital flows on economic growth, which if successful would actually make the environment more attractive for longer-term direct investment.[38] It should also be stressed that most transition economies possess extremely small financial sectors in relation to global capital flows, most of which come from the more advanced market

---

[32] On the broader agenda for reform see United Nations, "Toward a new international financial architecture", *Report of the Task Force of the Executive Committee on Economic and Social Affairs of the United Nations*, New York, January 1999 (known as "the Ocampo Report"); and J. Eatwell and L. Taylor, *International Capital Markets and the Future of Economic Policy. A Proposal for the Creation of a World Financial Authority*, paper available at www.newschool.edu/cepa.

[33] Resignation letter of Philippe Maystadt addressed to the Managing Director of the IMF, *IMF Survey*, 20 July 1998, pp. 227-228.

[34] The Chilean approach includes sterilized intervention, to avoid excessive appreciation of the exchange rate, supported by restrictions on short-term capital flows as to minimum entry amounts and a one-year delay before they can be repatriated. In addition there are reserve requirements which differentiate in favour of long-term as against short-term capital inflows. The advantage of these types of control over the much-discussed Tobin tax on foreign exchange transactions is that they can be applied by individual countries whereas the tax requires wholesale international compliance.

[35] Harry Dexter White was chief international economist at the United States Treasury in the early 1940s and, with Keynes, one of the two principal architects of the IMF and the World Bank.

[36] Capital controls came to an end with the collapse of the Bretton Woods system of fixed exchange rates in the early 1970s; that collapse, by transferring the management of foreign exchange risk to the private sector was a major factor behind the general move to financial deregulation in the 1970s. Eatwell and Taylor, op. cit.

[37] See chap. 3.2(ii) below.

[38] The distinction between short- and long-term investment becomes increasingly less significant with full capital account convertibility as access to modern derivatives markets can be used to reduce the differences in liquidity between different assets.

economies. A minor portfolio adjustment for a large hedge fund such as LTCM could deliver a major shock to such an economy. If import surcharges and import disruption clauses can be provided for under WTO rules for merchandise trade it is difficult to see why similar provisions cannot be allowed in the case of foreign capital flows, especially when the strongest supporters of capital liberalization claim that the arguments for liberalizing trade and capital are equivalent.

One of the standard objections to such controls is that it is too late to "turn the clock back", that the process of capital liberalization is unstoppable. This is often little more than self-interested determinism by market operators and there seems to be no reason why Chilean-type controls could not be adopted by a country if it so chooses,[39] although it is probably advisable to introduce them during a period of relative calm in the financial markets rather than as an emergency measure during a crisis. More to the point, however, is that the majority of central European transition economies still retain a wide array of capital controls;[40] for the most part inward direct investment is generally free but controls remain on many portfolio flows. These have helped to insulate these economies from the worst effects of financial contagion by the crisis in emerging markets elsewhere and it would appear to be unwise to abandon them hastily, if at all.

Another objection to direct controls is to argue that if countries dislike the results of foreign capital inflows they should simply let the exchange rate rise. But this is not very helpful – how far it would have to rise is uncertain and may increase rather than ease the country's problems. In fact if direct controls are ruled out of court, countries will inevitably seek alternative ways to protect themselves from instability in the international capital markets which may be more damaging to the market economy system. In the absence of alternatives, the need for such protection will lead to attempts to increase the levels of reserves, which implies aiming for a current account surplus. By definition, not every country can achieve this, but if they all try there will be ever stronger pressure to resort to the traditional range of "beggar my neighbour" policies which will risk undermining the

liberal trading system – precisely the consequence that was feared by Keynes and White in the 1940s but ignored by the liberalizers of the 1970s.[41]

(v) Conclusions

This brief review of a selection of current policy attitudes suggests that they share a number of characteristics. None of them in themselves can be said to be "wrong" or undesirable, but the confidence with which they are pursued and applied ignores the fact that the empirical support for them is more uncertain and more ambiguous than is usually recognized. In particular, the tendency to downplay or even ignore the differences in institutional structures, which would appear to be a major source of the intercountry variations in their acceptance of and response to market forces,[42] increases the risk of outcomes which are not only less than optimal but actually opposite to those intended. Without the appropriate institutional infrastructures in place premature liberalization can cause considerable damage to economic and social systems and create a severe backlash against programmes for reform and transition to a market economy. (There are signs that since the Asian crisis this is increasingly recognized vis-à-vis the financial sector[43] but the lesson applies across the board. Failure to deal with monopolistic structures, to create appropriate legal (and enforcement systems), to build patiently popular support for the reform programme,[44] and so on and so forth, can all undermine attempts to create a market economy and drive the existing system into stagnation or recession rather than create a new basis for sustained growth.) Adapting policies to the particular conditions of individual economies and taking into account a wider range of factors undermines the simplicity of the ruling paradigm, but that may well be a price worth paying if the transition process is ultimately strengthened and opposition to market reforms diminished by more optimistic expectations.

The other characteristic that most of these policies share is a tendency towards deflation. This is fairly clear in the case of current policies directed at inflation and unemployment but is less often acknowledged in the case

---

[39] On the effectiveness of capital controls in a number of developing countries and on the dangers of capital account liberalization in a global system that has still to find ways to prevent the international transmission of financial shocks, see UNCTAD, *Trade and Development Report, 1998* (United Nations publication, Sales No. E.98.II.D.6), especially chap. IV.

[40] Slovenia is often singled out as an economy where capital controls have helped to maintain stability in the domestic economy. See H. Davidson, "Slovenia's splendid isolation", *Central European*, November 1998. A useful summary of selected capital controls in 11 transition economies is given in R. Feldman, et al., *Impact of EMU on Selected Non-European Union Countries*, IMF Occasional Paper, No. 174 (Washington, D.C.), 1998, table 2.9. According to the IMF's index of capital account liberalization (varying from zero to 100, the latter representing maximum liberalization), the least liberalized country was Romania (12.5) and the most was the Czech Republic (73.7). For Hungary it was 59.5 and for Poland 55.3; for all the others it was under 50.

[41] The Secretary-General of UNCTAD recently emphasized the role of financial instability in bringing about the collapse of world trade growth from almost 10 per cent in 1997 to some 3.7 per cent in 1998. R. Ricupero, *Keynote Address to the High Level Symposium on Trade and Development*, WTO (Geneva), 17 March 1999.

[42] Although some of these institutional arrangements are inimical to market forces and decentralized decision-making, there is no unique set of institutions which describe a market economy. Capitalism comes in a number of institutional variations.

[43] *"Now we know* that the incentive structure – critical for the behaviour of people and firms – is not only indicated by prices. Prices are critical, markets are absolutely essential, but they are not the only things that create the incentive structure of the economy. It's institutions as well" – "Institutions matter, says chief economist for Latin America", *World Bank News*, 2 July 1998, p. 5 (emphasis supplied).

[44] UN/ECE, *Economic Survey of Europe in 1992-1993*, pp. 10-15.

of attempts to implement structural reform at a pace which is too rapid to be supported by a country's institutional framework. When the required adjustment in structure is very large – and for most transition economies the requirements are far from the marginal changes assumed in standard economics textbooks – and the institutional support for transition very weak, rapid liberalization is unlikely to lead to growth.

The broader conclusion, however, is that growth and employment have to be restored to a more prominent position among the objectives of policy. The idea that liberalization, structural reform, and economic growth can be tackled in a temporal sequence is as mistaken for the transition economies as for the mature western market economies. Instead, measures directed at supporting growth need to be introduced alongside stabilization and reform programmes in order to establish a mutual support between them.[45]

The triumph of capitalism in the second half of the 20th century was largely based on its ability to regain popular legitimacy via the intervention of government to ensure low levels of unemployment and more acceptable distributional outcomes – capitalism with a "human face". This, essentially, was "the third way" and derived from a conjunction of the welfare state with "Keynesian" economic policies. (Keynes, it should be remembered, was a liberal who was acutely aware in the 1930s that if ways were not found to make capitalism more socially acceptable then the likely outcome would be a swing to one of the two totalitarian alternatives then on offer.) To put it crudely, for any economic system to survive it must deliver the goods and distribute them in a reasonably equitable manner. The former centrally planned economics failed this test and they have been dismantled; but there are many people now living in some of the transition economies who are wondering whether the new market economy, however embryonic, will fail the test as well.

Another aspect of late 20th century capitalism is that it comes in many varieties and is supported by different institutional arrangements. This tolerance of national varieties, however, is increasingly under threat from those who see globalization in normative terms and insist that transition and developing economies should adopt all the values and institutions of the currently dominant market economies. This approach, which is partly reflected in the post-Uruguay agenda of the WTO and which seeks to harmonize policies and to set rules in areas which have traditionally been regarded as matters for national policy and national preferences, carries considerable risks. It represents a radical change from the original philosophy behind the creation of the Bretton Woods institutions which was to create an environment

of international financial stability that would underpin the development of world trade and allow countries to develop according to their own preferences, subject to their avoiding actions that would "beggar their neighbours". The pursuit of the globalization agenda, however, increasingly appears to deny much room for any national preferences which clash with those of the major market economies.

The crucial danger from this is to the market economy system itself, because economic and social preferences are closely entwined in the broader framework of social and political values which underpin a country's institutions including its form of economic organization. This is why in previous issues of this *Survey* there has been repeated stress on the problems of institutional hiatus in transition economies and on the necessity to allow them sufficient time – and to provide them with significant support – to enable the new market institutions to become embedded in the social and political values of the population and to give the institutions time to start working effectively. In a few of the central European economies this process is well advanced, but in many others it is not. If the process does not advance, the new market economies will not function properly and they will not achieve popular legitimacy. But, equally, if those social and political values – and preferences – are attacked in the name of the new global economy, the chances are that there will be a backlash against that economy rather than a change in values. It is therefore not surprising that an increasing number of distinguished market economists have recently warned of the dangers of pushing the liberalizing agenda too rapidly and too widely.

The stability of any socio-political-economic system ultimately rests on three crucial conditions: *one*, on whether it has *legitimacy*, i.e. whether the rules and procedures according to which authority is conferred and exercised can be justified and can be seen to be rooted in Adam Smith's "moral sentiments of the population"; *two*, on whether the agreed rules, conventions of behaviour, etc., maintain *order* in the system by encouraging acceptable behaviour and penalizing the unacceptable; and *three*, on the *welfare outcome*, which recognizes that popular support for institutions and economic arrangements will not be sustained if the distribution of costs and benefits is considered by too many of the population to be unjust. The instability in the international financial system in the last decade, the aggressive pursuit of an ever-widening liberalization agenda, and the enormously costly turbulence of the last 18 months or so all suggest that the present global system may be moving closer to violating all three conditions.

---

[45] On this see J. Kornai, "Lasting growth as the top priority: macroeconomic tensions and government economic policy in Hungary", EBRD, *Working Paper*, No. 15 (London), December 1994, and the quotation therefrom in chap. 3.4 below.

CHAPTER 2

THE GLOBAL CONTEXT AND THE SITUATION IN THE WESTERN MARKET ECONOMIES

2.1 The global context

(i) The broad pattern

Uncertainties in international financial markets have continued to prevail after the decision of the Brazilian government on 15 January 1999 to abandon the exchange rate peg and to float the domestic currency, the real, which has since depreciated sharply. The Brazilian crisis is the latest episode in a succession of contagion effects from the Asian crisis which were also an important factor in the Russian crisis which unfolded in mid-1998.[46] Basically, all these crises have to do with a major reappraisal of risk exposure by international investors, which has been mirrored in a sudden and large-scale redirection of short-term capital flows from emerging markets to safe havens in industrialized countries. Reduced net capital inflows, or even net capital outflows, have been associated with a considerable rise in the costs of borrowing, often tantamount to a "credit crunch" for emerging markets. High short-term interest rates required to check capital flight and defend established fixed or quasi-fixed exchange rates, in turn, have had considerable domestic economic costs, often triggering a vicious circle, in which the ensuing recessionary tendencies reinforced the selling pressure on the currency.

The adjustment policies implemented in emerging markets to cope with these changes have led to a steep fall in their domestic absorption, which, in turn, has had a deflationary effect on world economic activity. These deflationary effects have also led to a considerable fall in commodity prices since the Asian crisis which adversely affected real incomes in those countries for which commodity exports are a major source of foreign exchange. These adverse effects have only been partly offset by the potential stimulus of falling interest rates – associated with the retreat of capital flows to "safe havens" – and the gains in real income, ensuing from the fall in commodity prices, in western Europe and North America.

The cumulative effects of these successive crises on world economic activity has been considerable. Real GDP in the world economy rose by only 2¼ per cent in 1998, a marked slowdown from the growth rate of 4.2 per cent the previous year. This was the lowest growth rate of world output since 1991 (chart 2.1.1). This outcome reflects in the main the deepening recession in Japan and the sharp contractions of economic activity in several other east Asian countries, developments which have been mutually reinforcing as a result of the strong regional trade links. But there was also a marked deceleration in economic growth in other parts of the world economy, viz. Latin America, the Middle East and the transition economies, which contrasts with continuing robust growth in western Europe and, especially, in North America for the year as a whole.

It not only proved very difficult to anticipate correctly the deflationary effects of the Asian crisis but, with hindsight, the choice of the traditional policy response seems to have been inappropriate.[47] In any case, the much deeper than expected economic crisis in Japan and in the east Asian emerging markets and its adverse spillover effects to other regions has been the major factor in the successive and significant lowering of growth forecasts for the world economy in 1998 and beyond (chart 2.1.2).

The slowdown in world output growth has also led to a marked weakening of the rate of expansion of world trade. World merchandise imports rose in volume by only 3¼ per cent in 1998, down from some 10 per cent in 1997.[48] Import demand in the developing countries was depressed on account of the domestic adjustment measures required to cope with reduced capital inflows and a significant deterioration in their terms of trade. These adverse effects on world trade were amplified by the steep fall in import demand in Japan and a slowdown in import growth in North America and western Europe.

---

[46] UN/ECE, *Economic Survey of Europe, 1998 No. 3.*

[47] UNCTAD, *Trade and Development Report*, 1998 (United Nations publication, Sales No. E.98.II.D.6), p. 69.

[48] IMF, *World Economic Outlook and International Capital Markets. Interim Assessment* (Washington, D.C.), December 1998, p. 164, table 5.

CHART 2.1.1

Changes in world output, 1990-1999 [a]
(Percentage change over previous year)

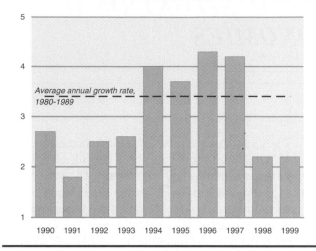

Source: IMF, *World Economic Outlook and International Capital Markets, Interim Assessment* (Washington, D.C.), December 1998, p. 160, table 1.

[a] Real GDP. Data for 1998 and 1999 forecasts.

CHART 2.1.2

Changing forecasts of world output growth, 1998-2000
(Annual percentage change)

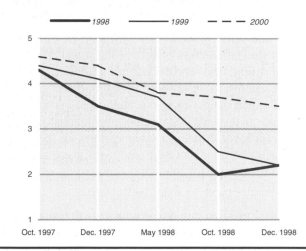

Source: IMF, *World Economic Outlook and International Capital Markets, Interim Assessment* (Washington, D.C.), December 1998, p. 7, table 1.1.

Note: The dates refer to the issue dates of the IMF, *World Economic Outlook.*

World trade prices in dollar terms fell by some 4.5 per cent in 1998, following a decline of more than 6 per cent in 1997. The terms of trade of industrialized countries improved by some 1 per cent in 1998, while those of developing countries deteriorated by 5 per cent. Since 1990, the terms of trade of developing countries have fallen by a cumulative 12 per cent.[49]

TABLE 2.1.1

World commodity prices, 1995-1998
(Percentage change over previous year)

	Weights[a]	1995	1996	1997	1998
Food and beverages	9.9	1.6	-1.6	5.6	-12.3
Industrial raw materials	29.5	16.3	-12.1	-1.8	-14.5
Energy	60.5	8.3	15.4	-3.9	-29.0
Crude oil	55.5	8.6	17.1	-3.6	-31.1
Total	100.0	9.6	3.3	-1.4	-22.3
Total, *excluding energy*	39.5	12.0	-9.8	1.3	-13.8

Source: Hamburg Institute for Economic Research (HWWA).

Note: Growth rates calculated on the basis of current dollar prices.

[a] Weights refer to average commodity shares in total imports of western industrialized countries in 1989-1991.

The sharp fall in *international commodity prices* in 1998 was the main factor behind these differential changes in the terms of trade. Oil prices declined by some 30 per cent to their lowest level in more than 20 years.[50] Non-oil commodities fell at about half that rate (table 2.1.1). These price developments are largely due to the direct and indirect effects of the Asian crisis, including the deep recession in Japan, on the demand for commodities.[51] This shortfall of demand amplified an already existing oversupply in a number of commodity markets, notably for oil, which was reflected in rising stocks. Oil demand was also dampened by the mild winter of 1997/98 in the Northern Hemisphere and the economic downturn in the CIS in 1998. Some OPEC countries stepped up oil production in an unsuccessful attempt to offset the impact of falling oil prices on revenues.[52] In the markets for several other commodities, producers also appear to have expanded output in response to the appreciation of the dollar vis-à-vis domestic currencies. Commodity producers, in general, have been reluctant to cut back output to limit or reverse the fall in prices; instead, they have preferred to build up stocks which has led to a large overhang. The completion of new plants has also added to the downward pressure on metal prices.

Seen in a longer-term perspective, recent developments continue the tendency for commodity prices to fall in real terms, i.e. relative to changes in the prices of manufactured goods exported by developed market economies (chart 2.1.3). This reflects a combination of supply and demand factors, *inter alia,*

---

[49] Ibid.

[50] The average price of the OPEC crude oil basket fell to $12.44 in 1998, its lowest level since 1977, when it was $12.40.

[51] Net imports of commodities into East Asia rose strongly during the period of rapid economic growth since the mid-1980s with the result that the region's share of global raw material consumption was larger than its corresponding share in world output. But with the onset of recession, commodity consumption has been falling.

[52] Economic and Social Commission for Western Asia, *Preliminary Overview of Economic Developments in the ESCWA Region in 1998* (United Nations document E/ESCWA/ED/1998/6), p. 8.

CHART 2.1.3

Changes in international energy and non-energy commodity prices, 1970-1998
(Indices, 1990=100, quarterly average)

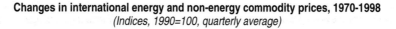

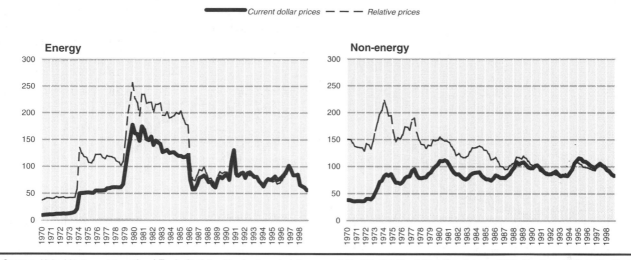

Source: United Nations, *International Trade Statistics Yearbook,* various issues and *Monthly Bulletin of Statistics,* January 1999; Hamburg Institute for Economic Research (HWWA).

Note: Data are annual averages. Relative prices are nominal prices divided by the United Nations unit value index of exports manufacture from developed countries.

reduced raw material and energy intensity of production, substitution by other materials and the fall in production costs of commodities themselves.[53] These long-term factors will continue to exert downward pressure on commodity prices in the future, underlying the cyclical movements of prices.

(ii) Lingering instability in financial markets

The Russian devaluation and debt default in mid-August 1998 triggered severe tensions in international financial markets.[54] These tensions were reflected in a sharp rise in the risk aversion of international investors vis-à-vis emerging markets, a feature which had occurred, albeit less pronounced, already in the aftermath of the Asian crisis. The Russian crisis accelerated the flight to quality (i.e. to financial instruments in industrialized countries) and this was mirrored in significant downward pressure on long-term interest rates in the western market economies.[55] At the same time there was a substantial widening of yield spreads between bonds issued in emerging markets and comparable

benchmark government bonds in the United States and other western countries. This effectively prevented new borrowing by the former countries in the international bond markets in September and October 1998.[56] But the general sense of uncertainty which had afflicted financial markets also became visible in a perceptible widening of interest rate differentials between private sector corporate bonds and government bonds within the industrialized countries themselves. In the United States, the yield difference between triple-A rated corporate bonds and 10-year treasuries rose from some 1.1 percentage points to 1.84 percentage points between June and October 1998. This combined with a marked increase in investors' preference for more liquid instruments and concerns about the possible risks of a credit crunch if banks were to tighten lending standards.

These tensions in financial markets receded in the autumn after the decision of the United States Federal Reserve to lower interest rates in three consecutive steps between end-September and mid-November 1998 and an easing of monetary policy in western Europe, which reflected the need for convergence of short-term interest rates among the prospective member countries of the euro area prior to the start of EMU on 1 January 1999.

Nevertheless, as yet there has been no return to the status quo ante. Although yield spreads on emerging market bonds have fallen again, they remain significantly above the levels prevailing in the months before the Russian crisis. And in the United States, the differential between yields on triple-A corporate bonds and 10-year

---

[53] Technological change in production methods and the larger scale of operations have caused productivity to increase and costs to fall over the past two decades. This has been especially the case for oil exploration and extraction and for metal mining, smelting and refining, which have also benefited from the deregulation of energy markets in some producing countries. At the same time, advances in agronomic and genetic research have led to higher yields in agriculture.

[54] UN/ECE, *Economic Survey of Europe, 1998 No. 3*, pp. 15-18.

[55] The general sense of enlarged risk and uncertainty engulfing investors was probably also related to the near failure of a large United States hedge fund, which was averted by a rescue operation organized by the United States monetary authorities. To this was added the shock that Russia was not considered, as widely believed, to be "too big to fail".

[56] Institute of International Finance, Inc., *Capital Flows to Emerging Market Economies* (Washington, D.C.), 27 January 1999.

CHART 2.1.4

International share prices, January 1994-February 1999
(Indices, January 1994=100)

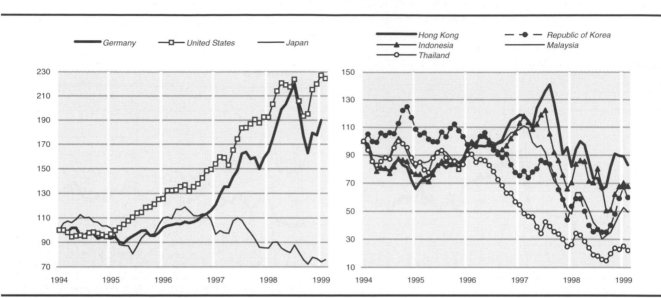

Source: Reuters News Service.

Note: National currency basis; data are monthly averages. Germany: CDAX; Japan: Nikkei 225; United States: New York Stock Exchange Composite; Hong Kong: Hang Seng; Indonesia: Jakarta Composite; Malaysia: Kuala Lumpur Composite; Republic of Korea: Korea Composite Exchange; Thailand: Bangkok SET.

treasuries was still 1.5 percentage points at the end of January 1999, about half a percentage point more than during the months before the Russian crisis. In contrast, United States share prices, which fell sharply in August and September 1998, have more than recovered their losses. Share prices also recovered in western European markets (chart 2.1.4).

The increasing risk aversion of international investors towards emerging markets is reflected in the sharp drop of net private credit flows to some $38.5 billion in 1998, down from $119 billion in 1997 and $196 billion in 1996. There was also a sharp fall in portfolio investment. But foreign direct investment has remained relatively stable, a reflection both of the longer time horizon of investment decisions pertaining to fixed assets and also of the favourable asset prices prevailing in emerging markets, notably in East Asia. In the event, total net private capital flows to emerging market economies fell to $152 billion in 1998, a decline by nearly $90 billion from their level in 1997.[57]

(iii) The crisis in Brazil

Brazil had introduced a new currency, the real, in July 1994 as part of a wider plan (the Plano Real) to achieve price stability following a long period of extremely high inflation during the 1980s and early 1990s. The main element of the monetary policy strategy was to peg the exchange rate of the real to the dollar in order to anchor the domestic wage-price process.

Inflation did, indeed, fall to quite low levels and it is against this background that the government strongly resisted speculative attacks on the currency which occurred as part of the contagion effects of the Asian crisis in the autumn of 1997 by tightening monetary policy. But the combination of a large budget deficit and a large current account deficit, together with evidence that the real was overvalued,[58] made the currency vulnerable to speculative attack. The trigger for this was the Russian crisis, which led to massive capital outflows and associated selling of the currency. In response, official interest rates were raised to nearly 50 per cent and the government announced fiscal austerity measures. But the high interest rates created a vicious circle by depressing domestic activity and, given the strong reliance on variable interest rates for financing the budget deficit, by significantly raising the cost of domestic debt servicing. The immediate consequence was a further deterioration in the public finances.

Against the background of lingering instability in the international financial markets in the second half of 1998, there were concerns that a disorderly devaluation of the real would have significant adverse contagion effects on other countries of Latin America, with concomitant risks to other regions as well. An emergency support package of $41.5 billion was agreed with the IMF in mid-November 1998 to support domestic policies designed to defend the exchange rate policy and to curb the budget deficit. But when domestic political

---

[57] Ibid. For an analysis of recent changes in net capital flows into the transition economies see chap. 3.7.

[58] The cumulative inflation in Brazil was significantly higher than in the United States since the onset of the Plano Real.

support for the fiscal retrenchment programme faltered, capital outflows resumed on a massive scale in January 1999 and the attempt to defend the exchange rate threatened to exhaust the stock of foreign reserves. The key official interest rate was raised to 39 per cent to arrest these outflows. On 13 January 1999, the government attempted a controlled devaluation by widening the fluctuation band for the exchange rate which immediately fell to its new floor. In the face of persistent strong selling pressure the authorities decided on 15 January 1999 to float the real. By the end of February 1999 the Brazilian currency had depreciated by some 40 per cent against the dollar.

In early March 1999, the Brazilian government concluded the renegotiation of the support package agreed with the IMF in November 1998. The basic policy strategy is to keep inflation in check and to avoid an extended wage-price spiral. This will also depend on the extent of the currency depreciation. As in the Asian emerging markets, high real interest rates are expected to arrest and reverse capital outflows, with concomitant positive effects on the exchange rate. The earlier tightening of monetary and fiscal policy has now pushed the economy into recession. Current forecasts are for real GDP to fall by some 3-4 per cent in 1999 compared with 1998, but this may prove to be too optimistic. The contagion effects on other emerging markets have so far been much more limited compared with those that followed the Russian devaluation and default. This probably reflects the fact that the currency depreciation had been widely anticipated and that the exposure of investors to emerging markets, notably as regards highly leveraged investments, had already been substantially reduced in the final months of 1998.

The large currency depreciation has significantly improved price competitiveness of Brazilian firms and this could lead to tensions within Mercosur, the free trade zone which, besides Brazil, includes Argentina, Paraguay and Uruguay. In fact, foreign trade and investment links can constitute an important channel for contagion.[59] But Mercosur is a relatively closed trade area,[60] which accounts only for some 3 per cent of United States and extra-EU exports. This means that the trade effects will be largely felt inside Mercosur. The main impact will be on Argentina, the third largest economy in Latin America, which relies strongly on the Brazilian market for its exports. Argentina has raised interest rates to defend its own currency, the peso, which is pegged to the dollar in the framework of a currency board.[61]

Overall economic developments in *Latin America* in 1998 were strongly affected by the repercussions of the Asian crisis on international capital flows and commodity prices. Monetary policy was tightened significantly to prevent capital outflows and the associated loss of international reserves. On current trends a recession in 1999 cannot be excluded.[62]

This episode can be seen as a confirmation of lessons for the ECE transition economies already drawn from the Asian crisis.[63] Strong dependence on short-term foreign capital can lead to an inherently unstable economic situation once foreign investors start pulling out. The increase of official interest rates, even to very high levels, is then no guarantee for arresting capital outflows, in fact, it may even make matters worse, given the adverse consequence of tight policies for domestic activity levels. Any official exchange rate peg, moreover, must be backed not only by an adequate level of foreign reserves but, more importantly, by credible economic policies designed to prevent the emergence of major domestic and external imbalance. Otherwise, governments simply sow the seeds for a speculative attack on the currency with attendant risks of a serious overshooting of the ensuing depreciation. More generally, when significant imbalances begin to emerge, governments must design credible adjustment policies and be seen to implement them in order to maintain or restore investor confidence. Governments should also be prepared for contagion effects if a financial crisis occurs in another country in the region or beyond. This holds independently of the state of the so-called "fundamentals" given that international investors in times of crisis often fail to differentiate between national markets.

(iv) Recent developments in East Asia

In *Japan*, the economic situation deteriorated significantly in the course of 1998. Real GDP fell in the four consecutive quarters[64] since the final quarter of 1997 and for 1998 as a whole a decline by some 2¾ per cent is estimated, the worst recession since 1974, when there was a decline of nearly 1 per cent. The unemployment rate rose above 4 per cent, a postwar record. Deflationary tendencies are discernible, *inter alia*, in a very large and rising output gap, falling wholesale and producer prices as well as asset prices, a severe crisis in the banking sector, a credit crunch for small- and medium-sized enterprises, and depressed business profits. Private households' spending behaviour has become very cautious on account of the worsening outlook for jobs

---

[59] R. Glick and A. Rose, "Contagion and trade: why are currency crises regional?", *NBER Working Paper,* No. 6806 (Cambridge, MA), November 1998.

[60] The degree of openness (measured as the arithmetic average of the sum of merchandise exports and imports as a proportion of total GDP) is only about 8 per cent compared to some 35 per cent of the aggregate of five Asian economies most affected by the recent crises.

[61] There has even been a proposal by the government to "dollarize" the economy, i.e. to introduce the United States currency as legal tender.

[62] Economic Commission for Latin America and the Caribbean, *Preliminary Overview of the Economies of Latin America and the Caribbean 1998* (United Nations publication, Sales No. E.98.II.G.15).

[63] UN/ECE, *Economic Survey of Europe, 1998 No. 1,* pp. 73-75.

[64] At the time of writing, national accounts data were available only for the first three quarters of 1998. But forecasts are for a further fall in real GDP in the fourth quarter of 1998. This would then be the fifth consecutive quarterly decline in aggregate output.

CHART 2.1.5

**The exchange rate of the yen against the dollar,
January 1994-February 1999**
(Monthly averages)

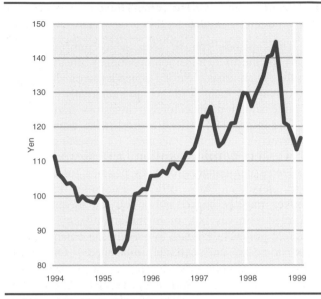

Source: United States Federal Reserve.

and incomes and concerns about the pension system. As a result, the savings propensity rose markedly in 1998. Weak domestic demand has translated into a marked fall in imports. Exports to western Europe and North America rose strongly but this was more than offset by the continuing weak demand from other countries in the region. The current account surplus rose to some $140 billion or 3.3 per cent of GDP in 1998.

The sharp appreciation of the yen between the beginning of August 1998 and mid-January 1999 has raised concerns about its adverse impact on export growth, the mainstay of economic activity in the current malaise. The Bank of Japan intervened in early January 1999 to arrest the strengthening of the yen against the dollar, which has since been partly reversed (chart 2.1.5). The appreciation of the yen has probably offset to a large degree the potential effects of the new fiscal stimulus package adopted in April 1998. In any case, significant positive effects of this package were hardly discernible until late 1998, when there were signs of a strengthening in public investment. A further package of fiscal measures, which envisages additional public works spending as well as income and corporate tax reductions, was adopted in November. Given the persistence of recessionary forces, the successive fiscal stimulus packages have propelled the budget deficit and government debt to high levels. Gross general government debt rose to about 100 per cent of GDP in 1998, compared with some 75 per cent in 1995.

Official interest rates in Japan are at very low levels. The discount rate has been at a historic low of 0.5 per cent since September 1995. The overnight lending rate was reduced to 0.25 per cent in September 1998. The effects of this monetary easing, if any, were probably offset by the appreciation of the yen. There was a further lowering of the lending rate to 0.15 per cent in mid-February 1999 and in early March, the bank pushed it down to 0.02 per cent. This move led to a fall in long-term interest rates as investors shifted funds from the money market to the bond market. But, since for some time there has been no evidence that the monetary transmission mechanism is still effective, there have been demands for an outright monetization of government debt by the Bank of Japan, a demand which it has so far resisted.

Reform of the banking sector is underway, but small- and medium-sized companies continue to be faced with the restrictive lending policy of banks ("credit crunch"). Public funds were made available in the autumn of 1998 to enable banks to tackle the bad loans problem, but although they have made large write-offs, the volume of bad loans did not change significantly in the first half of 1998, as new firms became insolvent.

In the *five Asian economies* most affected by the crisis in the region (Indonesia, Malaysia, Philippines, Republic of Korea and Thailand) there was a sharp fall in output in 1998, except in the Philippines, where the recession was rather shallow (table 2.1.2). The current account balances of these countries have moved from deficit in 1997 into surplus in 1998, reflecting the domestic adjustment process to the net outflow of private capital from the region. Falling import demand has played a major role in this reversal of the current account balance. Export values have remained depressed with, in some countries, a strong recovery in export volumes offset by falling dollar prices. National currencies have tended to appreciate against the dollar in 1998, thus partly reversing the earlier sharp depreciations. Exchange rate pressures were also reduced on account of the strong appreciation of the yen against the dollar in the second half of 1998. This provided scope for lowering domestic interest rates, which was supported in some countries (Indonesia, Republic of Korea, Thailand) by a more accommodative stance of fiscal policy. Equity prices have also edged upwards but displayed considerable volatility in view of the turbulence in international financial markets (chart 2.1.4). The recession is expected to bottom out in 1999 reflecting the more conducive stance of economic policy and improved prospects for export earnings, but this will also depend on the extent of the cyclical slowdown expected in western Europe and North America.

Among other Asian emerging market economies, Hong Kong moved into deep recession in 1998, while the forces for growth have weakened significantly in Singapore, driving the economy to the brink of recession. In contrast, the Taiwan economy has displayed a striking resilience to the recession in the region, although the financial sector has started to experience some difficulties (table 2.1.2).

TABLE 2.1.2

Annual changes in real GDP in east Asian countries, 1996-1999
(Percentage change over preceding year)

	1996	1997	1998	1999
Asean-4	7.1	4.6	-8.9	-1.2
Indonesia	8.0	4.6	-13.7	-3.9
Malaysia	8.6	7.7	-6.4	0.2
Philippines	5.8	9.7	-0.5	1.5
Thailand	5.5	-0.4	-7.9	0.7
NIEs	6.3	6.0	-2.0	0.1
Hong Kong	4.6	5.3	-5.0	-1.5
Republic of Korea	7.1	5.5	-6.1	-2.2
Singapore	6.9	7.8	1.3	–
Taiwan Province of China	5.7	6.8	4.8	4.4
China	9.7	8.8	7.8	7.3
Japan	5.0	1.4	-2.6	-0.5
Total above	7.4	5.6	0.8	2.7

Source: Consensus Economics Inc., *Consensus Forecasts*, February 1999 (internet website).

Note: Growth rates of regional aggregates have been calculated by the ECE secretariat as weighted averages of growth rates of individual countries. Weights were derived from 1996 GDP data converted from national currency units into dollars using purchasing power parities.

In *China*, the pace of economic expansion slowed down further in 1998, although the growth rate of real GDP remained very high by international standards. Despite the significant adverse trade effects of the east Asian crisis and the associated repercussions on domestic employment and income levels, the official target of an increase in real GDP by 8 per cent was broadly met. Strong overall growth, however, contrasts with sluggish consumer demand and falling consumer and producer prices in 1998. It appears that a large part of output is simply being added to already large inventories, which may not be saleable. In fact, to counter the slowdown in economic growth and reverse deflationary tendencies the stance of monetary policy was eased and the government boosted expenditure on public investment projects. These measures appear to have been effective in supporting economic growth in the second half of 1998.

A matter of concern has been the signs of crisis in the so-called International Trust and Investment Corporations (ITICs), which have been channelling funds borrowed abroad to domestic projects. In October 1998, a large ITIC was declared bankrupt after defaulting on its foreign loans. The government announced in early 1999 that most of the ITICs will have to be restructured. International banks have reacted to the prospect that their loans might not be repaid with a credit squeeze on Chinese corporate borrowers, refusing to extend new loans and calling in some existing loans. A matter of dispute remains the reliability of macroeconomic statistics published by the Chinese Statistical Office and to what degree output growth is overstated.[65] Faced with a deteriorating domestic

_____

[65] See IMF, *World Economic Outlook ...*, op. cit., pp. 147-150, box 4.1, which tries to reconcile strong output growth with low increases in electricity production and falling freight traffic in 1998.

economic environment, the authorities have maintained their commitment not to devalue the renminbi, which has fluctuated within an unchanged narrow band against the dollar since May 1994. But the domestic economic costs of this exchange rate policy have been increasing and its sustainability will depend strongly on a recovery not only of demand in the neighbouring Asian economies and sustained import growth in western markets but also on the restoration of domestic consumer and investor confidence. Growth prospects for 1999 could also be affected by potential adverse spillover effects of the crisis in Brazil, which so far, however, have failed to occur.

2.2 The economic situation in western Europe and North America

(i) General economic developments

In the western market economies, the contractionary effects of the crisis in Asia and other parts of the world economy were increasingly restraining export growth in the second half of 1998. In western Europe, this weakening of exports was not offset by a strengthening of domestic demand; instead, the growth of domestic demand also slowed down. Real GDP rose by only 0.6 per cent between the second and third quarters of 1998 and was only 2.5 per cent above its level in the third quarter of 1997 (chart 2.2.1). Partial data suggest that economic growth decelerated further in the final quarter of 1998: real GDP in the four major economies combined stagnated between the third and fourth quarters, masking falling aggregate output levels in Germany and Italy. Rough estimates suggest that economic growth in western Europe as a whole was only about one quarter of a percentage point in the final quarter of 1998. This stands in sharp relief to developments in the United States. Propelled by buoyant domestic demand, real GDP rose by 1.5 per cent between the third and last quarters. These relative changes have led to an increasing divergence in the cyclical positions of western Europe and the United States, a tendency which appears to have continued in early 1999. For 1998 as a whole, real GDP in western Europe is currently estimated to have increased by 2.7 per cent, down from 2.9 per cent in 1997. Within this aggregate, there was a slight increase in the average annual growth rate in the European Union and the euro area to 2.8 per cent in 1998 (table 2.2.1). In the United States, real GDP rose by 3.9 per cent in 1998, the same as in 1997.

(a) Western Europe

Against a background of deteriorating prospects for sales and profits, industrial confidence in western Europe has fallen sharply since mid-1998, a feature which contrasts with a further rise of consumer confidence to very high levels (chart 2.2.2). Industrial and consumer confidence have been highly correlated in the past, and the recent divergence between the two is therefore quite

CHART 2.2.1

Quarterly changes in real GDP, 1995-1998
(Percentage change over same quarter of preceding year)

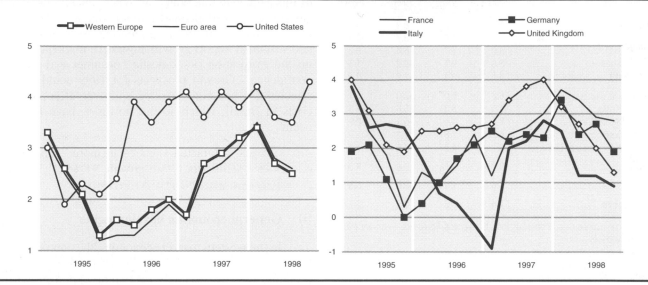

Source: National statistics.

Note: Data are seasonally adjusted. Euro area excludes Ireland and Luxembourg. Western Europe: euro area plus Denmark, Norway, Sweden, Switzerland and the United Kingdom.

striking. To some extent the relative optimism of consumers may reflect the prevailing low interest rates and the gains in financial wealth of private households, which have supported the purchase of consumer durables (notably cars) and favourable financing of residential investments. There could be considerable myopia, however, on the part of consumers. Thus, the effects of the recent deterioration in the short-run economic outlook will become visible in the labour markets only with a lag in the course of 1999. It is also striking that, on balance, households perceived an improvement in the general economic situation between September 1998 and February 1999,[66] although forecasts of economic growth were being steadily revised downwards since last autumn.

Manufacturing production turned increasingly sluggish in the course of 1998, a marked contrast to its buoyancy in 1997 (chart 2.2.3). This reflected to a large degree the adverse effects of the spreading crisis in emerging markets, including the transition economies, on net exports of manufactures. These effects then spilled over via weaker activity levels and depressed demand for imported intermediate goods and raw materials between west European countries themselves. As a result, manufacturing output in western Europe is estimated to have fallen between the third and fourth quarters of 1998. In view of the significant statistical carry-over effect from the end of last year, output rose, nevertheless, by some 3.5 per cent for the year as whole.

This average includes considerably stronger growth rates in Finland (8.5 per cent), Ireland (16.5) and Spain (6¼). In view of the sharp slowdown in output growth, capacity utilization rates fell in the second half of 1998 and in January 1999 they were nearly 2 percentage points lower than in August 1998 (chart 2.2.3).

Among the major components of demand, private consumption held up relatively well in 1998, and although the underlying tendency was for a slight weakening in the course of the year (chart 2.2.4), it was the mainstay of domestic demand. Aggregate households' disposable incomes in 1998 were supported by continued moderate growth in average earnings and by stronger gains in employment than in 1997. In several countries, consumers' expenditure was also supported by falling saving ratios. In addition, real disposable incomes were boosted by falling inflation and the sharp fall in oil prices.

Quarterly changes in real fixed capital formation have been rather volatile since the second half of 1997, but the momentum which has normally accompanied earlier cyclical upswings has been lacking. The rise in capacity utilization rates until mid-1998 stimulated business investment, as did favourable financing conditions and improved profitability. But with the deteriorating economic outlook, many firms appear to have postponed or scaled down their investment plans. The main focus of business investment has continued to be rationalization and modernization. Expenditure on machinery and equipment rose in real terms by some 8 per cent in 1998 (compared with 1997). In contrast, construction investment remained sluggish with

_____

[66] European Commission, *Business and Consumer Surveys, First Results: February 1999* (Brussels), 4 March 1999.

TABLE 2.2.1

Real GDP in the developed market economies, 1996-1999
(Percentage change over previous year)

	1996	1997	1998	1999[a]
Western Europe	2.0	2.9	2.7	1.9
4 major countries	1.5	2.3	2.4	1.5
France	1.6	2.3	3.1	2.2
Germany	1.3	2.2	2.8	1.5
Italy	0.9	1.5	1.4	1.8
United Kingdom	2.6	3.5	2.3	0.5
17 smaller countries	3.1	3.9	3.3	2.5
Austria	2.0	2.5	3.3	2.1
Belgium	1.3	3.0	2.8	2.0
Cyprus	2.0	2.5	5.0	4.0
Denmark	3.3	3.1	2.4	1.6
Finland	4.1	5.6	4.9	3.0
Greece	2.4	3.2	3.0	3.2
Iceland	5.5	5.0	5.6	4.3
Ireland	7.4	9.8	8.5	6.3
Israel	4.7	2.7	2.0	1.7
Luxembourg	3.0	4.8	4.7	3.4
Malta	3.8	4.4	7.6	7.5
Netherlands	3.1	3.6	3.7	2.3
Norway	5.5	3.4	2.0	1.0
Portugal	3.2	3.7	3.5	3.0
Spain	2.4	3.5	3.8	3.4
Sweden	1.3	1.8	2.9	2.0
Switzerland	–	1.7	2.1	1.5
Turkey	7.0	7.5	2.4	1.8
North America	3.3	3.9	3.8	3.0
Canada	1.2	3.8	3.0	2.7
United States	3.4	3.9	3.9	3.0
Total above	2.7	3.4	3.3	2.4
Japan	5.0	1.4	-2.9	-0.5
Total above, *including Japan*	3.0	3.1	2.3	2.0
Memorandum items:				
European Union	1.8	2.6	2.8	1.9
Euro area	1.6	2.5	2.8	2.1

Source: National statistics and national economic reports.

Note: All aggregates exclude Israel. Growth rates of regional aggregates have been calculated as weighted averages of growth rates in individual countries. Weights were derived from 1991 GDP data converted from national currency units into dollars using purchasing power parities.

[a] Forecasts.

persistent excess capacities in many countries. Falling mortgage interest rates stimulated households' residential investment and there was also a stronger growth of investment in industrial buildings. On average, however, construction investment rose only by some 1¼ per cent in 1998. Altogether, total real gross fixed capital formation increased by 4.7 per cent in 1998, up from about 3.4 per cent in 1997 (table 2.2.2).

Changes in stockbuilding tended to support domestic activity in 1998, although there was a weakening in stock accumulation in the second half of the year. For the year as a whole, stockbuilding contributed half a percentage point to the overall growth of GDP.

Growth in real exports of goods and services slowed down significantly in 1998 from the very high rates of 1997, a reflection of the fall in demand from Asia, Russia and the OPEC countries. But also demand from central and eastern Europe weakened. This general shortfall of demand was increasingly less offset by rising demand in the other west European economies, which was reflected in a weakening of their import growth. In addition there were competitive pressures from the recovery of export growth in Asia, which tended to crowd out producers from western Europe in their domestic markets and abroad.

On average, the changes in real net exports of goods and services subtracted somewhat more than half a percentage point from the growth in total domestic demand of 3.4 per cent to yield an increase in real GDP in western Europe of 2.7 per cent.

Developments in the *labour markets* were relatively positive in 1998. The rise in aggregate output was associated with an increase in total employment in western Europe by some 1¼ per cent in 1998 (table 2.2.3). This was the largest annual increase since 1990 (chart 2.2.5), but the weakening of cyclical growth forces in the course of 1998 increasingly weakened the demand for labour.

Employment growth continued quite strongly in the smaller economies in 1998, also a reflection of rapid output growth in the past few years. In contrast, changes in employment were more divergent among the four major economies, where the average increase was small (about half a percentage point). There was, however, a strong upturn in the demand for labour in France, in fact the largest annual increase in employment in this decade. This reflected the combined effect of robust economic growth and special labour market measures aimed at providing jobs for young persons in the public sector.[67] Employment growth also remained relatively strong in the United Kingdom, but weakened in the course of the year in response to the cyclical downturn. In Germany, the fall in employment since 1991 petered out into broad stagnation in 1998. There was, however, a rise in manufacturing employment in the course of 1998 but this levelled off in the final months of the year as output growth weakened. Employment in eastern Germany continues to be supported by special job creation programmes. In Italy, sluggish economic activity produced only a slight rise in employment.

Increased employment was also reflected in a further small decline in the average unemployment rate to 9.2 per cent in 1998, down from 9.9 per cent in 1997 (table 2.2.4 and chart 2.2.6). Some offset to the falls in unemployment was due to the growth in the labour force, which was also influenced in many countries by the increased incentives for "discouraged workers" to seek

---

[67] This accounted for about one third of all the additional jobs created in 1998 and was reflected in a decline of youth unemployment.

CHART 2.2.2

Business cycle indicators for the European Union and the United States, January 1994-February 1999

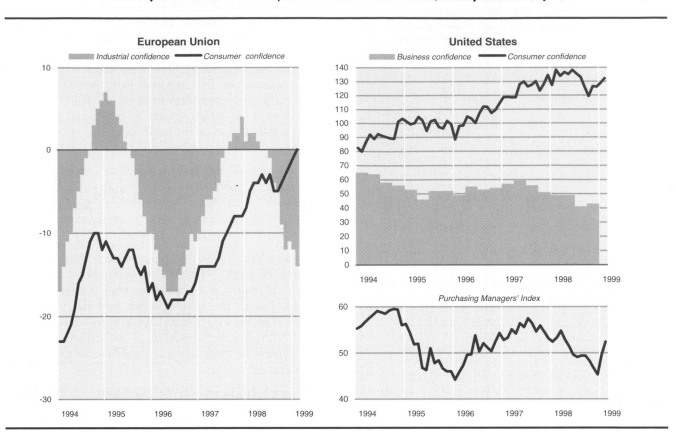

Source: Data for the European Union: Commission of the European Communities, *European Economy*, Supplement B (Luxembourg), monthly and direct communications. Data for the United States: consumer and business confidence: the Conference Board, New York (internet website), and direct communications. Purchasing Managers' Index: website of the National Association of Purchasing Management, Arizona, and direct communications.

Note: European Union data show net balances between the percentages of respondents giving positive and negative answers to specific questions. For details see any edition of the source. United States: consumer confidence is measured in index form with base year 1985=100. Business confidence is compiled on the basis of answers to specific questions, with the following scale applying: 100 = substantially good; 75 = moderately good (+); 50 = moderately good (-); 25 = moderately bad; (0) = bad. The Purchasing Managers' Index (PMI) is a composite index pertaining to the business situation in manufacturing industry. An index value above (below) 50 per cent indicates that manufacturing industry is generally expanding (contracting). A PMI above (below) 44.5 per cent, over a period of time, indicates that overall economic activity, as measured by real GDP, is generally expanding (contracting).

jobs again against a background of tighter labour markets. On the other hand, special labour market measures also played a role in reducing unemployment in France and Germany. Given the modest recent declines, the average unemployment rate has remained close to its peak of the past two decades in France, Germany and Italy. This contrasts with the sharp fall of the unemployment rate in the United Kingdom since the start of the cyclical upswing in 1993, to 6.3 per cent in 1998, the lowest rate in the past two decades. Unemployment rates have fallen significantly in many of the smaller economies and to relatively low levels in 1998 (table 2.2.4).

The negative social and economic consequences of persistently high unemployment rates in most of western Europe has increased the pressure on governments to strengthen their *labour market policies*. At the "Jobs Summit" of November 1997 the European Union launched the *Luxembourg process*, which aims at reorienting policies towards a more preventive and active approach to the problem. Guidelines were agreed, which

should be translated into National Action Plans for employment. The 1999 version of these guidelines reaffirms the tenets of the strategy and puts the accent on active measures (e.g. changes in benefits and taxes so as to provide incentives for unemployed or inactive people to seek and take up work and training opportunities and to reduce recourse to early retirement schemes) and on lifelong learning (especially in the area of information and communication technologies). However this process is still incipient and the shift in the focus of policies is likely to take place only in the medium term.[68]

Consumer price inflation in western Europe continued the declining trend established at the beginning of the decade and in 1998 reached its lowest level in almost 40 years (see chart 2.2.7). The main factor

---

[68] European Commission, *European Commission Adopts 1999 Employment Guidelines,* IP/98/887 and *European Commission Adopts 1998 Joint Employment Report,* IP/98/889 (Brussels), 14 October 1998.

CHART 2.2.3

Manufacturing output and capacity utilization in the euro area and the United States, January 1996-January 1999

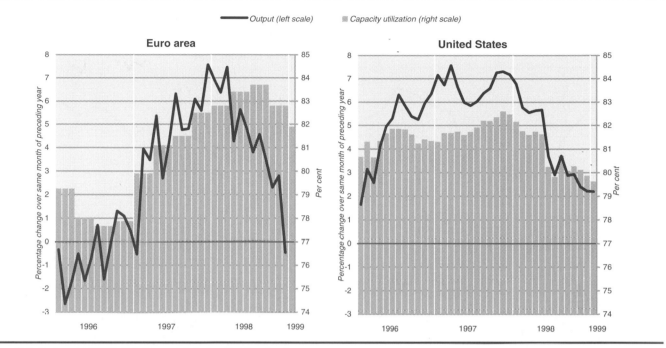

——— Output (left scale)   ▨ Capacity utilization (right scale)

Source: Eurostat; OECD, *Main Economic Indicators* (Paris), various issues.

Note: Data are monthly and seasonally adjusted. Capacity utilization rates for the euro area refer to January, April, July and October of each year. Data for the euro area excludes Austria.

underpinning the latest fall in inflation rates was the steep decline in the prices of international commodities (section 2.1 above). Labour cost pressures have remained largely absent. Prices of international manufactures fell against the background of excess capacities in several sectors (e.g. steel, automobiles, textiles, information processing equipment) and fierce price competition in the wake of the Asian crisis and the marked slowdown in world output growth.[69]

Falling commodity prices depressed not only the prices of industrial raw materials (a major component of producer price indices) but they also exerted downward pressure on the energy and food prices paid by final consumers. The pass-through of falling non-fuel commodity prices contributed to lower average price increases faced by private households. *Producer prices* actually fell not only in many west European countries[70] but also in North America and Japan in 1998. In western Europe, their fall was accentuated by the depreciation of the dollar in the second half of the year, which put additional downward pressure on import prices in domestic currencies. Consumer price inflation averaged only 1.6 per cent in 1998 (table 2.2.5), with virtual

stability in the monthly price indices in the second half of the year. Core inflation (i.e. excluding food and energy prices) has been stable at an annual rate of some 2 per cent since early 1997. The differential changes in producer and consumer prices (chart 2.2.7) reflect not only differences in the composition of the indices but also the fact that consumer prices also include services. There is evidence that service suppliers have been more successful in raising their prices in recent years than goods suppliers,[71] who have been facing intensified import competition.

An alternative measure of inflation in the euro area is the Harmonized Index of Consumer Prices (HICP), which has a less comprehensive coverage than the traditional national indices. The HICP rose by 1.2 per cent in the euro area in 1998, down from 1.6 per cent in 1997. The general tendency is for the annual inflation rate in the individual countries according to HICP to be slightly lower than the rates based on the national definitions (table 2.2.5). Outside the euro area, there is a considerable difference (some 2 percentage points) between these two measures in the United Kingdom.

---

[69] International trade prices of manufactures (in dollars) fell by 2.5 per cent in 1998 compared with a fall of 8.1 per cent in 1997.

[70] Average annual producer price indices fell in 10 out of 17 countries in 1998. The fall in prices was even more pervasive, in 14 out of 17 countries, in the final months of 1998.

---

[71] In the United Kingdom, for instance, 27 per cent of goods' prices included in the retail price index fell in 1998, as compared with just 14 per cent of service prices. The difference between producer price and consumer price changes may also partly reflect past increases in the cost of labour or bought-in services, which together account for a large portion of manufacturers' total costs. Bank of England, *Inflation Report* (London), February 1999, pp. 35-36.

CHART 2.2.4

Quarterly changes in real GDP and major demand components in western Europe, 1995-1998

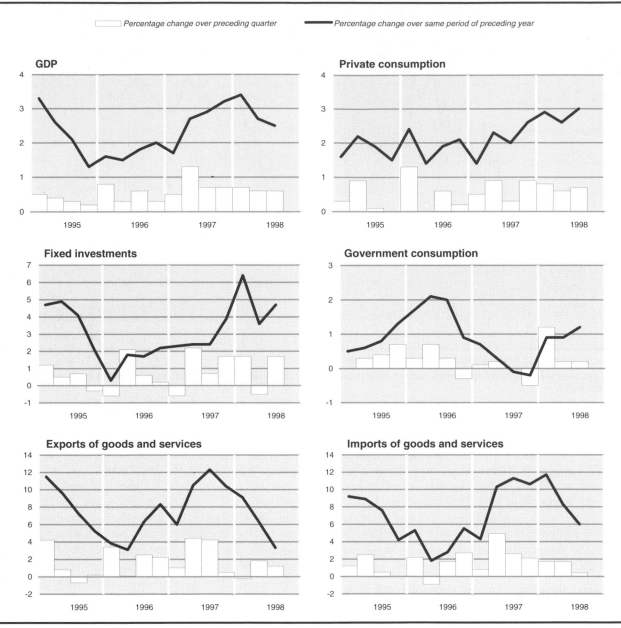

Source: National statistics.

Note: Data are seasonally adjusted. Data cover 14 countries, i.e. 12 member states of the EU (except Greece, Ireland and Luxembourg) plus Norway and Switzerland.

Inflation differentials between countries of the euro area had narrowed significantly in early 1997, but since then the gap between the highest and lowest rates has tended to rise again (chart 2.2.8). While the average increase in the HICP continued to be pulled down by the further decline of inflation in countries such as Austria, Finland, France and Germany, this was partly offset by somewhat stronger inflation in a number of other countries (Portugal, Ireland, the Netherlands) in the course of the year.

The continued moderate growth in labour costs in most western European countries was to a large extent offset by gains in productivity. GDP per person employed, a crude measure of productivity, rose by 1.6 per cent in 1998, less than the 2.5 per cent gain in 1997. This limited the average increase of *unit labour costs* to just 0.6 per cent. In several countries (Germany, Italy, Spain, Netherlands, Switzerland) unit labour costs even fell slightly. The major exceptions to this general pattern were Denmark, Norway and the United Kingdom, where unit labour costs rose by some 4 per cent in 1998.

Among the four major economies, there was a marked strengthening in the average yearly rate of GDP growth in France and Germany. The pace of economic

TABLE 2.2.2

Major components of demand in the ECE market economies, 1997-1998
(Percentage change over preceding year)

	Private consumption		Government consumption		Gross fixed investment		Stock building [a]		Total domestic demand		Exports		Imports		Net exports [a]	
	1997	1998	1997	1998	1997	1998	1997	1998	1997	1998	1997	1998	1997	1998	1997	1998
Western Europe	2.3	2.7	0.3	1.3	3.4	4.7	0.4	0.6	2.6	3.4	10.2	4.8	9.7	7.4	0.2	-0.7
4 major countries	1.8	2.4	-0.1	1.2	1.6	4.1	0.6	0.8	2.0	3.3	9.5	3.9	8.8	7.1	0.3	-0.9
France	0.9	3.4	1.2	1.5	0.1	4.6	0.1	0.6	0.9	3.8	12.6	5.7	8.1	8.2	1.4	-0.7
Germany	0.5	1.9	-0.7	0.6	0.1	1.6	1.2	1.5	1.4	3.1	11.1	5.4	8.1	6.6	0.8	-0.3
Italy	2.6	1.9	-0.8	1.4	0.8	3.5	0.7	0.5	2.4	2.6	5.0	1.3	9.9	6.1	-0.9	-1.1
United Kingdom	3.9	2.6	–	1.5	6.6	8.0	0.2	0.2	3.8	3.5	8.7	2.7	9.5	7.8	-0.3	-1.7
17 smaller countries	3.4	3.2	1.1	1.5	6.9	5.8	–	0.3	3.9	3.8	11.5	6.5	11.4	7.8	0.1	-0.5
Austria	0.7	1.8	-3.9	1.5	2.8	4.8	1.4	0.3	1.8	2.8	10.1	7.5	8.7	6.8	0.7	0.4
Belgium	2.1	2.8	0.8	1.1	5.4	4.8	-0.3	0.1	2.2	3.0	7.1	5.1	6.3	5.5	0.9	-0.1
Cyprus	2.4	7.0	3.4	7.7	-8.4	0.6	0.4	0.1	0.7	5.6	2.1	-2.0	1.3	3.6	0.3	-3.0
Denmark	3.6	3.4	1.1	2.2	10.6	5.0	0.1	0.3	4.5	3.8	5.5	1.2	9.8	4.8	-1.3	-1.3
Finland	2.2	5.1	2.9	0.4	14.2	8.2	0.7	–	5.4	4.6	14.2	6.6	11.4	8.1	2.0	0.2
Greece	2.5	1.9	-0.4	0.8	9.6	8.0	-0.2	-0.2	3.5	3.0	5.3	5.5	5.4	4.5	-0.8	-0.4
Iceland	6.0	10.3	1.5	3.0	11.2	28.2	-0.2	0.2	5.8	12.4	5.6	5.7	8.0	25.0	-0.6	-6.6
Ireland	6.3	8.3	4.8	3.0	10.9	13.0	0.4	-0.6	7.3	7.6	16.9	19.5	15.6	21.3	3.7	2.2
Israel	4.1	3.3	1.9	2.3	-2.3	-3.3	-0.9	-1.0	1.4	0.9	7.6	6.0	2.8	2.1	1.1	1.0
Luxembourg	2.5	2.6	1.7	2.8	14.1	6.5	-0.7	–	4.7	3.7	6.0	7.5	6.1	7.0	0.8	1.5
Malta	2.4	2.9	-1.2	-4.6	-7.6	-4.1	2.1	5.3	1.6	5.6	2.0	5.2	-2.4	1.6	2.8	2.3
Netherlands	3.0	4.4	1.5	2.5	6.8	3.9	–	–	3.6	4.0	6.7	5.9	7.1	6.8	0.3	–
Norway	3.4	3.2	3.0	2.8	12.6	6.6	0.2	0.6	5.6	4.5	5.8	0.5	12.3	6.9	-1.8	-2.3
Portugal	3.0	3.6	2.5	2.8	11.3	7.8	0.2	–	5.2	4.5	8.4	10.5	10.4	10.0	-2.1	-1.2
Spain	3.1	3.5	1.4	1.3	5.1	8.8	-0.3	0.1	2.9	4.4	14.8	10.1	12.2	11.5	0.5	-0.7
Sweden	2.0	2.7	-2.1	2.0	-4.8	10.5	0.7	0.3	0.4	4.1	12.8	5.1	11.7	8.9	1.4	-0.9
Switzerland	1.7	1.8	-0.7	0.6	1.5	3.8	–	1.7	1.3	3.8	9.1	4.1	7.9	8.7	0.5	-1.7
Turkey	8.4	2.1	4.1	0.5	14.8	-2.0	-0.9	1.0	9.0	1.7	19.1	3.3	22.4	1.8	-1.9	0.3
North America	3.4	4.7	1.1	1.0	7.5	9.3	0.5	-0.1	4.3	4.8	12.4	2.1	13.8	10.3	-0.4	-1.2
Canada	4.1	2.7	-0.8	0.7	11.1	4.2	0.8	-0.4	5.2	2.2	8.0	8.1	13.3	6.4	-1.5	0.7
United States	3.4	4.8	1.3	1.1	7.1	9.7	0.5	-0.1	4.2	5.1	12.8	1.5	13.9	10.6	-0.4	-1.4
Total above	2.9	3.7	0.7	1.2	5.4	7.0	0.5	0.3	3.5	4.1	11.3	3.4	11.8	8.8	-0.1	-1.0
Japan	1.0	-1.1	1.5	0.6	-1.9	-9.0	-0.1	-0.2	0.1	-3.6	11.6	-2.3	0.5	-7.7	1.4	0.6
Total above, including Japan	2.6	2.9	0.8	1.1	4.3	4.5	0.4	0.2	2.9	2.9	11.3	2.5	10.0	6.2	0.1	-0.7
Memorandum item:																
European Union	2.0	2.7	0.1	1.3	2.8	5.0	0.5	0.6	2.3	3.5	9.9	5.0	9.1	7.6	0.4	-0.7
Euro area	1.7	2.7	0.2	1.3	2.0	4.2	0.5	0.7	2.0	3.4	10.2	5.5	9.0	7.6	0.5	-0.5

Source: OECD national accounts and national statistics.

Note: All aggregates exclude Israel.

[a] Percentage point contribution to annual GDP growth.

expansion remained sluggish in Italy. In the United Kingdom, there was a marked slowdown in the rate of economic growth.

In *France*, the acceleration in economic growth to a rate of 3.1 per cent in 1998, markedly above the west European average, was mainly supported by domestic demand. Export growth weakened markedly reflecting, *inter alia*, a fall in shipments to Asia. In the presence of strong import demand, changes in real net exports subtracted significantly from overall economic growth. The most striking feature was the recovery in private consumption expenditures, which rose by nearly 3.5 per cent. Aggregate real incomes were boosted by gains in employment, falling inflation and reduced social security charges. Business fixed investment was stimulated by

high capacity utilization rates and lower costs of finance. The favourable outcome for the year as a whole, however, masks a deceleration in the pace of expansion in the second half of 1998, as the effects of the weakening of global growth forces began to increasingly affect activity in industry despite a partial offset by sustained growth in services. Despite the weakening of export growth and strong demand for imports, the merchandise trade surplus fell only slightly and the overall current account remained in comfortable surplus. Developments in 1999 will depend heavily on the impact of the deteriorating international economic environment on consumer and industrial confidence and investment behaviour. A major uncertainty is how the implementation of the 35-hour legal working week will affect industrial competitiveness.

TABLE 2.2.3

Total employment in the ECE market economies, 1995-1998
(Percentage change over previous year)

	1995	1996	1997	1998[a]
Western Europe	1.0	0.8	0.2	1.2
4 major countries	0.3	0.2	0.1	0.6
France	1.0	0.2	0.2	1.4
Germany	-0.4	-1.3	-1.3	–
Italy [b]	-0.3	–	-0.2	0.2
United Kingdom [c]	1.1	2.4	1.9	0.9
17 smaller countries	2.0	1.6	0.3	2.1
Austria	0.2	-0.5	0.3	0.9
Belgium [c]	0.5	0.4	0.5	1.2
Cyprus	3.4	1.0	0.2	..
Denmark	1.1	0.8	2.0	1.9
Finland	1.7	1.0	2.0	2.7
Greece	0.9	1.2	-0.5	1.4
Iceland [b]	0.8	3.0	1.7	2.1
Ireland [d]	5.1	3.9	3.2	6.7
Israel	5.2	2.4	1.4	1.8
Luxembourg	2.5	2.8	3.2	4.5
Malta [e]	3.8	1.0	0.5	0.4
Netherlands [b]	1.4	2.0	2.6	2.7
Norway	2.1	2.5	2.9	2.3
Portugal	-0.7	0.7	1.9	2.8
Spain	2.7	2.9	3.0	3.1
Sweden	1.5	-0.5	-1.0	1.4
Switzerland	0.1	0.3	-0.3	1.2
Turkey	3.7	2.0	-2.5	1.5
North America	2.3	1.8	2.5	2.6
Canada	1.6	1.3	1.9	2.5
United States [f]	2.4	1.9	2.6	2.6
Total above	1.6	1.2	1.2	1.8
Japan	0.2	0.5	1.1	-0.6
Total above, including Japan	1.3	1.1	1.2	1.4
Memorandum items:				
European Union	0.6	0.6	0.5	1.1
Euro area	0.5	0.2	0.2	1.1

Source: National statistics; OECD, *National Accounts Detailed Tables*, Vol. II, 1998 and *OECD Economic Outlook*, No. 64, December 1998 (Paris); UN/ECE secretariat estimates.

Note: All aggregates exclude Israel. Unless otherwise indicated, data refer to the annual average number of persons employed, i.e. no adjustment is made for part-time workers. Comparisons with previous years are limited due to changes in methodology in Israel (1996).

[a] Provisional.

[b] Full-time equivalent data.

[c] June.

[d] Mid-April estimates.

[e] End of year.

[f] Full-time equivalent employees plus the number of self-employed workers (unpaid family workers are not included).

In *Germany*, real GDP rose by 2.8 per cent in 1998 compared with 2.2 per cent in 1997. This improved performance was solely due to the strengthening of domestic demand. Export growth weakened significantly and changes in real net exports subtracted slightly from overall economic growth in 1998 (table 2.2.2). None of the domestic demand components, however, developed any significant upward momentum during the course of

the year. Households' consumption expenditures were supported by larger gains in nominal wage rates which, combined with the fall in inflation and the stabilization of employment levels, led to higher growth in real disposable incomes. Disposable incomes were also supported by a lowering of the income tax burden, which was only partly offset by the rise in VAT at the beginning of April 1998, and by the fall in the savings ratio to historically low values. Business expenditures on machinery and equipment rose strongly, by some 8.5 per cent year-over-year, but this was mainly due to a strong recovery in the first quarter of 1998 which petered out into broad stagnation for the rest of the year. Construction investment fell sharply, by some 5 per cent. The contribution of changes in stockbuilding to overall growth in GDP was some 1¼ percentage points in the past two years, which is very high by international standards.[72] In the labour market, the fall in employment in recent years finally bottomed out in 1998, but there was very little growth during the year. The number of unemployed, which was at a postwar high at the end of 1997, fell steadily in 1998, a reflection, as in France, of special labour market measures. Labour cost pressures were negligible and unit labour costs continued to fall. The merchandise trade surplus rose somewhat in 1998, in part a reflection of the fall in import prices, but this was more than offset by the deterioration in the invisibles balance; as a result, the current account deficit increased to some DM 15 billion in 1998 (or 0.4 per cent of GDP), about twice its level in 1997.

In *Italy*, overall economic activity remained very sluggish in 1998. Real GDP rose by only 1.4 per cent slightly less than in 1997. Fiscal policy was more neutral, following the sharp retrenchment in 1997, but monetary policy was relatively tight for most of the year. Private consumption remained subdued, reflecting little growth in real disposable incomes which was only partly offset by a fall in the household savings ratio. The weakness of private consumption was partly counterbalanced by a moderate strengthening of fixed investment. Government consumption expenditures rose in real terms, more than offsetting their decline in 1997 (table 2.2.2). Private sector domestic demand was restrained in the second half of 1998 by the ending of the special incentive scheme for the purchase of new cars introduced by the government in 1997. The ensuing fall in car sales was a factor behind the weakness of industrial activity in the second half of 1998. The overall deterioration in export performance in 1998 reflects also the adverse effects of the Asian crisis on the domestic textile and clothing sector, which still accounts for an important part of Italian industry. Changes in real net exports subtracted from overall economic growth in 1998. Employment rose only slightly and the high rate of

_____

[72] There is a presumption that these inventory changes are overstated as they are difficult to reconcile with advances in inventory management and general economic developments. Given that inventory changes for recent years are typically calculated as a residual, this would therefore point to biases in other national accounts aggregates. DIW, "Grundlinien der Wirtschaftsentwicklung 1999", *Wochenbericht 1/99* (Berlin), 7 January 1999, p. 18.

CHART 2.2.5

Changes in total employment in industrialized countries, 1990-1998

(Percentage change over previous year)

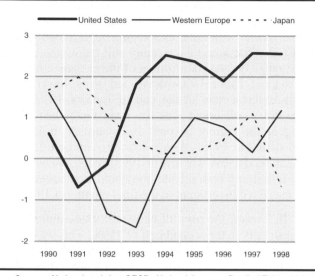

Source: National statistics; OECD, *National Accounts Detailed Tables*, Vol. II, 1998 and *OECD Economic Outlook*, No. 64, December 1998 (Paris); UN/ECE secretariat estimates.

unemployment remained unchanged. The merchandise trade surplus fell in 1998, but the current account remained in comfortable surplus corresponding to some 2.5 per cent of GDP.

In the *United Kingdom*, the pace of economic expansion slowed down from the high rates of 1997 to near stagnation in the final quarter of 1998. The lagged effects of tight economic policies were amplified by the dampening impact of the appreciation of the pound sterling and the effects of the Asian crisis on net exports. The growth of both private consumption and fixed investment has slowed down significantly; this has affected mainly manufacturing industry, which was on the edge of recession throughout the second half of 1998. But there are increasing signs that activity in the services sector has also started to slow down. In response to the weakening of GDP growth and a favourable inflation performance in line with the official target, the stance of monetary policy has been progressively relaxed since early October, although nominal and real interest rates are still significantly higher than in the euro area. Real GDP rose by 2¼ per cent in 1998 down from 3.5 per cent in 1997. Changes in the real foreign balance subtracted about 1.5 percentage points from overall economic growth. Overall employment growth slowed down significantly in 1998, although there were continuing gains in services. The unemployment rate fell to 6.3 per cent in 1998, the lowest in nearly 20 years. But the improvement in the labour market has petered out. Labour cost pressures are difficult to gauge since the suspension of the Average Earnings Index in November 1998, but there are some indications that they have been easing recently. The question is whether in the face of weakening external and domestic demand, a recession can be avoided in 1999.

TABLE 2.2.4

Standardized unemployment rates [a] in the ECE market economies, 1995-1998

(Per cent of civilian labour force)

	1995	1996	1997	1998 [b]
Western Europe	10.1	10.1	9.9	9.2
4 major countries	9.8	10.1	10.2	9.7
France	11.7	12.4	12.4	11.9
Germany	8.2	8.9	9.9	9.4
Italy	11.9	12.0	12.1	12.2
United Kingdom	8.7	8.2	7.0	6.3
17 smaller countries	10.4	10.1	9.5	8.5
Austria	3.9	4.4	4.4	4.4
Belgium	9.9	9.7	9.2	8.8
Cyprus [c]	2.6	3.1	3.4	3.2
Denmark	7.3	6.8	5.6	5.1
Finland	15.3	14.6	12.7	11.4
Greece	9.2	9.6	9.6	9.3
Iceland	5.0	4.4	3.9	2.8
Ireland	12.3	11.6	9.9	7.8
Israel	6.9	6.7	7.7	8.6
Luxembourg	2.9	3.0	2.8	2.8
Malta [c]	3.8	4.4	5.0	4.9
Netherlands	6.9	6.3	5.2	4.0
Norway	5.0	4.9	4.1	3.4
Portugal	7.3	7.3	6.8	4.9
Spain	22.9	22.2	20.8	18.8
Sweden	8.8	9.6	9.9	8.2
Switzerland	4.2	4.7	5.2	3.8
Turkey	6.9	6.0	5.7	5.6
North America	6.0	5.8	5.4	4.9
Canada	9.5	9.7	9.2	8.3
United States	5.6	5.4	4.9	4.5
Total above	8.3	8.3	7.9	7.3
Japan	3.2	3.4	3.4	4.1
Total above, *including Japan*	7.5	7.5	7.2	6.8
Memorandum items:				
European Union	10.7	10.8	10.6	9.9
Euro area	11.4	11.6	11.6	10.9

Source: National statistics; OECD, *Quarterly Labour Force Statistics*, No. 4, 1998, *Main Economic Indicators*, various issues and *OECD Economic Outlook*, No. 64, December 1998 (Paris); UN/ECE secretariat estimates.

Note: All aggregates exclude Israel.

[a] Adjusted to achieve comparability between countries, except for Cyprus, Iceland, Israel, Malta, Switzerland and Turkey.

[b] Provisional.

[c] End of year.

Among the *smaller west European economies*, the pattern of performance was as diverse as among the four larger economies, but the general factors shaping outcomes were much the same. The dominating feature was for weakening export growth in the second half of 1998, accompanied by a slowdown in the growth of domestic demand. For the year as whole, real GDP rose by 3¼ per cent, down from nearly 4 per cent in 1997 (table 2.2.1). This outcome reflects to a large degree a pronounced weakening of economic growth in Denmark, Norway and Turkey. In contrast, the rate of economic expansion remained quite vigorous in most of the other countries, notably Finland, Ireland, Luxembourg, the Netherlands, Portugal and Spain.

CHART 2.2.6

Unemployment rates in industrialized countries, 1990-1998

(Per cent of civilian labour force, quarterly average, standardized rate)

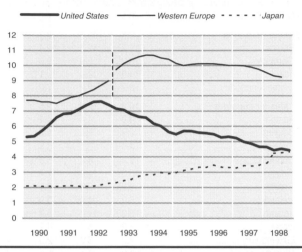

Source: National statistics; OECD, *Quarterly Labour Force Statistics*, No. 4, 1998, *Main Economic Indicators*, various issues and *OECD Economic Outlook*, No. 64, December 1998 (Paris); UN/ECE secretariat estimates.

Note: The average unemployment rate for western Europe does not include data for east Germany before 1993.

CHART 2.2.7

Inflation in four major European countries, 1994-1998

(Percentage change over same month of previous year)

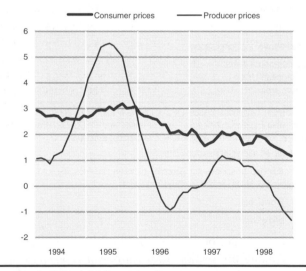

Source: National statistics.

Note: Four major European countries: France, Germany, Italy and the United Kingdom.

In *Denmark*, in addition to the adverse changes in real net exports, the deceleration in economic growth also reflects the effects of restrictive fiscal measures introduced to prevent the overheating of domestic activity.

In *Norway*, a cyclical peak was passed in 1998 after a long and high rate of economic expansion which started in 1993. Monetary policy was significantly tightened

between March and August 1998 in response to considerable capital outflows which put downward pressure on the exchange rate. These capital ouflows were associated with the sharp fall in oil prices and mounting wage cost pressures originating in the increasingly tight labour market. In late August, the central bank abandoned its attempt to maintain the exchange rate within the established target range against the ECU. The krone is currently still below the official target range but the stabilization of the exchange rate and the marked cyclical slowdown led to a lowering of official interest rates at the end of January 1999. The sharp fall in oil prices was the main factor behind the swing in the current account from surplus in 1997 to small deficit in 1998. As a reaction to falling prices, oil and gas production was cut in 1998. High interest rates were restraining both private household expenditures and business fixed investment in the final months of 1998.

In *Turkey*, the pace of economic expansion slowed down sharply in the second half of 1998. This was partly in response to the tightening of economic policies within the framework of the government's three-year stabilization programme which was launched in the first half of the year and which aims to curb very high inflation and reduce high fiscal deficits. The restraining effects of tighter macroeconomic policy, however, were significantly amplified by the adverse effects of the Asian and Russian crises. Exports were depressed by the fall in demand from Russia[73] and increasing competitive pressures from Asian producers in domestic and foreign markets. In addition, the Russian crisis triggered capital outflows which were mirrored in a significant rise in yields on short-term treasury bills and of overnight lending rates in the interbank market. High real domestic interest rates and a tightening of lending standards have restrained private sector borrowing, with concomitant negative effects on consumption and investment spending.

The steady economic recovery in Switzerland during 1997 increasingly lost momentum in 1998, reflecting mainly the effects of slowing export growth and the adjustment of business inventories, which offset the steady growth of consumption and fixed investment.

Among the remaining countries, annual rates of economic growth were rather favourable but, again, the annual average masks a more or less pronounced slowdown in domestic demand and exports during the course of the year. In Portugal and Spain, domestic demand was stimulated by falling interest rates in the course of 1998 but despite high levels of activity the deteriorating international environment appears to have alleviated fears of overheating.

In *Greece,* macroeconomic policies are focused on meeting the key Maastricht convergence criteria by mid-2000. Economic growth in 1998 was largely supported

---

[73] The sharp depreciation of the Russian rouble eroded the incentives for the so-called "suitcase trade" with Russia and other members of the CIS, which was estimated to exceed official exports by a large margin.

TABLE 2.2.5

Consumer price indices in ECE market economies, 1996-1998

(Percentage change over previous year)

	According to national definitions			HICP[a]
	1996	1997	1998	1998
Western Europe	2.3	1.9	1.6	..
4 major countries	2.4	1.9	1.6	1.1
France	2.0	1.2	0.7	0.7
Germany	1.5	1.8	0.9	0.6
Italy	3.9	1.7	1.8	2.0
United Kingdom	2.4	3.1	3.4	1.6
16 smaller countries [b]	2.3	1.8	1.5	1.8
Austria	1.9	1.3	0.9	0.8
Belgium	2.0	1.6	1.0	0.9
Cyprus	2.9	3.6	2.2	..
Denmark	2.0	2.2	1.9	1.4
Finland	0.5	1.2	1.4	1.4
Greece	8.3	5.5	4.8	4.6
Iceland	2.3	1.8	1.7	1.4
Ireland	1.7	1.4	2.4	2.2
Israel	11.3	9.0	5.4	..
Luxembourg	1.3	1.4	1.0	1.0
Malta	2.5	3.2	2.2	..
Netherlands	2.0	2.2	2.0	1.8
Norway	1.3	2.6	2.3	1.9
Portugal	3.1	2.3	2.8	2.3
Spain	3.6	2.0	1.8	1.8
Sweden	0.5	0.5	-0.1	1.0
Switzerland	0.8	0.5	0.1	..
Turkey	79.8	84.8	86.2	..
North America	2.8	2.2	1.5	..
Canada	1.6	1.6	0.9	..
United States	3.0	2.3	1.6	..
Total above	2.6	2.1	1.5	..
Japan	0.1	1.8	0.6	..
Total above, *including Japan*	2.2	2.0	1.4	..
Memorandum items:				
European Union	2.4	1.9	1.6	1.3
Euro area	2.4	1.7	1.3	1.2

Source: National statistics and Eurostat.

Note: All aggregates exclude Israel.

[a] Inflation according to the Harmonised Index of Consumer Prices (HICP).

[b] Thirteen smaller countries in the case of inflation according to the HICP.

CHART 2.2.8

Inflation rate differentials in the euro area, 1996-1998

(Harmonized Index of Consumer Prices, percentage change over same month of previous year)

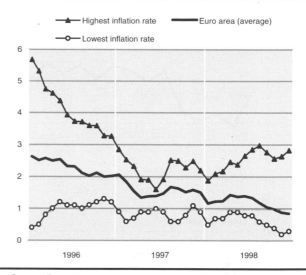

Source: Eurostat.

the average change of the consumer price index. Growth prospects for 1999 will be affected by the expected near stagnation of the United Kingdom economy, the major trading partner.

Outside Europe, economic growth in *Israel*[74] has been sluggish since the second half of 1996. Economic developments in 1998 were influenced by the cumulative effects of the Asian crisis which affected capital inflows and depressed export growth. Domestic demand remained weak against a background of tight economic policies and the petering out of the capital stock adjustment process that had been triggered by the earlier surge in immigration and which stimulated notably residential investment.

(b) North America

In the *United States,* the last recession ended in March 1991. This was followed by the longest period of peacetime expansion (96 months in April 1999) since the dating of business cycles began in 1854.[75]

The marked acceleration in economic growth, by 1.5 per cent, between the third and final quarters of 1998 was not expected by economic forecasters (chart 2.2.9). The growth of personal consumption expenditures remained very high and business fixed investment accelerated sharply following moderate growth in the

by fixed investment in both the private and public sectors, with the latter partly financed by EU structural funds. Inflation was below 3.7 per cent in January 1999 down from 6.8 per cent in the same month of 1997. The general government budget deficit fell below 3 per cent in 1998, but government debt, which is more than 100 per cent of GDP, fell only slightly.

In *Ireland*, the economy has so far displayed a striking resilience to the repercussions of the Asian and Russian crises on the global economy. Continued buoyancy of exports and domestic demand led to an increase in real GDP of 8.5 per cent in 1998, down from 9.8 per cent in the previous year. Mounting inflationary pressures on labour costs and asset prices in some sectors of the domestic economy have failed so far to show up in

---

[74] Israel has been a member of the UN/ECE since July 1991.

[75] National Bureau of Economic Research, *US Business Cycle Expansions and Contractions* (internet website). The longest expansion so far lasted 106 months starting from February 1961 (trough) until December 1969 (peak) – but this was influenced by the Viet Nam war.

CHART 2.2.9

Quarterly changes in real GDP and major demand components in the United States, 1995-1998

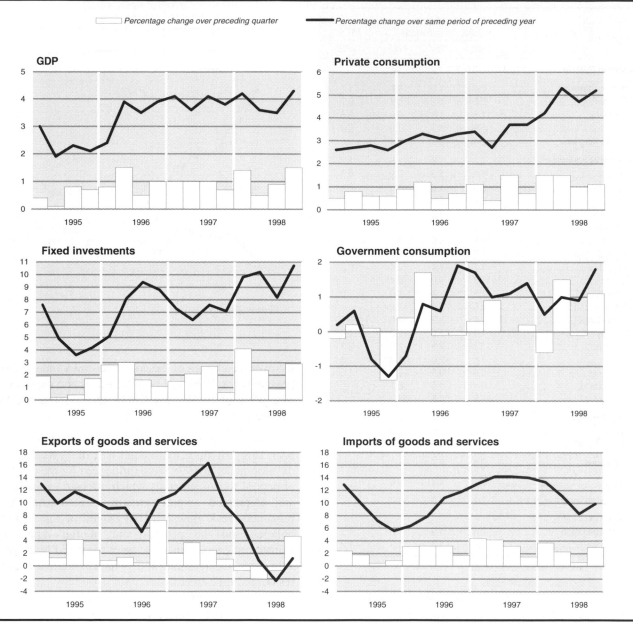

Source: National statistics.

Note: Data are seasonally adjusted.

third quarter. Residential investment maintained its high momentum. Real exports of goods and services also rose markedly following three consecutive quarters of decline. Import demand growth remained strong in the presence of buoyant domestic demand but, following seven consecutive quarters of negative contributions to quarterly GDP growth, real net exports even provided some slight support to domestic activity.

For the year as a whole, real GDP rose by 3.9 per cent in 1998, the same rate as in 1997. Total domestic demand rose by more than 5 per cent, but this was significantly offset by adverse changes in real net exports. Real exports rose only 1.5 per cent for the year as a

whole, restrained by the strong dollar (for most of the year) and weakening demand in foreign markets. Personal consumption expenditure rose at its strongest rate since 1985, and continued to be supported by the combined effect of continuing employment growth, increases in average nominal earnings, and falling inflation. Consumer confidence rose to very high levels, a tendency which was only temporarily interrupted by the financial market turbulence in late summer 1998 (chart 2.2.2). Household savings fell to only 0.1 per cent of disposable incomes in the fourth quarter, down from an already low 1.1 per cent in the first quarter. This willingness of households (in the aggregate) to spend all of their disposable income is associated with the significant gains in financial wealth stemming from the rise in share prices. One result of the favourable gains in incomes and wealth and low mortgage interest rates, was a considerable demand for single-family housing, which contributed to a boom in the construction sector. The buoyancy of business fixed investment reflects to a large degree the continuing surge in expenditure on information processing equipment which, in real terms, was some 31 per cent higher in the fourth quarter of 1998 than a year earlier.[76] Manufacturing production was relatively sluggish in the course of 1998, a result of the Asian crisis and competitive pressures from the strong dollar. Production rose only slightly in the course of the year, and the relatively strong average annual growth rate of 4 per cent largely reflects a significant statistical carry-over effect from 1997.[77] As a result of the continuing strong growth in productive capacity, due to high levels of fixed investment, there was a significant fall in capacity utilization rates (chart 2.2.3). Capacity output in January 1999 is estimated to have been 5.5 per cent higher than in the same month of 1998. Capacity utilization rates fell by more than 3 percentage points over the same period and were some 6 percentage points below their previous peak in 1988-1989. Business confidence recovered slightly in the final quarter of 1998 after falling to a seven-year low in the third quarter, which was marked by turbulence in financial markets (chart 2.2.2).

The continuing economic expansion in the United States supported further large gains in employment and a fall in the unemployment rate to 4.3 per cent at the end of 1998. Increased demand for labour in services, financing, insurance and the construction sectors was partly offset by labour shedding in manufacturing industry during the year. Driven by strong output growth, there was a considerable rise in labour productivity (output per hour worked) in the non-farm business sector by some 2.5 per cent in 1998. This partly reflects the rise in capital intensity associated with the surge in fixed investment during the current expansion. Strong growth in productivity offset to a large degree the rise in labour costs, unit labour costs in the non-farm business sector rising by somewhat less than 2 per cent in 1998. Changes in the consumer price index have remained quite moderate: in addition to the favourable changes in productivity and unit labour costs, this also reflects falling prices of energy and imported finished goods, as well as the pass-through of lower commodity prices (chart 2.2.10). But core inflation (excluding food and energy prices) also did not rise significantly in 1998.

Given the differential strength of domestic and foreign demand, there was a large increase in the foreign trade deficit to $169.1 billion in 1998. This was

CHART 2.2.10

Inflation in the United States, 1994-1998
(Percentage change over same month of previous year)

Source: National statistics.
Note: Producer prices of finished goods.

amplified by the weakening of net investment income from abroad, leading to a current account deficit of $233.4 billion or 2.7 per cent of GDP and a further rise in United States net foreign indebtedness. The mirror image to the current account deficit is an excess of domestic investment over national savings, which occurred despite the general government financial balance moving into surplus.

Economic growth also strengthened in *Canada* in the final quarter of 1998. This followed two quarters of only moderate expansion, which was partly due to labour strikes in various sectors of the economy. Apart from the return to normal production levels, the rebound in economic growth was also supported by the stronger demand for goods from the United States, Canada's major trading partner. Fixed investments also edged upward but personal consumption expenditure was rather sluggish, as gains in disposable incomes were used to rebuild savings, which had fallen significantly over the first three quarters.

For the year as a whole, real GDP rose by 3 per cent, down from 3.8 per cent in 1997. This slowdown was entirely due to the weaker growth of domestic demand, the increase in real net exports supporting overall economic growth in 1998 (table 2.2.2). Export growth remained quite robust because the negative effects from Japan and developing countries were offset by the strong import demand from the United States. Exports were also supported by strong gains in price competitiveness stemming from the significant depreciation of the Canadian dollar. Natural resource industries reacted to falling commodity prices and the associated decline in profits by cutting output and

---

[76] Spending on computers rose in real terms by 70 per cent over the same period. This contrasts with an increase by some 17 per cent in nominal terms, the implication being that prices fell by 31 per cent.

[77] The output level in December 1997 was 3 per cent above the annual average, which ensured *ceteris paribus* an annual growth rate of the same amount for 1998.

investment expenditures. Despite the various disturbances, nearly half a million jobs were created in 1998, the largest gain since 1987. The unemployment rate fell in December 1998 to its lowest level since July 1990.

(ii) Monetary conditions and fiscal policy

In western Europe the framework for monetary policy has changed radically with the launching of the euro at the beginning of 1999.[78] In the second half of 1998, the orientation of monetary policy in the future member countries of EMU was increasingly determined by the objective of achieving convergence of official interest rates before the end of the year, an aim which entailed a progressive lowering of official interest rates in the so-called periphery countries. The final step to complete convergence was taken on 3 December 1998, when the central banks of the 11 member countries agreed on a coordinated cut of interest rates to 3 per cent. This decision also reflected concerns about the increasing evidence of a cyclical slowdown, notably in France and Germany, where the repo rate was reduced by 0.3 percentage points (or 30 base points). In other countries with interest rates significantly above those prevailing in France and Germany, the cuts were correspondingly larger.[79] The European Central Bank (ECB) decided to maintain the 3 per cent rate for its first major refinancing operation[80] which was conducted on 7 January 1999. This key official interest rate has since remained unchanged in spite of the continuing cyclical slowdown in the euro area. The three-month EURIBOR,[81] has accordingly been rather stable at some 3.1 per cent in the first few months of 1999 with a slight tendency to move closer to 3 per cent in mid-March (chart 2.2.11).

The average real short-term interest rate in the euro area was 2.3 per cent in January 1999, down from 2.8 per cent[82] in the same month of 1998, but still about 0.3 percentage points higher than in January 1997. Falling inflation has more than offset the significant decline in nominal rates by 1 percentage point between January 1997 and January 1999. In view of the deteriorating economic situation and the modest rate of inflation in the euro area it is generally expected that the ECB will reduce official interest rates in the near term. Overall

monetary conditions have already eased slightly as a result of the depreciation of the euro against the dollar (see below).

In the *United Kingdom*, the significant weakening of economic growth led to a progressive relaxation of monetary policy in the final quarter of 1998 and this has been continued in early 1999. The base lending rate was reduced by half a percentage point to 5.5 per cent in February, which is two percentage points below its recent peak in June 1998, when monetary policy was still being tightened.[83] Short-term interest rates in the United Kingdom have fallen significantly since the autumn but they were still some 2.5 percentage points higher than in the euro area in February (chart 2.2.11).

In the *United States*, monetary policy has been on hold after the target for the federal funds rate was cut in three steps from 5.25 per cent to 4.5 per cent between end-September and mid-November 1998. These moves helped to ease the severe tensions in the international financial markets in the wake of the Russian crisis, but they also provided a potentially significant monetary stimulus to the United States economy. The unexpected strengthening of economic growth in the final quarter of 1998 has made it more difficult for the Federal Reserve to find an appropriate balance between the timely countering of potential inflationary pressures and the avoidance of any further shocks to the still fragile stability of the financial markets. One source of concern could be the high rate of growth of money supply. Broad money (M3) in the final quarter of 1998 was 11 per cent higher than in the same period of 1997, far above the range of 2-6 per cent growth fixed by the FOMC[84] and the most rapid increase since 1981. But the Federal Reserve has argued that this strong growth of broad money reflects to a large degree the combined impact of temporary special factors which led to large fall in velocity with correspondingly few consequences for inflation.[85]

---

[78] For a more detailed discussion see sect. 2.3 below.

[79] The largest cut, by some 0.7 percentage points, occurred in Ireland. In contrast, the repo rate in Finland had to be increased by 0.4 percentage points to achieve convergence at 3 per cent. But in Italy, for domestic policy reasons, the central bank lowered its key official interest rate to only 3.5 per cent on 3 December 1998; a further reduction to 3 per cent took place later in the month.

[80] This was a so-called fixed rate tender, which involves commercial banks submitting bids for funds at an interest rate fixed by the monetary authorities. The advantage of a fixed rate against a variable rate tender, where the interest rate on the latter adjusts to demand pressures, is that it sends a clear signal about the intentions of the monetary authorities.

[81] Euro Interbank Offered Rate.

[82] GDP-weighted average.

---

[83] This decision was influenced by the publication of statistics showing strong growth in average earnings, a development which raised fears of mounting inflationary pressures. But these figures were subsequently shown to be overstated; publication of the Average Earnings Index has been suspended and its calculation is currently under independent review. This has led to considerable uncertainties about the cost pressures arising from the labour market, especially after the recent introduction of a working time directive and a national minimum wage.

[84] M2 rose by 8.5 per cent over the same period, also significantly above its target range of 1-5 per cent. It should be noted that the Humphrey-Hawkins Act requires the Federal Reserve to announce a target range for money supply growth but these targets have been ignored in the conduct of monetary policy since about 1992 because of the weakening link between changes in money supply and economic activity.

[85] The fall in velocity is, *inter alia*, attributed to a shift of portfolios away from equities to monetary assets against the background of the increased volatility in the financial markets and to the increased sensitivity of the demand for monetary assets to changes in long-term interest rates and the slope of the yield curve, which was inverse in the second half of the year with long-term rates falling below short-term rates. Federal Reserve Board, *Humphrey-Hawkins Report*, 23 February 1999 (internet website).

CHART 2.2.11

Nominal interest rates, January 1997-March 1999
(Average monthly rate, per cent per annum)

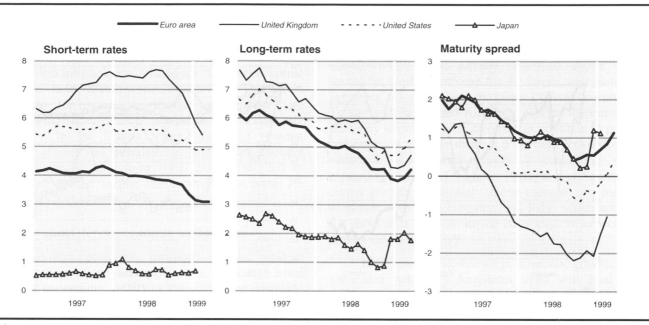

Source: National statistics; OECD, *Main Economic Indicators (*Paris), various issues; European Central Bank; *Financial Times*, various issues.

Note: Short-term interest rates: three-month money market rates. Long-term interest rates: yields on 10-year government bonds. Maturity spread: long-term interest rates less short-term interest rates. The interest rates for the euro area prior to 1999 are GDP weighted averages of national rates. The figures for March are the average rates of the first half of the month.

Another difficult issue in the formulation of monetary policy in the near future is the current level of equity prices in the United States. These have recovered strongly after the financial market turbulence receded last autumn and have helped to sustain domestic demand, both directly through wealth effects and indirectly by easing the availability and terms of credit. How monetary policy should respond to asset prices, however, is difficult to determine.[86] It cannot be excluded, of course, that the current level of asset prices also reflects excessive money creation in the past, and that a tightening of monetary policy may provoke a major fall in equity prices, with considerable downside risks for the United States economy.

Long-term nominal interest rates are still very low, though they have tended to rise slightly in the United States in early 1999: yields on 10-year treasuries rose to some 5.3 per cent in early March. There has also been some upward pressure on interest rates at the shorter end of the maturity spectrum, but increases were larger at the longer end, with the result that the yield curve is no longer inversed as in the second half of 1998 (chart 2.2.11). This change in the slope of the yield curve also reflects changing expectations in the financial markets

about future changes in official interest rates. Given the stronger than expected rate of economic growth, no further easing of monetary policy is expected in the near term.

Long-term interest rates also edged upward in the euro area in early 1999, partly reflecting the spillover effects from the United States bond market. As expected, there is no complete convergence of long-term interest rates among the various member countries of EMU. Yield spreads on national 10-year government bonds over German bonds were very small for France (about 0.05 percentage points) and the Netherlands (0.15 percentage points) in February. For the other countries they were within a range of 0.2 to 0.3 percentage points. Among the possible elements affecting these spreads are the risks of default and of exit from the EMU. The exchange rate or realignment risk, which was a major factor in the relatively high yield spreads in the former EMS, has been eliminated with the adoption of a single currency.

In the *foreign exchange markets* the depreciation of the dollar against the deutsche mark and other west European currencies in the wake of the Russian crisis was partly reversed in the last two months of 1998. This reflected changing assessments about the relative strength of economic growth and expectations of monetary easing, which did indeed occur in the form of the coordinated interest rate cut in early December 1998 (see above). Nevertheless, in December 1998 the deutsche mark had appreciated, on average, by 8.9 per cent against the dollar compared with January 1998.

---

[86] BIS, *67th Annual Report* (Basle), June 1997, pp. 74-75. For a study on the role of asset prices in obtaining inflation forecasts see F. Smets, "Financial asset prices and monetary policy: theory and evidence", Centre for Economic Policy Research, *Discussion Paper*, No. 1751 (London), November 1997.

1.5-1.8 per cent in 1999. This was not significantly different from private sector forecasts, the consensus of which in the autumn was for an increase in real GDP by 2 per cent.[94] These forecasts basically assumed that the sharp weakening in export demand, in combination with the strong dollar and rising labour costs, would squeeze corporate profits and lead to a sharp deceleration in the rate of expansion of business fixed investment. Private consumption was also seen to slow somewhat, but still to grow at a relatively robust rate, reflecting further large gains in real disposable incomes – in turn a reflection of further increases in employment and stronger earnings growth – which was only partly offset by a rise in the savings ratio.

This "baseline scenario" now appears to have been overtaken by the continuing buoyancy of domestic output and demand in late 1998 and which has persisted in the first two months of 1999.[95] The acceleration in GDP growth in the final quarter of 1998, moreover, has led to a considerable statistical carry-over effect which implies that even if total economic output stagnates for the entire year at the level attained in the final quarter of 1998 the average level of real GDP in 1999 would still be 1.7 per cent higher than in 1998. It is against this background that growth forecasts for the United States economy were increased significantly in early 1999. Forecasts of annual GDP growth now range from some 2.5-3.5 per cent. Most private sector forecasters see only a relatively mild deceleration in the growth rate, on average, to some 3¼ per cent in 1999.[96]

The upshot is that the "virtuous circle" which has characterized the United States economy in recent years is now widely expected to persist in 1999: strong increases in fixed investment lead to gains in productivity, profits, real wages and asset prices, which in turn boost consumer demand and fixed investment and, hence, overall economic growth. Inflationary pressures continue to be held in check in spite of increasingly tight labour markets because intensive competitive pressures and business restructuring have led to changes in the wage-price process which restrain the scope for price increases with subsequent moderating effects on wage demands. But inflation has also been moderate because of the fall in commodity prices and because the strong dollar and the sharp rise in imports have limited domestic resource utilization. The consequence of this is the surge in the foreign trade deficit, which attained a record level in January 1999.

There are several factors, however, which will, nevertheless, work towards a slowdown in the rate of economic expansion in 1999. Business investment will

be dampened by the adverse effects on corporate profits associated with the squeeze on margins stemming from rising labour costs and falling capacity utilization rates in manufacturing industry. Real incomes of households will no longer benefit from falling oil prices, which have started to rise in early 1999. Also, more moderate gains in share prices will reduce the support from favourable wealth effects on spending. And weakening economic activity abroad at the same time as robust domestic demand will lead to further adverse changes in real net exports, which will pull down overall economic growth.

The progressive lowering of the target for the federal funds rate from 5.25 per cent to 4.5 per cent in the autumn of 1998 has not yet been officially reversed. But informally the Fed appears to have shifted to a more neutral stance in 1999 with possibly a slight bias towards tightening. This is mirrored in the rise of the federal funds rate above the official target to 5 per cent in mid-March 1999.

Altogether, real GDP in western Europe and North America is now forecast to increase by some 2.5 per cent in 1999, down from 3.3 per cent in 1998.

This benign scenario, however, is confronted by considerable downside risks, the effects of which could be amplified because they are partly interrelated.[97] A major cause of concern is whether the recession in Japan will bottom out or deepen in 1999. This will depend on sufficient progress being made in the restructuring of the banking sector which, if significant, could boost business and consumer confidence. A deepening recession in Japan would, via reduced domestic demand and a depreciation of the yen, have significant spillover effects on the other countries in the region and beyond.

The outlook for the emerging markets of Asia and Latin America will also depend on their ability to return to the capital markets at more favourable terms than have prevailed in the wake of the Russian crisis. Any renewed capital outflows and a concomitant rise in the costs of external and domestic financing would deepen their recession.

Another important downside risk is the high level of equity or share prices in many industrialized countries. This is especially the case in the United States, where the Dow Jones index broke through 10,000 for the first time in mid-March 1999. It was already being repeatedly stated last year that the level of share prices appeared to be increasingly difficult to reconcile with the expected growth in corporate profits in 1998. This appears to be even more so in 1999. A major sustained downward correction of share prices in the United States would have potentially large negative effects on both consumer spending and business investment, with significant financial spillover effects on western Europe.

---

[94] Consensus Economics Inc., *Consensus Forecasts* (London), November 1998.

[95] Federal Reserve Board, *The Beige Book*, 17 March 1999 (internet website).

[96] Consensus Economics Inc., op. cit., March 1999.

[97] See also *OECD Economic Outlook*, op. cit., pp. 13-19 and IMF, *World Economic Outlook ...*, op. cit., pp. 110-112.

The projected rise in the United States current account deficit to very high levels (and the concomitant rise in net foreign indebtedness) could eventually arouse concerns of international investors about its sustainability and trigger a large-scale withdrawal from dollar denominated assets. The associated depreciation of the dollar would then affect activity levels in western Europe and other regions of the world economy.

The international environment facing the western market economies has continued to deteriorate since the final months of 1998. This reflects in the main the deepening recession in Japan and the deteriorating economic situation in Latin America triggered by the crisis in Brazil. Current forecasts point to a further fall in real GDP in Japan by some 0.5 per cent or slightly more in 1999. It is now also unlikely that a recession in Latin America can be avoided in 1999. Little growth is forecast for the transition economies in aggregate and a continued deterioration in the external environment could push many of them into recession.[98] In the Asian emerging markets directly affected by the crisis of 1997, the steep fall in output appears to have bottomed out, but no significant upturn is expected in 1999. Also, the continuing depression in commodity prices will dampen activity levels and import demand in most of the commodity exporting countries. All these factors will feed through to the western economies via foreign trade and restrain their domestic output growth.

How far these risks materialize will depend to a large extent on the policy responses to the weakening forces for economic growth.

2.3 The start of EMU

(i) Introduction

On 1 January 1999, 11 member states[99] of the European Union adopted a common currency, the euro. The conversion rates between the euro and national currencies were fixed on 31 December 1998.[100] The

national currencies have become *uno actu* (non-decimal) subunits of the euro until they will be withdrawn in the course of the first half of 2002 and replaced by euro notes and coins. Private households, companies and public administrations can already use the euro in the form of "write money" (e.g. cheques, bank transfers, credit cards). More importantly, however, all transactions in the money, capital and foreign exchange markets, which were formerly made in the national currencies of the members of the euro area, are now done on the basis of the new currency.

EMU will have a major impact on international financial markets and foreign exchange markets. Indeed, the introduction of the euro is certainly the most important change in the international monetary system since the collapse of the Bretton Woods system of fixed exchange rates in 1972.

Aggregate GDP of the 11 member states (measured at purchasing power parities) corresponds to some 75 per cent of the GDP of the United States and is nearly twice as high as Japan's. The size of the population is somewhat larger in the euro area than in the United States and more than twice as high as in Japan (table 2.3.1). The share of the euro area and the United States in world merchandise trade are broadly the same, but exceeding the share of Japan by a very large margin.

From a monetary perspective, the trade of goods and services among countries in the euro area is no longer considered foreign trade: what were previously external exchanges have now become domestic transactions. Given that intra-area trade constitutes on average some 50 per cent of total trade, the effect is that the degree of openness of the euro area[101] will be significantly reduced (by about half). The relative exposure to foreign trade is therefore only slightly higher than that of the United States but significantly more than for Japan (table 2.3.1). EMU also means that the balance of payments problem is eliminated for the individual member countries.

The international role which the euro will play in the longer run as an international investment currency, as a component of official reserves, in international trade invoicing and in foreign exchange transactions is necessarily subject to a large degree of uncertainty. But from its inception, the euro has been the second most important currency in all these functions, albeit occupying a considerably smaller role than the dollar. Given its economic base, the role of the euro area in international trade and the fact that introduction of the euro should lead to a closer integration of national financial markets (an increase in breadth, depth and liquidity), however, "the potential for the euro as an international money comes into view".[102]

---

[98] See chap. 3.1.

[99] Austria, Belgium, Finland, France, Germany, Ireland, Italy, Luxembourg, the Netherlands, Portugal and Spain.

[100] Two constraints had to be observed: first, the conversion rates between national currencies and the euro had to be based on the bilateral central rates prevailing in the ERM and, second, the conversion from the ECU to the euro had to be made at parity. The first condition was agreed upon in May 1998 and was designed to prevent speculative tensions in the ERM in the run up to EMU. Tensions failed indeed to occur, a reflection of the credibility of the exchange rate commitment. But the strong dollar was also helpful given that in the past dollar weakness was often associated with an asymmetric appreciation of the deutsche mark, with concomitant tensions in the ERM. The second condition was stipulated in the Maastricht Treaty (Article 109l(4)). It was this condition which allowed the euro conversion rates to be fixed only on the eve of monetary union, because the ECU is a currency basket which includes currencies of countries (Danish krone, the Greek drachma and the pound sterling) not participating in EMU. For a detailed account of the technical steps involved see European Union, *Joint Communiqué on the Determination of the Irrevocable Conversion Rates for the Euro*, 2 May 1998 (internet website).

---

[101] It should be noted that statistics about the extra-area trade in goods and services of the euro area are relatively uncertain. The estimate of the degree of openness in table 2.3.1 should therefore be regarded with some caution.

[102] R. McCauley, "The euro and the dollar", *BIS Working Papers*, No. 50 (Basle), November 1997, p. 44. A key factor will be the role that the

TABLE 2.3.1

Comparison of economic indicators for the euro area, Japan and the United States

	Period	Euro area	United States	Japan
GDP [a] (billion dollars)	1997	6 016.9	7 824.0	3 100.4
Population (millions)	1997	290.4	271.8	126.0
GDP per capita [a] (thousand dollars)	1997	20.7	28.8	24.6
Degree of openness [b] (per cent of GDP)	1996	14.2	12.3	9.7
Balance on current account (per cent of GDP)	1998	1.9	-2.7	3.2
General government financial balance (per cent of GDP)	1998	-2.3	1.6	-6.1
Inflation [c] (per cent)	1998	1.3	1.6	0.6
Unemployment [d] (per cent)	1998	11.0	4.5	4.1

Source: National statistics; OECD, *National Accounts, Main Aggregates 1960-1997*, Vol. 1, 1999 and *OECD Economic Outlook*, No. 64, December 1998 (Paris); United Nations Comtrade Database.

[a] At current prices and purchasing power parities.

[b] Arithmetic average of imports and exports of goods and services as a per cent of GDP. Intra-euro area trade is excluded. It was assumed that the share of intra-euro area trade in services is the same as the share of intra-euro area trade in goods.

[c] Consumer price index; percentage change over previous year.

[d] Standardized unemployment rate. Per cent of civil labour force.

To what extent the euro will become a serious competitor with the dollar is, however, more difficult to gauge. This will depend largely on the speed and extent of integration of financial markets in the euro area and the role which the euro will play in foreign trade invoicing in other regions of the world economy, notably Asia, where the dollar is well established. Also relative long-run dynamics will play a role, as these affect the importance of the euro area in the world economy. The existing economies of scale will tend to preserve the competitiveness of the dollar for quite some time and they may also affect the different functions of money differentially. This points to a more gradual extension of the international role of the euro, which could well remain much more limited than the role of the dollar even in the long run.[103]

On the macroeconomic plane, the transfer of monetary policy authority from sovereign national states to the independent (supranational) European Central Bank and the establishment of rules governing fiscal policy will radically alter the framework for the conduct of economic policy in the euro area. National monetary policy is no longer available to respond via changes in interest or exchange rates to adverse economic shocks. A single monetary policy implies a single short-term interest rate, which will be set with a focus on the *average* economic conditions in the euro area.[104] Nevertheless, in view of the marked differences in the economic size of the countries in the euro area, this "average" will be dominated by France, Germany and Italy, which together account for some 75 per cent of GDP in the euro area (table 2.3.2). A general concern with regard to monetary policy is whether "one size will fit all". As this is unlikely to always be the case, EMU will put an increased adjustment burden on fiscal policy and on the goods and factor markets, notably the labour markets.

A centralized monetary policy in the presence of decentralized fiscal policies across 11 countries will make the ECB the "single most important policy-making body in the new Europe".[105] There are many challenges facing this new institution which has not only to build its reputation, but also to operate, at least in the initial years, in uncharted territory. The regime shift to a new currency and a single monetary policy will not only trigger structural changes in financial markets but will also influence the expectations and behaviour of economic agents. This, in turn, will affect the stability of relationships between economic variables observed in the past, rendering it more difficult to predict the effects of changes in monetary policy.[106] Different cyclical positions of member states and different degrees of aversion to inflation, and, more generally, different rates of trade-off between policy objectives, moreover, may be potential sources of tension in the formulation of monetary policy within the ECB on the one hand and between the central bank and governments on the other hand. This in turn raises the issue of the proper policy mix, notably between monetary and fiscal policy.

euro can occupy in foreign exchange transactions which, by a significant margin, dominate the transactions in security markets and international merchandise trade. The dominant role of the dollar in forex transactions reflects its role as "vehicle currency", i.e. it is used as the medium of exchange between third currencies. The reason for this is reduced exchange related transaction costs, reflecting network externalities (economies of scale) from its wide use. This (virtuous) circularity implies a tendency for a single currency to dominate in forex transactions. Any change in this pattern is likely to occur only gradually over time. See, for example, P. Hartmann, *Currency Competition and Foreign Exchange Markets. The Dollar, the Yen and the Euro* (Cambridge, Cambridge University Press, 1998).

[103] For an optimistic scenario in which the international role of the euro and the dollar as means of payment and stores of value will be broadly similar, see R. Portes and H. Rey, "The emergence of the euro as an international currency", *Economic Policy*, 26 April 1998, pp. 307-343.

[104] An often made comparison is with the tightening of monetary policy by the Bundesbank in the wake of German unification which was designed to curb inflationary pressures. In the context of the ERM this forced other countries to raise their interest rates as well, although this was not necessarily appropriate for their cyclical positions. If German unification had occurred when EMU was in place then the ECB would have raised interest rates by less than the Bundesbank, because it would have responded to the *average* inflationary pressures in EMU rather than to *above average* rate of price increases in Germany.

[105] C. Allsopp and D. Vines, "The assessment: macroeconomic policy after EMU", *Oxford Review of Economic Policy*, Vol. 14, No. 3, Autumn 1998, p. 3.

[106] This is the so-called *Lucas critique* of the use of standard economic models to predict effects of economic policy in the presence of major regime changes. R. Lucas, Jr., "Econometric policy evaluation: a critique", *Studies in Business Cycle Theory* (Cambridge, MA), 1981, pp. 104-130.

In fact, EMU has started against the background of weakening growth in western Europe, which is part and parcel of a significant slowdown in the world economy.[107] This is not a situation that will induce governments to provide a generous grace period to the ECB. High unemployment is the major economic and political problem in the euro area and governments have declared its reduction as their main priority. Faced with the rigid rules of the game established in the Stability and Growth Pact for the conduct of fiscal policy, pressures have mounted on the ECB to further lower interest rates, which were reduced by a coordinated action of the national central banks of the euro area to 3 per cent in early December 1998.

At the same time there have been suggestions for exchange rate management to limit movements in the bilateral exchange rates of the dollar, the euro and the yen.[108] Economic developments in each of the three major economic powers in the global economy will have a bearing on the economic performance of the remaining two. This raises the important issue as to what extent EMU increases the need for and the possibility of global macroeconomic policy coordination, notably in the area of exchange rates.[109]

(ii) The new institutional framework for monetary policy

The European System of Central Banks (ESCB) was created on 1 June 1998, but it assumed its full functions only as from the beginning of 1999. The ESCB is composed of the ECB and the national central banks of EU member states.[110]

The ESCB has four main tasks, namely:

- To define and implement monetary policy for the euro zone with the primary objective of maintaining price stability;

- To conduct foreign exchange operations;

- To hold and manage the official reserves of the countries in the euro area;

- To promote the smooth operation of payment systems.

All decisions in matters of monetary policy are taken by the Governing Council, which is composed of the 11 national central bank governors of the countries which have adopted the euro and the six members of the Executive Board of the ECB.[111] Decisions in the Governing Council are, as a rule, taken by simple majority, with each member having one vote.[112] The President of the ECB has the casting vote in case of a tie. The fact that the national central bank governors have a clear majority in the voting on monetary policy points to the problem that their voting behaviour may be excessively influenced by the specific economic conditions prevailing in their own countries. This could contribute to some inertia, always inherent in group decision-making, in changing the course of monetary policy.[113] The Executive Board of the ECB has to implement the decisions taken by the Governing Council. The actual implementation of monetary and foreign exchange rate operations, however, is delegated to the national central banks, based on corresponding instructions received from the ECB. The President of the Ecofin Council can participate at the meetings of the Governing Council. Although this government representative does not have the right to vote (Article 109b of the Maastricht Treaty), she/he can participate in the debate on the orientation of monetary policy, present the assessment of the Council, and thus possibly influence decision-making.

The existing national competencies relating to the prudential supervision of credit institutions and the stability of the financial system have been maintained. The ECB is to "contribute to the smooth conduct of policies pursued by the competent authorities." (Article 105(5) of the Treaty). It is in line with these arrangements that there are no explicit provisions for the ECB to assume the role of lender of last resort in the event of financial crisis. This could be problematic because it may affect the ability to arrange for an effective monetary policy response to a liquidity crisis in the financial sector of one country which threatens to spread rapidly across the euro area. In the absence of close central control and authority by the ECB, the responses of a national central bank to a banking crisis may prove to be inadequate since the transboundary

---

[107] This is discussed in more detail in sects. 2.1 and 2.2 above.

[108] See also sect. 2.3(iv) and box 2.3.1 below.

[109] This is in contrast to the classical gold standard, which included all the most advanced economies at that time. The consequence was that the economic performance and policies of countries outside the gold standard area did not have a significant impact on policies inside the area. M. Panic, *European Monetary Union. Lessons from the Gold Standard* (New York, St. Martin's Press, 1992), p. 130.

[110] The basic rules governing monetary policy in the euro area are enshrined in the Treaty on European Union (Articles 105-109) and the Protocol on the Statute of the European System of Central Banks and of the European Central Bank, which is annexed to the Treaty.

[111] There is also a General Council, with all 15 central bank governors as members together with the President and Vice-President of the ECB. But this body has no decision-making authority in matters of monetary policy.

[112] This was a major concession of the larger countries (notably Germany) to the group of smaller countries. The strong independence of the ECB and the emphasis on price stability as the single major goal may be regarded as the counterpart to this. In certain matters votes will be weighted according to central banks' shares in the subscribed capital of the ECB. This is the case if decisions have to be taken concerning the capital of the ECB, the transfer of foreign assets from central banks to the ECB, the allocation of monetary income of central banks and of profits and losses of the ECB (see Article 10 of the Protocol annexed to the Treaty).

[113] This need not necessarily be negative because it can also create an internal system of checks and balances. A. Blinder, *Central Banking in Theory and Practice* (Cambridge, MA/London, The MIT Press, 1998), pp. 20-22.

spillover effects may not be given the appropriate weighting.[114] In the absence of a centralized and regulatory supervisory authority, this points to the need for very close coordination of the various national authorities in the area of bank regulation and supervision.

The ECSB is a supranational institution, which is independent of national governments and the general political process.[115] Article 107 of the Treaty stipulates that "neither the ECB nor a national central bank, nor any member of their decision-making bodies shall seek or take instructions from Community institutions, from a government of a Member State or from any other body". Given that central bank independence does not have a tradition in many of the countries which have adopted the euro, their national legislation had therefore to be adapted as part of the required convergence process towards EMU.

In the economic literature, central bank independence is generally seen to shield monetary policy from the so-called time inconsistency problem of government behaviour. The presumption is that governments tend to conduct monetary policies only with a short-term view, which is revealed in a temptation to exploit any short-run tradeoff between inflation and output growth, which would lead to an inflationary bias of monetary policy.[116] Thus, the delegation of monetary authority to an independent central bank is tantamount to governments deliberately tying their hands with regard to monetary policy. Although a negative correlation has been shown to exist between an index of central bank independence in industrialized countries and their corresponding rate of inflation, the association is not very robust and does not necessarily reflect a casual relationship. Rather, central bank independence may be simply the institutional complement to the preference which a society already attaches to low inflation. There is evidence that central bank independence per se does not ensure a more favourable "sacrifice ratio", i.e. the output costs associated with disinflationary polices are not necessarily lower.[117] This trade-off depends also on the credibility (reputation) of the central bank, which will influence expectations and actions of economic agents.

There has been much speculation as to what extent the ECB will inherit some of the credibility of the Bundesbank. This will be difficult to establish. In general, a reputation can only be built over a fairly long time, allowing observers to see whether, in fact, central bankers are "matching deeds to words".[118] But the ECB is a new institution with no track record and it will therefore have to build up a constituency which supports its goals and policy actions. A key factor for this is effective accountability and communication with the broader public.

Accountability is the natural counterpart to central bank independence in a democratic society.[119] In fact, the ECB cannot operate outside the political context; "it must be able to justify its policies to the general public and to political leaders".[120] As a supranational institution, the ECB is not accountable to national governments or national parliaments. But to sustain its legitimacy, the ECB will have to provide the public with a coherent account of its assessment of the general economic conditions and an explanation of policy measures taken to meet the established goals. An important channel for this are regular reports and hearings. Apart from a monthly bulletin, which will be addressed to the public at large, annual reports will be presented by the President of the ECB to the European Parliament, the Ecofin Council, the Commission and the European Council. The European Parliament can invite the ECB to hearings by the competent committees of the Parliament, and ECB itself may also take the initiative for such events to take place.

(iii) Monetary policy goals and strategy

The ECB has a single primary objective, namely to maintain price stability. Although the central bank is called upon to support the general economic policies in the euro area, this will only be done if it does not conflict with the primary objective (Article 105(1) of the Treaty). Apart from this general mandate, it is up to the ECB to define what price stability shall mean in practice, and in addition, it is free to choose the policy instruments and strategy to pursue this goal. In other words, it is independent both in setting the target and in deciding how to reach it.[121]

---

[114] B. Eichengreen, "Designing a central bank for Europe: a cautionary tale from the early years of the Federal Reserve system", in M. Canzoneri, V. Grilli and P. Masson (eds.), *Establishing a Central Bank: Issues in Europe and Lessons from the US* (Cambridge, Cambridge University Press, 1992), pp. 13-40.

[115] R. Smits, "The European central bank has been devised as the epitome of an independent central bank", *The European Central Bank* (The Hague/London/Boston, Kluwer Law International, 1997), p. 151.

[116] C. Bean, "The new UK monetary arrangements: a view from the literature", *The Economic Journal*, Vol. 108, November 1998, pp. 1795-1809. Alternatively, the emphasis has been put on the time profile of disinflationary policies, with costs up front and benefits emerging only gradually over time, which may not be convenient for policy makers. A. Blinder, op. cit., pp. 55-57.

[117] A. Blinder, op. cit., pp. 62-63.

[118] Ibid, p. 64.

[119] This is an area which is not well defined. The United States Federal Reserve is "generally, but not precisely accountable to the Congress" and the Bundesbank is "accountable to the public". S. Fischer, "Central bank independence revisited", *The American Economic Review*, Papers and Proceedings, Vol. 85, No. 2, May 1995, p. 205.

[120] These are the words of P. Volcker, a former chairman of the United States Federal Reserve. P. Volcker, "An American perspective on EMU", in P. Masson et al., op. cit., p. 256.

[121] An alternative arrangement would be for the government to set an inflation target and then give the central bank the necessary power to achieve this goal. Examples of this are Canada, New Zealand, Sweden and the United Kingdom. Central banks can also have multiple goals. In the United States, the Federal Reserve Act stipulates that the Federal Open Market Committee has "to promote effectively the goals of maximum employment, stable prices and moderate long-term interest

The most important policy instrument for steering short-term interest rates and refinancing conditions of financial institutions will be open market operations.[122] The main refinancing operations are so-called "reversed transactions", i.e. the buying or selling of domestic currency assets, which will be reversed at an agreed later date. Purchasing of assets ("repos") is equivalent to injecting liquidity, while sales do the opposite. The difference between the buying and selling price corresponds to the (very short-term) interest rate, which is typically known as the "repo-rate".

Only monetary targeting and inflation targeting were seriously considered as potential candidates for the monetary policy strategy.[123] Monetary targeting involves the use of a more or less broad monetary aggregate as an intermediate target, which is linked via the monetary transmission mechanism to the ultimate goal of price stability. Inflation targeting involves the definition of an explicit preferred rate (or range) of inflation, which the central bank aims to attain via changes in interest rates or other policy instruments.[124] Hence, the ultimate goal is common to both approaches and in practice elements of both strategies are often combined. Thus, the Bundesbank conducted its monetary policy within the framework of a monetary target, but this involved the definition of an implicit inflation target. The Bundesbank also displayed significant flexibility when it came to meeting the monetary target, provided that the inflation rate was regarded as satisfactory.[125]

The link between money supply and inflation, however, requires a stable demand for money function (i.e. the relationship between money demand, real incomes and interest rates) for policy to be effective. The demand for money function, however, has become quite unstable (or less stable) in many countries, a phenomenon which is partly attributed to significant financial sector innovations, and this has forced many central banks to move away from monetary targeting. Although a stable aggregate demand for money function was found to exist in the individual member states of the euro area, and for

selected groups of EU countries,[126] there are strong doubts as to whether this stability will persist, at least initially, in EMU. The shift to a single currency is a major structural break (a "regime change") which will affect behavioural relationships, the structure of financial markets and, therefore, the monetary transmission mechanism. Similarly, direct inflation targeting has to rely on stable and predictable effects of changes in monetary policy on inflation. Given the long and variable time lags with which the effects of monetary policy appear, such forecasts are surrounded in general by large margins of error, which are likely to be amplified by the uncertainty surrounding the monetary transmission mechanism in EMU.

Against this background, the ECB has opted for a more discretionary strategy, which combines elements of both monetary and inflation targeting, but leaves open their relative importance in the overall conduct of monetary policy.[127] These elements are:

- The quantitative definition of a preferred inflation rate;

- A reference value for the growth of a broad monetary aggregate (M3);

- A continuous assessment of overall economic developments in the euro area with emphasis on the inflation outlook.

The measurement of price stability is based on the HICP and the target is to keep the average year-on-year inflation rate for the euro area below 2 per cent. This asymmetry, i.e. the absence of a definite floor, will leave markets guessing as to which inflation rate is low enough for the ECB and this will therefore affect the transparency of monetary policy. Also, it is possibly an excessively ambitious target, notably in view of the well-known upward biases of inflation measures, which over time will also affect the new HICP.[128] At very low levels of inflation these could risk imparting a deflationary bias to monetary policy and raises the wider issue of the costs of targeting such low rates of inflation.[129]

One factor which will affect the average inflation performance in the euro area is the significant variation in real incomes across the member countries of the EMU.

---

rates". Goals which are not precisely defined leave the central bank with room for interpretation, which is tantamount to a de facto enhancement of power. A. Blinder, op. cit., pp. 54-55.

[122] For a detailed overview of the various instruments see European Central Bank, *The Single Monetary Policy in Stage Three* (Frankfurt am Main), September 1998.

[123] The other main alternative would have been exchange rate targeting, which would have been unusual for such a large economic area and would have risked coming into conflict with the main goal of price stability.

[124] It has been argued that in the case of an inflation target, the central bank's inflation forecast becomes the intermediate target of monetary policy.

[125] What speaks, in principle, in favour of a monetary target is that the money supply is more closely under the direct control of the central bank and is a variable which can be directly observed by the public, which enhances the transparency of monetary policy. In contrast, inflation cannot be directly controlled and inflation forecasts are inherently less transparent. C. Bean, "Monetary policy under EMU", *Oxford Review of Economic Policy*, Vol. 14, No. 3, Autumn 1998, p. 43.

[126] European Central Bank, *Monthly Bulletin*, February 1999, p. 36; K. McMorrow, "Is there a stable money demand equation at the Community level?", European Commission, *Economic Papers*, No. 131, November 1998; V. Clausen, "Money demand and monetary policy in Europe", *Weltwirtschaftliches Archiv*, Vol. 134, No. 4 (Kiel), 1998, pp. 712-740.

[127] European Central Bank, "A stability-oriented monetary policy strategy for the ESCB", *Press Release*, 13 October 1998 (internet website).

[128] UN/ECE, *Economic Survey of Europe, 1998 No. 1*, pp.39-40.

[129] In the case of downward rigid nominal wages, very low inflation would be more or less equivalent to real wage rigidity which, in case of adverse output shocks, would drive up unemployment. G. Akerlof, W. Dickens and G. Perry, "The macroeconomics of low inflation", *Brookings Papers on Economic Activity*, 1 (Washington, D.C.), 1996, pp. 1-76.

TABLE 2.3.2

Selected economic indicators for the euro area

	GDP[a] (percentage share in total) 1997	GDP per capita[a] (average euro area=100) 1997	Degree of openness[b] (per cent of GDP) 1996	Unemployment rate[c] (per cent of civil labour force) 1998	General government financial balance[d] (per cent of GDP) 1998	Inflation rate[e] (annual percentage change) 1998	Memo. item: Conversion rates (national currency units per euro)
France	22.3	111	11.0	11.9	-2.9	0.7	6.55957
Germany	33.3	118	13.3	9.7	-2.4	0.7	1.95583
Italy	18.1	92	12.5	12.2	-2.6	2.0	1936.27
Austria	3.3	118	15.8	4.4	-2.2	0.8	13.7603
Belgium	3.9	111	25.8	8.8	-1.5	0.9	40.3399
Finland	1.9	106	23.5	11.8	0.8	1.4	5.94573
Ireland	1.2	92	46.8	7.8	2.5	2.2	0.787564
Luxembourg	0.3	175	25.8	2.2	2.2	1.0	40.3399
Netherlands	5.8	108	23.8	4.1	-1.2	1.8	2.20371
Portugal	1.6	47	11.9	4.9	-2.3	2.3	200.482
Spain	8.4	62	10.5	18.9	-1.9	1.8	166.386
Euro area	100.0	100	14.2	11.0	-2.3	1.3	..

Source: National statistics; OECD, *National Accounts, Main Aggregates 1960-1997,* Vol. 1, 1999 and *OECD Economic Outlook,* No. 64, December 1998 (Paris); United Nations Comtrade Database.

a GDP at current prices and current dollar exchange rates.

b Arithmetic average of imports and exports of goods and services as a per cent of GDP. Intra-euro area trade is excluded. It was assumed that the share of intra-euro area trade in services is the same as the share of intra-euro area trade in goods.

c Standardized unemployment rate.

d OECD estimates.

e Harmonized Index of Consumer Prices (HICP).

In the catching up process, the relative prices of non-tradeables in countries with below average real incomes will tend to rise faster than in the other countries. This reflects the tendency of wages in this sector to outpace productivity growth.[130] The direct consequence is an appreciation of the implicit real exchange rate of the "periphery" within the monetary union. Although currently the inflation differentials among the various countries in the euro area are relatively small (table 2.3.2), this need not remain so. Evidently, any significant inflation differentials across countries would make the task of monetary policy more difficult.[131]

The reference value for the growth of money supply (M3) has been set at a year-on-year increase of 4.5 per cent in 1999.[132] This figure was derived on the basis of the standard money equation[133] using estimates for the

trend growth rate of GDP (2-2.5 per cent), a trend decline in velocity between 0.5 and 1 per cent, and the inflation target (less than 2 per cent). The ECB has opted for a single reference value rather than a reference range to avoid any connotation with monetary targeting, which has traditionally involved defining upper and lower bounds for the growth of money supply. Along these lines, the ECB has emphasized that the public should not expect that any deviation of money supply growth from the reference value will automatically trigger a change in official interest rates.[134]

Despite all the uncertainty surrounding the growth of potential output and money velocity, this nevertheless appears to be quite a cautious estimate of the adequate growth of money supply in view of the existing large margins of spare capacity in the euro area. Taking the values at the upper range of the corresponding variables would have led to a money supply growth of nearly 6 per cent. The lower range values (assuming an acceptable inflation rate of 1.5 per cent) imply a growth rate of money supply of 4 per cent. This illustrates the cautiousness of the ECB in setting the reference value. An additional indication of this is that the growth rate of M3 was only slightly above 4.5 per cent in the final quarter of 1998 against the background of very low

---

[130] This is the implication of the Harrod-Balassa-Samuelson theorem, which states that countries with higher productivity levels in tradeables have higher price levels than other countries.

[131] In case of large relative price changes this could even go so far that the average inflation rate targeted by the ECB could well have "no meaning for consumers in any particular country". C. Bean, "Monetary policy ..." op. cit., p. 44.

[132] European Central Bank, "The quantitative reference value for monetary growth", *Press Release,* 1 December 1998 (internet website).

[133] This equation states that the product of money supply and velocity is equal to the product of real output and the price level. Accordingly, estimates of the rate of the change of the latter three variables allow money supply growth to be calculated.

[134] To prevent irregular fluctuations from distorting the underlying trend, monthly money supply figures will be smoothed, using three-month moving averages. European Central Bank, "A stability-oriented monetary policy strategy", *Press Release,* 13 October 1998 (internet website).

inflation and increasing evidence of a cyclical slowdown in the euro area. This could point to a procyclical bias of the current stance of monetary policy (if the reference value were strictly adhered to) with detrimental repercussions for economic growth.

An important source of uncertainty surrounding the effects of monetary policy is the existing variation in the financial structures of the countries in the euro area. This concerns, for example, the importance of short-term relative to long-term interest rates in private sector borrowing or the share of short-term government bonds in private households' financial assets. These differences could lead, via the various channels of monetary transmission, to monetary policy having asymmetric effects across countries. In fact, recent research points to notable differences in the degree to which output in various EU countries is affected by a change in interest rates. This holds, however, only for the medium-term, i.e. over a period of some two years.[135] Similarly, effect of changes in the euro exchange rate on output might also differ across countries. Fluctuations of the euro-dollar exchange rate are estimated to have a potentially much larger effect on output in the euro area than in the United States.[136] But these results will have to stand up to the Lucas critique, i.e. it is not clear to what extent these effects will materialize under the new monetary regime. It can be expected that over time there will be a closer integration of financial markets in the euro area, with the consequence that these asymmetric effects in the transmission mechanism will be largely eliminated. In the intermediate period, however, the uneven effects of monetary policy could be a source of tension not only within the Governing Council of the ESCB but also in the Ecofin Council.

Another conflictual consequence of the change in policy regime may be that trade unions in the individual countries perceive the existence of a more favourable inflation-unemployment trade off. The reason for this is that the impact of a given wage increase in a country will have less of an impact on the aggregate inflation rate in the euro area compared with the national inflation rate. As the ECB will focus on the average inflation rate in the euro area, the restrictive monetary policy response will be smaller than under the pre-EMU regime. This might arise notably in Germany where the trade unions, traditionally, have anticipated the Bundesbank's reaction to high wage claims, behaviour which has probably contributed to the wage restraint observed in the past. The large wage claims of the metal workers in the current wage round illustrate this potential problem. However, a fallacy of composition could arise if unions in several countries pursued a wage bargaining strategy on this assumption, because the resulting euro area-wide inflationary shock would trigger a tightening of monetary policy. The upshot would be that, at least temporarily, the ECB might be confronted with an

inflation output trade-off that could be worse than that previously faced by the Bundesbank.[137]

(iv) Exchange rate policy

Given that the euro is fluctuating against other currencies,[138] notably the dollar and the yen, the ECB is also in a position to influence, via changes in interest rates and foreign exchange operations, the exchange rate of the euro. EMU member governments, however, have retained influence on exchange rate policy. The Ecofin Council can decide, although only unanimously, to conclude formal exchange rate arrangements for the euro (Article 109(1) of the Treaty). The term "formal" points to fixed exchange rate systems such as Bretton Woods or a mechanism like the ERM with countries outside the EU. The second lever which governments have is the right to provide "general orientations for exchange rate policy" (Article 109(2)) in the context of floating exchange rates. Informal exchange rate target zones (without any obligatory intervention mechanism) would probably fall into this category. These orientations, however, are subsidiary to the goal of price stability, a provision which provides the ECB with considerable scope for blocking the implementation of such recommendations. Evidently, any attempt to formulate an explicit exchange rate policy could create tensions between the ECB and governments because it would effectively limit the room for manoeuvre of the Governing Council in matters of monetary policy. In December 1997, the Ecofin indicated that it will issue such orientations only in exceptional circumstances, for example, in the case of a clear exchange rate misalignment. But even then a conflict between the ECB and governments cannot be excluded.[139]

The adoption of a single currency has eliminated exchange rate instability within the euro area, which in the aggregate is much less open than its individual member countries. But should the euro exchange rate therefore be treated with "benign neglect"? In fact, although the euro area resembles more a large, relatively closed economy in which domestic prices are less influenced by fluctuations in the euro exchange rate (for a given level of foreign prices) this is not per se a sufficient reason for being indifferent to exchange rate movements, especially if these are very large. A potential source of conflict among countries is that their vulnerability to adverse exchange rate movements will vary because of their different degrees of exposure to trade with the rest of the world (table 2.3.1).

---

[135] R. Dornbusch, C. Favero and F. Giavazzi, "Immediate challenges to the European Central Bank", *Economic Policy*, No. 26, April 1998, pp. 15-64.

[136] Ibid., p. 48.

[137] Ibid., p. 51; D. Soskice and T. Iversen, "Multiple wage-bargaining systems in the single European currency area", *Oxford Review of Economic Policy*, Vol. 14, Autumn 1998, pp. 110-124.

[138] The ERM2 limits, in principle, exchange rate fluctuations between the euro and currencies of EU member states which did not adopt the single currency at the beginning of 1999. But of these four countries, only Denmark and Greece have entered this mechanism.

[139] It is significant that the ECB has pointed out that the announcement made by the Ecofin Council is not legally binding. European Central Bank, *Monthly Bulletin*, January 1999, p. 41.

An argument against "benign neglect" – at least in the initial years – is that "not only financial market participants but also domestic wage and price setters would look to the ECB's reaction for evidence bearing on its credibility"[140] if the euro were to weaken significantly against the dollar. It can also be argued that the considerable uncertainties surrounding both monetary and inflation targeting in the early years of the euro should induce the ECB to give greater weight to the exchange rate when setting monetary policy. "In these circumstances, coordination with the United States and Japan to limit exchange rate fluctuations may naturally emerge."[141]

In fact, trans-Atlantic exchange rates and capital flows have received considerable attention since the start of EMU. Some governments, although by no means all, have expressed their preference for a more or less large measure of exchange rate stability between the three major currencies of the world economy. Suggestions have ranged from explicit exchange rate target zones to a more informal monitoring of exchange rates with the possibility of coordinated intervention in the case of emerging misalignments. Box 2.3.1 provides a brief overview of some of the salient issues involved.

The potential, in the longer run, for greater exchange rate volatility of the euro-dollar exchange rate (compared with the deutsche mark-dollar exchange rate in the past) should certainly not be underestimated, especially if both the United States and the euro area were to adopt an attitude of "benign neglect".[142] This could result in prolonged misalignments between the major three currencies with the associated risk of trade protectionism and competitive depreciations.[143]

(v) Domestic economic policy coordination

The abandonment of national monetary policies should, in principle, argue in favour of increased flexibility of fiscal policy to cope with adverse shocks. But there may be a need to avoid possible negative externalities if diverging fiscal policies were to lead to excessive deficits and debts in individual countries. This points to the need for rules and the desirability of a mechanism for fiscal policy coordination.[144] It is also important to ensure a sound policy mix between fiscal and monetary policy. More generally, coordination will also be required to prevent "free rider problems" and the emergence of "prisoner's dilemma" situations.[145]

The institutional foundations for economic policy coordination and multilateral surveillance in the euro area are embodied in the Maastricht Treaty.[146] The Ecofin Council is the sole decision-making body in all matters of economic policy coordination. As not all EU member states have adopted the single currency, a euro-11 group was set up to provide a platform for informal discussion of policy issues related to EMU. Put simply, the role of the euro-11 group is to reach agreement on all those issues (e.g. exchange rate management) that are not the responsibility of the ECB, to ensure that despite the decentralization of fiscal policy there is effective coordination when needed and a single voice in the discussions of macroeconomic policy with the ECB and in other international policy fora such as the Group of Seven. Although the euro-11 group cannot take any legally binding decisions it can be expected to become de facto a strong political counterweight to the ECB.

The Stability and Growth Pact, which was adopted in June 1997, is intended to ensure that national budgetary policies do not conflict with the objectives of the single monetary policy. The Pact restricts the room for manoeuvre of fiscal policy by putting a ceiling on government budget deficits (3 per cent of GDP) and debt (60 per cent of GDP). The deficit can exceed the 3 per cent threshold only in the case of severe recession. The latter is defined as an annual decline in real GDP by at least 2 per cent, but under certain conditions an "excessive deficit" may also be permitted if the fall in real GDP lies within a range of 0.75 to 2 per cent. The target is to achieve broadly balanced budgets in the medium term (i.e. over the business cycle).[147] Countries have pledged to achieve this by the year 2002. This is to provide sufficient scope for the working of automatic stabilizers in the case of a subsequent cyclical downturn. There will be surveillance of how countries intend to observe these targets on the basis of annual stability programmes to be elaborated by the individual governments. Significant deviations from targets can lead to recommendations of corrective policy measures.

[140] R. McCauley, op. cit., p. 18.

[141] P. Masson and B. Turtelboom, "Characteristics of the euro, the demand for reserves and policy coordination", in P. Masson et al., op. cit., pp. 216-217.

[142] P. Volcker fears that, "If markets sensed that governments and central banks were neglectful, benignly or otherwise, of the desirability of exchange rate stability, huge amounts of capital could be easily mobilized to ride a trend", P. Volcker, op. cit., p. 258.

[143] C. Bergsten, "The impact of the euro on exchange rates and international policy cooperation", in P. Masson et al., op. cit., pp. 42-43. Bergsten argues in favour of a target zone system between the euro, the dollar and the yen, but only in the medium term, i.e. after it has been possible to calculate the fundamental equilibrium exchange rate of the euro.

[144] It should be noted that fiscal policy, including the potential need for fiscal federalism, is "an aspect of monetary union on which consensus

remains most elusive". B. Eichengreen, "European monetary union: a tour d'horizon", *Oxford Review of Economic Policy*, Vol. 14, No. 3, Autumn 1998, pp. 27-29.

[145] A prisoner's dilemma arises (in game theory) if the combined outcome of policies, which are rational from the point of view of each player (here, governments and the central bank) are socially undesirable.

[146] Article 103(1) stipulates that "Member States shall regard their economic policies as a matter of common concern and shall coordinate them within the Council". The Ecofin Council will also formulate "broad guidelines of the economic policies of the Member States" (Article 103(2)) and "monitor economic developments in each of the Member States" (Article 103(3)). Article 104c arranges for the surveillance of the government financial positions (budget deficits and stock of debt).

[147] The implication is that there will be little scope for borrowing for the sole purpose of financing investment (the so-called "golden rule").

BOX 2.3.1

Exchange rate target zones for major currencies

An explicit target zone consists of pre-announced limits on the deviations of the exchange rate from a central parity, which are enforced through foreign exchange intervention. As such, it is an example of an exchange rate arrangement with limited flexibility: the exchange rate is fixed at the limits, but fluctuates freely within them.

Its behaviour, however, is different from that of a flexible rate. This is due to the effect of the target zone on exchange rate expectations in financial markets. In the case of an explicit target zone, these derive not only from economic fundamentals, such as the money supply or short-term interest rates, but also from expected central bank interventions, the more so the closer the exchange rate is to its floor or ceiling. As a result, in a target zone the exchange rate displays less sensitivity to fundamentals than a flexible rate, a feature sometimes dubbed the "honeymoon effect".

Given these properties, exchange rate target zones have been proposed as a means of combining both the scope for policies oriented towards domestic objectives that exists under flexible rates and the exchange rate stability usually associated with fixed rates. Like fixed exchange rate arrangements, they can also be viewed as a defence against exchange rate overshooting that could be triggered by capital flows of a purely speculative nature. Moreover, they prevent the deliberate use of the exchange rate as a strategic variable to achieve a temporary competitive advantage.

The properties of target zone exchange rates, however, hinge crucially on the credibility of the zone, i.e. whether financial markets believe in the commitment, or the willingness, of the authorities involved to defend it. If credibility is lacking, a target zone may actually be destabilizing and the exchange rate may be more sensitive to fundamentals than a flexible rate (the "divorce effect").

One factor that determines credibility is the level of reserves available for the defence of the zone, another characteristic that target zones share with fixed exchange rate systems. If the level of reserves is low, it is likely that the zone will be attacked and abandoned. In addition, there is the possibility that speculative attacks may be self-fulfilling, in the sense that although the exchange rate is consistent with economic policies the zone will be abandoned once an attack occurs, as the domestic policy costs of defending it become too high.

Another factor that affects the credibility of a target zone is the extent to which the central parity or fluctuation margins are adjustable.[1] The possibility of frequent and large adjustments tends to lower credibility, as it implies less of a constraint on the participating currencies.

An alternative to explicit rule-based target zones is an informal monitoring of exchange rates with intervention in support of undisclosed target values (parity or margins) decided on an ad hoc basis. An arrangement of this kind has more flexibility than an explicit target zone, but does not ensure as much stability, because it does not lead to strong expectations of intervention.

In the past, there was such monitoring of exchange rates for the major currencies (at that time, the dollar, the yen and the deutsche mark) during the second half of the 1980s, in the context of the Plaza Agreement and Louvre Accord of September 1985 and February 1987, respectively.[2] These agreements did not contain any reference values, but they did reveal the general concern at exchange rate movements that did not reflect economic conditions.

The Plaza Agreement followed a substantial appreciation in the dollar, which arose from a mix of tight monetary and lax fiscal policies and a concomitant rise in United States interest rates, but nevertheless went beyond what was considered to be consistent with economic fundamentals. Its objective was to foster an orderly depreciation of the dollar, which had turned around earlier in the year, as a means of correcting the considerable current account imbalances in Japan, the United States and, to a lesser extent, Germany. When the fall in the dollar was considered to be sufficient the Louvre accord then sought to stabilize exchange rates at around the prevailing levels.

This period was marked by concerted interventions, which seem to have influenced the external value of the United States dollar, especially at its peak in February 1985 and trough in April 1987.[3] There were other factors, which may have contributed as well, for instance an increased awareness in the financial markets of the major currencies' misalignments. This period has also shown the difficulties inherent in exchange rate management.

One difficulty is focusing monetary policies on the exchange rate objective. Following the Plaza Agreement, for example, further coordination on interest rates was resisted in May 1986 by Germany and Japan because they feared excessive money growth and asset inflation, respectively. As a result, the United States acted unilaterally to cut rates and manage the dollar exchange rate. Similarly in late 1987, interest rates in the United States were kept low to limit the fallout from the October stock market crash, despite the fact that the dollar had resumed the downward trend that was supposed to be avoided under the Louvre Accord.

Since the Plaza-Louvre period, coordinated attempts to manage exchange rates have receded. To some extent this can be attributed to the absence of any pronounced trends in the major exchange rates. But it may also reflect relatively greater attention to domestic policy issues, as Germany experienced the economic impact of unification, Japan the consequences of asset price deflation, and the United States the 1990-1991 recession and credit crunch. In fact, the only recent episode of concerted intervention was in June 1998, when the Federal Reserve and the Bank of Japan intervened jointly in reaction to a large rise in the dollar against the yen.

context, chronic economic weaknesses – if left unchecked – may set the stage for a full-scale financial and economic crisis. One of the main lessons from this recent experience is thus related to the dangers of complacency: a deliberate, consistent and long-term policy effort – combining prudence and a dedication to reform – is the major prerequisite for successful transformation; otherwise recovery and macroeconomic stabilization may be easily reversed.

(ii) Short-term outlook

Due to the considerable volatility of output in the second half of 1998, the short-term outlook for the ECE transition economies is very uncertain. At the moment of writing this *Survey* it was not clear how much deeper the current downturn might go and how much longer it would last. However, if the deterioration in west European economic performance continues in 1999, as well it might, then a number of transition economies, including some of those that have grown rapidly in recent years, could even move into recession. The rising uncertainties (and the increased downside risks) are a serious handicap in attempting to quantify even the short-term outlook and this, in itself, presents a serious challenge to economic policy in the transition economies.

Most of the official government forecasts reported in table 3.1.1 are those associated with the formulation of the 1999 budgets. Although the budget procedures and their timing vary widely among countries, in the majority of cases the 1999 budgets were prepared before the worsening of output became clear, when expectations about 1999 in general were much more optimistic.[163] Since that time some governments have lowered their growth forecasts for 1999 and some of these revisions are reflected in table 3.1.1. However, on average, most of the forecasts in table 3.1.1 still appear to be somewhat optimistic, especially in view of the possible further weakening of west European demand and the continuing volatility of output in some transition economies in the first few months of 1999.[164]

According to the available official forecasts, governments in all the east European and Baltic countries (with the exception of the Czech Republic and Romania) still expect positive economic growth in 1999. Among the central European transition economies, the growth projections underlying the budgets were highest in Hungary and in Poland where some 5 per cent GDP

growth is envisaged in 1999. However, in recent statements government officials in both countries have warned that these targets were unlikely to be met.[165] The Czech budget was drafted under the assumption of 1.5 per cent GDP growth in 1999, but with the dramatic worsening of output in the fourth quarter of 1998, when quarterly GDP fell year-on-year by 4.1 per cent, this forecast has been lowered and it is likely that recession will continue in 1999.[166] The 1999 budget adopted by the new Slovak government assumes a considerable slowdown in economic activity but positive GDP growth (of 3 per cent) is still expected in 1999. However, given the scale of the required adjustment effort in Slovakia, even this reduced growth rate may turn out to be optimistic. Official expectations were also cut substantially in Croatia: preliminary estimates of some 5 per cent GDP growth in 1999 were first lowered to some 3 per cent and at the beginning of the year the central bank reduced it further, to 1.5-2 per cent.[167] Recession is likely to continue in Romania in 1999 but its depth remains uncertain. The government forecast of a 2 per cent decline in GDP is conditional on renewed financial support from the IMF which is still under negotiation. In the absence of IMF finance Romania may face a serious balance of payments constraint due to the problem of servicing its foreign debt and in this case, the actual decline in GDP may be even worse.

As output kept decelerating in 1998 in the Baltic states, so did the official forecasts for 1999. In October 1998, the official forecasts for the three Baltic countries still envisaged that GDP growth in 1999 would be in the range of 5-7 per cent.[168] Since then, the forecasts have been lowered in all three countries, and in mid-March their GDP, on average, was expected to grow by 4.5 per cent (table 3.1.1), some 1.5 percentage points below the expectations of five months ago.[169]

---

[163] The actual deterioration in output performance became evident only towards the end of 1998 and in the beginning of 1999.

[164] These difficulties are also reflected in private sector forecasts as well, but a clear downward trend of expectations can be traced in the most recent forecasts. For example, between September 1998 and March 1999, the mean of available private forecasts of 1999 GDP growth in the Czech Republic decreased by almost 2 percentage points to -0.4 per cent; in the case of Hungary it was lowered by 0.5 percentage point to 3.8 per cent; in Poland it was reduced by 1.6 percentage points to 3.7 per cent. Consensus Economics Inc., *Eastern Europe Consensus Forecasts*, March 1998.

[165] In the case of Poland, Prime Minister Jerzy Busek stated in March that he expected GDP to grow by 4.5 per cent in 1999. Oxford Analytica, "Poland: slowdown response", *Oxford Analytica Brief*, 15 March 1999. The National Bank of Poland has also lowered its 1999 growth forecast to 4-5 per cent (statement by Central Bank Governor Hanna Gronkiewicz-Waltz as reported by *Reuters News Service*, 2 March 1999). In Hungary, the Economics Minister Attila Chikan stated, also in March, that GDP growth would not reach 5 per cent in 1999 and that the Ministry of Economics was preparing a revised forecast envisaging growth in the range of 3-4 per cent (*Reuters News Service*, 17 March 1999).

[166] Both the Ministry of Finance and the Central Statistical Office in the Czech Republic prepare independent forecasts. At the beginning of February the Central Statistical Office had already revised its 1999 GDP forecast to a 0.8 per cent decline. The forecast of the Ministry of Finance was also revised downwards but as of February it still envisaged some 1 per cent GDP growth in 1999 (*Reuters News Service*, 3 February 1999).

[167] Statement by Central Bank Governor Marko Skreb, as reported by *Reuters News Service*, 12 February 1999.

[168] UN/ECE, *Economic Survey of Europe, 1998 No. 3*, p. 49.

[169] The downward revision of forecasts has since continued. On 18 March Lithuania's Ministry of Economics announced a reduction in its 1999 GDP forecast to 3.7-4.1 per cent. *Reuters News Service*, 18 March 1999.

Official forecasts envisage falling GDP in 1999 in three of the CIS countries – the Republic of Moldova, the Russian Federation and Ukraine (table 3.1.1). Moderate but still positive GDP growth is projected for Kazakhstan and Kyrgyzstan, whereas in the rest of the CIS countries for which official forecasts were available relatively high rates of GDP growth are envisaged. While the reliability of many of these forecasts remain questionable, one feature is common to all of them: economic prospects in the CIS as a whole by and large depend on the performance of the Russian economy. However, at the beginning of 1999, numerous uncertainties surround the economic prospects of Russia. Among them, the unsettled issue of servicing of the foreign debt is probably the most acute problem facing the Russian economy in 1999. These uncertainties are reflected in the different forecasts for the Russian Federation: as late as March, the official forecasts for the decline in GDP in 1999 ranged between -2 and -10 per cent.[170] But whatever course the Russian economy takes in 1999 will determine to a large extent the growth path in many of the other CIS countries as well.

As regards inflation, the short-term outlook varies considerably among the transition economies. The better than expected 1998 inflation performance in a number of transition economies was largely determined by external factors, in the first place, the considerable fall in world commodity prices. In the short run there does not appear to be much room for further falls in these prices, but on the other hand an abrupt upward reversal also seems unlikely. Under these circumstances price developments in the transition economics in 1999 are likely to be determined mostly by domestic factors. Hence, while it can be expected that the medium-term trend of disinflation will continue in the more advanced economies, price developments in 1999 on average will probably not match the disinflation record of 1998. On the other hand, the series of currency crises in 1998 resulted in currency devaluations in a large group of transition economies (for details see section 3.2(ii)), and a renewed upsurge of inflation in these can probably be expected in 1999.

Another issue that is likely to have an important bearing on economic performance in 1999 is the level of current account deficits and their financing. Despite some easing in borrowing conditions, at least for some borrowers, it can be expected that international financial markets will in general remain tight, and that borrowing will be more limited and relatively more expensive than it

was before the global financial crisis. Given the increasing divergence in the performance of individual transition economies, the accessibility of financial markets is also likely to remain highly differentiated: while some countries will probably continue to enjoy a privileged status, others will find it increasingly difficult to borrow. Thus, balance of payments constraints may emerge in some cases as the dominant factor in determining the performance of individual economies. The tightening of balance of payments constraints in some transition economies that previously were able to finance relatively large external imbalances may force them to make unwelcome macroeconomic adjustments and thus dampen further their rates of economic growth.

3.2 Issues in transformation policy

(i) Policy challenges in the current stage of transition

The transition from plan to market posed a double challenge for policy makers in the transition economies. On the one hand, the process of economic transformation was unprecedented in terms of both the nature of the policy issues involved and the severity of the problems to be solved. On the other hand, due to their decades of isolation and adherence to central planning dogmas, policy makers in these countries had little, if any, experience with modern economic policy-making. The policy-making background was also rather weak: with the exception of a small number of (mainly central European) countries, there were actually very few trained economists and there was a general deficiency of administrative know-how and skills. Transition was thus also a "learning-by-doing" process for policy makers in these countries and, inevitably, one characterized by "trial-and-error".

Almost a decade after the start of economic transformation, the policy scene in many of these countries now looks rather different. Many of the transition economies have made remarkable progress in the policy process in terms of developing both its conceptual basis and the actual policy mechanisms and instruments required for effective implementation. However, as with many other aspects of the transition process, there are also growing disparities among countries in the general stance of economic policy. The "leading" reform countries, in terms of institutional and structural questions, are often also ahead as regards the depth and sophistication of their policy process. In most of the central European and Baltic countries, the cardinal regime changes which were typical of the initial stages of the transition – and which as a rule involved some macroeconomic turbulence – have already been implemented, albeit with varying degrees of success. It is sometimes asserted that these countries have more or less completed the "first phase" of the transformation process and have now entered a new one where the policy issues and problems are of a rather different nature.

---

[170] The latest available forecast by the Russian Ministry of Economics was drafted in February and it assumed that GDP would fall by 2.5 per cent in 1999 (*Interfax News Agency*, 12 February 1999). Subsequently, the Analytical Department of the Duma published a report in March ("On the forecast of socioeconomic development in Russia for 1999") which contained three basic scenarios: according to the first (which was in agreement with that of the Ministry of Economics) GDP would decline by 2-3 per cent in 1999; in the second scenario the fall in GDP amounted to 5-6 per cent; and in the third GDP declined by 9-10 per cent. WPS Inc., *Banks and Exchanges Weekly*, 9 March 1999.

For example, in this second phase the macroeconomic policy process is turning towards fine-tuning and is becoming more routine, combining longer-term objectives with current day-to-day management. This requires continuous policy coordination, especially between fiscal and monetary policy, and although this does not always work smoothly, the accompanying policy debate has contributed to improving the quality of the policy process. Painful setbacks can still occur within this group of transition economies (as indicated by the recent experience of the Czech Republic); however, these disturbances are starting to resemble cyclical downturns in mature market economies. The composition of the macroeconomic policy mix in the more advanced reform countries has also changed significantly. The apparent eclecticism in defining the nature of macroeconomic policy and its components which marked the early stages of the transition has gradually diminished and even disappeared altogether. In particular, a clearer distinction has developed between the policy issues addressed by monetary and fiscal policy; there has also been growing emphasis on creating automatic countercyclical mechanisms and increasing the flexibility of the available macroeconomic policy tools.[171]

It is worth stressing that the aspiration for reintegration in the European economy – and ultimately for future EU membership – has been a very strong driving force for the positive changes in the economic policy process in these countries. The necessary legislative harmonization and policy synchronization with the EU – in itself a formidable policy challenge – is not only an essential element of the preparations for EU accession but has also been a strong stimulus for upgrading the policy process and the functioning of the public administration in these countries. Moreover, the more energetic has been the effort to achieve the medium-term objective of harmonization with the EU, the stronger has been the positive externality of policy-specific administrative knowledge and skills being diffused towards the aspirant countries.

Despite the progress in reforms and the refinement of the policy process, policy makers still face numerous challenges even in the more advanced transition economies. Within the principal macroeconomic policy mix, the dualism of monetary and fiscal policy in general probably calls for a better balance between the macroeconomic policy goals pursued through the instruments of monetary and fiscal policy. At the start of economic transformation the monetary-fiscal dualism was somewhat disproportionately biased towards monetary policy: the main macroeconomic policy objectives were primarily pursued through monetary policy tools while fiscal policy apparently lagged behind, especially as regards its role in demand management. Indeed, as mentioned above, in recent years the policy

process has improved considerably (notably, in this direction) in the advanced reformers; however many transition economies still have a long way to go.

The background of this policy imbalance was both conceptual and technical in nature. Conceptually it was a reflection of the philosophy of the transformation paradigm embodied in the reform packages, especially those applied in the early phases of transition. These were in many cases strongly influenced by the "Washington Consensus" (see chapter 1) which in principle assigns higher priority to monetary policy than demand management. Technically, it was a consequence of the fact that it takes relatively much less time, resources and effort to constitute an operating monetary authority, capable of pursuing well defined monetary objectives than to establish a similar policy infrastructure for the pursuit of (macroeconomic) fiscal policy goals.

As discussed in section 3.2(ii), the monetary authorities in a number of transition economies have made considerable progress in this respect: they are capable of setting a wide range of monetary objectives and have developed the policy instruments to pursue such objectives. This notwithstanding, the central banks in the transition economies often face difficult policy dilemmas in implementing their agenda and in the day-to-day conduct of monetary policy. In addition to that, the underdeveloped money and capital markets and the still limited arsenal of available policy tools at the disposal of central banks, may limit the efficiency of monetary policy. Thus – as argued in section 3.2(ii) – when faced with conflicting policy objectives (as appears to have been the case in 1998), the monetary authorities may sometimes be forced to revert to "second best" policy decisions. In part, this conflict may also be a consequence of the imbalance between the monetary and fiscal policy noted above: due to this imbalance monetary policy may sometimes turn out to be overburdened with macroeconomic policy objectives, some of which may in principle be possible to pursue (and probably to pursue more efficiently) through other policy means, in particular through fiscal policy.

In fact, through a large part of the 1990s, and especially in the first phase of transition, fiscal policy in many transition economies has predominantly concentrated on the containment of endemic fiscal crises, largely stemming from the legacies of the communist past and the transformational recession.[172] At the extreme (which however was not uncommon in this period), this one-sided notion of fiscal policy was merely reduced to the pursuit of quantified budget deficit targets. Regrettably, such a simplistic approach fails to take into account the fact that not only the deficit position but any

---

[171] See, for example, National Bank of Hungary, *Monetary Policy Guidelines 1999* (Budapest), pp. 5-7.

[172] J. Campbell, "Reflections on the fiscal crisis of post-communist states," pp. 84-112, and S. Owsiak, "Financial crisis of the post-socialist state. The Polish case", pp. 149-167, in J. Hausner, B. Jessop and K. Neilsen (eds.), *Strategic Choice and Path-Dependency in Post-Socialism: Institutional Dynamics in the Transformation Process* (Aldershot, Edward Elgar, 1995).

fiscal action has macroeconomic implications – even if these are not explicitly spelled out or intended. Thus, sometimes (Russia is the most conspicuous example in this regard) the blind pursuit of deficit targets, disregarding complex causal relations and the actual factors (including microeconomic and institutional ones) that cause the fiscal deficit in fact did lead to perverse macroeconomic outcomes.[173]

More recently, and especially with the emergence of new, transition-specific imbalances, the scope of fiscal policy in some of the more advanced reformers has been broadened to incorporate some of the features of more conventional demand management. Thus, as discussed in section 3.3, when faced with unsustainable external or domestic imbalances, a number of transition economies have in recent year been compelled to restore equilibrium (or at least to reduce the imbalances) largely through the use of fiscal policy. However, so far, the widening of the scope of macroeconomic fiscal management has leaned almost exclusively towards its use in cutting expenditure.[174] Besides, there appears to be ample room for a more sophisticated use of fiscal policy through the differentiated management of the individual component of the fiscal accounts.

The unexpected slowdown of economic growth in the second half of 1998 poses further challenges for the conduct of fiscal policy. It is natural to expect larger fiscal deficits in the downward phase of a cycle and this should be borne in mind in designing the proper policy response. An excessive fiscal austerity in response to lower revenue and the desire to meet targeted fiscal deficits (planned under different conditions and assumptions) at any cost, may in fact have perverse effect: such policies may further dampen output and the end result may be even larger deficits. Thus the current downside risks in the economic outlook call for more policy flexibility and innovation as well as greater coherence and closer coordination of all elements in the macroeconomic policy mix to counterbalance these adverse effects.

In contrast to the notable progress in economic transformation in some (mostly central European and Baltic) countries, important reforms have been stalled or have suffered serious setbacks in a number of transition economies, especially in the Commonwealth of Independent States but also in south-eastern Europe. Policy makers in these countries are still faced with

problems that are typical of the first phase of transition, such as the existence of major macroeconomic disequilibria and, hence, persistent sources of macroeconomic instability. Indeed, some transition economies have been in a state of "permanent crisis" since the very start of the transformation process. While these problems are largely due to the considerable difficulties in the implementation of the transformation agenda, they also – at least partly – reflect gaps and flaws in the policy process itself: inconsistencies and incoherence in the policy mix; the absence of policy discipline; poor policy coordination; and a lack of public debate about the policy course, with the consequent failure to gain public support for difficult but necessary reforms.

Due to the lack of experience and expertise, the economic policy process in some transition economies is still embryonic and this adds to the overall fragility of their economies and their vulnerability to disturbances and shocks. It is not uncommon for important policy decisions to be taken in an ad hoc manner and without a coherent and consistent framework for policy and long-term objectives. In the absence of overall policy consistency and due to a myopic bias caused by a state of "permanent crisis", policy is often inefficient and sometimes produces unintended or perverse macroeconomic consequences. In turn, the lack of transparency in the policy process encourages corruption and rent-seeking behaviour which further reduces the efficiency of the policy-making process.

Ironically, it is this group of lagging countries, which is most in need of outside assistance for improving the policy-making process but which de facto has received less than the leading reformers. The international financial institutions (IFIs) have indeed been active in this region and maintain operations in most of the less advanced transition economies. However, the main problem is that when economic performance in these countries goes off-track (and it tends to do so more often in their fragile economic environment), the IFIs, due to the nature of their assignment and their terms of reference, tend to withdraw as well. Consequently, national policy makers are left on their own exactly at the moment when they are most in need of external assistance.

In addition, the less advanced transition economies tend to have less intensive relations with the EU and some of them in fact have not even been part of the debate on the future enlargement of the EU.[175] Despite the existence of some forms of EU financial assistance, the countries without association agreement have been left outside the accompanying policy discussions and, hence, have not benefited to the same extent from the infusion of policy-related know-how from the EU. The decision to start pre-accession negotiations with only five

---

[173] For example the mechanical sequestration of budgetary spending to meet deficit targets (in view of revenue shortfalls) had highly detrimental macroeconomic repercussions for the Russian economy. UN/ECE, *Economic Survey of Europe, 1998 No. 3*, pp. 31-41.

[174] A notable exception has been the use of fiscal policy to boost domestic demand, via public investment, in Slovakia. However, as argued in sect. 3.3, the policy wisdom of this experience is rather questionable: due to its unsustainable scale and because it was not designed in the framework of an overall consistent macroeconomic policy, this fiscal boost led to a dangerous escalation in the external and domestic imbalances.

---

[175] Only 10 ECE transition economies have association agreements with the EU and none of them are CIS countries.

of the 10 associated transition economies is also likely to add to the existing disparities. With the start of the pre-accession negotiations, the "fast track tier" of countries (which is anyway more advanced in the reform and policy process) will begin to receive a disproportionately large share of financial and technical assistance from the EU[176] while the flow of assistance to the countries left out of the negotiations at this stage (and which are less advanced in the reform process) will decline, at least in relative terms.

The unprecedented difficulties and policy challenges in the implementation of the transformation agenda are mirrored in the recent series of transformation crises in several ECE transition economies. Given the severity of these crises as well as their unprecedented nature and character, various issues of this *Survey* have been devoting special attention to them, in an attempt to identify their causes and the mechanisms through which they evolve and escalate.[177] Following this tradition, section 3.2(iii) contains an analytical assessment of the difficult transition process in Romania, focusing both on the underlying roots of the "permanent crisis" in Romania and on the causes of the recent acute deterioration of the economic situation in this country. The nature of many of the economic problems that Romania has been facing throughout the entire decade of the 1990s – as well as the roots of these problems – are not only confined to Romania; for the most part they are also characteristic of most transition economies. It is mainly the frequency and scale of the problems that differ from country to country and that define whether or not they have the potential to develop into a crisis.

As argued in chapter 1, the series of transformation crises poses a number of questions about the wisdom of the prevailing transformation paradigm (at least as regards its success in some transition economies) which was heavily influenced by the "Washington Consensus". This philosophy – underlying the transformation agenda in many transition economies (and especially in the programmes implemented in the first phase of transition) – presumed that sustainable macroeconomic stabilization could be easily and rapidly achieved through rapid liberalization and monetary austerity; it was supposed (at

least implicitly) that this would then pave the way for setting the economy on a path of high and self-sustained growth. This paradigm embodied strong reliance on the automatic operation of the market mechanisms in restructuring the economy, an assumption incorporated – at least implicitly – in the design of the transition programmes. The main ingredient of success, it was believed, was the strong political will to press ahead with a reform agenda so formulated.

The increasing number of transformation failures has shown that in many cases this paradigm did not perform in accordance with expectations. In particular, it was found to pay insufficient attention to a number of factors which were crucial for the transformation process. Among these are several that are clearly identified in the analysis of the Romanian crisis (section 3.2(iii)), namely, the crucial importance of the starting conditions for the success of economic restructuring and transition in general; the key role of institutions, not only for the establishment and proper functioning of markets (an issue that has been repeatedly stressed in previous issues of this *Survey*) but also for avoiding a vicious circle of "path dependence" in economic performance during the transition; and the fact that the endogeneity of the policy process may become a dominant factor during a period of severe structural adjustment.

As shown in section 3.2(iii), the starting conditions can in principle be presented in terms of the transition economy's "distance" from the "normal" state of mature market economies (or, equivalently, from any desired "end-point"). This quantifiable measure (which is country-specific and which in general depends on the inherited distortions in the domestic allocation of resources and in relative prices) helps to define the magnitude of the required adjustment effort to be made in the course of the transformation process. As adjustment is costly and painful, and because there is a limit to the pain that will be endured by the population, (beyond which social cohesion will be threatened) the needed adjustment time basically depends on two parameters: 1) the "distance" from the starting point to the desired structure and 2) the available (locally or attracted from abroad) resources required to make the necessary adjustment.

The transition economies that have made the most progress in the transformation process so far are those that had to cover a smaller "distance" and/or were capable of attracting more external resources (in the first place FDI). In contrast, the most severe transformation crises have occurred in countries where both these conditions were most unfavourable. The fact is that 10 years after the start of economic transformation, some transition economies are still incapable of sustaining their own economic performance and can only keep functioning with the continued support of international assistance.

However, the issue of regaining economic sustainability is intimately related to economic restructuring in the broader sense, that is, to the

---

[176] Since the Essen Council of December 1994, EU assistance programmes, PHARE in particular, are to be increasingly directed at preparing the potential candidates for accession. The Court of Auditors has interpreted this to mean "that a substantial part of the PHARE Programme should be oriented towards a larger-scale and more adequate preparation of the administrations of the candidate states concerned for the understanding, the adoption and the implementation of the main Community policies and the related regulations". See the *Annual Report* concerning the financial year 1994 together with the institutions' replies, OJC303 (Luxembourg), 14 November 1995, p. 216. On the strategic influence of the EU on the development of policies and institutions in both candidate and non-candidate transition economies, see UN/ECE, "Enlarging the European Union to the transition economies", *Economic Bulletin for Europe*, Vol. 48 (1996), pp. 7-18.

[177] An analytical account of the transformation crisis in Bulgaria is given in UN/ECE, *Economic Survey of Europe in 1996-1997*, pp. 75-84; the Czech exchange rate crisis is discussed in UN/ECE, *Economic Survey of Europe, 1998 No. 1*, pp. 75-82; and the crisis in Russia is analysed in UN/ECE, *Economic Survey of Europe, 1998 No. 3*, pp. 31-41.

establishment of a sufficiently large number of viable businesses that would pull the whole economy onto a viable performance path. In this respect, some transition economies appear to be unrestructurable on their own – that can only be done if there is an inflow of external resources on a significant scale (and considerably larger than current levels of official assistance). Obviously, the international financial markets would hardly be willing to supply such funds on such a scale, especially, given their current sentiment towards emerging markets. This underlines the need for a more differentiated approach by the international community towards the transformation process in individual transition economies.

Wide public support is crucial for the success of complex and painful reforms. This aspect of the reform process has been repeatedly emphasized in the recent policy reform literature.[178] An important part of this literature has studied the importance of political constraints for the success of policy reforms: it has been argued that political constraints may be a key factor in the reform process and may impede the successful implementation of a reform package even in the presence of the political will to push it forward, and even if the latter increases long-term social welfare.[179] Other important findings concern the endogeneity of the policy process: the policy process can be strongly affected by the actual outcome of the ongoing reform process.[180]

It can be argued that, given the scale of the required adjustment effort which needs to be engineered through policy reforms in the course of economic transformation (and which is largely determined by the starting conditions) and the available resources at the disposal of the authorities, the endogeneity of the policy process by and large determines the plausible speed of restructuring. As shown in the case of Romania (section 3.2(iii)), when the required adjustment is very large, the endogeneity of the policy process (i.e. the extent to which policy can be followed independently of previous outcomes) may

become a dominant factor that determines the plausibility of the policy course and de facto sets upper limits to the possible speed of restructuring. If adjustment is pushed at a greater speed than the plausible one (in terms of social cohesion), policy is likely to generate perverse results and resistance to reforms.

In this context, public resistance to transformation reforms and the emergence of political structures that are strongly opposed to the policy of reforms in some countries is not solely based on ideological grounds as is often suggested. These reflect the emergence of large numbers of people who are not only losers in the transformation process but who also see no chance of becoming winners.[181] These processes are at the same time the regrettable outcome of wrong policy prescriptions made in the first phase of economic transformation; had this first phase been more successful – and more successful in a greater number of countries – the political environment could have been much more reform-friendly in the transition economies in general and in each individual country.

On the other hand, domestic policy can affect the level of resources deployed in support of an adjustment effort (especially those attracted from abroad), and hence may also have a positive impact on the plausible speed of restructuring. Establishing a favourable investment climate, policy transparency and predictability, the establishment of the rule of law, legislative as well as political stability, are all factors that can affect the inflow of external resources, in particular FDI. Thus, Hungary provides a good example of policy attracting FDI at the early stages of transition when there was relatively much greater interest by direct investors in expanding business in the former centrally planned economies. At the same time Hungary never applied shock-therapy type of liberalization-cum-monetary austerity and never pushed for speedy disinflation; rather, a more gradualist approach was followed towards macroeconomic stabilization coupled with a pragmatic and non-doctrinaire approach to foreign participation in the economy.

On balance, despite the considerable progress in transformation reforms, the policy challenges and dilemmas in the current phase of transition still appear to be formidable. The questions are still much more numerous than the readily available answers and most transition economies, even the most advanced ones, still have a long way to go before they reach the mature state. The international community, the IFIs as well as the European Union – the leading regional economic power – have a great responsibility in assisting and guiding this difficult process.

---

[178] This literature analyses the process of policy reform in the context of motivated behaviour of policy agents (representing interest groups, in particular, "winners" and "losers" from policy reforms) who operate under political constraints (support or resistance to the reform process).

[179] For example, some studies have analysed the importance of uncertainty as a political constraint for policy reforms. If there is considerable *ex-ante* uncertainty about the outcome of reforms, political support for the reform may be weak and these expectations may negatively affect electoral results. R. Fernandez and D. Rodrik, "Resistance to reform: status quo bias in the presence of individual-specific uncertainty," *American Economic Review*, Vol. 81, No. 5, 1991, pp. 1146-1155; A. Drazen, "The political economy of delayed reform," *Journal of Policy Reform*, Vol. 1, No. 1, 1996, pp. 25-46. Other studies have focused on the political constraints to microeconomic restructuring due to the resistance of workers that are threatened by displacement. M. Dewatripont and G. Roland, "Economic reform and dynamic political constraints," *Review of Economic Studies*, No. 59, October 1992, pp. 703-730.

[180] The endogeneity of reform policies and public attitude to reforms (and the fact that they may and do change endogenously over time) have been studied in the same vein of literature. A. Krueger, "Virtuous and vicious circles in economic development," *American Economic Review (AEA Papers and Proceedings)*, Vol. 83, No. 2, 1993, pp. 351-355.

---

[181] Russia and Ukraine are among the countries that are most frequently quoted as examples of where public resistance to reforms has taken the form of organized political structures which even dominate the current political spectrum. However, similar processes have taken place in other transition economies as well.

(ii) Monetary policy

(a) Overview of monetary policy in 1998-1999

In pursuing their main objective – maintaining the general price level within a specified range – national monetary authorities use indirect levers which affect prices through the monetary transmission mechanisms.[182] Hence, in most cases, the monetary policy goals are defined in terms of intermediate targets which, in turn, depend on the chosen monetary and exchange rate regime. In the case of a fixed or pegged exchange rate regime the target is the nominal exchange rate and the main policy tool of the central bank is its own lending rate (which serves as a reference point for the level of domestic interest rates) while money supply is more or less treated as endogenous.[183] In the extreme case of a currency board regime, there is no room for an independent monetary policy as the monetary authority cannot act as a lender of last resort and loses the interest rate as a policy tool.[184] In the case of a pure floating regime, the monetary authorities usually target the level of money supply (as defined by a selected monetary aggregate) while the exchange rate is left to be determined on the market. The main policy tool is again the interest rate but in some cases direct controls over the monetary aggregates are also applied. In the intermediate cases of a pegged exchange rate with a fluctuation band or a managed float, the central bank may set multiple targets (with explicit or implicit priorities among them).

The central banks in the transition economies still face numerous challenges in implementing monetary policy. The conduct of monetary policy is largely hampered by the inefficient monetary transmission mechanisms which, in turn, is a consequence of underdeveloped money and capital markets. The institutional infrastructure of these economies (even in the more advanced let alone the less advanced reform countries) is still relatively fragmentary and weak. Markets are marred by inherited or transition-specific distortions and are far from being efficient. In general the transition economies lack robustness: they remain quite fragile and prone to disturbances, and policy makers cannot afford to neglect these imperfections in setting their policy agenda.

These inherent weaknesses have come to the forefront of the policy debate since the beginning of the Asian crisis which was marked by high volatility on global financial markets. The Russian crisis – apart from being a major domestic shock – had a further destabilizing impact on the ECE transition economies. These external developments served as a detonator to the internal pressures which had been building up in a number of transition economies in recent years. The exchange rate regimes were especially vulnerable to these pressures and several countries were faced with full-blown currency crises. Many ECE transition economies are now in the process of painful adjustments which, *inter alia*, require some major macroeconomic policy changes.

Contagion from the turmoil in the international financial markets also posed serious challenges to the monetary authorities in the transition economies; on several occasions in this period some of them were forced to revert to emergency measures such as excessive tightening of monetary policy (in some east European and Baltic countries) or even restrictions on the convertibility of the currency (in some CIS countries) to prevent financial and macroeconomic destabilization. Moreover, the immediate impact in terms of direct contagion, strong as it was, was not the only negative consequence of the recent crisis. With time it became clear that the global financial instability and the resulting, unexpectedly strong slowdown of global economic activity would have lasting negative implications not only for output in the transition economies but also, more broadly, on their macroeconomic balances.

The negative developments in the global environment will almost certainly require changes in the focus and priorities of monetary policy. Among the major developments are the possible further weakening of external demand (especially in western Europe) and the rising costs of financing current account deficits. In the two years or so prior to mid-1998 the central banks in the fast-growing transition economies were concerned at the prospect of overheating and the consequences of significant capital inflows; but they are now facing the opposite problem: an economic slowdown and emerging balance of payments constraints. Thus the focus of monetary policy in the more advanced reform countries has been gradually shifting from seeking a balance between growth and stability towards invigorating domestic economic performance and growth. Indeed, some changes in policy priorities along these lines were already observable in the second half of 1998; others were made explicit with the setting of the 1999 monetary policy guidelines.

The introduction of the euro so far does not appear to have had any major impact on the monetary stance of the transition economies. However, in purely practical terms it did affect the conduct of monetary policy insofar as all the transition economies that used the deutsche mark as a reference currency (for a direct peg or as a component of a currency basket) switched to the euro as the reference currency as of 1 January 1999.

---

[182] During the last decade, a number of developed market economies have turned to "inflation targeting", a regime under which the government or the central bank sets directly an explicit inflation target. G. Debelle, *Inflation Targeting in Practice*, IMF Working Paper WP/97/35 (Washington, D.C.), March 1997. Since 1998, some transition economies (notably the Czech Republic and more recently Slovakia and Poland) have introduced elements of this regime in their policy framework. However, the monetary authorities in these countries have continued, de facto and in parallel, to meet other targets as well and it will probably take some time before inflation targeting will emerge in its pure form.

[183] See, for example, E. Koch, "Exchange rates and monetary policy in central Europe – a survey of some issues", *MOCT-MOST*, Vol. 7, No. 1, 1997, pp. 1-48.

[184] For a description of the currency board regime see UN/ECE, *Economic Survey of Europe in 1996-1997*, p. 70.

Exchange rates

The ECE transition economies apply a wide variety of exchange rate arrangements, covering practically the whole range of existing currency regimes. The various regimes in 1998-1999 were as follows:[185] currency boards in Bosnia and Herzegovina, Bulgaria, Estonia and Lithuania; a fixed exchange rate in Latvia; an adjustable peg in Yugoslavia (where there was a forced devaluation and multiple rates now exist); a fixed rate with a fluctuation band in Slovakia (until 1 October 1998, managed float afterwards); a crawling peg against a currency basket with a fluctuation band in Hungary and Poland; a target band in Russia (until 18 August 1998, managed float afterwards) and in Ukraine (however, with forced changes in the band in this period); a managed float in Croatia, The former Yugoslav Republic of Macedonia, and Slovenia. The rest of the CIS countries formally have floating exchange rate regimes, with varying degrees of intervention by the central banks; however, in most of these countries currency convertibility is limited and multiple exchange rates exist de facto in some of them.

For much of 1998, public attention was focused on the escalating financial and economic crisis in Russia.[186] The crisis culminated in August, when the persistent loss of investor confidence led to a massive outflow of capital from Russia, to the collapse of the exchange rate regime (which had been maintained since 1995), and default on domestic public debt. After the rouble was floated, it lost much of its value[187] and has been under intense pressure ever since; without the reintroduction of some administrative controls over the currency market it would have depreciated even more in this period.

The global financial turmoil and the Russian crisis had a negative impact on the financial markets of all the transition economies. The currencies of a number of them came under growing pressure both as a result of changing investors' sentiments (see next section) and the inherent internal weaknesses of some of these economies. In addition, the collapse of the rouble in August 1998 reduced the competitiveness of Russia's trading partners and especially those neighbouring countries with which it has relatively intense trade relations (see section 3.6). This resulted in import substitution by Russia and lost revenue for the affected exporters.

In effect, the Asian and the Russian crises triggered a series of currency crises in the region which unfolded in an almost identical manner: a persistent run on the currency leading to a drain of the limited currency reserves forced the monetary authorities to give up futile attempts to maintain the exchange rate within its targeted range. Thus on 4 September 1998, Ukraine was forced to abandon the previous fluctuation corridor of 1.8-2.25 hryvnia per dollar and to adopt a new band of 2.5-3.5 hryvnia per dollar, a significant effective currency devaluation. As pressures on the currency continued, a further devaluation occurred on 9 February 1999 when the trading band was raised to 3.4-4.6 hryvnia per dollar.

In the second half of the year pressures also started to increase on the Moldovan leu.[188] After losing some one third of its reserves in defence of the currency,[189] the central bank was forced to discontinue intervention on the foreign exchange market on 2 November. In the week after this decision the leu depreciated by more than 30 per cent. Towards the end of the year, following a worsening of the fiscal balance in the aftermath of the Russian crisis, the Georgian lari also became the target of a speculative attack and on 4 December the central bank abandoned its support of the currency. Within a month the lari lost almost half of its value against the dollar only to recover slightly in the first months of 1999. Following a significant deterioration in the trade and current accounts, the Kyrgyz som also fell victim to a currency run losing over 50 per cent of its value in the second half of 1998.

Among the most affected CIS currencies was the Belarussian rouble. For some time now the Belarussian authorities have been engaged in soft-lending to ailing companies and to the agricultural sector (for which Russia has been the main export market) which had resulted in the weakening of the currency already in 1997. The drying-up of Russian import demand in the second half of 1998 resulted, *inter alia,* in increasing pressure on the currency. Between September 1998 and the time of writing this *Survey* the Belarussian rouble has been falling steadily, resulting in a considerable loss in its value and in the persistent widening of the margin between the official and the trading rates.[190]

---

[185] For an overview of exchange rate regimes and their implications for monetary policy in the transition economies see P. Desai, "Macroeconomic fragility and exchange rate vulnerability: a cautionary record of transition economies", *Journal of Comparative Economics*, Vol. 26, 1998, pp. 621-641; H. Wagner, *Central Banking in Transition countries*, IMF Working Paper WP/98/126 (Washington, D.C.), August 1998.

[186] These developments have been analysed in more detail in previous issues of the *Survey*. UN/ECE, *Economic Survey of Europe, 1998 No. 2*, pp. 22-26; and *1998 No. 3*, pp. 31-41.

[187] Some 70 per cent between September 1998 and February 1999.

[188] Apart from the negative impact of the Russian crisis, the economy of the Republic of Moldova has been marked for several years by serious domestic and external imbalances (a "twin" deficit problem). The lack of progress in correcting these prompted the International Monetary Fund in mid-1997 to discontinue disbursements under a 1996 agreement which rendered the balance of payment constraint even more acute. IMF financing resumed in January 1999 after a tough 1999 budget was approved; however, the current imbalances (and the further weakening of the economy by the Russian crisis) will require a major policy effort to restore equilibrium.

[189] According to a statement by the Central Bank Chairman Leonid Talmaci, intervention by the bank in the period September-October resulted in a fall in the country's hard currency reserves from $300 million to $200 million. RFE/RL, *Newsline*, Vol. 2, No. 212, Part II, 3 November 1998.

[190] It is difficult to be precise about the actual extent of the devaluation due to the complicated system of multiple exchange rates which exists in Belarus as a result of the numerous currency regulations. The official rate is in practice only applied to transactions between the central bank and the government. The trading rate at the interbank market, although formally subject to regulation, has in fact been deviating considerably from the official rate. The exchange bureaus operate at a cash rate which is also subject to regulation. In addition, apparently there exists a black market rate.

TABLE 3.2.1

Short-term interest rates in selected transition economies, 1995-1998

(Per cent)

	Short-term credits				Short-term deposits (domestic currency)				Average yield on short-term government securities			
	1995	1996	1997	1998[a]	1995	1996	1997	1998[a]	1995	1996	1997	1998[a]
Bulgaria	79.8	300.3	209.8	14.2	43.7	146.4	80.8	3.0	61.7	278.7	200.8	6.2
Croatia	20.2	22.5	15.5	15.8	5.5	5.6	4.3	4.6	20.7	18.1	8.8	10.2
Czech Republic	12.7	12.4	13.2	13.7	7.0	6.8	7.7	8.1	..	..	..	..
Hungary	32.6	27.3	21.8	19.3	26.1	22.2	18.5	16.2	32.0	24.0	20.1	17.7
Poland	33.5	26.1	24.9	24.6	22.7	18.5	18.1	17.0	25.6	20.3	21.6	19.1
Romania	48.9	55.3	72.5	55.4	36.5	38.1	55.8	37.3	41.4	51.1	85.7	64.0
Slovakia	17.7	14.3	17.3	20.6	9.0	6.7	8.0	10.1	..	..	..	..
Slovenia	23.4	22.6	20.0	16.1	15.3	15.0	13.2	10.6	10.3	5.7	5.0	4.4
The former Yugoslav Republic of Macedonia	..	..	21.4	21.1	..	..	11.5	11.7	..	..	..	..
Estonia	19.0	14.9	11.8	15.0	8.8	6.1	6.2	8.1	..	..	..	..
Latvia	34.6	25.8	15.2	14.3	14.8	11.7	5.9	5.3	28.2	16.3	4.7	5.3
Lithuania	27.1	21.6	14.4	12.2	20.1	13.6	8.1	6.5	29.3	21.0	8.6	10.7
Belarus	148.0	64.3	32.9	27.0	80.4	32.3	15.5	14.3	..	..	..	..
Russian Federation	319.5	146.8	46.2	43.6	102.0	55.1	16.4	15.1	168.0	85.8	26.0	45.2
Ukraine	122.7	79.9	49.1	54.4	70.3	33.6	18.2	21.9	..	..	..	..

Source: Central bank publications and direct communications to UN/ECE secretariat; IMF, *International Financial Statistics* (Washington, D.C.), various issues.

Note: Definition of interest rates:

Credits – Belarus: weighted average rate on short-term loans; Bulgaria: average rate on short-term credits; Croatia: weighted average rate on new credits; Czech Republic: average rate on total short-term loans; Estonia: weighted average rate on short-term loans; Hungary: weighted average rate on loans of less than one year; Latvia: average rates on short-term credits; Lithuania: average rates on loans of one to three months; Poland: median of the rate on low-risk short-term loans. Beginning January 1995, weighted average rate; Romania: average short-term lending rate; Russian Federation: weighted average rate on loans of up to one-year maturity; Slovakia: average rate on new short-term loans; Slovenia: average rate on short-term working capital loans; The former Yugoslav Republic of Macedonia: midpoint rates for short-term loans to all sectors; Ukraine: weighted average rate on short-term loans.

Deposits – Belarus: weighted average rate on short-term deposits; Bulgaria: average rates on one-month time deposits; Croatia: weighted average rate on new deposits; Czech Republic: average rate on short-term time deposits; Estonia: weighted average rate on short-term deposits; Hungary: weighted average rate on deposits fixed for more than one month, but less than one year; Latvia: average rates on short-term deposits; Lithuania: average rates on deposits of one to three months; Poland: weighted average rate (according to information collected from 15 biggest commercial banks) on short-term households' deposits in domestic currency; Romania: average short-term deposit rate; Russian Federation: prevailing rate for time deposits with maturity less than one year; Slovakia: average rate on time deposits; Slovenia: average rate on time deposits of 31-90 days; The former Yugoslav Republic of Macedonia: lowest reported interest rate on household deposits with maturities of three to six months; Ukraine: weighted average rate on short-term deposits.

Yields of government securities – Bulgaria: yield on government securities is computed as the average weighted yield of all issues during the calendar month; Croatia: interest rate on NBC bills, due in 91 days; Hungary: weighted average yield on 90-day treasury bills sold at auctions; Poland: yield on bills purchased, weighted average, 13 weeks; Romania: rate on 91-day treasury bills; Slovenia: BS tolar bills, 14 days overall nominal rate; Latvia: weighted average auction rate on 91-day treasury bills; Lithuania: average auction rate on treasury bills with maturity of 91-days; Russian Federation: weighted average rate on government short-term obligations (GKO) with maturities of up to 90 days. Beginning in April 1997, the rate is calculated on the basis of GKOs with remaining maturity of up to 90 days.

[a] January-November for Bulgaria, Hungary, Slovakia and Russian Federation.

Despite significant progress in a wide range of reforms, the financial systems in many transition economies remain relatively underdeveloped, a state which is largely a reflection of the legacies of the former economic systems. Even in the more advanced economies financial markets are still rather shallow in terms of product diversification and the extent of their penetration into the economy.[204] This is clearly demonstrated by the monetization ratios (table 3.2.2) which with the possible exception of the Czech Republic and Slovakia (where they reflect specific historic factors) remain rather low by international standards.[205]

Moreover, the transition experience so far has indicated that changes in this sphere take place only very slowly: in fact, on average there has been very little change in the level of monetization since the start of reforms[206] and it will probably take decades for the depth of financial markets in these countries to reach levels comparable to those in the developed market economies.

The remonetization of the transition economies involves a number of delicate policy issues related to the balance between stability and growth. The evolution of commercial credit in the transition economies in recent years (credit to the non-government sector as a proportion

[204] Actually the range of products offered by the banks in some of the transition economies has increased enormously in recent years and continues to grow rapidly; however, this improvement still touches only a tiny segment of the market so far.

[205] UN/ECE, *Economic Survey of Europe in 1996-1997*, p. 75.

[206] It is noteworthy that in the cases where radical changes did occur, as in Bulgaria in 1996-1997, they were in the reverse direction: the financial crisis provoked scaling down of the level of monetization due to the erosion of the value of domestic assets by very high inflation.

TABLE 3.2.2

Monetization in selected transition economies: share of monetary aggregates [a] in GDP, 1995-1998

(Per cent)

	M1 [b]				Total broad money [c]				Total credit [d]			
	1995	*1996*	*1997*	*1998 [e]*	*1995*	*1996*	*1997*	*1998 [e]*	*1995*	*1996*	*1997*	*1998 [e]*
Albania	21.3	34.7	..	..	39.1	62.6	..	..	5.5	6.4	..	..
Bulgaria	9.3	7.4	6.5	9.7	56.9	44.4	23.9	26.8	35.5	34.5	17.4	15.7
Croatia	7.9	9.0	10.0	9.8	21.2	28.4	36.0	39.5	30.2	33.2	33.1	40.4
Czech Republic	30.6	29.1	25.7	22.3	68.5	69.9	69.3	67.6	64.8	63.5	65.2	63.6
Hungary	16.4	15.2	14.7	14.7	37.2	36.4	35.6	33.0	27.8	23.3	24.2	23.8
Poland	9.9	10.9	13.9	13.3	32.0	33.5	41.2	43.0	16.0	17.2	20.4	22.7
Romania	6.9	7.3	5.0	5.1	18.0	20.8	18.5	21.0	17.6	19.2	14.9	14.6
Slovakia	23.8	25.8	23.5	21.3	66.1	64.6	64.3	63.1	57.5	58.9	55.9	52.8
Slovenia	7.9	7.8	7.9	8.9	37.7	40.6	42.5	47.3	23.0	26.9	26.3	28.4
The former Yugoslav Republic of Macedonia	..	..	6.4	..	..	..	12.7	..	..	..	26.7	..
Yugoslavia	6.0	5.3	6.4	6.2	29.4	36.6	31.3	36.5	..	..	..	..
Estonia	17.4	17.9	19.1	17.9	22.0	23.3	26.4	25.4	13.2	16.6	24.7	33.2
Latvia	12.7	12.4	14.3	16.4	27.4	19.7	23.0	26.1	15.4	7.3	9.1	14.8
Lithuania	11.7	10.6	10.7	11.9	20.8	16.5	16.3	17.6	16.5	12.3	10.4	12.1
Belarus	..	6.7	6.4	7.6	..	12.4	12.1	14.0	..	4.3	3.9	4.9
Russian Federation	7.0	7.8	10.9	10.4	13.9	14.8	16.5	17.8	11.2	10.1	10.7	11.3
Ukraine	..	6.6	8.5	8.8	..	9.5	11.9	13.0	..	7.1	7.6	8.0

Source: National statistics and direct communications from national statistical offices to UN/ECE secretariat; IMF, *International Financial Statistics* (Washington, D.C.), various issues.

[a] Averages of monthly or quarterly figures.

[b] Currency in circulation plus demand deposits.

[c] M1 plus time deposits in domestic currency and foreign currency deposits.

[d] Total outstanding claims on firms and households.

[e] January-November for Bulgaria, the Czech Republic, Hungary, Poland and The former Yugoslav Republic of Macedonia; GDP data for 1998 are estimates.

of GDP, see table 3.2.2) shows that in a number of the faster growing countries (for example Croatia, Poland, Estonia, Latvia, among others) the share of credit also increased in 1996-1998. An increasing share of credit in GDP indicates an intensification and widening scope of banking activity. Moreover, when credit to the corporate sector increases faster than the narrow components of money supply (M0 and M1), this suggests an increase in the value of the money multipliers and thus a deepening of financial intermediation in the country. Such a development also suggests that the improved access of firms to finance may have contributed to the strong economic performance of these countries.[207] It is noteworthy that in most of the countries where there was an economic downturn in this period there was also a shrinking share of commercial credit: this was the case in Bulgaria, the Czech Republic, Romania and Russia. It is difficult to draw general conclusions about the direction of causation in these cases; most likely the shrinking share of credit reflects the outcome of a vicious circle of contracting money demand and more cautious lending policy due to the unfavourable economic environment.

As argued in previous issues of this *Survey*,[208] money demand in the transition economies tends to be highly unstable and it is imperative that the day-to-day conduct of monetary policy takes due account of that.[209] Financial volatility and, in particular, rising concerns about the stability of the currency or of the exchange rate regime may provoke rapid changes in money demand, and ultimately, a run on the currency. Foreign exchange reserves can be used to protect the currency in the case of a speculative attack and the extent to which domestic assets can be matched by reserves is one of the indicators of financial vulnerability.[210] Hence, in overseeing and monitoring the rate of monetary expansion, central banks need to take into account the extent to which domestic currency assets (including the broader definitions of domestic monetary aggregates) are backed by reserves. As indicated by the monetary ratios in table 3.2.3, most east European and Baltic countries can be regarded as

---

[207] It should be stressed, however, that credit expansion is a healthy development only when banks perform proper credit screening and finance viable economic projects. As indicated by the painful experience of some transition economies (Bulgaria is an example), providing credit to unviable firms leads to a snowballing of bad loans which, if unchecked, can lead to a financial crisis.

[208] For example, UN/ECE, *Economic Survey of Europe in 1996-1997*, pp. 73-75.

[209] Moreover, abrupt ad hoc financial market interventions by the monetary authorities may themselves trigger unwelcome shifts in money demand which, in turn, may have a destabilizing impact on the financial markets.

[210] When markets panic, the restructuring of investors' portfolios in response to the changes in money demand usually involves attempts to convert all domestic currency assets into a reserve currency.

TABLE 3.2.3

Monetary ratios for selected transition economies, 1995-1998

(Per cent)

	Dollarization: share of foreign currency in broad money				Official foreign exchange reserves as percentage of M1				Official foreign exchange reserves as percentage of broad money, domestic currency			
	1995	1996	1997	1998[a]	1995	1996	1997	1998[a]	1995	1996	1997	1998[a]
Bulgaria	27.2	34.8	49.8	41.0	107.2	77.0	222.1	200.3	24.5	21.3	119.9	131.3
Croatia	52.9	59.8	62.1	65.1	124.3	125.7	123.6	124.5	98.3	98.7	91.0	88.3
Czech Republic	7.5	8.0	10.3	11.3	64.2	78.2	81.5	91.7	31.0	35.5	33.6	34.3
Hungary	25.1	26.6	23.4	19.4	110.8	150.2	126.1	109.5	65.6	85.5	68.0	60.4
Poland	22.0	17.0	14.1	12.9	83.1	111.9	96.6	116.0	32.8	43.7	37.9	41.3
Romania	22.5	23.0	32.0	29.7	71.9	67.5	160.6	160.3	34.6	30.8	63.4	55.7
Slovakia	12.7	10.6	10.7	12.0	57.3	70.9	68.5	74.9	26.5	31.7	28.8	28.8
Slovenia	33.3	34.9	31.5	27.2	113.0	129.3	214.9	206.3	35.6	38.2	54.3	53.1
The former Yugoslav Republic of Macedonia	..	..	..	..	..	34.0	53.4	85.3	..	..	..	..
Yugoslavia	69.7	79.4	72.1	75.4	..	..	..	..	..	..	..	..
Estonia	12.1	11.1	12.7	17.5	86.8	77.0	71.7	80.4	78.2	66.4	59.4	60.1
Latvia	..	32.2	32.6	30.7	..	89.2	85.1	77.2	..	83.1	78.7	70.0
Lithuania	30.5	25.7	25.3	23.4	91.0	85.2	87.8	100.3	73.2	73.2	76.6	88.3
Belarus	..	..	..	..	..	..	44.1	33.4	..	..	..	..
Russian Federation	..	19.5	17.9	21.7	..	37.4	37.7	31.9	..	24.5	25.7	24.1
Ukraine	..	18.9	14.3	17.6	..	34.0	53.4	41.4	..	28.9	44.6	33.5

Source: National statistics and direct communications from national statistical offices to UN/ECE secretariat; IMF, *International Financial Statistics* (Washington, D.C.), various issues.

[a] January-November for Bulgaria, Czech Republic, Hungary, Poland and The former Yugoslav Republic of Macedonia.

relatively safe on this account. In some of the CIS countries, however (for example Belarus, Russia and Ukraine), the level of reserves as a share of the money supply has on average been much lower in recent years, a situation which made their currencies more vulnerable to speculative attacks and added to the currency turmoil in 1998.

While the overall level of dollarization of an economy may reflect some country-specific features (in particular, historical traditions and persistent habits), its evolution largely reflects changes in the overall level of confidence in the national currency. Indicative of this is that in many of the more advanced transition economies (for example, Hungary, Poland, Slovenia and Lithuania), the level of dollarization has been shrinking rapidly in recent years (table 3.2.3). Conversely, a deterioration in the economic situation, and especially a financial crisis, usually results in currency substitution and growing level of dollarization. Such a change occurred even in the Czech Republic after the 1997 currency crisis (table 3.2.3).

To sum up, the remonetizing of the transition economies needs to be conducted with utmost caution. Thus, in targeting the money supply (or in assessing the state of the money supply when the latter is not being directly targeted by policy), the central banks need to distinguish the different nature of the various forces driving money demand. A clear distinction needs to be made between money demand generated by robust economic performance and growing sophistication of the economy (in fact, by the catching-up process in which some of the transition economies have already engaged)

and the "appetite" for permanent access to easy finance emanating from an inconsistent fiscal policy (or a malfunctioning economy in general). Monetizing "healthy" money demand is beneficial and essential for the normal functioning of the economy (indeed, not monetizing such demand would risk the creation of unnecessary obstacles to improved economic performance). Conversely, accommodating monetary claims arising from chronic fiscal (or quasi-fiscal) deficits can set the stage for macroeconomic destabilization and persistently high inflation.

One of the greatest policy dilemmas facing a transition economy at present is how to remonetize the Russian economy while minimizing the negative side effects. The artificial macroeconomic stabilization programme pursued in 1995-1998 was founded on what turned out to be an unsustainable exchange rate regime based on an unnecessarily restrictive monetary policy. This resulted, *inter alia*, in a mushrooming of monetary surrogates. The size of these flows and the extent of their propagation put them on a comparable level with the official monetary circulation.[211] The return to a normal functioning of the economy necessitates the remonetization of all commercial and fiscal relations. However, this is not a minor task and no easy solutions appear to be at hand. The greatest source of apprehension is the likely macroeconomic impact of

_____

[211] For details see UN/ECE, *Economic Survey of Europe, 1998 No. 3*, pp. 31-41.

remonetization: injecting new liquidity is likely to have a strong inflationary impact and to cause a further weakening of the exchange rate. The main dilemma arises from the doubts as to whether, at this stage, there exists a workable solution to the problem of non-monetary payments (and, for that matter, of non-payments as well) and whether it can be resolved in a one-off operation. While the existing "stock" of non-monetary instruments can in principle be removed in the framework of a one-time monetary emission, the difficult issue is how to address the "flow" of non-monetary payments.[212] If this problem remains unresolved, simply monetizing a continuous flow of payments in non-monetary form will not only produce a one-step increase in the price level but will result in a persistent and very high rate of inflation.

The policy issues related to the remonetization of the Russian economy are also relevant for a number of other transition economies facing similar problems. Thus finding an efficient, workable solution to the problem in Russia may have important policy implications for other countries as well.

(b) Selected policy issues: can monetary policy be efficient when trapped between conflicting targets?

Policy makers often face difficult choices between conflicting goals and the monetary authorities in the transition economies are especially prone to policy dilemmas in implementing their agenda. There are no universal prescriptions as to how to proceed in such situations: in some cases it may turn out that the de facto optimal solution goes against the conventions of economic theory; in other cases it may turn out that an optimal solution simply does not exist and that the choice is between "second-best" or even "third-best" solutions. Yet another source of confusion is the fact that policy decisions are as a rule judged by the public in accordance with their *ex-post* efficiency which may not necessarily coincide with the *ex-ante* efficiency due to the fundamental uncertainty characteristic of the environment in which decisions are taken.

The Asian and Russian crises and the ensuing global financial turbulence in 1998 created a difficult and equivocal environment for the monetary authorities in the transition economies in which they were faced with conflicting goals and the need to compromise between controversial alternatives. Apart from the fundamental uncertainties of the transition environment, there were several additional sources of external disturbance in this period that generated monetary pressures with a variety of consequences.

First, there was a general increase in financial market volatility which affected practically all the transition economies.[213] The change in investors' sentiment about emerging markets in the aftermath of the Asian crisis provoked an outflow of foreign capital (mostly short-term) from the transition economies which had a destabilizing effect on their financial markets and put downward pressure on their currencies. One of the conventional policy responses in such circumstances is to tighten monetary policy and, in particular, raise interest rates.

The rationale behind such a move is related to the change in the investors' perception of the risk of holding assets denominated in the currencies affected (directly or indirectly) by financial instability. The series of crises in 1997-1998 increased investors' perception of the risk associated with financial investments in all emerging markets (including the ECE transition economies). Consequently investors started to require higher interest premia to compensate for the increased risk of investing in the affected currencies. If, as a result of the change in expectations, the returns on the financial assets denominated in the local currency do not match the expected risk premium, investors may decide to pull out of the currency and of the country and, as noted above, this is what happened in many transition economies in 1998. In an attempt to counter this outflow, the monetary authorities often revert to tightening monetary policy in order to engineer a rise in the yields of local assets sufficient to match the higher risk premium. The result is a general upward pressure on interest rates, and a tendency for them to rise above the level at which the monetary authorities would have set them in the absence of the external pressure.

During the same period, however, there were other external factors at play that acted in the opposite direction. In the wake of the Asian crisis, the weakening of global demand for primary commodities and semi-processed goods generated strong downward pressures on prices, especially those for tradeables, in many parts of the world. On average, world market prices of internationally traded goods probably declined in nominal terms in 1998. The transition economies are basically price-takers and, given their openness and very little domestic price protection, lower import prices resulted on average in a much faster rate of disinflation in 1998 than in 1997.

In the course of 1998 it became clear that actual inflation in many of the transition economies was going to be lower than the *ex-ante* targets (either the explicit inflation targets or the inflation expectations on which monetary policy in general was focused). After years of fighting inflation this was an unexpected outcome, and for a number of transition economies this was the first time since the start of economic transformation that actual inflation was below expectations. At the same time, output growth throughout the region was losing pace, prompting the possibility of a need for a change in policy. Due to its nature and focus, it is usually monetary policy that bears the brunt of policy adjustments in the short run. Did policy makers – in particular, the monetary authorities – respond to the increasing gap between expectations and outcomes?

---

[212] This aspect of the remonetization of the economy is one of the issues that has not been properly addressed in recent proposals to establish a currency board in Russia. If non-monetary payments re-emerge after a currency board is put into operation, they may easily compromise this monetary regime.

[213] UN/ECE, *Economic Survey of Europe, 1998 No. 3*, pp. 41-43.

As discussed in the previous section, the monetary authorities throughout the region but especially in central Europe were rather active during the second half of the year in moderating monetary austerity. In fact, in terms of the number of changes in key interest rates, 1998 was probably the most "activist" year since the start of transition. These policy changes not only reflected some revision of inflation targets or expectations by the central banks but also the worldwide fall in interest rates which allowed interest differentials to be maintained at lower local rates.

However, in terms of actual real interest rates, these policy moves were far from sufficient in moderating the restrictive character of monetary policy. On the contrary, real interest rates actually increased in many transition economies in 1998. This is especially striking in terms of the forward-looking *ex-post* real lending rates (chart 3.2.1):[214] while not necessarily resulting from deliberate policy actions, the actual outcomes point to a considerable de facto tightening of the stance of monetary policy in a number of countries in 1998. Thus, rather than providing the required (and probably desired) support to activity, the persistently (in some cases increasingly) restrictive character of monetary policy may have actually depressed it, reinforcing the deceleration of economic growth.

It is difficult to be definite as to the exact set of country-specific factors that could have led to such an unwelcome outcome. Besides, as seen on chart 3.2.1, there was considerable variation in the extent of monetary tightening in those countries where the information on real lending rates is available. Moreover, at the moment of writing this *Survey*, it was not quite clear what direction this trend would take in each individual country. However, the fact that monetary tightening was not an isolated phenomenon but occurred in a large group of countries, suggests that it may have been influenced by some common factors related to the nature of the monetary policy process and the policy instruments available in the transition economies.

Leaving aside the question of whether the monetary authorities were actually ready to respond quickly to rapidly changing external conditions, the real issue is whether they had efficient policy alternatives and policy instruments at their disposal. The basic problem is that as a result of the two divergent and externally induced trends, monetary policy became trapped between two conflicting objectives: on the one hand, central banks were faced with capital outflows and downward pressure on their currencies; on the other, with an unexpected deflationary impulse from the prices for imports.

The degrees of freedom of the monetary authorities to cope with such a situation are determined by the monetary and exchange rate regime as well as by the actual monetary targets (nominal anchors) and the tools available to pursue these targets. As noted above, when the exchange rate is chosen as the intermediate target of monetary policy (as is the case in fixed or pegged exchange rate regimes), the main policy instrument at the disposal of the central bank is the nominal interest rate. Assuming that the exchange rate provides a reference point to the price level in the country (or country zone) of the peg, keeping the exchange rate within the targeted range acts as an anchor for the level of domestic prices.

One basic requirement for the proper functioning of the monetary transmission mechanism in countries with fixed or pegged exchange rates, following the logic outlined above, is that there are no major and systemic misalignments in the change in foreign trade prices relative to the change in prices in the reference country. However, such a misalignment is exactly what happened in 1998: there was a substantial drop in the relative prices of many internationally traded goods which produced a "third party" bias (that is, a bias that did not originate in the reference country). This created a serious distortion for monetary policy in transition economies that adhered to exchange rate targeting, since the exchange rate failed to provide the relevant reference point for monetary targeting; in reality, the trade-induced price effect was different in magnitude and probably in direction.[215] An interest rate policy aimed at defending an exchange rate target under these circumstances would tend to create (and is likely to have done so) an undesirable rigidity in monetary policy.

An indirect argument in support of this conjecture is the fact that countries where monetary policy did not target the exchange rate directly were much less affected by such a policy bias as regards the level of real interest rates. This especially seems to be the case in Slovenia but also, to some extent, in Croatia (chart 3.2.1).[216] There was, indeed, an upsurge of real interest rates in these countries towards the end of 1997, largely due to the Asian crisis, but afterwards the pressure on real lending rates subsided rapidly. Since the intermediate target of the central banks in these countries is the money supply and the monetary aggregates were not affected by the above-mentioned price misalignment, there was no "instrumental" upward bias generated by monetary policy.

---

[214] The *ex-post* forward-looking real interest rate is the nominal rate deflated by the prevailing inflation rate in the period when the loan is actually being taken up. For practical purposes this means that the prevailing interest rate at time t should be deflated by the average inflation rate prevailing in the period (t+T), where T is the maturity of the loan. Note that this is the period following the drawing of the loan, so that interest rates reported at time t have to be deflated by average inflation reported in a subsequent period of time (hence, forward-looking). Such a quantitative assessment can only be performed *ex post*. Another important detail is the price index to be used for this assessment. Conventional logic suggests that if the loan is used to finance a production cycle, then the proper price deflator should be that of the goods produced. Thus the closest aggregate proxy for assessing the real interest rate on corporate loans is the Producer Price Index (PPI). On chart 3.2.1 the short-term nominal lending rates are deflated by the average PPI in the subsequent three-month period.

---

[215] A major shift in the cross exchange rates of the currencies comprising a currency basket may create similar distortions for monetary policy in an economy whose currency is pegged to such a basket.

[216] It is more difficult to make a clear judgement about the recent trends in real interest rates in Romania because of the major regime change that took place at the beginning of 1997: monetary policy was tightened considerably and the long-standing practice of soft bank lending (often at negative real rates) was discontinued.

CHART 3.2.1

Nominal and real lending rates *a* **in selected transition economies, 1996-1998**
(Three-month moving averages)

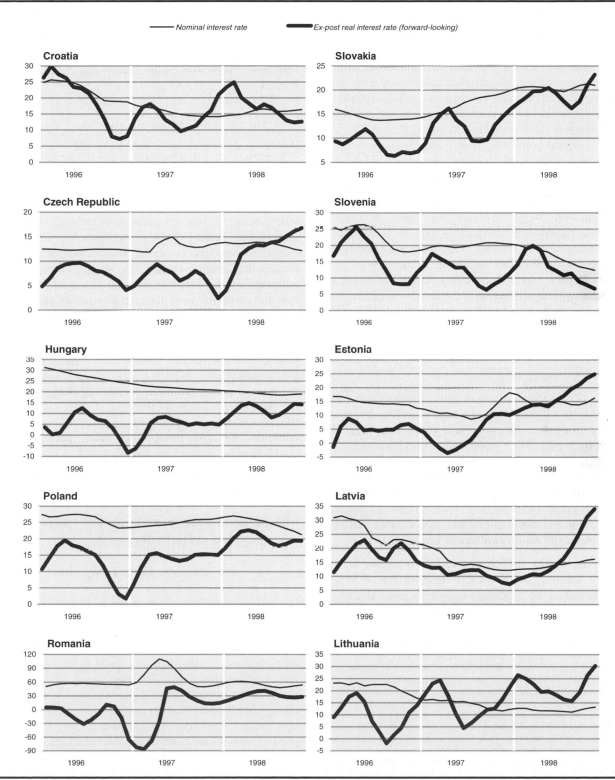

Source: UN/ECE secretariat calculations, based on national statistics and direct communications from national statistical offices.

a *Ex-post*, forward-looking rates computed by deflating the nominal rates quoted for a given month by the average producer price inflation in the three-month period following this month.

However, there is another possible cause of the unwelcome upsurge in real lending rates in some of the transition economies in 1998 and it is related to the actual set of policy tools used to pursue the monetary targets. The fact is that by and large the central banks used one and the same instrument (interest rates) both to prevent rapid capital outflows and to pursue a targeted level of the exchange rate. Hence, when faced with conflicting objectives, they were trapped with no efficient strategies to pursue these two goals simultaneously and thus they were compelled to give up one objective at the expense of the other. Related to this issue is a sequencing problem: initially, interest rates were kept too high for too long (to serve as "capital controls"); but then, when they were lowered, they were not allowed to fall enough (due to the policy misalignment).

In short, in 1998 monetary policy in the transition economies has been revealed to have a certain "downward rigidity" in the face of negative, externally induced price shocks due to a reluctance or failure to respond quickly. Whether deliberate or unintended, the de facto outcome was that monetary policy turned out to be unnecessarily restrictive in the post-shock period and this probably contributed to the slowing down of output growth in 1998 and in early 1999. Although so far there has been little debate over this episode, and the future evolution of policy is still not clear, some policy lessons can already be suggested.[217]

One of the lessons is that monetary policy did not apply the most efficient tools to target the two divergent trends (or to pursue the two conflicting objectives). In line with the discussion in chapter 1, it can be argued that interest rates are probably not the most efficient policy instrument to regulate the movement of short-term capital flows: arguably, if the latter were targeted by other policy instruments (for example by some form of capital controls), the monetary authorities could have lowered interest rates more rapidly and more aggressively.

Another policy lesson concerns the impact of the quality of banking assets on real lending rates. When banks' portfolios are burdened with substantial shares of

substandard and non-performing loans, they tend to charge higher interest rates to their "good" clients in order to be able to compensate for the lost income. This results in higher spreads between lending and deposit rates. Although in recent years interest rate spreads in some transition economies have declined considerably, they still remain stubbornly high in others (table 3.2.1). Undoubtedly, the existence of high nominal spreads played a negative role in supporting the rise in real lending rates in 1998, at least in some transition economies.[218]

The negative impact of high interest rate spreads becomes especially pronounced at low nominal rates. When rates of inflation and interest are high, a wide interest rate spread alone would have a relatively small impact on real rates as it would be diluted by the high nominal values. However, in a period of disinflation, when nominal interest rates are falling, a persistent markup on lending rates caused by the low average quality of bank assets would create a permanent upward bias in real lending rates. This is one more reason for emphasizing the fact that the soundness of the banking system is a prerequisite for effective policy and a healthy economy.

Finally, another lesson concerns the set of monetary policy tools: a further diversification of the monetary policy instruments is highly desirable in order to avoid a situation of policy paralysis or "second best" solutions in the face of conflicting objectives. Closer monitoring of the components and driving forces of inflation (in particular, the trade-induced impact on domestic prices) could also be helpful in enabling policy to assess the situation more accurately and respond with adequate policy instruments.

(iii) Structure, strain and economic adjustment: the crisis in Romania

(a) Introduction: the starting point

This section discusses restructuring and macroeconomic adjustment during the post-communist transition in Romania and links them to two major issues: the legacy of resource misallocation, or what can be termed inherited structure, and institutional fragility. The legacy of resource misallocation leads to very intense strain in the system when there is a brutal and dramatic change of relative prices to market-clearing levels. At the new prices resources should flow from low to high productivity areas, a process which can generate much pain and friction in a real economy. The strain or tension involved explains why there is much opposition to change, and why coalitions of interests emerge to hinder

---

[217] In terms of the policy lessons of this episode it might also be useful to consider the hypothetical "mirror image" of the 1998 developments, that is, what would have been the likely outcome of a symmetric policy overshooting in the opposite direction. Consider a transition economy using an exchange rate anchor in the hypothetical but not unrealistic situation of a positive shock to world commodity prices and the prices of internationally traded goods in general (i.e. the relative prices of internationally traded goods increase vis-à-vis the general price level in the reference country). In this case there will be a higher than normal trade-induced upward pressure on local prices which will not necessarily be targeted by monetary policy due to the inherent misalignment of the exchange rate target. Assume at the same time a situation of non-negligible net capital inflows. If the central bank relies on interest rate policy to discourage an unwanted capital inflow, it might be tempted to lower interest rates in order to reduce the premium. Thus, apart from the direct impact of higher imported inflation, such a monetary policy overshooting (due to the delayed response by the monetary authorities to the changing external conditions, implemented entirely through interest rates) may in fact lead to an inappropriate easing of monetary policy and, consequently, an even stronger upsurge in the rate of inflation.

[218] A detailed assessment of the impact of spreads on real interest rates would require a detailed comparative analysis of individual banks' portfolios and lending practices, information which was not available at the time of writing this *Survey*.

deep restructuring. Strain also explains why large fiscal and quasi-fiscal deficits, of varying degrees of visibility, are a feature of post-command economies which create an endemic proclivity to high inflation.

Some analysts relate inflation, primarily, to the breakdown of the political process and rent-seeking activities by old elites.[219] While this is not implausible, the approach adopted in this section emphasizes the magnitude of the required resource reallocation, which is sometimes so large that it undermines attempts to achieve durable stabilization. It is arguable that the success of the leading transition economies is due, primarily, to policy being able to deal with the magnitude of required resource reallocation while not being "captured" by vested interests.

Institutional fragility is another dimension of the transformation process which underlines the complicated nature of change, restructuring included. The lack of institutions, of organized markets, hinders a smooth reallocation of resources and has a negative effect on performance at both the micro and macroeconomic levels; it also helps to explain the intense friction in the system, especially rising transaction costs, that arises during the passage between two regimes. This line of reasoning finds substantial analytical support in recent work.[220]

Together with strain, institutional fragility helps to explain stop-go policies, as well as many of the setbacks and inconsistencies in the transition process. Fuzziness and a lack of transparency characterise the realm of public finance. For example, banks are frequently the vehicle for the granting of subsidies. Primitive banking systems, in the grip of redundant structures, are likely to perpetuate much of the old pattern of resource allocation (or misallocation) and engage in significant quasi-fiscal operations, with the latter showing up in high rates of inflation or of bank failures.

Romania's experience is a highly relevant example of how strain[221] and institutional fragility condition macroeconomic stabilization.

In the following review of economic developments during 1990-1998, stop-go policies, resurgent inflation and macro-disequilibria, as well as bank failures, all emerge as an inevitable outcome of a feeble pace of restructuring and fragile institutions. It is emphasized that without large inflows of foreign direct investment (FDI) and the creation of appropriate institutions, the economy is unlikely to be able to escape from the grip of the old structures. It is also clear that a more rapid rate of privatization would help to increase the inflow of foreign capital. The slow pace of restructuring has maintained intense strain in the system and has led to a bad "path dependency". Romania started the transition process at a disadvantage, with significantly worse initial conditions than those prevailing in the leading reform countries,[222] which suggests that her policy makers have also had less room for manoeuvre. Nonetheless, the end result is that they have not yet been able to find a clear way forward to a well-functioning market economy. Under the current unfavourable conditions in the world economy it will be increasingly difficult for the Romanian economy to escape from this path dependency.

In comparative analyses of the transition economies insufficient attention has been paid to the initial conditions prevailing when the transformation process got underway.[223] Communist Romania, particularly in the 1970s and 1980s, provides an interesting and instructive case of "immiserising-growth" which was caused by the logic of the system, in particular, the rush to speed up industrial growth and to increase ties with market economies on a very weak functional basis (by totally ignoring market mechanisms). In the literature, this phenomenon is explained by the existence of various price distortions which harm resource allocation, worsen the terms of trade, and lower welfare.[224] But it can also be argued that it was the way the economy functioned as a whole (including the genesis of wrong industrial choices) which constituted *the* distortion that led to immiserising growth. It has been shown that the inner dynamics of the system – its incapacity to cope with

[219] P. Boone and J. Hoerder, "Inflation: causes, consequences, and cures" in P. Boone, S. Gomulka and R. Layard (eds.), *Emerging from Communism. Lessons from Russia, China and Eastern Europe* (Cambridge, MA, MIT Press, 1998), pp. 42-72.

[220] O. Blanchard, *The Economics of Post-communist Transition* (Oxford, Clarendon Press, 1997).

[221] A formal development of the idea of strain was given in D. Daianu, *The Changing Mix of Disequilibria during Transition: A Romanian Background*, IMF Working Paper WP/94/73 (Washington, D.C.), 1994, and D. Daianu, "An economic explanation of strain", in J. Bachaus (ed.), *Issues in Transformation Theory* (Marburg, Metropolis, 1997). Essentially, strain (J) measures the distance or dissimilarity between two vectors of prices and quantities, namely:

$$J = \sum_i qi \mid pi - pi^* \mid / \sum_i pi^* qi^*$$

where pi and qi refer to prices and quantities at the start of the transition for sector i and the asterisk denotes their level after full adjustment

towards international prices and a new, "western-like" economic structure. The higher the value of J the greater the required change in relative prices and the greater is the strain of adjustment. Obviously other variables such as quantities, employment or relative wages, can be substituted for the price vectors in the index. For empirical estimates of strain, made by OECD, see table 3.2.7.

[222] Romania practised late Stalinism until the very end of the communist regime. Initial conditions can be related to the magnitude of resource misallocation, the institutional ingredients of a market environment, the existence of a private sector, to a certain industrial culture, etc.

[223] An IMF report of 1997 acknowledges that "Romania emerged from communism with an economy that was suffering from considerably more deep-seated structural problems than most former communist countries in the region". IMF Staff Country Report No. 97/46, *Romania, Recent Economic Developments* (Washington, D.C.), July 1997, p. 7.

[224] J. Bhagwati, "Immiserising growth – a geometrical note", *The Review of Economic Studies*, Vol. 25, June 1958, pp. 201-205; H. Johnson, "The possibility of income losses from increased efficiency of factor accumulation in the presence of tariffs", *The Economic Journal*, Vol. 77, 1967, pp. 151-154.

increasing complexity and its inability to assimilate and generate technological progress – led to a "softening" of output, characterized by its expansion with a strong bias towards low value added industrial goods, which led to a steady deterioration of the terms of trade.[225]

Since "immiserising growth" limited the potential to increase exports, the targeted trade surpluses in the 1980s – required to pay back the external debt – were achieved through very large cuts in hard currency imports. Apart from the reduced level of investment, growth possibilities were also impaired by a sharp reduction in imports of machinery and equipment from the western countries. The heavy overtaxation of domestic absorption that took place during this period subsequently resulted in lower growth rates of production, reduced welfare (consumption), and bigger domestic imbalances (both visible and hidden). In addition, shortages were rising in both production and consumption.

The immiserising nature of "growth" in communist Romania is well illustrated by its income per capita (which has remained one of the lowest in Europe) and the very high energy intensity of its GDP.[226] Another telling fact is that whereas the GDP grew – allegedly – by almost 28 per cent during the 1980s exports decreased over the same period.

The structure of industry also revealed a strong bias towards the creation of gigantic units, with no regard for the important sources of flexibility in an economy, namely, the small and medium-sized enterprises. Thus, in 1989, 1,075 enterprises with more than 1,000 employees each, represented more than 51 per cent of all units, provided jobs for 87 per cent of all industrial workers and supplied almost 85 per cent of all industrial output; enterprises with over 3,000 workers (which accounted for about 16 per cent of the total) supplied over 50 per cent of total industrial output and provided jobs for 53 per cent of all employees in industry. At the same time, the small- and medium-sized enterprises (with less than 500 employees) accounted for 4 per cent of all workers and 6 per cent of total industrial output.

The forced reduction of the external debt in the 1980s (actually a *sui generis* shock-therapy), accentuated the decline in the competitiveness of the economy, exacerbated imbalances among sectors, increased shortages, and generally lowered the welfare of the people.

(b) The high inflation period, 1990-1993

The early years of post-communism in Romania were marred by severe economic difficulties, including a very large fall in output (table 3.2.4), an institutional

hiatus,[227] and "systematic" policy incoherence. Institutional hiatus refers to the melting down of much of the old institutional structures without a rapid build up of market-based institutions. This, obviously, contributed to increasing uncertainty, fuzziness, and volatility in the national economic environment. At this stage "the entrenched structures are being broken and changed, which means that the quantity of friction in the system goes up considerably and important energies (resources) are consumed in order to accommodate change. A lot boils down to a change of the organizational behaviour of actors, to the buildup of new organizational capital. In this phase of transition there exists a territory over which market coordination failures combine with an "abandoned child" feeling of many enterprises, which are no longer able to rely on central allocation of resources and customers. For these enterprises information and transaction costs skyrocketed".[228]

In spite of its tortuous path some institutional change did take place during those years; through spontaneous processes, such as massive land privatization and the emergence of a private sector (which preceded Law 54 of 1990 on the setting up of private enterprises),[229] as well as measures "from above" initiated by government. Among the latter are the start of the two-tiered banking system (in 1990), the commercialization of state owned enterprises (Law 15 of 1990), and the privatization Law 58 of 1991 which aimed at giving 30 per cent of the equity of commercial companies to Romanian citizens.[230] What happened with the privatization law is symptomatic of the vacillations and inconsistencies of reform policies during that period; Law 58 of 1991 created much confusion regarding the actual structure of property rights and the need for enhanced management of assets. What was totally lacking was a concern for building institutionally organized markets for factors of production.

Overall and in a formal sense, it can be said that policy makers practised a sort of "institutional mimetism" by trying to adopt, although in a highly inconsistent way, institutions found in the western world. A problem with institutional mimetism, however, is that it cannot deal with the fine print of reforms (institutional change) and, frequently, it lacks substance since the real functioning of institutions is driven by vested interests.

---

[225] D. Daianu, "A case of immiserising growth", *Revista Economica*, No. 20 (in Romanian), 1985.

[226] The energy consumption per unit of GDP is twice as high in Romania as in Hungary, and more than 4 times larger than the OECD average. EBRD, *Transition Report 1995* (London), p. 77.

[227] R. Kozul-Wright and P. Rayment, "The institutional hiatus in economies in transition and its policy consequences", *Cambridge Journal of Economics*, Vol. 21, No. 5, September 1997, pp. 641-661.

[228] D. Daianu, *The Changing Mix of Disequilibria during Transition: A Romanian Background*, IMF Working Paper WP/94/73 (Washington, D.C.), 1994.

[229] In 1991 the number of private companies rose quickly to 72,277; they operated mainly in trade and services. By the end of 1995 the number had risen to almost half a million. It should be recalled that, in contrast with Hungary or Poland, the communist regime in Romania did not allow any form of private property.

[230] It should be said that commercial companies represented only 60 per cent of state assets; the rest belonged to the so-called "*régies autonomes*", which were created according to the French model.

TABLE 3.2.4

Macroeconomic indicators of Romania, 1990-1998

(Per cent)

	1990	1991	1992	1993	1994	1995	1996	1997	1998
GDP *(annual change)*	-5.6	-12.9	-8.8	1.5	3.9	7.1	3.9	-6.9	-7.3
Unemployment rate *(end of period)*	–	3.3	8.2	10.4	10.9	9.5	6.6	8.8	10.3
Inflation									
Average	5.1	170.2	210.4	256.1	136.7	32.3	38.8	154.8	59.1
December/December	37.7	222.8	199.5	295.6	61.9	27.7	56.8	151.7	40.7
M2 *(end of period)* growth rate	22.0	101.2	79.6	141.0	138.1	71.6	66.0	104.9	27.4[a]
Nominal devaluation									
Average	50.3	240.5	303.1	146.8	117.8	22.8	51.6	132.5	23.8
December/December	140.4	444.5	143.3	177.4	38.4	45.9	56.5	98.8	36.5
M2/GDP	55.7	27.4	20.1	13.8	13.3	18.1	20.5	18.1	..
Budget deficit [b]/GDP	1.0	3.3	-4.6	-0.4	-1.9	-2.6	-3.9	-3.7	-4.0[c]
Current account/GDP	-8.5	-3.5	-8.0	-4.5	-1.4	-5.0	-7.2	-6.7	-6.6
Real wage index	5.1	-18.3	-13.0	-16.7	0.4	12.6	9.5	-22.2	4.7[a]

Source: National Bank of Romania.

[a] November 1998.

[b] Consolidated budget.

[c] Estimates.

After December 1989 there was tremendous *pressure from below* to consume tradeables, to reduce exports and boost imports of both consumer and intermediate goods, after the years of severe deprivation in the 1980s. The switch in favour of tradeables was almost instantaneous and virtually unstoppable; it was also strengthened by a "shunning of domestic goods" syndrome. In 1990 the boost in consumption was financed primarily by dissaving (the depletion of foreign exchange reserves).

However, there is another side of the story that needs to be highlighted, namely, that policy makers complicated the state of the economy both by commission and omission. By commission, since they faltered in the face of pressures from below and were influenced also by the prospect of elections in May 1990. This resulted in the concession of large wage rises[231] and the introduction of the five-day workweek, despite the fact that output was plummeting, together with the maintenance of wide-ranging price controls, a greatly overvalued exchange rate, and mismanagement of the foreign exchange reserves. By omission, for there were no serious attempts to deal with macroeconomic imbalances before November 1990. Events during that year revealed a fundamental flaw in the transformation process, namely, the considerable decision-making power of enterprises when they do not have to face hard-budget constraints.

Confronted with a rapid deterioration of the economy and unable to contain growing disequilibria (unsustainable trade deficits, rising prices, vanishing

investment) a stabilization plan, supported by the IMF, was introduced at the start of 1991.[232] The middle-of-the-road, gradualistic stabilization programme that took shape included the following: a tightening of fiscal and monetary policy (although real interest rates remained highly negative), a tax-based incomes policy, a new devaluation and introduction of a two-tier exchange rate system (through the initiation of an interbank foreign exchange auction system, in February 1991). The programme failed to stop inflation.

At the end of 1991 there were growing tensions in the system: for example, an overvalued official exchange rate; artificially low prices for energy and raw materials which encouraged their overconsumption; and insufficient inflows of foreign capital to compensate for the low levels of domestic saving and the weakness of fixed investment. Many exporters and importers found a way out of the *impasse* in making barter deals, which introduced an *implicit* exchange rate into the functioning of the economy; this rate mitigated the pernicious effects of overvaluation but entailed considerable information and transaction costs. However, capital flight and insufficient exports were becoming matters of major concern.

In the spring of 1992 policy makers were compelled to act. Interest rates were raised considerably, the refinance rate of the National Bank reaching 80 per cent; the exchange rate was devalued substantially and exporters were granted full retention rights in the hope of overcoming their mistrust of policy makers and encouraging the repatriation of capital. The full retention measure was thought necessary since enterprises still had a vivid memory of the "confiscation" of their hard-

[231] This development should be seen in the context of the elections in May 1990. Measured real wages rose by 11 per cent between December 1989 and October 1990, while output continued to fall. The removal of price controls began in November of that year.

[232] D. Demekas and M. Khan, *The Romanian Economic Reform Program*, IMF Occasional Paper, No. 89 (Washington, D.C.), 1991.

currency holdings at the end of 1991. But the policy turnround was incomplete and interest rates remained negative as a result of a large array of preferential credits and very low deposit rates – the latter reflecting a high propensity to shun the domestic currency in favour of the dollar. Political factors, resulting from the elections of September 1992, also weakened the determination of the government to pursue a consistent policy.

(c) A policy breakthrough, 1993-1994: "the interest rate shock"

Rising inflation and the persistence of a large trade imbalance eventually forced a reconsideration of policies. A breakthrough occurred in the last quarter of 1993 when several key decisions were made in order to contain and reverse the dynamics of inflationary expectations, to start the remonetization of the economy and to create a transparent, functioning foreign exchange market. The major omission in the whole strategy, however, was privatization, which would have had a major influence on the size of capital inflows and on the scope and intensity of restructuring.

The main decision, a dramatic rise in nominal interest rates, led to positive real interest rates. Thus, the central bank's average refinancing rate rose from an annual rate of 59.1 per cent in September 1993 to 136.3 per cent in January 1994 and remained at that level for another three months. Commercial banks' lending rates followed suit with a two-month lag. This measure had two major consequences: first it stemmed the flight from the leu and started a rapid rate of remonetization; and, second, it greatly helped the formation of a transparent foreign exchange market and, thereby, strengthened the potential for an export drive. The scale of remonetization explains why the policy shock of 1994 did not lead to a decline of output as was the case in 1997 (when the economy was subject to a credit crunch).

Another key decision was the substantial devaluation (in several stages) of the official (interbank market) exchange rate which lowered it to more or less the rate prevailing on the grey market; this also increased the transparency of the foreign exchange market which in turn reduced considerably the entry costs for those in need of foreign exchange.

The third measure involved a stricter control of base money and consequently a reduced rate of money creation. And finally, the fiscal stance was tightened to aim at a low budget deficit when corrected for the removal of explicit and implicit subsidies.[233]

The results of this policy breakthrough were much as expected. Inflation fell to an annual rate of 62 per cent (December-on-December) in 1994 and there was a large

reduction in the trade deficit to $411 million.[234] The economy absorbed the shock of high positive real interest rates and of the exchange rate unification – which meant the suppression of some implicit and explicit subsidies to inefficient producers – and there was no decline of output. The removal of subsidies explains why the budget deficit went up to 4.3 per cent in 1994, with a large part of its financing being obtained from external sources.

The export drive played a major role in the recovery, but it cannot explain why so many enterprises in the weak sectors also did well in 1993, especially as arrears did not "appear" to be rising sharply in 1994.[235] Several explanations can be suggested. One is the existence of important market imperfections, such as monopolies that can extract rents and which operate in the less efficient sectors. Another is that there are huge amounts of "X-inefficiency" in the system.[236] This means that potential micro-efficiency gains are ubiquitous and that, when under pressure, even firms in the backward sectors can realize some of them and cope with the situation. But accepting this explanation requires an evaluation of the resilience of *organizational routines* in the system. An implication of the X-inefficiency explanation is that the pressure for fundamental restructuring begins to bite only when most of the efficiency reserves are exhausted. A third explanation is that there was more reliance on self-financing, although in fact many companies were plagued by a lack of working capital. Last, but not least, unwarranted bank lending (rollover of loans) may have played a significant role in supporting the weaker enterprises.

(d) Fragile growth and relapse into inflation, 1995-1996

In 1995 there was a rapid growth of GDP in Romania, 7.1 per cent against just under 4 per cent in 1994 and under 2 per cent in 1993; at the same time the inflation rate at the end of 1995 was about 28 per cent. The remonetization of the economy continued, as indicated by the expansion of the money supply (72 per cent) far exceeding the rate of inflation (table 3.2.4 and chart 3.2.2); money velocity (for the aggregate M2, which includes hard currency deposits) fell below 5 – from over 7.5 in 1993 – reflecting a rise in money demand. While exports continued to grow rapidly (by over 20 per cent) imports increased by more than 30 per cent, causing the trade imbalance to increase again to more than $1,570 million and putting pressure on the foreign exchange (interbank) market.

---

[233] The budget deficit was actually higher in 1994 than in 1993, but most of the implicit and explicit subsidies had been removed, which was a key objective.

[234] It can be argued, however, that the *ceteris paribus* condition does not apply in this assessment since there were favourable external "shocks" as well.

[235] Caution is required with the numbers since arrears can be obscured by inefficient activities being kept afloat by bank lending (via rollovers). Ultimately, these "hidden" arrears will show up in a deterioration in the portfolios of the banks. This is what appears to have happened in 1996 and thereafter.

[236] H. Leibenstein, "Allocative efficiency vs. X-efficiency", *American Economic Review*, Vol. 56, No. 3, 1996, pp. 392-410.

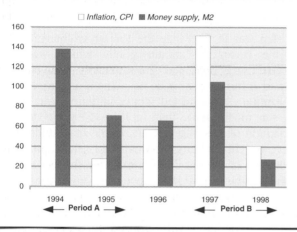

CHART 3.2.2

Remonetization vs. demonetization in Romania, 1994-1998
(Per cent, December over December)

Source: National Bank of Romania.

Note: The change in M2 for 1998 refers to November over November.

What caused the trade imbalance to deteriorate again, bearing in mind that the real exchange rate did not appreciate in 1995 (although it did so in the second half of 1994) and that there were no major changes in the terms of trade in this period? One explanation is that an import and consumer spending boom started in the last months of 1994, which, arguably, might have been encouraged by perceptions that the exchange rate was unsustainable. But this explanation would have to be reconciled with the fact that in 1994 the trade and current account imbalances improved dramatically and the foreign exchange reserves of the banking system (including the central bank) increased substantially, which might have suggested that the exchange rate was in fact sustainable. It is also possible that the various economic agents were unused to stability of the nominal exchange rate and therefore anticipated an inevitable depreciation which, paradoxically, may not have been justified by the economic fundamentals. Another conjecture is that some of the improvement in the trade balance in 1994 was caused by temporary factors; their removal in the following year then put additional pressure on an exchange rate that was already overvalued. Without dismissing these factors, the more important explanation is probably that the higher growth rate of the economy, driven by highly import-dependent branches, led to overheating and the rapid growth of imports.

In 1996 there was a clear link between inflation and the way the budget deficit was financed. Whereas the target for the consolidated budget deficit was 2.2 per cent, it turned out to be 5.8 per cent, on an accrual basis. More significant was that its financing was inflationary as a result of the commercial banks buying an increasing volume of three-month treasury bills. The scale of inflationary financing was augmented by the injection of base money in order to cover the quasi-fiscal deficit which arose because of the losses of agriculture and of the *régies autonomes*. Together with the quasi-fiscal

deficit the fiscal imbalance reached 8.4 per cent (on an accrual basis) in 1996 (table 3.2.5).

The process of remonetization had supported the efforts to subdue inflation in 1994 and 1995. Regarding remonetization several aspects should be emphasized:

- It facilitated the subsidization of various sectors of the economy (agriculture, energy) from the central bank's resources, allowing the central bank to pursue simultaneously the reduction of inflation. The sectoral financing mirrored the existence of major structural disequilibria in the economy;

- It "helped" put off dealing resolutely with the two failed banks – Dacia Felix and Credit Bank; more then 1,700 billion lei (approximately $400 million) were injected in both through special credits during 1995-1996. If money demand had not grown for most of 1995 and 1996 the size of the special credits would have certainly fuelled inflation. The reason for this injection was that there was no insurance scheme for small depositors and so it was felt necessary to forestall a run on the banks and, therefore, a possible systemic crisis;

- It involved the expansion of base money through the increase of net domestic assets, and not through the accumulation of net foreign assets. Ideally, remonetization should have taken place as an outcome of a rise in net foreign assets – that is, as a result of capital inflows or of net exports – and not, primarily, via base money injections which supported the expansion of domestic credit;

- It can be argued that this remonetization slowed down the development of monetary policy instruments, namely open market operations. This is because the central bank did not face the pressure to cope with a surge of liquidity as would have been the case with substantial capital inflows. The main reasons why such inflows did not occur are the feeble pace of privatization during 1994-1996, the poor functioning of the domestic capital markets, and the credibility problem surrounding domestic policies.

By the end of 1996 several worrying tendencies had emerged: a very sharp rise in the monthly inflation rate which was in double-digits in the last quarter of the year; the sharp rise in the trade and current account deficits, although the growth rate of GDP was lower than in 1995 (3.9 per cent as against 7.1 per cent); and still greater distortions in relative prices due, especially, to the delay in adjusting energy prices and to the administrative control of the exchange rate. Overall, the macroeconomic stabilization programme was losing steam. The inflation rate at the end of the year was 57 per cent. Furthermore, in spite of heavy borrowing (over $1.5 billion) on the international capital markets,[237] the foreign exchange

---

[237] During 1995 Romania was rated BB- by the principal western rating agencies (and BB+ by JCRA), which helped the raising of money on the international capital markets. These accommodating capital inflows fended off a major balance of payments crisis in 1996.

TABLE 3.2.5

Fiscal and quasi-fiscal deficits of Romania, 1993-1997

(Percentage share in GDP)

	1993	1994	1995	1996	1997
Budget balance					
Total					
Cash	-0.4	-1.9	-2.6	-3.9	-4.5
Accruals	-0.4	-1.9	-3.0	-5.8	-3.5
Primary					
Cash	80.6	-0.5	-1.2	-2.2	-0.5
Accruals	0.6	-0.5	-1.6	-4.1	0.5
Quasi-fiscal deficit *a*	-3.1	-3.6	-0.3	-2.6	–
Budget balance including quasi-fiscal deficit					
Total					
Cash	-3.5	2-5.5	-2.9	-6.5	-4.5
Accruals	-3.5	-5.5	-3.3	-8.4	-3.5
Primary					
Cash	-2.5	-4.1	-1.5	-4.8	-0.5
Accruals	-2.5	-4.1	-1.9	-6.7	0.5
Memorandum item:					
Interest payment	0.9	1.4	1.4	1.7	2.4

Source: National Bank of Romania.

a National Bank of Romania refinancing.

reserves of the national bank stood at about $600 million at the end of 1996. The external debt of the country was rising rapidly with peak payments looming in the following years. In addition, the policy mix being pursued by the government (multiple exchange rates, price controls, subsidies, etc.) was making it unlikely that it would be possible to reach a new arrangement with the IMF. Such developments were clearly leading to a dead-end and a policy change was urgently required.

The events of 1995 and 1996 underscored both the importance of privatization for inducing autonomous capital inflows and for enhancing restructuring, as well as the danger of "populist macroeconomics".[238]

(e) The "policy shock" of 1997 and its consequences, 1997-1998

At the end of 1996 the economic situation was as follows: the monthly inflation rate was over 10 per cent; the consolidated budget deficit and the quasi-fiscal operations of the central bank were in excess of 8 per cent of GDP; the current account deficit was about 7.2 per cent of GDP; and foreign exchange reserves were down to some $600 million, less than a month's imports in spite of the large loans that had been raised in the international capital market. At the same time, financial indiscipline (total arrears) had reached a magnitude that was causing serious concern (about 34 per cent of GDP), while inadequate steps were being taken toward privatization and restructuring. Last but not least, the remonetization of the economy had allowed massive

subsidies to be given to agriculture and other sectors in 1995 and 1996 without raising inflation; as the remonetization process came to a halt in the latter half of 1996, maintaining subsidies without igniting inflation was to prove an impossible endeavour.

What happened in 1997? The new government's first step was to liberalize the foreign exchange market and the prices of certain goods which were still administratively regulated. Paradoxically, in a year when renewed efforts were made to achieve macroeconomic stabilization, the expected annual inflation rate, 90 per cent, was much higher than in 1996 (57 per cent). The explanation of this paradox lies in the magnitude of the effect of liberalizing prices and the anticipated devaluation of the leu.[239] Nevertheless, the assault upon several of the major imbalances led to some positive results: the foreign exchange market began to function adequately; the consolidated budget deficit (including quasi-fiscal deficits) was reduced to 3.5 per cent of GDP;[240] the current account deficit shrank a little, from 7.2 per cent to 6.7 per cent of GDP; and the central bank's foreign exchange reserves soared to about $2.6 billion.[241] The size of the fiscal adjustment should also be seen against the backdrop of the sharp fall in output, which greatly reduced the tax base. But despite all this, there was another side to the coin: the actual inflation rate was 152 per cent and GDP fell by much more than expected (6.9 per cent as against 2 per cent). Both demand and supply shocks were behind the decline of the economy.

One consequence of the programme, which is not often mentioned, was its severe impact on the emerging private sector. The large contraction of real credit lowered considerably the prospects for many small- and medium-sized companies and was a major factor in the fall of output. Thus, total real credit (in domestic and foreign currency) declined by 52.5 per cent and its non-government component by as much as 61.3 per cent. This should be set against the growth of real credit in previous years when the non-government component increased by 19.7 per cent, 35.6 per cent, and 4.1 per cent in 1994, 1995, and 1996, respectively.[242] In many sectors sales fell by 20-25 per cent. This development was the reason behind the growing chorus of demands in the private sector for fiscal relaxation, demands which became very intense during 1998. Ironically, a programme which was meant to advance reforms,

---

[238] The elections of 1996 clearly had an impact on macroeconomic policy and, subsequently, on the performance of the economy.

---

[239] From some 4,000 lei/$1 at the end of December 1996 the rate rose sharply to about 9,000 lei/$1 in late February 1997, after which a nominal appreciation took place and the rate stabilized at around 7,000 lei/$1.

[240] This is an overstatement to the extent that arrears stood at a high level and even increased. The bail-out of Banca Agricola and Bancorex in 1997 indicated how serious the problem of arrears was and how they can obscure quasi-fiscal deficits.

[241] Significant amounts of portfolio capital entered the country, which tested the ability of the central bank to sterilize them when base money represented no more then 4.6-4.7 per cent of GDP.

[242] National Bank of Romania data.

affected negatively the emerging entrepreneurial class and encouraged the expansion of the underground economy because of the degree of austerity involved.

There are several factors that explain the high rate of inflation. First, the corrective component of inflation (price de-control plus a rise in some administered prices) came strongly into play in March when inflation reached almost 30 per cent. Secondly, the overshooting of the leu. Thirdly, the programme underestimated the role of monopolies and the slow response of supply as sources of inflation. Another factor lay in the economic policy slippages in the latter half of the year when there was a premature relaxation of monetary policy: there was an extensive and abrupt indexation of wages, redundancy payments were granted to laid-off workers, and large amounts of money were pumped into banks that were in difficulty. It was obvious that the macroeconomic policy mix was not well balanced and that the supply-side response had been greatly overestimated.

Belated moves were made to restructure some of the major "producers" of arrears. The delay was due to the inherent problems of undertaking such an operation in a year when the economy was in steep decline: on the one hand, the overall measures aimed at restructuring implied the need for layoffs, but on the other hand, the troubles confronting the small and medium-sized enterprises in the private sector, a direct consequence of the austerity measures, were discouraging the creation of new job opportunities. Privatization of large enterprises dragged on at a snail's pace and as for bank privatization, the various projects were left in abeyance. Such a situation could not provide incentives for direct foreign investment nor promote restructuring.

In the last months of 1997 the big losses of state banks, accumulated over a long period and mirroring the state of the real economy, attracted increasing attention. In the last quarter of the year, the central bank and the Ministry of Finance converted 8,000 billion lei ($1 billion) of poor credits granted by the Agricultural Bank and Bancorex into government bonds as a way of recapitalizing the two banks. While the Dacia Felix and the Credit Bank failures were caused by large-scale fraud and embezzlement, the failure of the state banks was the result of a chronic misallocation of resources and of poor performance in a number of large economic sectors, which in turn was due to slow restructuring and feeble capital inflows.[243]

GDP continued to decline in 1998, according to preliminary data, by 7.3 per cent. At the end of the year unemployment stood at about 10 per cent (as against 6.6 per cent in December 1996). Inflation in December (year-on-year) fell to 40.6 per cent, and the consolidated budget deficit was kept to just below 4 per cent. The latter should be seen against the background of a further reduction of the tax base (because of the fall in output)

and the implications for government spending of the rescue package for the two state owned banks. Actually, the budget deficit was kept under control by a very severe cut in public expenditure undertaken in August.

Real interest rates stayed high in 1998[244] as a result of the tight monetary conditions and a lack of sufficient credibility in macroeconomic policy. Their level indicated how small the room for manoeuvre available to policy makers was. Interestingly, real credit started to grow again in 1998 although output did not. Between December 1997 and November 1998 real domestic credit rose by some 24 per cent with the non-government component increasing even more. A note of caution is needed here, however, since over the same period, the net foreign assets of the banking system fell by almost a half and the real money supply shrank (see table 3.2.4).

Based on consumer prices, the exchange rate appreciated in real terms by about 30 per cent since mid-1997 (after the sharp devaluation at the start of that year), which helps to explain the rising trade and current account deficits in 1998. The foreign exchange reserves of the national bank declined to less than 1.9 billion at the end of the year, a result of its interventions to stem the fall of the leu. It should also be mentioned, that excessively lax income policies also help to explain the size of domestic absorption in a year when there was a further contraction of output. Real wages actually grew by about 4.7 per cent in the year to December (table 3.2.4).

Because of the fallout from the financial crisis in Russia external bond issues were postponed, which in turn casts doubt on the possibility of rolling over a portion of the external debt in 1999. Because of the size of payments due in 1999 (about $2.9 billion) there is a threat of a financial crisis and default unless an agreement with the international financial organizations is reached early in 1999. This threat explains the considerable efforts to conclude privatization deals at the end of 1998 (Romtelecom, Romanian Development Bank, etc.) and the attempt to close down large loss-making companies.

(f) A comparison of the two stabilization programmes, 1994-1995 and 1997-1998

There are several features which differentiate the two attempts at macroeconomic stabilization in 1994-1995 (hereafter policy A) and in 1997-1998 (policy B). These differences help to explain why output grew, albeit on a very fragile basis, during the first attempt whereas it declined in 1997 and 1998. It should be stressed that in both cases the pace of restructuring was feeble.

Both policies were accompanied by interest rate shocks. However, policy A did not involve a credit crunch; on the contrary, M2 grew rapidly and so did

---

[243] Behind these developments was the slow pace of privatization which failed to attract capital inflows and thereby help restructuring.

[244] In the second half of the year *ex-post* dollar returns on three-month treasury bills hovered at about 50 per cent.

lending. As was mentioned already, this was due to the rapid remonetization of the economy, which was enhanced by a psychological factor: for the first time people found it worthwhile to put their savings into banks (because of positive real interest rates). Consequently, bank deposits grew rapidly. The psychological-cum-savings reorientation factors were no longer strong in the second period, and the sharp rise in interest rates (in 1997) could not be accompanied by remonetization. Policy B, as a matter of fact, involved a major credit crunch.

It should also be emphasized that the process of remonetization came to a halt in the second half of 1996, which created a major constraint for policy in 1997. The increase in the velocity of money forced policy makers to consider a much tighter monetary policy. The issue at stake was how much tighter it should be.

Policy B involved exchange rate unification via a large overshooting of the leu, which magnified inflation and the decline of money balances in real terms. Policy A included multiple exchange rates and controls on key prices such as energy.

Policy B involved a major fiscal adjustment, including a large reduction in explicit and implicit subsidies, which affected certain sectors more heavily than others.

Policy B used as a nominal anchor base money (which actually recovered its 1996 December level in the second quarter of 1997), whereas policy A was quite eclectic, relying on both the control of the money supply and a certain degree of stability in the exchange rate[245] during the phase of intense remonetization.

Macroeconomic imbalances persisted, or even developed, over the 1994-1996 period. Arrears rose to over 34 per cent of GDP in 1996 (from an average of 22-23 per cent in previous years), which was increasingly worrisome since, as the economy had been growing, restructuring should have been encouraged. A factor here is that policy makers ignored the need for a restructuring policy, an industrial policy conceived as a damage-control device.[246] The growth of arrears indicated the unsound basis of economic growth. The rising trade deficits in 1995 and 1996 were financed by substantial accommodating or compensatory capital inflows, which created a dangerous situation for the following years. With the benefit of hindsight, one can imagine various scenarios against the backdrop of the world financial crisis.

Policy B tried to speed up privatization and used the stock market to this end. This explains the large inflows of portfolio capital in the first half of 1997 and the accumulation of foreign exchange reserves by the central bank. In 1997 Romania, for the first time, received substantial autonomous capital inflows, which tested the sterilization capacity of the central bank. These flows later subsided as policy ran into an impasse.

An apparent puzzle comes out of comparing the two programmes. In the period 1994-1996 the trade and current account deficits rose in the wake of the expanding economy. With the very severe compression of domestic absorption in 1997 and 1998 an improvement in the current account deficit might have been expected. There was a slight reduction of the deficit in 1997 (as against 1996), but it started to grow again in 1998. The fact is that, after a fall in GDP of more than 13 per cent in just two years, the current account deficit remained in the vicinity of 7 per cent of GDP. The immediate explanation is that this was due to the real appreciation of the exchange rate (see chart 3.7.1) and the lax incomes policy in 1998.

Whether the fall in output could have been smaller, or even avoided, in 1997 can only be a matter for speculation. It is clear nonetheless that, owing to very tight credit conditions, a continuation of growth was hardly possible and this is why the programme anticipated a decline of 2 per cent in GDP. One policy issue for analysis is the appropriateness of the nominal reduction of base money in the first quarter of 1997, instead, for instance, of keeping M0 fixed for a while. The reasons for the reduction – a rising velocity of money and the desire to mitigate the size of the correction in the price level – are plausible but not indisputable. In addition, the appropriateness of moving at the same time on two tracks, the cut in M0 and floating the exchange rate, can be questioned. It is possible to conceive of a sequence of moves so that the floating of the exchange rate would have followed the correction of the inflationary surge that had been set off by the too rapid expansion of base money in late 1996. There might also have been a closer and more critical look at the size of tariff reductions proposed for agriculture. The conclusion is that policy makers underestimated the scale and extent of supply rigidities in the economy.

As for the 1994-1995 programme, it should again be emphasized that the slow pace of privatization and restructuring damaged its effectiveness. A faster rate of privatization, and consequently more capital inflows, especially of FDI, could have changed significantly the structure of the economy. Even if the then government had not allowed the official exchange rate to float, a dual system – a commercial rate with rationing, and a free rate for financial transactions – could have created an exit window for potential foreign investors in the local equity market. The government might have also used the favourable circumstances of an expanding economy to deal with the large loss-making units. The failure to do so represents a missed opportunity.

---

[245] The plural "exchange rates" is emphasized since a de facto quasi-unification of the rates occurred during 1994. The relative stability of the rates helped the stabilization effort at that time.

[246] Such an industrial policy, seen as managing the gradual phasing-out of chronically inefficient companies, was advocated already in the early 1990s. D. Daianu, "Transformation and the legacy of backwardness", *Économies et Sociétés*, No. 44, May 1992, pp. 181-206.

(g) What next?

In early 1999 Romania faces three major interlinked threats and policy challenges: the risk of an external payments default;[247] the danger of a banking crisis owing to the scale of bad loans in the banking system and the size of the foreign exchange reserves of the central bank, which were less than base money and insufficient to stem a run on the banks;[248] and a possible financial crisis as a result of persistently high real interest rates and the consequences of a further bail-out of Bancorex (about $400 million in December 1998). Other important constraints on policy are social and policy fatigue,[249] and an increasingly unfavourable external environment.

In February 1999 the parliament approved a budget that envisages a deficit of 2 per cent of GDP and which relies on a rise in taxation and further cuts in expenditure.[250] The big unknown in the whole picture, however, is the real quasi-fiscal deficit in the economy which is hidden by arrears and the accumulation of bad loans to enterprises. What happened with Bancorex and Banca Agricola is an illustration of the result of years of weak restructuring, which shows up in the balance sheets of the banks[251] and, ultimately, in the consolidated budget deficit when the "day of reckoning" cannot be postponed any longer.

In the short run, in order to avoid default on external payments, it is essential for the government to reach an agreement with the IMF and the World Bank. The difficulties of concluding such agreements stem from the requirements of further drastic cuts in the consolidated budget deficit and of finding resources to finance substantial lays-offs in a year when GDP is expected to fall again. As already mentioned, a very critical challenge for policy is to avert a banking crisis. Over the longer term, the government needs to design a strategy which will help the export-orientation of the economy, lead to better management of the external debt, and create conditions for sustainable economic growth.

(h) Concluding remarks

If it is accepted that a command system allocates resources inefficiently because of the impossibility of economic calculation, the implication is that the freeing of prices and the functional opening of the economy put

the latter under tremendous strain since resource reallocation cannot take place quickly enough and without friction. One effect of this strain are massive interenterprise arrears, which appear as a *sui generis*, and unintended financial innovation and create a structural trap for stabilization policy.[252] Strain is also intensified by the disorganization in the system which results from the institutional hiatus during the process of regime change.

The magnitude of the required resource reallocation can seriously qualify the attempt to pursue a low inflation rate in the short run – particularly if the lack of capital markets, the presence of large and growing budget deficits, low savings rates, and meagre foreign capital inflows and external aid are taken into account. In a system subject to substantial strain there are strong forces that create a high propensity to generate inflation as a way of diffusing tension by spreading out, or putting off, the costs of adjustment. The *inflation tax* and *negative real interest rates* are implicit subsidies for those that are unable to make ends meet financially in a competitive environment. Inefficient enterprises develop a vested interest in raising prices at a faster pace than the increase in costs (wages), and, in addition, tend to form strong lobbies to obtain cheap credit. Their endeavours are made easier since markets tend to be heavily monopolized, the control of money supply is shaky for both technical and political reasons, and a fixed exchange rate – as an anchor and source of market discipline – is virtually a practical impossibility.

Analysts have frequently highlighted the relatively tighter financial discipline in countries such as the Czech Republic, Hungary and Poland (table 3.2.6), as compared with Romania, the Russian Federation or Ukraine. Nonetheless, the pernicious effects of arrears are a problem for policy makers in all the transition economies. It is noteworthy that even where macrostabilization has been seen as comparatively successful – as in the Czech Republic where the underlying inflation rate was already below 10 per cent in the early 1990s – arrears remained resilient and were a warning of substantial *strain* in the system.[253] But the question remains: why have the first three countries fared better in this respect? It is suggested here that the answer can be pursued by looking at the *structure* of these economies,[254] their ability to export to

---

[247] Despite a moderate level of external debt (which does not exceed 30 per cent of GDP), it has nevertheless been increasing rapidly. Questions, however, can be raised about the management of the external debt, with a peak payment approaching $3 billion in 1999.

[248] At the start of 1998 the $500 limit to the purchase of hard currency by individuals was lifted. This measure may increase the risk of a run on the banking system.

[249] The result of an austerity policy underway for two years in which GDP has fallen by more than 13 per cent.

[250] Particularly worrisome are the low shares in the state budget of expenditure on education and healthcare, and the plunging share of capital expenditure (especially on infrastructure).

[251] Non-performing loans were 57 per cent of total outstanding loans at the end of 1997.

[252] D. Daianu, *Inter-Enterprise Arrears in a Post-Command Economy. Thoughts from a Romanian Perspective*, IMF Working Paper WP/94/54 (Washington, D.C.), September 1994. For the history of arrears in Romania see also E. Clifton and M. Khan, "Inter-enterprise arrears in transforming economies. The case of Romania", IMF, *Staff Papers*, Vol. 40, No. 3 (Washington, D.C.), 1993, pp. 680-696.

[253] In the Czech Republic it was noted that, "Many companies are locked in a circle of bad debt caused by unpaid bills from customers ... Officials fear that many other companies could be affected if major companies are allowed to go bankrupt". P. Blum, "Czechs set to act on bankruptcy", *Financial Times*, 17 February 1993, p. 2.

[254] A World Bank study shows the median number of employees in a sample of firms in Romania to be 1,327, whereas in other countries it was very low: Slovenia, 213; Poland, 820; Hungary, 241; Bulgaria, 291.

TABLE 3.2.6

Government revenues in selected east European economies, 1990-1996

(Per cent of GDP)

	1990	1991	1992	1993	1994	1995	1996
Romania	39.7	41.9	37.4	33.9	32.1	31.9	29.6
Albania	46.8	31.5	23.5	25.6	24.5	24.0	..
Bulgaria	52.9	40.4	38.4	37.2	39.9	36.2	33.6
Czech Republic	..	..	48.2	50.5	49.4	48.4	..
Hungary	52.1	50.9	50.0	50.7	49.6	46.6	45.8
Poland	45.4	42.4	43.9	47.6	47.2	47.2	45.7
Slovakia	..	..	46.1	44.2	46.3	46.8	..

Source: Country authorities and IMF estimates.

western markets and to attract foreign investment, their size, and their economic policies. Furthermore, *structure* is influenced by whether or not there was a history of partial reforms (that, in some cases, brought about several of the ingredients of a market environment), the degree of concentration of industry, and the prior existence of a private sector. Policy credibility[255] can be singled out as a major explanatory factor, but credibility itself depends on how much structural adjustment can be brought about by that policy over a stated period; and the *capacity to adjust* is influenced by the initial *structure* and the scale of *resource misallocation* that it contains.

If it is accepted that the roots of financial indiscipline are to be sought in *structure* – however multifaceted – and the *strain* to which the economy is subjected, the obvious conclusion is that both *structure* and *strain* have to be targeted by policy. Dealing with *structure* includes a focus on both property rights and corporate *governance*. Also attention must be paid to the development of appropriate and effective market institutions and to finding ways to erode the existing economic power structure and to change enterprise behaviour. *Strain,* which reflects the scale of the required resource reallocation, should be approached by starting with the simple truth that structural adjustment is always difficult even in an advanced market-based economy and even when reform is credible.[256]

The structure of the economy has to be tackled firmly and industrial restructuring must be enhanced by privatization and supported by capital inflows: both must take place if real interest rates are to fall significantly.

---

[255] Defining *policy credibility* in post-command economies needs qualification since, with the exception of Hungary and Poland, there is no history of stabilization attempts. Without such a history agents react according to entrenched behavioural patterns, and not on the basis of what they have learned about past policy intentions and their possible reversal. Certainly, when widespread bail-outs represent a reversal of a major policy goal, stabilization history starts on the wrong foot and policy credibility is impaired from the very beginning.

[256] M. Bruno, "Stabilization and reform in eastern Europe: a preliminary evaluation", IMF, *Staff Papers*, Vol. 39, No. 4, (Washington, D.C.), December 1992, p. 753.

Otherwise, high real interest rates will maintain intense strain in the system and make it prone to macroeconomic instability. High real interest rates will also maintain the fragility of banks, particularly of domestic ones.[257]

The situation of potentially viable enterprises, but which are burdened with heavy debts, should be dealt with more carefully and creatively. It should be kept in mind that many companies are heavily in debt because they were undercapitalized (without working capital) by design, and not by choice, as was the case of firms in South-East Asia. The fact is that tight monetary conditions and high real interest rates can kill even potentially viable companies. One way of reducing this risk would be to distinguish between past and current payments. On past debts the interest rate applied should be slightly above an average inflation rate whereas current interest rates should concern only current payments.[258] Something along this line could mitigate the plight of many potentially sound companies.

There is much need for foreign capital to act as a powerful influence for modernization and restructuring. The more this capital is committed long term, the easier it will be for post-communist economies such as Romania to weather the inherent risks of a market environment. Policy makers, however, need to be aware that the competition for capital is intensified by the effects of the redistribution of economic power in the world. The nature of capital inflows needs to change. Currently, most of them are of an accommodating nature, a result of the existing pattern of production and consumption in the Romanian economy, rather than a force for structural change.

Romania's experience emphasizes once again the principle and problems of continuity, that *natura non facit saltum,* that making institutions function properly takes time, and that there is a grip of *structure* – the product of history – that is hard to loosen. It would be naive to assume that the institutions of the post-communist economies can quickly and easily perform according to the various role models of western Europe or North America; they need time to develop in order to perform effectively. Realism is needed not only in designing policies, but also in making balanced judgements as to "what constitutes good performance" and "what is to be done next".

A crucial lesson is that institutions in the making are fragile, and that their very *fragility* makes the economic system more vulnerable to both internal and external shocks. This institutional fragility magnifies the *strain* in

---

[257] This is because foreign banks will cater less to the needs of Romanian companies and will be less dependent on the vagaries of the local environment.

[258] Martin Feldstein has proposed something similar for Asian companies hurt by the high real interest rates resulting from austerity measures. M. Feldstein, "All is not lost for the won", *Wall Street Journal,* 4 June 1998.

TABLE 3.2.7

Levels of strain in labour market adjustment
(Percentages)

	Romania 1990	Romania 1995	Hungary 1992	Hungary 1995	Poland 1992	Poland 1995	Czech Republic 1991	Czech Republic 1995	Slovakia 1991	Slovakia 1995	Slovenia 1993	Slovenia 1995	France 1992	United Kingdom 1994
Relative wages *(average monthly earnings=100)*														
Agriculture and forestry	104.2	81.6	68.9	76.8	82.3	90.6	97.2	84.2	99.7	81.7	105.3	95.5	72.5	77.9
Industry	98.6	107.6	99.0	104.0	98.7	108.9	104.5	99.2	101.4	104.3	84.9	85.0	111.1	116.5
Construction	110.9	106.4	90.2	84.4	106.1	92.5	106.2	108.0	102.4	104.8	83.0	82.5	98.6	109.2
Trade, hotel and restaurant	86.1	78.2	97.0	90.0	90.3	88.9	85.8	88.2	89.3	94.0	102.2	99.8	90.9	69.9
Transport, communications	108.5	121.0	105.8	106.5	102.1	101.2	102.1	100.7	102.1	108.4	115.0	110.9	105.4	144.6
Financial, banking and insurance, real estate and other services	109.3	126.8	144.7	137.4	147.7	137.3	99.9	130.7	103.9	131.4	143.8	124.6	128.0	136.8
Education, health and social assistance	96.5	85.3	93.5	86.5	86.9	81.7	93.2	91.2	97.6	87.2	111.8	109.6	75.8	53.0
Public administration and defence, other branches	88.9	88.6	118.0	111.3	115.7	108.9	88.5	103.8	103.4	102.5	127.8	132.7	91.0	93.6
Index of "strain" on prices	23.0	9.8	24.1	19.7	18.3	17.0	21.1	19.1	23.8	17.2	33.9	33.1	11.7	..
Excluding agriculture	21.2	12.9	26.0	21.3	22.9	18.1	21.2	20.0	24.0	18.6	34.5	34.8	12.0	..
Employment shares *(per cent)*														
Agriculture and forestry	29.0	34.4	11.4	8.1	25.5	22.6	12.1	6.6	15.8	9.2	10.7	10.4	5.2	2.0
Industry	36.9	28.6	30.2	27.1	25.2	25.9	41.0	33.2	35.9	30.3	38.7	38.0	20.6	20.2
Construction	6.5	5.0	5.4	6.0	6.6	6.1	5.7	9.2	8.2	8.6	5.4	5.1	7.2	6.4
Trade, hotel and restaurant	6.9	10.4	14.8	15.9	10.7	13.6	7.8	15.7	8.1	13.1	14.6	15.4	17.4	20.8
Transport, communications	7.0	5.9	8.6	8.8	5.5	5.8	9.0	7.7	5.5	7.8	6.5	5.9	5.8	5.8
Financial, banking and insurance, real estate and other services	3.9	4.2	5.2	5.9	1.3	2.0	5.4	6.7	5.4	5.8	4.6	6.1	10.8	12.5
Education, health and social assistance	6.7	8.1	13.6	15.6	13.1	13.3	13.8	12.1	16.5	14.5	10.2	11.4	6.9	14.5
Public administration and defence, other branches	3.1	3.4	10.6	12.5	12.1	10.7	5.1	8.8	4.6	10.7	9.2	7.6	26.2	17.9
Index of "strain" on quantities	91.4	76.6	47.6	37.2	60.4	56.7	68.1	47.1	68.7	45.9	62.2	56.7	13.8	..
Excluding agriculture	76.4	57.5	41.5	33.7	46.0	42.4	63.1	44.4	63.4	43.2	52.9	48.3	21.8	..
Indicator of total "strain"	94.2	77.2	53.3	42.1	63.1	59.2	71.3	50.8	72.6	49.0	70.9	65.6	18.1	..
Excluding agriculture	79.3	59.0	49.0	39.9	51.4	46.1	66.6	48.7	67.8	47.0	63.2	59.5	24.9	..

Source: OECD, Centre for Cooperation with Non-members (CCNM); *OECD Economic Surveys 1997-1998, Romania* (Paris), 1998, p. 171; D. Daianu, *The Changing Mix of Disequilibria during Transition: A Romanian Background*, IMF Working Paper WP/94/73 (Washington, D.C.), 1994 and D. Daianu, "An economic explanation of strain", in J. Bachaus (ed.), *Issues in Transformation Theory* (Marburg, Metropolis, 1997).

the system caused by the resource misallocation inherited from the command economy. The time constraint is increasingly short for the Romanian economy and society, but time (and breathing space) is precisely what policy makers need after years of indecisiveness in dealing with a complicated and burdensome legacy, a legacy which is indicated by the intensity of the foreign exchange constraint and the persistence of soft budget constraints throughout the economy.

3.3 Output and demand

(i) Output

Output performance in the ECE transition economies as a whole deteriorated in 1998: aggregate GDP fell by over 0.5 per cent from its previous year's level, a considerable slide from the 2 per cent growth achieved in 1997. Output performance worsened most in the Commonwealth of Independent States where after a modest 1.1 per cent rise in 1997, aggregate GDP declined by 2¾ per cent in 1998, mostly as a result of the Russian crisis. Economic growth in the Baltic states decelerated

rapidly in the second half of the year but the average increase in GDP remained relatively high (around 4¼ per cent), although below the 7.6 per cent in 1997. GDP growth in eastern Europe as a whole (some 2 per cent) was lower than in 1997 (2.8 per cent); but within this aggregate, output in central Europe increased by 3.6 per cent, while it actually declined by almost 2 per cent in south-eastern Europe. In all parts of the region, the deterioration of performance occurred in the second half of 1998; in the first half, GDP was growing more or less at the same rates as in 1997.

Performance in the transition economies in 1998 remained highly differentiated across countries and subregions. While the shrinking of external demand had strong negative repercussions on economic activity across the board, the central European countries managed to a large extent to shield their economies from contagion and financial turmoil. However, for a large number of transition economies, the external demand shock was amplified by the deepening of internal problems and this undoubtedly reinforced the negative trends in these countries.

CHART 3.3.1

Gross industrial output in selected transition economies, 1995-1998
(Year on year percentage changes)

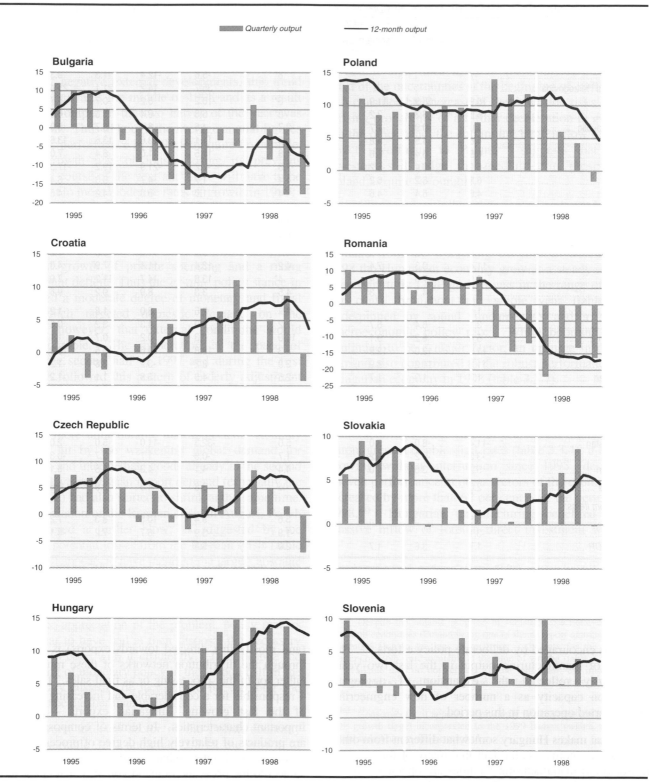

(For source and notes see end of chart.)

CHART 3.3.1 (concluded)

Gross industrial output in selected transition economies, 1995-1998
(Year on year percentage changes)

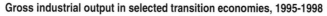

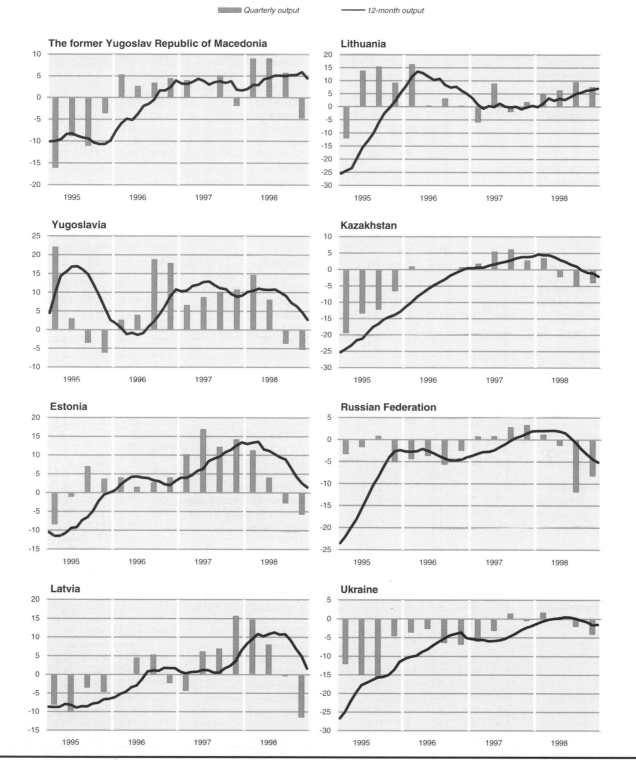

Source: National statistics and direct communications from national statistical offices to UN/ECE secretariat.

Note: The coverage of industrial output in the monthly statistics may differ from the coverage in the annual data.

TABLE 3.3.2

Share of major sectors in GDP [a] in eastern Europe and the Baltic states, 1993-1998
(Per cent of GDP, at current prices)

	1993	1994	1995	1996	1997	1998 [b]		1993	1994	1995	1996	1997	1998 [b]
Albania							**Romania**						
Agriculture	54.6	54.6	54.6	52.8	..	..	Agriculture	21.6	20.6	20.7	20.1	19.7	17.6
Industry	13.9	12.5	11.7	12.5	..	..	Industry	34.9	37.6	34.5	34.8	38.6	35.0
Construction	9.1	9.6	10.3	11.4	..	..	Construction	5.4	6.8	6.9	6.8	5.7	5.7
Wholesale and retail trade	..	..	..	..	..	..	Wholesale and retail trade	10.6	8.5	11.0	12.2	10.8	–
Transport and communication	..	..	..	..	..	..	Transport and communication	10.4	9.1	8.1	9.4	11.0	..
Financial services, real estate	..	..	..	..	..	..	Financial services, real estate	8.6	8.2	8.8	7.0	7.4	..
Other services [c]	22.5	23.2	23.4	23.3	..	..	Other services	8.6	9.2	9.9	9.7	6.9	14.7[c]
Bosnia and Herzegovina							**Slovakia**						
Agriculture	..	..	25.0	20.7	18.3	..	Agriculture	4.9	6.9	6.0	5.5	5.1	5.2
Industry	..	..	24.4	21.5	21.7	..	Industry	32.0	25.1	34.6	32.0	29.6	26.9
Construction	..	..	3.0	4.3	6.1	..	Construction	4.9	4.7	4.9	5.0	5.5	5.7
Wholesale and retail trade	..	..	..	..	..	..	Wholesale and retail trade	21.7	..	19.3	23.7	22.9	25.3
Transport and communication	..	..	..	..	..	..	Transport and communication	8.4	8.9	9.0	8.9	8.5	8.3
Financial services, real estate	..	..	..	..	..	..	Financial services, real estate	14.2	..	13.0	12.0	15.1	16.1
Other services [c]	..	..	47.6	53.5	53.9	..	Other services	13.9	54.4	13.2	12.9	13.2	12.5
Bulgaria							**Slovenia**						
Agriculture	10.6	12.3	13.9	15.4	26.2	20.0	Agriculture	5.1	4.5	4.5	4.4	4.2	..
Industry	29.2	27.0	28.5	25.9	26.7	26.8	Industry	33.4	34.7	32.6	32.0	31.8	..
Construction	5.8	5.1	5.2	4.3	2.8	3.5	Construction	4.7	4.7	5.0	5.6	5.6	..
Wholesale and retail trade	..	..	..	11.8	9.6	..	Wholesale and retail trade	14.0	14.8	15.0	14.6	14.5	..
Transport and communication	..	..	..	7.3	7.4	..	Transport and communication	7.8	7.5	7.7	7.6	8.0	..
Financial services, real estate	..	..	..	26.7	18.3	..	Financial services, real estate	14.6	14.6	15.7	16.0	15.6	..
Other services	54.4[c]	55.6[c]	52.5[c]	8.6	9.1	49.7[c]	Other services	20.5	19.2	19.5	19.8	20.3	..
Croatia							**The former Yugoslav Republic of Macedonia**						
Agriculture	13.3	11.2	10.4	10.0	9.3	..	Agriculture	10.3	10.6	12.8	13.1	13.7	..
Industry	29.7	27.4	23.1	25.6	25.9	..	Industry	24.9	18.9	22.2	22.4	22.4	..
Construction	4.8	5.1	5.9	6.6	7.1	..	Construction	5.5	4.9	5.4	5.7	5.2	..
Wholesale and retail trade	..	..	..	15.2	15.6	..	Wholesale and retail trade	11.6	14.4	16.8	17.3	18.3	..
Transport and communication	..	..	..	8.8	8.7	..	Transport and communication	7.0	5.8	6.9	6.8	6.8	..
Financial services, real estate	..	..	..	14.7	14.0	..	Financial services, real estate	20.5	26.0	12.2	10.5	10.1	..
Other services	52.3	56.3	60.5	19.1	19.5	..	Other services	20.1	19.4	23.7	24.1	23.6	..
Czech Republic							**Estonia**						
Agriculture	5.2	4.4	4.6	..	..	..	Agriculture	11.0	10.3	7.9	7.5	7.1	6.4
Industry	32.5	32.1	33.2	..	..	..	Industry	24.5	24.1	23.1	22.2	22.1	20.9
Construction	7.1	7.6	8.1	..	..	..	Construction	6.6	6.4	5.9	5.8	5.5	6.3
Wholesale and retail trade	14.5	16.2	14.9	..	..	..	Wholesale and retail trade	18.3	16.6	17.6	18.4	19.1	19.7
Transport and communication	7.7	7.2	7.7	..	..	..	Transport and communication	12.4	11.6	10.5	10.8	11.8	14.3
Financial services, real estate	20.2	18.8	17.5	..	..	..	Financial services, real estate	10.2	11.6	13.1	14.3	15.0	13.3
Other services	12.8	13.8	14.0	..	..	..	Other services	17.0	19.6	21.8	21.0	19.4	19.1
Hungary							**Latvia**						
Agriculture	6.6	6.7	6.7	6.6	5.8	..	Agriculture	11.8	9.5	10.8	9.0	7.4	7.1
Industry	26.2	25.3	26.3	26.3	28.2	..	Industry	30.8	25.4	28.1	26.4	25.6	24.0
Construction	5.3	5.1	4.6	4.3	4.6	..	Construction	4.3	5.9	5.1	4.7	5.0	4.6
Wholesale and retail trade	13.3	12.6	13.3	13.3	13.3	..	Wholesale and retail trade	9.6	11.4	12.4	16.5	17.7	18.7
Transport and communication	8.8	8.5	9.0	9.2	9.6	..	Transport and communication	23.1	20.5	16.0	17.0	17.2	17.2
Financial services, real estate	17.8	19.7	19.6	21.1	19.6	..	Financial services, real estate	7.8	12.1	9.9	9.0	8.1	7.1
Other services	22.0	22.1	20.5	19.3	18.8	..	Other services	12.7	15.3	17.7	17.5	19.0	21.3
Poland							**Lithuania**						
Agriculture	7.2	6.9	7.0	6.5	5.6	5.6	Agriculture	14.2	10.7	11.7	12.2	11.7	12.3
Industry	35.7	31.1	31.9	30.3	29.5	29.6	Industry	34.2	27.0	26.1	25.8	25.2	22.5
Construction	7.1	7.4	7.3	7.5	8.0	7.7	Construction	5.1	7.2	7.1	7.1	7.7	9.0
Wholesale and retail trade	16.8	21.2	20.9	22.0	22.1	..	Wholesale and retail trade	15.3	18.9	19.3	18.4	18.2	17.5
Transport and communication	6.6	7.4	6.6	6.5	6.5	..	Transport and communication	9.8	10.1	9.4	9.5	9.6	9.1
Financial services, real estate	6.9	9.3	9.2	9.8	11.2	..	Financial services, real estate	11.5	11.7	10.5	10.5	9.6	10.7
Other services	19.7	16.7	17.1	17.5	17.1	57.1[c]	Other services	9.9	14.4	15.8	16.5	18.0	18.8

Source: National statistics and direct communications from national statistical offices to UN/ECE secretariat.

Note: Data are presented in terms of the NACE/ISIC classifications. For Bosnia and Herzegovina, Croatia (for 1993-1995) and The former Yugoslav Republic of Macedonia, the three countries not reporting in NACE/ISIC, industry includes mining, manufacturing and water management; wholesale and retail trade includes trade, hotels and restaurants, tourism and crafts; financial services, real estate includes financial and other business services; other services include community services, education and culture, health care and social welfare and public administration.

[a] Percentage shares of total value added.

[b] Full year for Romania; January-September for other countries.

[c] All services.

TABLE 3.3.3

Share of major sectors in GDP [a] in the CIS economies, 1993-1998

(Per cent of GDP, at current prices)

	1993	1994	1995	1996	1997	1998		1993	1994	1995	1996	1997	1998
Armenia							**Republic of Moldova**						
Agriculture	50.8	43.5	40.8	..	..	..	Agriculture	30.3	28.1	32.2	29.8	28.8	27.5
Industry	22.5	29.1	24.3	..	..	..	Industry	37.8	32.2	27.5	25.0	22.5	25.3
Construction	4.0	6.7	6.5	..	..	..	Construction	3.2	4.6	3.9	4.1	5.3	4.9
Wholesale and retail trade	2.6	5.1	10.2	..	..	..	Wholesale and retail trade	9.1	9.3	9.7	9.8	9.9	10.0
Transport and communication	5.9	4.2	4.3	..	..	..	Transport and communication	4.3	6.4	5.7	6.1	7.0	8.3
Financial services, real estate	1.4	3.6	4.0	..	..	..	Financial services, real estate	5.9	7.0	6.1	9.6	9.5	10.8
Other services	12.8	7.9	9.8	..	..	..	Other services	9.5	12.3	15.0	15.6	17.0	13.2
Azerbaijan							**Russian Federation**						
Agriculture	26.7	31.4	26.7	27.2	21.9	21.8	Agriculture	8.2	6.5	8.0	7.7	7.4	6.9
Industry	24.5	19.8	29.0	28.4	27.1	23.9	Industry	34.4	32.8	30.7	29.8	28.5	28.1
Construction	7.2	7.1	3.9	10.2	15.0	17.6	Construction	7.9	9.1	8.8	8.2	7.8	7.1
Wholesale and retail trade	3.9	3.9	5.2	5.9	6.0	6.1	Wholesale and retail trade	19.0	18.4	18.6	15.9	16.6	19.2
Transport and communication	7.9	11.9	18.4	11.3	13.0	13.7	Transport and communication	8.6	9.9	11.3	13.5	12.3	12.1
Financial services, real estate	7.1	5.5	2.8	1.1	1.1	0.1	Financial services, real estate	6.9	5.8	3.6	2.8	3.8	4.0
Other services	22.7	20.3	13.9	15.9	15.9	16.8	Other services	15.0	17.6	18.9	22.1	23.6	22.6
Belarus							**Tajikistan**						
Agriculture	16.8	13.9	17.0	15.7	14.5	..	Agriculture	22.2	21.5	38.0	38.0	38.6	..
Industry	28.4	28.7	30.2	34.0	35.2	..	Industry	34.7	24.8	33.3	28.1	28.1	..
Construction	7.7	5.7	5.9	5.4	6.4	..	Construction	9.5	11.7	1.8	2.8	3.0	..
Wholesale and retail trade	11.0	15.2	11.5	10.3	10.1	..	Wholesale and retail trade	6.1	15.4	5.6	16.9	15.4	..
Transport and communication	12.0	12.2	13.3	12.6	11.9	..	Transport and communication	1.4	2.7	1.8	2.3	2.0	..
Financial services, real estate	9.1	8.2	5.2	3.4	3.3	..	Financial services, real estate	5.2	12.5	8.2	4.6	5.3	..
Other services	15.0	16.0	16.9	18.6	18.5	..	Other services	20.8	11.4	11.2	7.3	7.5	..
Georgia							**Turkmenistan**						
Agriculture	69.7	65.1	44.4	32.1	29.6	26.1	Agriculture	19.2	32.9	16.9	13.1	21.0	..
Industry	8.5	8.3	10.1	10.7	10.1	9.6	Industry	49.0	38.7	55.3	56.6	34.6	..
Construction	0.9	1.7	2.3	4.8	5.0	6.1	Construction	12.0	6.9	6.1	10.8	11.8	..
Wholesale and retail trade	7.6	8.4	27.6	23.0	23.1	22.9	Wholesale and retail trade	4.1	5.6	4.3	3.3	3.9	..
Transport and communication	3.8	5.1	9.0	6.5	10.4	13.9	Transport and communication	5.2	4.8	5.0	5.9	10.8	..
Financial services, real estate	2.6	2.5	0.2	..	..	..	Financial services, real estate	1.7	2.3	1.4	1.9	2.9	..
Other services	7.1	8.8	6.4	22.8	21.8	21.4	Other services	8.8	8.9	11.0	8.5	15.0	..
Kazakhstan							**Ukraine**						
Agriculture	16.4	15.2	12.8	12.7	11.9	..	Agriculture	20.0	15.3	15.0	13.7	12.6	..
Industry	28.6	29.7	24.4	22.1	22.3	..	Industry	27.6	36.7	33.8	30.6	33.5	..
Construction	8.3	9.8	6.7	4.6	4.4	..	Construction	6.4	7.8	7.5	6.6	5.9	..
Wholesale and retail trade	10.3	12.4	17.9	18.0	16.3	..	Wholesale and retail trade	11.5	7.6	7.6	7.8	6.4	..
Transport and communication	9.9	11.4	11.1	11.8	12.2	..	Transport and communication	10.9	8.5	13.1	14.6	9.5	..
Financial services, real estate	6.3	0.9	1.4	1.2	1.2	..	Financial services, real estate	9.5	7.8	3.2	2.9	..	..
Other services	20.2	20.6	25.7	29.6	31.7	..	Other services	14.1	16.3	19.8	23.9	32.2	..
Kyrgyzstan							**Uzbekistan**						
Agriculture	40.0	39.9	43.1	49.4	44.2	43.1	Agriculture	29.9	36.2	31.4	25.6	..	..
Industry	25.7	21.3	12.7	11.8	17.8	18.7	Industry	24.0	17.9	19.1	20.3	..	..
Construction	5.5	3.5	6.5	6.4	4.8	2.6	Construction	9.6	7.6	7.9	9.4	..	..
Wholesale and retail trade	7.9	10.5	12.0	11.2	11.3	12.3	Wholesale and retail trade	8.6	10.2	9.1	10.9	..	..
Transport and communication	4.0	4.7	4.8	4.9	4.5	4.7	Transport and communication	5.9	6.1	8.1	7.7	..	..
Financial services, real estate	5.8	5.3	4.3	1.1	1.9	2.0	Financial services, real estate	3.6	4.6	4.3	3.7	..	..
Other services	11.0	14.8	16.6	15.1	15.5	16.5	Other services	18.5	17.5	20.1	22.4	..	..

Source: National statistics; CIS Statistical Committee; direct communications from national statistical offices to UN/ECE secretariat.

Note: To compile sectoral statistics, CIS countries use national classifications which are modified versions of the former Soviet Union's branch classification. Although the figures in the table are presented according to NACE/ISIC categories, they are not fully comparable with those in table 3.3.2. Agriculture covers agriculture, fishing, hunting and forestry; industry covers mining and quarrying, manufacturing, production of electricity, gas and water and their supply for production purposes; wholesale and retail trade covers trade and catering, supplies and procurement, renting of machinery and equipment and trade-related intermediation services; financial services and real estate cover banking, insurance and pension funding, real estate, information, computing and other business services; other services cover geology and exploration, publishing houses, recycling, security, housing, community services (including electricity, gas and water supply to households), hotels, personal service activities, health care, recreational, cultural and sporting activities, education, science and public administration. In some years non-reported sectors are included in "other services".

[a] Percentage share of total value added.

However, the risk of a large overall exposure to a single market exists for Hungary as well and the negative impact of weakening west European demand began to be felt towards the end of 1998. Thus while the rate of growth of industrial output still remained high in the fourth quarter, it was considerably lower than in the first three quarters (chart 3.3.1). Also, it has to be borne in mind that the high rates of growth in 1997-1998 partly reflect the introduction of new production capacities; it is only natural to expect that with the phasing out of this one-time effect the growth of manufacturing output will moderate.

In contrast to Hungary, the crisis in the Czech economy – which initially was only associated with the collapse of the exchange rate regime in May 1997 – deepened in 1998. It had been expected that after a meagre 1 per cent GDP growth in 1997, economic performance would accelerate in 1998. Indeed, there were some positive signs at the beginning of the year: the 1997 depreciation of the exchange rate, together with the austerity measures including, in particular, a certain degree of wage restraint, boosted Czech exports and as a result, manufacturing output started to recover strongly in the last quarter of 1997 and the first quarter of 1998 (chart 3.3.1).

However, during the second quarter of 1998 this trend was reversed and throughout the rest of the year there was a steady weakening of economic activity. The pace of industrial output gradually decelerated and by the fourth quarter had started to fall (chart 3.3.1). Construction output also continued to fall in 1998, for a second consecutive year (table 3.3.6). The downturn became especially pronounced in the fourth quarter of the year with quarterly GDP declining by 4.1 per cent (year-on-year) and industrial output falling by 7 per cent.

A number of factors – both on the supply and on the demand side – were behind these developments. As all the transition economies, the Czech Republic was severely hit by the external demand shock. However, the Czech economy in 1998 was a case where the combination of domestic and external factors amplified considerably the negative trends and resulted in an output performance that was much worse than expected.

On the domestic side, both factors that had contributed to the relative improvement in manufacturing performance lost momentum in 1998. Wage restraint turned out to be short-lived: real unit labour costs increased again in 1998 (table 3.4.4) and this had a negative effect on the competitiveness of Czech exports. The substantial tightening of monetary policy in 1998 caused, *inter alia*, a relative strengthening of the Czech koruna and this also had a negative effect on competitiveness. In addition, monetary policy resulted in an unprecedented rise in real interest rates (chart 3.2.1) which further depressed economic activity and domestic demand. In fact, all the components of domestic demand contracted in 1998 (tables 3.3.10 and 3.3.12), a reflection of growing uncertainties about the future of the economy.

These negative developments – which are the background to the current recession – are likely to continue to affect Czech economic performance for some time to come.[265] Their persistence is largely due to the slow progress in structural reforms (in turn, a result of the obscure ownership structure after the rapid mass privatization), inefficiencies and gaps in the institutional infrastructure, and the malfunctioning of important markets which constitute the microeconomic foundations of the Czech crisis.[266] It remains to be seen whether the proper policy responses can be found to resolve these problems and reverse the negative trends.

The Slovak economy is in the process of going through a painful macroeconomic adjustment. In fact, the annual figures on Slovak growth in 1998 (GDP increased by 4.4 per cent and gross industrial output by 4.6 per cent – table 3.1.1), which followed several years of robust recovery, may be misleading insofar as they conceal the magnitude of the required adjustment effort. For several years the Slovak government had followed a rather hazardous policy of artificially boosting output through large, publicly-financed infrastructural investment projects; a large share of the finance was raised by borrowing abroad.[267] While this policy did boost domestic output and ensured high rates of economic growth, it also gave rise to escalating macroeconomic disequilibria, notably, large current account and budget deficits and a snowballing of foreign debt.[268] At the same time very little progress was made in structural reforms, particularly in restructuring inefficient industrial firms.[269]

In 1998 policy came under the influence of the electoral cycle and no changes were made in policy until after the September parliamentary elections; consequently, there was little change in the pattern of performance. Gross industrial output grew strongly (chart 3.3.1) but this was mostly due to the expanding operations of the new Volkswagen plant whereas other manufacturing branches were facing difficulties (table 3.3.4). However, the post-election period was marked by an abrupt reversal in performance. Already on 1 October the National Bank of Slovakia was forced to abandon the fixed exchange rate regime. Faced with large and growing macroeconomic imbalances, the new government announced its intention to reduce considerably its involvement in investment projects. Together with the negative external impact, this decision triggered a considerable weakening of output in the fourth quarter: industrial output declined by 0.1 per cent (year-on-year), after growing by 8.6 per cent in the third quarter (chart 3.3.1).

---

[265] The 1999 budget was drafted on the assumption of 1.5 per cent GDP growth, but in February the Czech Statistical Office reduced its 1999 growth forecast to -0.8 per cent. *Reuters News Service*, 3 February 1999.

[266] The Czech crisis is analysed in more detail in UN/ECE, *Economic Survey of Europe, 1998 No. 1*, pp. 75-82.

[267] An estimated $3 billion, as reported by *Reuters News Service*, 16 September 1998.

[268] Previous issues of this *Survey* have questioned the sustainability of this policy and warned of the imminent need for a major adjustment. UN/ECE, *Economic Survey of Europe in 1996-1997*, p. 87; *Economic Survey of Europe, 1998 No. 1*, p. 88 and *1998 No. 3*, p. 53.

[269] Moreover, in 1997 the government adopted a highly controversial programme of "revitalizing" ailing enterprises, which implied the provision of additional "soft credits" to these firms from public funds.

TABLE 3.3.4

Growth of industrial output by branch in eastern Europe and the Baltic states, 1997-1998

(Annual percentage change)

NACE codes	C-E	C	D	15, 16	17-19	20-22	23-25	26	27, 28	29-35	36, 37	E
	Total industry	Mining and quarrying	Manu-facturing	Food, beverages and tobacco	Textiles, apparel and leather	Wood, paper and printing	Chemical industry	Non-metallic mineral products	Basic metals and metal products	Machinery and equipment	Other manu-facturing industries	Electricity, gas, steam and water
Bosnia and Herzegovina												
1997	35.7	46.1	39.8	19.4	27.4	63.1	82.6	102.4	108.8	42.4	44.4	25.5
1998	23.8	22.8	29.7	13.8	17.7	16.9	32.6	27.3	121.4	14.3	-1.0	13.6
Bulgaria												
1997	-10.2	-10.2	-10.3	-18.1	-4.7	-21.3	-16.1	-2.9	12.4	-3.6	-26.4	5.9
1998	-9.4	0.6	-12.1	..	..	..	..	..	..	..	..	3.5
Croatia												
1997	6.8	-0.3	3.9	-6.7	1.8	35.1	-1.8	-11.2	20.9	14.0	31.5	24.2
1998	3.7	-2.4	3.2	3.6	-0.8	8.6	-2.8	14.0	12.5	2.9	-7.2	8.7
Czech Republic												
1997	4.5	-2.9	6.4	4.3	-6.2	10.5	2.8	8.2	4.1	17.7	4.6	-2.7
1998	1.6	-5.7	2.5	-0.4	-6.8	6.3	-1.8	1.1	-4.4	13.1	10.7	-1.5
Hungary												
1997	11.1	-8.5	14.8	-7.2	2.4	15.4	4.6	4.4	8.1	54.9	-0.7	1.2
1998	12.6	-18.2	16.2	0.8	10.6	5.4	3.2	12.6	2.8	41.4	24.1	-0.4
Poland												
1997	11.5	0.5	13.4	9.4	8.7	15.1	11.2	11.9	13.6	18.2	24.8	3.4
1998	4.7	-13.2	6.5	6.7	-2.4	12.4	-0.9	12.4	7.3	9.6	12.2	1.9
Romania												
1997	-5.9	-12.2	-4.7	-16.1	-9.3	-12.2	-16.1	-13.0	0.9	3.4	-8.1	-0.1
1998	-17.0	-13.9	-18.1	-1.0	-29.2	-34.5	-14.7	-16.8	-9.5	-17.3	-43.4	-12.4
Slovakia												
1997	2.0	7.3	2.6	-1.2	-15.2	14.2	0.2	2.0	6.3	9.2	-6.9	-3.9
1998	4.6	-11.1	6.1	3.0	-5.5	-2.0	-9.3	20.8	-2.5	37.5	-2.2	-5.8
Slovenia												
1997	1.0	1.8	0.2	-3.0	2.0	-17.1	6.6	4.8	-3.7	-6.9	16.4	8.2[a]
1998	3.7	-0.4	3.9	3.2	-1.3	-7.3	2.3	6.7	3.4	11.0	9.5	3.3[a]
The former Yugoslav Republic of Macedonia												
1997	1.6	-0.5	-2.1	7.5	-14.1	-12.4	-7.8	6.2	1.9	-1.0	-12.5	1.4
1998 [b]	5.7	2.4	5.8	-0.4	10.3	8.2	20.7	-8.8	18.1	-6.3	38.2	5.1
Yugoslavia												
1997	10.0	8.0	14.2	-3.4	8.1	2.4	33.6	3.4	29.9	12.3	2.7	6.0
1998 [b]	5.0	-0.2	6.8	7.1	7.0	-1.4	8.5	11.4	5.4	8.4	3.6	–
Estonia												
1997	13.4	5.6	16.9	18.6	11.7	36.0	2.3[c]	33.6	..	7.7[d]	17.9[e]	-3.1
1998	1.5	-1.4	2.9	-6.1	1.8	23.1	-14.2[c]	17.9	..	-14.7[d]	3.7[e]	-5.1
Latvia												
1997	15.0	7.5	15.8	14.3	11.0	35.9	18.8[c]	–	56.3	1.1[d]	7.9[e]	–
1998	2.0	6.2	2.5	1.1	-2.0	16.7	-7.1[c]	30.7	-4.8	-8.8[d]	0.8[e]	-1.0
Lithuania												
1997	0.8	12.3	4.9	-3.1	10.4	5.2	15.5	0.6	10.6	0.1	9.3	-11.8
1998	7.0	52.1	4.7	-3.6	-2.0	3.5	17.5	2.5	4.9	12.9	8.9	6.0

Source: National statistics and direct communications from national statistical offices to UN/ECE secretariat.

Note: Data are presented in terms of NACE classification except for The former Yugoslav Republic of Macedonia and Yugoslavia. For these two countries national classification data have been aggregated into NACE groups. Figures for total industry may differ slightly for some countries from those shown in other tables because of differences in coverage. (Statistics on industrial output by branches normally cover enterprises above a certain threshold defined in terms of the number of employed persons.)

[a] Production and distribution of electricity only (NACE 40.1).

[b] January-November.

[c] Excluding manufacture of coke, refined petroleum products and nuclear fuel (NACE 23).

[d] Excluding manufacture of office machinery and computers (NACE 30).

[e] Excluding recycling (NACE 37).

Obviously this is only the start of the adjustment necessary to restore macroeconomic equilibrium. In January 1999, in the framework of the budget debates, the government adopted a further package of austerity measures, mostly aimed at curbing the budget and external deficits. Given the magnitude of the imbalances, it appears that considerable further effort will be needed to reduce the current gaps. Judging from the experience of other transition economies that underwent similar adjustments (Hungary in 1995-1996 and the Czech Republic since 1997), this promises to be a long and painful process and is likely to entail an unwelcome economic downturn.[270]

In 1998 the Croatian economy followed a pattern of output performance which looked somewhat similar to that in Slovakia (table 3.3.1 and chart 3.3.1); however the underlying macroeconomic fundamentals and the policy stance were rather different. Indeed, the current account deficit had also reached dangerous proportions in 1997 (12.1 per cent of GDP, the highest among the east European and Baltic countries, table 3.1.2); however, Croatia's overall fiscal position was considerably more sound. As it was considered that the external imbalance reflected an overheating of domestic demand, a moderate and coordinated tightening of monetary and fiscal policy was made in 1998. Overall, this policy change produced in 1998 the required adjustment: the current account deficit was reduced substantially (table 3.1.2), and judging from the growth of retail trade (chart 3.3.2),[271] this was achieved mainly by curbing domestic demand. In terms of output, the adjustment was not costless either: the tightening of policy obviously dampened economic growth and by much more than was expected already in the first half of the year (table 3.3.1). In addition, and like most of the other transition economies, the Croatian economy was hit by the deteriorating external conditions in the second half of the year: industrial output fell strongly (by 4.2 per cent) in the fourth quarter (chart 3.3.1). Thus the 1998 pattern of output growth in Croatia reflects to a large extent the outcome of a policy-induced, "orderly" adjustment with increasingly negative external factors only adding to the further weakening of performance in the second half of the year.

In recent years, Slovenia has been following a cautious and balanced policy which has allowed moderate rates of economic growth (in the range of 3-4.5 per cent per annum in the period 1995-1998) while maintaining a relatively high degree of macroeconomic stability. At the beginning of 1998 the Slovenian economy benefited from a considerable surge in exports to western Europe which gave a considerable boost to economic activity (GDP grew by 6.4 per cent and industrial output by 9.8 per cent in the first quarter of the year – table 3.3.1). However, with the deterioration in external conditions, some manufacturing branches started to experience difficulties and this pace could not be maintained: average industrial output growth weakened considerably in the course of the year (chart 3.3.1).[272] A decline of output in the tourist industry[273] as well as in other services also contributed to the overall moderation of output.

(b) The Baltic states

Compared with the central European countries, the three Baltic states have a greater trade exposure to the Russian market;[274] moreover, some Baltic banks had accumulated sizeable exposure to Russian financial markets. Therefore the Baltic economies were more prone both to demand shocks and financial contagion from Russia. On the other hand, the recent strong recovery in these countries was predominantly driven by the rapid growth of exports, mostly to western Europe (to which trade exposure is much greater). They are thus highly susceptible to external demand shocks (see the argument in section 3.1). In addition, the persistently large current account deficit in the three countries (table 3.1.2) was another source of financial and macroeconomic vulnerability.

Financial markets throughout the Baltic region were shaken by the fallout from the Russian crisis and the pressure on them remained high during the second half of the year.[275] Banks were weakened by the incurred losses (especially in Latvia and to some extent in Estonia) and were forced to restructure partially their portfolios, which resulted, *inter alia*, in liquidity constraints and in a general tightening of credit. With monetary policy also remaining fairly restrictive (as discussed in section 3.2(ii)), this produced a significant rise in real interest rates (chart 3.2.1). In fact, despite the relatively high average annual growth figures, 1998 turned out to be a year of high volatility and deteriorating output performance in this region.

---

[270] The 3 per cent GDP growth forecast incorporated in the 1999 Slovak budget thus appears as overly optimistic, especially given the continuing slump in external demand.

[271] Regrettably, the national accounts data for Croatia are still complied only in current prices which creates considerable difficulties in accessing macroeconomic performance in more detail. In particular, with the exception of retail sales, the Croatian statistical office does not produce any indicators reflecting the dynamics of domestic demand in real terms.

[272] Actually, the relatively high annual manufacturing output growth (table 3.3.4) as well as the high rates of growth of total export that were maintained until the end of the year (table 3.6.1) were achieved to a large degree thanks to the rapid expansion in the motor vehicles industry which is mostly export oriented: according to preliminary estimates, the production of transport equipment in 1998 increased by more than 29 per cent. Institute of Macroeconomic Analysis and Development, *Slovenian Economic Mirror* (Ljubljana), January 1999.

[273] Compared with 1997, overnight stays in 1998 fell by 1.5 per cent while revenue from foreign tourists in the first 11 months dropped by 5.8 per cent over the same period of 1997. Institute of Macroeconomic Analysis and Development, op. cit.

[274] As suggested by the estimates in table 3.6.5, Estonia may have lost some 6-8 per cent of its total exports as a result of the Russian crisis, while in Latvia and Lithuania foregone exports amounted to some 7-10 per cent of total exports. These relative losses are much higher than those in other east European countries.

[275] UN/ECE, *Economic Survey of Europe, 1998 No. 3*, pp. 42-45.

CHART 3.3.2

Volume of retail sales in selected transition economies, 1996-1998
(Year on year percentage changes)

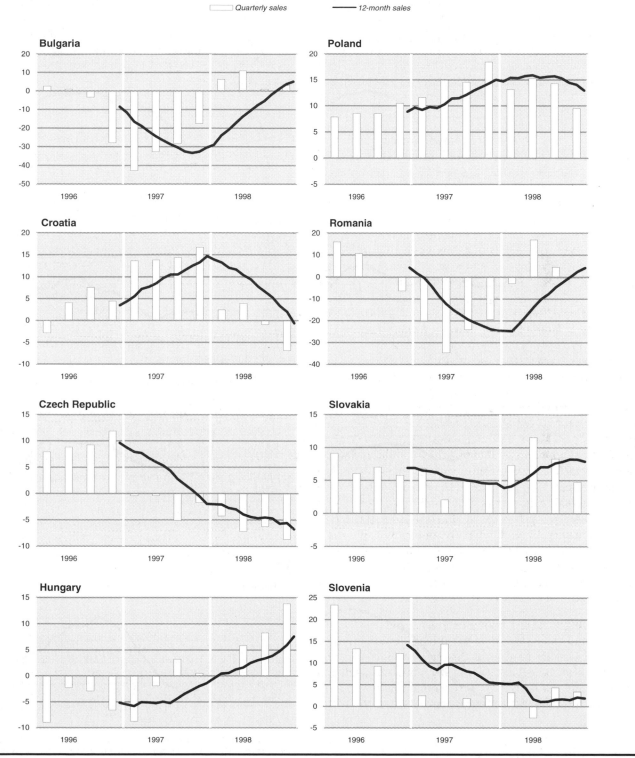

CHART 3.3.2 (concluded)

Volume of retail sales in selected transition economies, 1996-1998
(Year on year percentage changes)

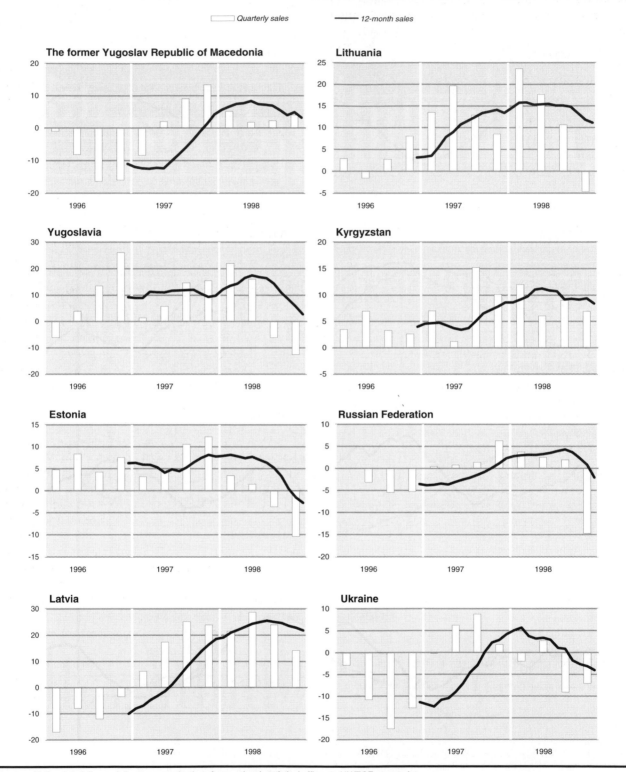

Source: National statistics and direct communications from national statistical offices to UN/ECE secretariat.

Note: The coverage of retail sales in the monthly statistics may differ from the coverage in the annual data.

In terms of their negative impact on the real economy, the repercussions from the Russian and the global crises were especially pronounced in Estonia and Latvia. The speed and the scale of the deterioration of industrial output performance in these two countries in the course of one year (chart 3.3.1)[276] indicate the fragility of transition economies in general, even those which have made considerable progress with reforms. In both countries, the biggest falls in annual output were in the chemical industry and in the manufacture of machinery and equipment (table 3.3.4); however, the industry that was probably worst hit by the Russian crisis was food processing, which incurred heavy losses in the second half of the year leading to the closure of many firms.[277] The Russian crisis also had a direct negative effect on other sectors of economic activity such as transport and other services. At the time of writing there were no clear signs of a reversal in these negative trends.[278]

Compared with Estonia and Latvia, the impact of the crisis on Lithuanian output so far has not been that strong. One of the factors that alleviated the negative impact was the relatively smaller exposure of Lithuanian banks to Russia. Another was the strong growth of output in mining and quarrying,[279] due to the start of a new oil-extraction facility; the latter probably also gave a boost to domestic oil refining. However, in view of the deteriorating conditions in other export markets, these factors could only provide a one-time cushion to external shocks. With falling exports and an emerging balance of payments constraint, economic activity is likely to weaken considerably in 1999.

(c) South-east Europe

Most of the south-east European transition economies have been experiencing serious difficulties in the process of economic transformation. A wide array of factors – unfavourable starting conditions, a lack of clear vision as to the course of reforms, stop-go policies as well as the numerous conflicts in some of the successor states of the former SFR of Yugoslavia – have created a difficult environment for the implementation of the transformation agenda in the countries of this region.

Given their poor performance in the 1990s, the gap between them and the more advanced reformers in central Europe is becoming ever wider.

The Romanian economy has been in deep recession since the beginning of 1997. As discussed in more detail in section 3.2(iii), it is plagued by structural weaknesses (mostly inherited from the communist period) which were not addressed at the earlier phases of transition; instead, the authorities attempted to alleviate the pressure of the necessary adjustments through accommodating, soft policies. The 1997 programme of policy reforms did not bring about the expected results either; in particular, it did not produce the urgently needed reduction in the trade and current account deficits. On the contrary, inadequate policies exacerbated the crisis and instigated a severe economic downturn: in 1997 GDP fell by 6.9 per cent and this was followed by a further decline of 7.3 per cent in 1998 (table 3.1.1). The abrupt reversal in monetary policy led to a sharp rise in real interest rates (chart 3.2.1) and a credit squeeze, while devaluation and high inflation have eroded real wages and incomes. In addition, being predominantly an exporter of intermediate goods, the Romanian economy was badly hit by the weakening of international markets in 1998. The combined supply-and-demand shock provoked a steep plunge in industrial output by 23 per cent over the period 1997-1998 (table 3.1.1). With output and exports continuing to decline and debt service problems looming on the horizon, the troubles facing the Romanian economy are by no means over.

Neighbouring Bulgaria underwent a similar crisis in 1996-1997 which was resolved with the establishment of a currency board in July 1997. This ended a period of very high inflation (in December 1998 the year-on-year rate of CPI inflation in Bulgaria was one of the lowest among the east European and Baltic transition economies, see table 3.1.1) and helped to strengthen the banking system (whose weakness had been one of the causes of the crisis). However, despite the obvious progress in macroeconomic stabilization, the economy remains in a very difficult situation. In particular, manufacturing industry is in an extremely precarious state: industrial output has been declining persistently since the beginning of 1996, a fall which was only briefly interrupted in the first quarter of 1998 (chart 3.3.1).[280] With a composition of exports similar to that of Romania, Bulgarian exporters also incurred considerable market and revenue losses in 1998; consequently the decline of industrial output accelerated substantially in the second half of 1998 (chart 3.3.1)[281]

---

[276] In Estonia, the year-on-year rate of growth of industrial output dropped from 11.3 per cent in the first quarter to -5.7 per cent in the fourth; the corresponding numbers for Latvia (14.7 per cent in the first quarter and -11.4 per cent in the fourth quarter) suggest that the shock was even there.

[277] The importance of this sector is illustrated by the fact that in Latvia it accounts for some 40 per cent of total manufacturing output while in Estonia it was responsible for about half of its exports to Russia. In the second half of the year about half of Latvia's licensed fish processors were closed down increasing unemployment by some 5,000 persons. Economist Intelligence Unit, *Country Report. Estonia,* 1st Quarter 1999 and *Country Report. Latvia,* 1st Quarter 1999 (London).

[278] According to preliminary estimates, industrial sales in Estonia in January 1999 continued to decline rapidly, falling by some 15 per cent from their level in January 1998.

[279] Gross annual output in mining and quarrying increased in 1998 by 52 per cent (table 3.3.4).

---

[280] On the inconsistency of the statistical reporting of Bulgarian industrial output for 1996 see the note to table 3.1.1.

[281] It was around 18 per cent lower than a year earlier in both the third and fourth quarters of 1998; according to preliminary statistics the decline has continued into 1999: in January industrial sales were 23 per cent below their January 1998 level.

TABLE 3.3.5

Growth of industrial output by branch in the CIS economies, 1996-1998

(Annual percentage change)

	Total industry	Fuels	Energy	Ferrous metals	Non-ferrous metals	Engineering	Chemicals	Building materials	Logging, wood and paper	Light industry	Food processing
Armenia											
1996	1.4	..	8.6	196.0	-9.5	-9.8	5.3	5.6	-11.1	-3.3	11.0
1997	0.9	..	-2.3	18.1	-25.4	-33.1	-1.6	6.2	..	50.4	24.3
1998	-2.5	..	-1.0	-25.6ᵃ	50.0	-20.0	-8.0	11.0	7.4ᵃ	10.0	12.0
Azerbaijan											
1996	-6.7	-1.6	-3.6	-72.8	-77.4	-18.0	25.0	7.1	-1.1	-40.6	-34.8
1997	0.3	0.2	-6.6	430.3	262.4	-0.7	-28.2	-4.4	7.3	-16.5	-6.6
1998	2.2	..	..	..	..	..	..	..	..	..	..
Belarus											
1996	3.5	-5.2	-1.6	23.4	31.9	1.6	7.2	-4.0	14.2	11.9	5.5
1997	18.8	-1.0	5.6	35.1	51.3	25.7	19.4	26.1	34.7	27.1	21.0
1998	11.0	0.6	-7.5	15.4	14.8ᵃ	13.2	6.0	14.3	21.2	22.2	19.0
Georgia											
1996	7.7	113.4	2.3	-16.8	23.8	15.0	47.3	52.2	21.6	-2.6	24.9
1997	8.1	64.7	3.2	14.0	-33.7	11.2	20.4	26.1	6.1	-12.6	10.7
1998 ᵇ	0.8	8.0	5.7	-10.1	57.4	10.9	-1.1	64.2	108.8	28.6	4.6
Kazakhstan											
1996	0.3	2.2	-10.3	-17.5	3.6	-9.2	-27.0	-33.6	10.1	19.8	35.1
1997	4.0	0.5	-14.2	25.2	13.8	-29.9	-29.9	-19.3	-27.4	-18.8	0.3
1998	-2.1	..	..	..	..	..	..	..	..	..	..
Kyrgyzstan											
1996	8.8	-11.2	11.0	-64.6	6.5	-6.0	0.1	25.9	-27.8	0.7	-3.0
1997	50.4	7.9	-6.9	..	280.3	5.9	-20.5	11.7	1.2	-7.0	-9.7
1998	4.6	-53.0	-15.0	..	30.0	–	-45.0ᵃ	10.0	-19.0	-26.0	20.0
Republic of Moldova ᶜ											
1996	-6.5	..	5.6	..	..	-19.8	6.5	26.8	-21.2	-0.2	-8.4
1997	–	..	1.1	..	..	-22.4	-52.6	9.5	-5.6	-3.3	2.8
1998	-11.0	..	4.0	..	..	-10.0	–	-16.0	-20.0	-14.0	-12.0
Russian Federation											
1996	-4.0	-1.5	-1.6	-3.6	-3.6	-4.6	-7.1	-17.3	-17.5	-22.5	-4.2
1997	1.9	0.3	-2.1	1.2	5.0	3.5	2.0	-4.0	1.2	-2.4	-0.8
1998	-5.2	-2.5	-2.5	-8.1	-5.0	-7.5	-7.5	-5.8	-0.4	-11.5	-1.9
Tajikistan											
1996	-23.9	-13.3	-2.2	-96.8	-19.3	-29.5	-19.7	-33.3	-30.4	-46.7	-33.0
1997	-2.0	-0.9	-5.9	..	3.3	-21.3	-2.8	-19.5	-24.4	-4.0	-18.8
1998	8.1	-25.0	2.0	..	4.0	16.0	-46.0	-19.0	25.0	3.0	19.0
Turkmenistan											
1996	17.9	10.8	6.3	..	..	155.7	-1.6	-3.4	39.1	63.8	-18.6
1997	..	..	..	..	..	..	..	..	..	..	..
1998	..	..	..	..	..	..	..	..	..	..	..
Ukraine											
1996	-5.1	-6.7	-6.9	11.9	8.0	-26.1	-3.4	-34.2	-18.6	-24.6	-7.2
1997	-0.3	6.2	-2.6	8.1	9.4	-0.2	2.1	-10.4	-0.9	1.1	-10.3
1998	-1.5	-2.0	-1.0	-8.0	11.0	-5.0	2.0	5.0	10.0	–	4.0
Uzbekistan											
1996	2.6	0.4	1.0	30.5	18.3	40.1	15.1	5.6	21.9	6.4	15.0
1997	4.1	4.2	-1.0	-17.1	7.6	44.2	1.3	-3.4	11.1	11.3	34.2
1998	5.8	8.0	-2.0	2.0	–	5.0	24.0	1.0	5.0	3.0	10.0

Source: National statistics; CIS Statistical Committee; direct communications from national statistical offices to UN/ECE secretariat.

Note: Data are presented in terms of national branch classifications comparable among the countries shown in the table. These classifications are not fully compatible with NACE or ISIC. Figures for total industry differ for some countries from those shown in other tables because of differences in coverage.

ᵃ January-September.

ᵇ January-June.

ᶜ Excluding Transdniestria.

TABLE 3.3.6

Gross output of agriculture and construction in the transition economies, 1993-1998

(Annual percentage change)

	Agriculture						Construction					
	1993	*1994*	*1995*	*1996*	*1997*	*1998*	*1993*	*1994*	*1995*	*1996*	*1997*	*1998*
Bulgaria	-18.3	6.8	16.4	-11.8	20.2	..	-10.4	-6.7	-4.4	17.5	-27.6	-10.3[a]
Croatia[b]	5.0	-3.0	1.0	2.0	3.0	..	-10.7	-4.6	-3.8	9.0	17.0	2.3[c]
Czech Republic	-2.3	-6.0	5.0	-1.4	-5.9	-1.3	-7.5	7.5	8.5	5.3	-3.9	-7.0
Hungary	-9.7	3.2	2.6	6.3	-3.8	-1.0	2.6	12.1	-15.7	-0.1	9.7	13.1
Poland	6.8	-9.3	10.7	0.7	-0.2	6.6	4.5	0.3	5.6	3.0	15.5	11.6[d]
Romania	10.2	0.2	4.5	1.3	3.4	-7.6	11.4	29.1	13.2	3.6	-24.4	-18.0
Slovakia	-8.1	4.8	2.3	2.0	-1.0	..	-32.4	-6.7	2.9	4.4	9.2	-3.7
Slovenia[b e]	-0.7	20.0	0.1	0.7	-0.6	..	-18.2	-0.1	0.9	-2.5	-5.2	1.7
The former Yugoslav Republic of Macedonia[b]	-20.0	8.0	4.0	-2.0	..	..	-5.8	-10.6	-3.0	2.0	-16.0	-9.0[c]
Yugoslavia[b]	-3.0	6.0	4.0	1.0	7.0	-6.0	-24.4	-15.0	-3.0	-9.0	-3.0	-6.0
Estonia[f]	-12.2	-12.9	0.2	-6.3	-1.5	-1.0	20.3	-4.2	4.0	21.0	15.0	..
Latvia[g]	-22.0	-20.0	-7.0	-6.0	0.2	..	-37.0	5.6	5.9	5.3	8.2	11.1
Lithuania[g]	-5.5	-20.2	6.1	10.3	6.5	-3.0	-38.8	0.8	-1.0	-7.2	12.3	21.8
Armenia	24.0	3.0	5.0	2.0	-6.0	13.0	..	..	..	..	..	..
Azerbaijan	-15.0	-13.0	-7.0	3.0	-7.0	4.0	..	..	..	..	..	..
Belarus[g]	3.7	-14.4	-4.7	2.4	-4.9	-0.4	-17.0	-31.0	-21.0	-2.0	15.0	11.0
Georgia	-12.0	11.0	13.0	6.0	6.5	-8.0	..	..	..	..	..	..
Kazakhstan[g]	-5.2	-19.8	-24.4	-5.0	-0.9	-18.9	-31.0	-11.0	-45.0	76.0	..	..
Kyrgyzstan[g]	-10.0	-18.0	-2.0	15.0	12.2	4.1	-23.0	-52.0	-3.0	-31.0	14.0	-47.7
Republic of Moldova[g]	10.0	-25.0	3.0	-13.0	12.0	-10.6	..	-48.0	-37.0	-13.0	..	-7.0[h]
Russian Federation[g]	-4.4	-12.0	-8.0	-5.1	1.3	-12.3	-8.0	-24.0	-9.0	-14.0	-6.0	-7.5
Tajikistan	-1.2	-6.5	-25.9	2.0	3.6	6.5	..	..	..	..	..	..
Turkmenistan	16.0	-4.5	1.3	-33.3	20.6	24.4	..	..	..	..	..	..
Ukraine[g]	1.5	-16.5	-3.6	-9.5	-2.0	-8.0	-9.9	-37.2	-38.4	-31.0	-10.4	..
Uzbekistan	1.0	-8.0	3.0	-6.0	4.0	4.0	..	..	..	..	..	..

Source: National statistics; CIS Statistical Committee; direct communications from national statistical offices to UN/ECE secretariat. The volume of construction output in the Russian Federation is from the joint database of the Working Centre for Economic Reform and the Russian European Centre for Economic Policy (internet website).

[a] January-March.

[b] Construction refers to effective working time.

[c] January-October.

[d] Excluding work abroad and by enterprises not classified in construction.

[e] Agriculture is final agricultural output, excluding intra-branch consumption.

[f] Construction refers to sales of construction work.

[g] Construction refers to the volume of work done by construction enterprises and companies.

[h] January-September.

The Ukrainian economy also suffered a setback in 1998 which was largely triggered by the Russian crisis, but it also reflected some deep-seated domestic economic problems, very similar in nature to those in Russia. At the beginning of the year it had been expected that the prolonged economic downturn in Ukraine had come to an end and that 1998 would be marked by the start of recovery (table 3.3.1). Indeed, in the first half of the year, there was a small increase in GDP growth for the first time since Ukraine gained independence. However, the subsequent loss of Russian markets, as well as the domestic financial squeeze in the second half of 1998, led to a substantial deterioration in Ukrainian output performance. Domestic demand also suffered a blow at the same time: after a modest recovery in 1997 and the first half of 1998, retail sales plunged abruptly in the third and fourth quarters of the year (chart 3.3.2). In addition,

a miserable grain harvest[295] led to a substantial decline in gross agricultural output (table 3.3.6). With IMF financing on hold, and growing uncertainties about macroeconomic stability (especially in view of the forced devaluation of the hryvnia), the negative trend in output intensified in the fourth quarter when industrial output declined, year-on-year, by 4.1 per cent (chart 3.3.1). As in the case of Russia, the key to the rehabilitation of Ukraine's economy lies in putting together a comprehensive and credible action plan, backed by sufficient resources, which will address not only the issue of macroeconomic stability proper but also the

---

[295] Ukraine harvested just 26.5 million tons of grain in 1998, some 25 per cent less than the 35.5 million tons collected in 1997. Interstate Statistical Committee of the CIS, *Commonwealth of Independent States in 1998. Statistical Abstract* (Moscow), 1999, p. 78.

of operations of the joint venture Kumtor gold mine, which boosted total industrial output by more than 50 per cent in 1997 (table 3.1.1). By mid-1998, the effect of this start-up was largely phased out and, with the rest of industry performing rather sluggishly and quite unevenly, total industrial output increased by just 4.6 per cent in 1998 (tables 3.3.1 and 3.3.5). Kyrgyzstan experienced a full-blown currency crisis in 1998 (see section 3.2(ii)) which also disturbed economic activity in the second half of the year.

The impact of the global crisis on economic activity in Uzbekistan was less pronounced: in 1998 GDP increased by 4.4 per cent which was close to the rate of the previous year (table 3.1.1). The growth of industrial output actually accelerated in 1998 thanks to the expansion of mining and quarrying,[306] which in turn gave a boost to some manufacturing branches, in particular, the chemical industry (table 3.3.5). Gross agricultural output also increased by 4 per cent in 1998 but within agriculture performance was mixed.[307] As cotton is one of the main export items, the sharp fall of cotton prices on international markets led to a large fall in export earnings and a forced cut-back of imports (table 3.6.7).

For several years until mid-1997, drawn out internal conflicts had caused major disturbances to Tajikistan's economy. Since the signing of the peace agreement in June 1997, the economy has started to recover and, according to the official data, GDP grew by 5.3 per cent in 1998 (table 3.1.1). Within industry, performance remained uneven but a marked recovery in some manufacturing branches (table 3.3.5) contributed to an increase of total industrial output by 8.1 per cent in 1998 (table 3.3.1). Gross agricultural output also increased by 6.5 per cent (table 3.3.6). Despite these positive developments, the economy of Tajikistan remains deeply depressed. Contagion from the Russian crisis generated a strong pressure on the Tajik rouble but in the absence of reliable data it is difficult to assess the actual impact with any pretence to accuracy. As in Uzbekistan, the sharp fall in the international price of cotton seems likely to have resulted in a de facto tightening of Tajikistan's balance of payment constraint.

Poor statistical reporting also makes it very difficult to assess properly the current economic situation in Turkmenistan.[308] The very limited data for 1998 suggest a partial recovery of output after the disastrous

performance in 1997 (table 3.3.1). The economic collapse in 1997 was caused by the suspension of gas deliveries to Ukraine[309] and the production of gas reportedly continued to decline in 1998.[310] With the signing of a new agreement in December,[311] gas exports to Ukraine resumed in the beginning of 1999 and this will contribute to some strengthening of economic activity. However, the Turkmen economy still remains in deep crisis. The fall in export revenue led to further restrictions on the convertibility of the currency and caused a severe liquidity squeeze in the final months of 1998.[312] The future prospects of the strategically important gas sector are also unclear mainly because of uncertainties and risks related to its transportation.[313]

(ii) Demand

(a) *The demand shock and its impact*

An external demand shock was one of the main factors behind the weakening of output performance in the transition economies in 1998. Due to the lags in statistical reporting (in particular, of national accounts) and to the fact that most of the output downturn occurred in the last quarter of the year, at the time of writing this *Survey* it was not possible to assess precisely the impact of weaker demand on growth performance. Thus, only a few signs of its negative impact can be traced in the partial and preliminary estimates of the contribution of the various components of final demand to GDP growth, as shown in tables 3.3.7 and 3.3.8.[314] For this reason, the discussion that follows on the transmission mechanisms of the demand shock in the transition economies is necessarily only tentative and mostly qualitative.

There were three main components of the 1998 demand shock: the direct impact from the weakening of global demand (which was most pronounced in primary commodities and intermediate products); the direct impact from the Russian crisis; and secondary effects

---

[306] Domestic extraction of gas increased by 7 per cent in 1998. Interstate Statistical Committee of the CIS, op. cit., p. 57.

[307] While official full-year figures for Uzbekistan were not available at the time of writing, some preliminary estimates indicate that the grain harvest was the largest in the 1990s. Economist Intelligence Unit, *Country Report. Uzbekistan* (London), 4th Quarter 1998. At the same time the cotton crop was the lowest in 20 years. Oxford Analytica, "Uzbekistan: poor harvest", *Oxford Analytica Brief*, 17 December 1998.

[308] Since the beginning of 1997 the officially released statistical information on Turkmenistan's economic performance has been extremely scanty even for basic economic indicators such as aggregate output or inflation.

[309] The stoppage was reportedly caused by a prolonged dispute with the Russian gas monopoly, Gazprom, over transit fees.

[310] According to estimates of the Turkmen Institute of Statistics and Forecasting, gas production in 1998 fell by 23 per cent. *Agence France Presse*, 28 January 1999.

[311] The issue of the transit fees paid to Gazprom was also settled in the framework of the new agreement. Oxford Analytica, *Oxford Analytica Executive Summaries*, 7 January 1999.

[312] Economist Intelligence Unit, *Country Report. Turkmenistan* (London), 1st Quarter 1999.

[313] For example, on 7 December 1997 the United States company Unocal announced that it was pulling out of the planned Turkmen-Afghan gas pipeline project. Oxford Analytica, "Turkmenistan: further decline", *Oxford Analytica Brief*, 15 December 1998.

[314] At the time of writing this *Survey* full-year national accounts (in preliminary and incomplete form) were only available for Kyrgyzstan, the Republic of Moldova and Romania; partial estimates on the basis of the preliminary national accounts for the first three quarters could be made for Bulgaria, the Czech Republic, Slovakia, Estonia and Latvia (tables 3.3.7 and 3.3.8).

TABLE 3.3.7

Contribution of final demand components to real GDP growth in eastern Europe and the Baltic states, 1994-1998

(Percentage points)

	1994	1995	1996	1997	1998 [a]		1994	1995	1996	1997	1998 [a]
Bulgaria						**Slovakia**					
Consumption	-4.1	-1.8	-5.8	-13.4	5.3	Consumption	-2.9	2.4	7.6	3.1	2.4
Fixed investment	0.1	2.2	-3.2	-3.0	1.0	Fixed investment	-1.4	1.5	10.9	5.2	4.3
Changes in stocks	-1.7	4.9	-5.1	5.8	3.2	Changes in stocks	-1.7	6.8	0.7	-7.0	-2.3
Net trade	7.5	-2.5	3.9	2.6	-6.6	Net trade	10.9	-3.7	-12.6	5.2	1.3
Exports	..	..	..	-0.1	-5.2	Exports	8.5	2.0	-0.2	3.6	5.6
Imports	..	..	..	2.7	-1.4	Imports	2.3	-5.7	-12.4	1.6	-4.3
GDP	1.8	2.9	-10.1	-6.9	4.3	GDP	4.9	6.9	6.6	6.5	5.8
Czech Republic						**Slovenia**					
Consumption	1.9	3.0	4.4	0.5	-1.9	Consumption	2.9	6.0	2.1	2.8	..
Fixed investment	4.9	6.2	2.9	-1.7	-1.0	Fixed investment	2.8	3.6	2.0	2.6	..
Changes in stocks	0.7	0.8	1.6	0.9	-1.3	Changes in stocks	0.4	1.6	-1.0	-0.2	..
Net trade	-5.3	-3.6	-5.0	1.4	2.1	Net trade	-0.8	-7.1	0.4	-0.6	..
Exports	0.1	8.5	3.1	6.0	9.7	Exports	7.6	0.7	1.8	6.2	..
Imports	-5.4	-12.1	-8.1	-4.6	-7.6	Imports	-8.4	-7.8	-1.4	-6.8	..
GDP	3.2	6.4	3.9	1.0	-2.1	GDP	5.3	4.1	3.5	4.6	..
Hungary						**Estonia**					
Consumption	-2.0	-5.6	-2.3	1.5	..	Consumption	0.9	7.3	4.5	6.9	4.7
Fixed investment	2.7	-1.0	1.3	1.9	..	Fixed investment	1.5	1.1	2.9	3.5	4.5
Changes in stocks	1.7	3.2	1.7	1.1	..	Changes in stocks	-1.4	0.2	0.4	3.0	-2.3
Net trade	0.5	4.9	0.6	0.2	..	Net trade	-6.1	-0.4	-4.4	-3.2	-2.2
Exports	4.3	4.6	3.1	10.4	..	Exports	2.6	3.9	1.6	21.6	11.9
Imports	-3.7	0.3	-2.5	-10.3	..	Imports	-8.7	-4.3	-6.0	-24.8	-14.1
GDP	2.9	1.5	1.3	4.6	..	GDP	-2.0	4.3	4.0	11.4	5.4
Poland						**Latvia**					
Consumption	3.2	2.6	5.6	4.8	..	Consumption	1.7	-0.8	6.9	3.4	0.8
Fixed investment	1.5	3.0	3.7	4.5	..	Fixed investment	0.1	1.2	3.4	2.0	1.1
Changes in stocks	–	1.3	0.2	0.1	..	Changes in stocks	2.6	-2.4	-2.3	-0.1	5.9
Net trade	0.6	0.1	-3.4	-2.6	..	Net trade	-3.8	1.2	-4.6	1.2	-1.4
Exports	2.7	5.4	3.1	3.0	..	Exports	-4.1	1.9	9.5	5.4	8.7
Imports	-2.1	-5.3	-6.5	-5.6	..	Imports	0.3	-0.7	-14.1	-4.2	-10.1
GDP	5.2	7.0	6.0	6.9	..	GDP	0.6	-0.8	3.3	6.5	6.4
Romania						**Lithuania**					
Consumption	2.9	8.3	5.7	-3.6	-3.2	Consumption	..	..	4.9	5.5	..
Fixed investment	3.7	1.4	1.2	-0.7	-4.0	Fixed investment	..	..	2.5	5.7	..
Changes in stocks	-6.3	-2.4	-0.6	-2.8	..	Changes in stocks	..	..	-0.1	1.2	..
Net trade	3.6	-0.2	-2.3	0.4	..	Net trade	..	..	-2.6	-6.3	..
Exports	4.4	4.2	0.6	3.2	..	Exports	..	..	10.3	13.3	..
Imports	-0.8	-4.4	-2.9	-2.8	..	Imports	..	..	-13.0	-19.6	..
GDP	3.9	7.1	3.9	-6.9	-7.3	GDP	..	..	4.7	6.1	..

Source: National statistics and direct communications from national statistical offices to UN/ECE secretariat.

Note: The sum of component changes may not equal the GDP change for some countries due to reported statistical discrepancies.

[a] January-September for Bulgaria, Czech Republic, Slovakia and Estonia; January-June for Latvia.

through the weakening of import demand in "third party" countries. These developments were interrelated and reinforced each other and their joint evolution in time resulted in a rapid acceleration of their combined negative effect on the transition economies.

The weakening of global demand started with the escalation of the Asian crisis in the second half of 1997 and continued in the course of 1998. It originated in a sharp contraction of import demand in South-East Asia caused by currency depreciation and the forced macroeconomic adjustment in the crisis-hit countries. The adverse effect on producers in the transition economies can be traced in the weakening of export performance in some transition economies already in 1997 and especially in 1998. For example, the sharp fall

of exports from eastern Europe and other transition economies to developing countries, which began already in 1997 (table 3.6.2) and continued through 1998, is most probably a direct real impact of the Asian crisis.[315]

As discussed in several parts of this *Survey*, the real effect of the Russian crisis was equivalent to a second external demand shock for many of the transition economies, especially those with intensive trade links with Russia.[316] The mechanism was very similar to that

---

[315] Exports from eastern Europe to developing economies declined in dollar terms by some 10 per cent both in 1997 and in 1998 (table 3.6.2).

[316] For an assessment of the "export losses" due to the Russian crisis for some transition economies see sect. 3.6.

TABLE 3.3.8

Contribution of final demand components to real GDP growth in selected CIS economies, 1994-1998

(Percentage points)

	1994	1995	1996	1997	1998		1994	1995	1996	1997	1998
Armenia						**Kyrgyzstan**					
Consumption	4.2	8.5	3.8	6.8	..	Consumption	-18.8	-15.6	5.9	-8.2	-0.6
Fixed investment	5.5	-3.5	1.7	2.2	..	Fixed investment	-3.8	7.3	-2.6	-6.6	-1.8
Changes in stocks	..	..	..	..	..	Changes in stocks	-0.3	1.4	4.7	6.8	-7.5
Net trade	-10.6	3.5	2.1	-6.2	..	Net trade	2.8	1.5	-0.9	17.9	11.7
Exports	15.3	-4.1	-1.3	4.4	..	Exports	-6.4	-5.9	2.0	6.5	3.9
Imports	-25.9	7.5	3.4	-10.6	..	Imports	9.1	7.4	-2.9	11.4	7.8
GDP	5.4	6.9	5.9	3.1	7.2	GDP	-20.1	-5.4	7.1	9.9	1.8
Azerbaijan						**Republic of Moldova**					
Consumption	-18.9	-2.8	7.9	10.5	..	Consumption	-9.8	7.1	8.7	11.1	-5.5
Fixed investment	18.6	-4.7	17.4	19.5	..	Fixed investment	-6.8	-0.7	4.0	-0.9	–
Changes in stocks	..	..	..	..	..	Changes in stocks	-22.2	-2.0	-3.9	-0.4	-0.2
Net trade	-2.3	-16.8	-19.9	1.1	..	Net trade	7.8	-5.9	-14.6	-7.9	-2.9
Exports	4.3	-2.7	0.3	11.2	..	Exports	11.5	17.9	-5.1	0.9	-10.6
Imports	-6.6	-14.1	-20.2	-10.1	..	Imports	-3.7	-23.7	-9.6	-8.8	7.7
GDP	-19.7	-11.8	1.3	5.8	10.0	GDP	-30.9	-1.9	-7.8	1.6	-8.6
Belarus						**Russian Federation**					
Consumption	-9.2	-7.6	2.6	7.6	..	Consumption	-1.9	-1.9	-1.5	1.1	..
Fixed investment	-4.6	-9.8	-0.8	5.1	..	Fixed investment	-5.2	-1.6	-3.4	-0.8	..
Changes in stocks	-7.4	0.4	2.6	-0.9	..	Changes in stocks	-3.1	-1.1	-0.1	0.8	..
Net trade	8.7	6.7	-1.6	-1.5	..	Net trade	-1.0	0.1	0.7	-0.5	..
Exports	0.1	-19.9	4.3	11.6	..	Exports	1.9	2.0	0.2	0.1	..
Imports	8.5	26.5	-5.9	-13.1	..	Imports	-2.9	-1.9	0.5	-0.7	..
GDP	-12.6	-10.4	2.8	11.4	8.3	GDP	-12.7	-4.1	-3.5	0.8	-4.6
Georgia						**Ukraine**					
Consumption	-7.3	9.1	..	..	..	Consumption	-6.2	-2.5	-6.4	2.6	..
Fixed investment	4.8	7.0	..	..	..	Fixed investment	-10.0	-7.2	-5.3	-1.4	..
Changes in stocks	..	..	..	..	..	Changes in stocks	0.1	-9.1	-1.6	-0.1	..
Net trade	-5.7	-1.4	..	..	..	Net trade	-6.7	2.2	–	-1.7	..
Exports	5.3	-0.9	..	..	..	Exports	2.7	0.4	7.9	-0.5	..
Imports	-11.0	-0.5	..	..	..	Imports	-9.4	1.8	-7.9	-1.2	..
GDP	-10.4	2.6	11.0	11.3	2.9	GDP	-22.9	-12.2	-10.0	-3.2	-1.7
Kazakhstan											
Consumption	-17.1	-16.5	-5.9	0.9	..						
Fixed investment	-3.2	-9.9	-5.5	0.6	..						
Changes in stocks	..	..	..	..	..						
Net trade	-1.6	11.2	8.2	-1.8	..						
Exports	-4.2	1.9	0.8	0.8	..						
Imports	2.6	9.4	7.4	-2.6	..						
GDP	-12.6	-8.2	0.5	1.7	-2.5						

Source: National statistics; CIS Statistical Committee; direct communications from national statistical offices to UN/ECE secretariat.

Note: The sum of component changes may not equal the GDP change for some countries due to reported statistical discrepancies.

experienced in the aftermath of the Asian crisis: the weakening of Russian exports led to a fall in imports from the transition economies already in early 1998 (chart 3.6.2); the subsequent collapse of the rouble in August provoked a plunge in Russian imports in the last months of 1998[317] and this had a severe impact on suppliers from many transition economies. In fact, the Russian crisis amplified the already deteriorating export conditions facing the transition economies and this process accelerated considerably in the second half of the year.

Also in the second half of the year, the negative impact of the weakening of the global economy (in addition to the Russian crisis) began to affect western Europe as well, causing a slowdown of economic activity in a number of countries. Although in terms of growth, the picture in western Europe remained mixed in the final months of 1998, the marked weakening of manufacturing output in several economies (Germany, Italy, the United Kingdom, among others) played an important role in the overall slowdown.

Because of the lag with which this secondary effect is felt, the data available at the moment of writing this *Survey* did not allow an accurate assessment of the actual magnitude of its impact on the transition economies. On the one hand, the available (preliminary and incomplete) export data for the fourth quarter of 1998 (table 3.6.1) do not suggest that all the transition economies experienced

[317] The average monthly dollar value of Russian imports during the last four months of 1998 were 44 per cent lower than their average monthly level during the first eight months of the year and 51 per cent lower than in the last four months of 1997. UN/ECE secretariat calculations on the basis of data from Russian Federation Goskomstat, *Sotsial'no-ekonomicheskoe polozhenie Rossii* (Moscow), various issues.

an additional fall in exports in the final months of the year; however, this may well be due to the inherent lags in the execution of export contracts. On the other hand, indirect evidence (and especially the unexpectedly sharp deterioration in output performance in a number of countries in the fourth quarter) suggests that some of the transition economies were subject to an additional demand shock in the closing months of 1998.[318]

The mechanisms through which changes in certain components of demand may affect output performance – or macroeconomic performance in general – can be extremely complex due to the heterogeneous causal relations involved.[319] Such an analysis requires a detailed assessment of the actual transmission mechanisms; usually, the latter are country-specific and their analysis requires taking into account the interrelations of both macro and microeconomic factors. Even the simple measurement of the statistical contribution of the components of final demand to economic growth (as shown in tables 3.3.7 and 3.3.8) – which is a purely statistical operation and does not imply any direction of causality – can only be made on the basis of the annual national accounts data.

Nevertheless, although the compositional mix of the factors of growth may have been different in the individual transition economies, the direction of change in their output performance in 1998 (as discussed in section 3.3(i)) suggests that the externally induced demand-side shock started to play the dominant role in most of them from the beginning of the year; and virtually all the indicators suggest that this dominance strengthened in the course of the year.

It is difficult to judge how and to what extent domestic demand in 1998 in the individual countries was affected by the external shock, as its impact was often mixed with various domestic factors. As noted already, tight macroeconomic policies (aimed at improving external or domestic balance) had already resulted in the curbing of domestic demand in some transition economies (Croatia in 1998 is a case in point; the policy effort in the Czech Republic in 1997 also aimed at a similar adjustment but the crisis turned out to be much deeper than expected). Full-blown economic crises have recently forced cuts in domestic demand in a number of transition economies (Bulgaria in 1996-1997, Romania since 1997, Russia and a number of CIS countries in 1998). It is difficult in all these cases to separate domestic from external factors.

On the other hand, the basic conjecture about the transmission mechanisms of the external shock is that it would first affect output while the eventual impact on domestic demand would be mostly indirect, albeit with certain time lags (through the negative impact on incomes and expectations and the effect of the latter on spending and investment decisions). Obviously, due to the inherent lags in the transmission processes, the proliferation of such indirect effects may continue for some time in the future. Thus while the effects of the shock are not always reflected in the 1998 performance indicators, they are likely to continue to have a negative effect on domestic demand in the transition economies in 1999 as well.

The magnitude of the external shock (already reflected in a considerable worsening of output performance), coupled with the deteriorating conditions on the international financial markets, suggests that a number of transition economies are likely to face increasingly tough balance of payments constraints in the short run. The main problem is that a number of transition economies will be facing increasing difficulties in financing current account deficits (which in some cases have been a necessary element in their recent recovery and in others are a reflection of chronic economic weakness). As already indicated by the experience of some transition economies, the weakening of global markets has also had a negative impact on their fiscal position, especially in cases where fiscal revenue is highly sensitive to export revenue. If these imbalances are to be kept under control, some transition economies will face the necessity of a macroeconomic adjustment, largely by further cuts in domestic demand and thus a further weakening of output performance.[320]

In this regard it is illuminating to consider how similar adjustment efforts have taken shape in some of the transition economies in recent years. Thus the Hungarian experience of 1995-1997 reflects the outcome of a deliberate policy response to the emerging twin-deficit problem, the simultaneous enlargement of the fiscal and current account deficits. This experience may thus be relevant for other transition economies that are facing, or may expect to face, similar problems in the near future.

As can be seen from the statistics in tables 3.3.7, 3.3.10 and 3.3.12, the policy of macroeconomic austerity resulted in a severe contraction of domestic demand in Hungary in 1995 (the year when the policy correction was initiated). The principal demand-side factor of growth in that year was net trade, mostly thanks to the continued expansion of exports, as real imports declined (table 3.3.7). This net trade effect was partly due to the trimming of costs (resulting from restrictive policies) and to the one-time depreciation of the currency. The following year, 1996, when investors' confidence started to recover, it was fixed investment that started to make a notable contribution to growth; the net trade effect also remained positive while consumption (both private and

---

[318] As discussed in sect. 3.2(ii), the upsurge in real interest rates towards the end of 1998, amplified the magnitude of the external shock in a number of transition economies.

[319] For example, a distinction is sometimes made between "supply-driven" and "demand-driven" types of growth in order to emphasize the dominant role of causality in one or the other direction.

---

[320] As noted above, a number of transition economies are already undergoing such a process for the reasons discussed. In these cases, the unfavourable external environment is likely to amplify substantially the downside factors and risks.

government) continued to subtract from the overall growth in output. By the time a rapid recovery started in 1997, the negative impact of austere policies was diminishing while the positive impact of enterprise restructuring was beginning to pay off, and in 1997 as a whole all the components of final demand made a positive net contribution to growth (table 3.3.7). The preliminary data for 1998 suggest that the rapidly growing private consumption (chart 3.3.2) probably took the lead as the largest net contributor to growth.

When analyzing country-specific policy experience, it is notoriously difficult to draw general conclusions or to come up with general policy recommendations for other countries. Nevertheless, it is tempting to ask whether, given the economic circumstances likely to prevail in 1999, other transition economies will be able to repeat, at least partly, the policy success of Hungary in engineering a painful – but effectual – adjustment effort. While it may be difficult to come up with any definite conclusions, several important, policy-relevant factors need to be taken into consideration when making such an assessment.

The first refers to external conditions. Hungary embarked on its policy adjustment when the external environment was rather favourable. The recovery in western Europe and its strong import demand supported the rapid growth of Hungarian exports after they had been given a boost by the adjustment effort. The strong export performance then became a major factor not only in reducing the macroeconomic imbalances but also in providing the main engine of recovery and growth. In addition to this favourable environment, the Hungarian policy package of 1995 also included a one-time – but significant – currency devaluation (by 8 per cent) and a switch from fixed to crawling peg exchange rate regime, which undoubtedly gave an additional impulse to export performance and the improvement in the external balance. Finally, the Hungarian adjustment effort was successful largely because it built on the success in restructuring the Hungarian economy, and especially manufacturing industry. As noted in section 3.3(i), the export-led revival of this sector, underpinned by a steady inflow of FDI over a period of several years, was the main factor behind the strong recovery that started in 1997. Without this support from a restructured manufacturing sector, the Hungarian economy would hardly have been able to grow at such rates, despite the reduction in the external imbalance.

The situation in early 1999 – featuring weak global trade, depressed commodity prices and hesitant import demand in parts of western Europe – looks quite different. It is highly unlikely that the transition economies will be able to rely on a strong growth of exports to check their external imbalances in the short run. Even if some transition economies were to resort to currency depreciation to boost exports,[321] it is questionable whether

this would in fact achieve the expected result because of the general weakness in export markets.[322] Nevertheless, if sluggish export performance continues, it can be expected that many transition economies will be facing increasing domestic pressures to resort to a competitive devaluation in order to boost economic activity.

Thus, if the weakness in external demand persists, it may have a long-lasting negative impact on the general level of economic activity in many transition economies since there will be very limited potential for an export-led adjustment and recovery in the short run.[323] The resilience of individual countries to the repercussions of the external demand shock will again depend on the general state of their economy which, in turn, will reflect the progress made in economic reform, in strengthening institutions, and in microeconomic restructuring. A sustained and robust growth of domestic demand (which does not lead to overheating and macroeconomic imbalance, but instead reflects rising confidence in the future) can provide another defence for domestic economic activity against the unfavourable external environment.

(b) The components of domestic demand

The composition of final demand in many transition economies is still undergoing substantial change (table 3.3.9).[324] Both the transition shocks and the uneven pace of economic growth have contributed to significant fluctuations and shifts in final domestic demand and, in some cases, to abnormal proportions in the composition of demand. One striking example is the proportion of domestic consumption in GDP in some transition economies: in several of the CIS countries, this share is close to, or even exceeding, unity. The fact that domestic output hardly covers (or even fails to cover) the level of domestic consumption is a conspicuous indication of the general weakness of these economies and their inability to create the basis for sustained economic performance.

The transformation crises recently experienced in a number of transition economies has brought about further distortions and detrimental changes in the composition of their final demand (table 3.3.9). One of the regrettable consequences of these crises has been a further reduction of already low shares of investment in GDP (especially manifest in Bulgaria and, in 1997-1998, in Russia and in a number of other CIS countries). This change in the

---

[321] Some transition economies were already forced to devalue as a result of the global financial and Russian crises (see sect. 3.2(ii)).

[322] For example, the Czech Republic introduced a policy package in 1997 that was similar to the Hungarian one of 1995; however, largely due to the unfavourable external environment, the adjustment process has been rather difficult and the accompanying recession has turned out to be much deeper than expected.

[323] As many of the transition economies are less advanced than Hungary in the reform process and few have enjoyed similar inflows of FDI, it is not very likely that the Hungarian experience of fast post-adjustment recovery and growth can be repeated in many other countries.

[324] The statistical offices in many transition economies started compiling national accounts only very recently. Despite an obvious improvement in statistical practices in recent years, the quality of the data often remains questionable; they often contain inconsistencies and/or puzzling discrepancies.

TABLE 3.3.9

Composition of final demand in current prices in selected transition economies, 1996-1998

(Percentage of GDP)

	Consumption			Fixed investment			Change in stocks			Net trade		
	1996	*1997*	*1998 [a]*	*1996*	*1997*	*1998 [a]*	*1996*	*1997*	*1998 [a]*	*1996*	*1997*	*1998 [a]*
Bulgaria	88.5	84.1	84.9	13.6	11.3	10.9	-5.2	0.5	3.5	3.1	5.5	2.4
Croatia	87.5	86.9	..	21.9	28.3	..	1.5	3.9	..	-9.5	-15.2	..
Czech Republic	71.5	71.6	70.8	33.0	30.7	25.9	2.5	3.2	3.8	-7.0	-5.5	-0.5
Hungary	74.3	72.3	..	21.4	22.1	..	5.4	6.1	..	-1.1	-0.5	..
Poland	79.6	79.6	83.1	20.9	23.6	22.2	1.1	1.1	0.9	-1.6	-4.3	-6.2
Romania	82.6	85.3	90.8	23.0	22.0	18.1	2.9	0.2	–	-8.4	-7.1	8.5
Slovakia	72.6	71.6	71.4	36.9	38.6	36.8	2.4	-3.2	2.7	-12.0	-7.1	-10.8
Slovenia	77.5	76.9	77.0	22.6	23.5	24.0	0.9	0.7	0.3	-1.0	-1.2	-1.3
The former Yugoslav Republic of Macedonia	90.2	..	..	17.4	..	..	2.7	..	..	-10.3	..	..
Yugoslavia	94.5	91.0	..	11.9	12.0	..	4.9	6.1	..	-11.6	-9.0	..
Estonia	84.8	81.4	81.3	26.7	26.5	29.0	1.1	3.4	0.6	-11.5	-11.4	-8.8
Latvia	89.3	90.4	84.9	18.1	19.3	15.7	0.7	0.4	8.2	-8.1	-10.1	-8.8
Lithuania	85.3	84.0	84.0	23.0	24.4	26.0	1.5	2.2	2.6	-9.8	-10.6	-12.6
Armenia	111.7	..	..	17.9	..	..	2.1	..	..	-32.8	..	..
Azerbaijan	99.7	90.4	93.0	29.1	37.8	45.2	-0.1	0.5	–	-31.0	-27.4	-35.9
Belarus	79.4	77.2	82.8	22.0	25.0	22.3	2.5	1.7	2.8	-3.9	-6.3	-7.0
Georgia	93.2	100.0	..	13.6	12.3	..	4.3	4.2	..	-7.4	-16.2	..
Kazakhstan	79.9	82.6	..	17.2	16.3	..	-1.1	-0.7	..	-0.7	-2.1	..
Kyrgyzstan	100.6	86.2	99.3	22.4	12.4	10.8	2.8	9.3	2.6	-25.8	-7.9	-26.9
Republic of Moldova	94.4	97.5	102.3	19.6	19.9	21.9	4.5	3.8	4.0	-18.8	-21.1	-28.3
Russian Federation	71.6	75.3	76.8	20.6	18.5	17.3	1.9	2.8	1.1	3.9	2.8	6.4
Tajikistan	62.0	..	..	12.5	..	..	9.0	..	..	9.7	..	..
Turkmenistan	56.3	81.7	..	41.3	40.9	..	8.2	7.3	..	-1.3	-31.1	..
Ukraine	79.9	83.7	..	20.7	18.3	..	2.0	1.8	..	-2.6	-3.8	..
Uzbekistan	..	..	85.0	..	..	33.7	..	..	-19.0	..	..	0.2

Source: National statistics; CIS Statistical Committee; direct communications from national statistical offices to UN/ECE secretariat.

Note: The sum of components does not add up to 100 per cent for some countries due to reported statistical discrepancies.

[a] January-September for Bulgaria, the Czech Republic, Poland, Slovakia, Estonia, Lithuania, Azerbaijan, Belarus and Uzbekistan and January-June for Latvia.

composition of final demand is among the factors contributing to the new dividing line among the transition economies. The proportionate decline in current investment in some transition economies (which are not among the advanced reformers anyway) is not improving their chances of catching up with the higher income levels prevailing elsewhere in Europe; on the contrary, it is likely to lead to a lower growth rate of output and a further falling behind in the future.

Due to the delays in compiling the national accounts, the assessment of changes in the various components of domestic demand in 1998 can only be tentative and partial at present. It is largely based on some surrogate indicators that are compiled and published by the statistical offices in their current (monthly and quarterly) statistical reviews.[325]

Consumption

The recent recovery of economic growth in many *east European and Baltic countries* has often been accompanied by very rapid growth of private

[325] Such as the volume of retail sales which is taken as a proxy for private consumption and the volume of investment outlays which is taken as a proxy for fixed investment.

consumption. In a number of cases (notably Poland, Slovakia and the three Baltic states),[326] the strong recovery of final consumption in 1996-1997 was a major support of economic growth (table 3.3.7). As the expansion of consumer spending was often accompanied by an upsurge in household credit, this started to give rise to fears of overheating in some of these countries. In fact, such concerns were among the arguments for the tightening of monetary policy that occurred in several transition economies in the second half of 1997.

The prevailing change in private consumption in the east European and Baltic countries in 1998 – as depicted by retail sales volumes (chart 3.3.2 and table 3.3.11)[327] –

[326] Croatia probably falls into this category as well, although the lack of full national accounts data do not allow this to be confirmed.

[327] Some words of caution are needed as regards the use and interpretation of retail sales as a proxy for private consumption. There are sometimes puzzling anomalies in the data which presumably are due to country-specific differences in statistical methodology and practice but which are not always explicitly spelled out in the publications of the national statistical offices. There are notable discrepancies between the reported rates of growth of retail sales and of private or total consumption for some countries (for example Latvia and Lithuania in 1997 and 1998; Romania and Estonia in 1998, among others – see tables 3.3.10 and 3.3.11). In some cases (Poland is an example – see the note to table 3.3.11), there are considerable discrepancies between monthly and annual

upsurge in precautionary purchases, notably of consumer durables, which gave a boost to the total volume of retail sales.[337] However, the deep downturn in consumer demand that occurred in the fourth quarter of 1998 probably indicates a major shift in aggregate demand in Russia which is unlikely to be reversed in the short run: at the beginning of 1999 the steep decline of retail sales was still continuing and there were no apparent signs of it coming to an end.[338]

After a modest recovery in 1997, private consumption in Ukraine fell again in 1998, especially in the second half of the year (chart 3.3.2). The renewed decline of retail sales reflected the general weakening of economic activity in Ukraine due to the shock from the Russian crisis. One important negative influence on private consumption was real income which started to decrease rapidly in the final months of the year due to the upsurge in inflation that followed the devaluation of the hryvnia in September.[339]

Investment

The level of business investment is generally regarded as one of the most reliable indicators of the overall economic perspectives of a country as it mirrors the collective perception of investors as to the prospects for profitable business. Each investment decision reflects a balance between the individual assessment of the overall business and economic risk and the expected return on the investment. Thus the aggregate level of current business investment can be regarded as representing an aggregate "consensus forecast" of the future economic prospects of a country made by the circle of prospective individual investors. In general, investment activity can be regarded as a lead indicator with respect to economic activity and growth; moreover, as regards mature market economies, there are well-documented cyclical elements in this relation.

It should also be borne in mind that, in purely statistical terms, the relation between investment and growth may be somewhat equivocal because of the presence of lags. Thus the "lead" of investment may not necessarily be reflected in the actual statistics on investment outlays, as there may be a long interval between the investment decision and its implementation depending on the scale of the project, technological complexity, etc. In such cases, recorded investment outlays (reflecting past investment decisions) may de facto be lagging behind actual changes in the level of economic activity (and may, for example, appear to be out of line with what might be expected given the current position in the business cycle). This can partly be observed in the pattern of investment in the transition economies in 1998.

Investment varied considerably among the transition economies in 1998. Although only partial and preliminary information was available at the time of writing this *Survey*, it allows some clear distinctions to be drawn about the investment pattern in a number of transition economies. Thus, in 1998, investment demand continued on average to be quite high in many central European and Baltic economies (with the notable exception of the Czech Republic) despite the slowing down of economic growth. In most cases (Hungary, Poland, Slovakia, Slovenia, Estonia and Lithuania, among the countries for which investment data were available)[340] investment grew at higher rates than GDP (table 3.3.12) and made significantly positive contributions to growth (table 3.3.7).

Business investment has been very buoyant in Poland since 1995: investment outlays have been growing at double-digit rates for four consecutive years and in 1997-1998 they increased by more than 20 per cent (table 3.3.12). There were also very high rates of investment in Slovakia in this period; however, as already noted, large-scale infrastructure projects, financed from public funds, accounted for a considerable share of the total.[341] In view of the post-election change in economic policy, it can be expected that this type of investment will be reduced substantially in the future (some deceleration was already visible in 1998 – table 3.3.12).

In contrast, the deteriorating economic situation in the Czech Republic led to a further marked weakening of investment in 1998: the volume of outlays and of investment in fixed capital fell for a second year running (table 3.3.12). Despite some recovery in 1998, investment remained rather weak in Bulgaria in absolute terms: the share of fixed investment in GDP in Bulgaria is the lowest among the east European and Baltic countries (table 3.3.9), a reflection of the sharp contraction in 1996 and 1997 (by over 20 per cent in both years). The preliminary 1998 national accounts figures for Romania indicate a similar process of collapse in fixed capital formation (table 3.3.12). Although the background to the current downturn of investment activity in these countries may be different (in the Czech Republic it reflects mostly uncertainties about the prospects of recovery in the short run, while in the other two countries, especially in Bulgaria, it is more the outcome of a persistent lack of investors' confidence)

---

[337] In August alone, the volume of retail sales of non-food items increased by 8.8 per cent from its level in July and by 6.6 per cent from August 1997. Russian Federation Goskomstat, *Sotsial'no-ekonomicheskoe polozhenie Rossii*, No. 12 (Moscow), 1998, p. 122.

[338] According to preliminary Goskomstat data, retail sales in January continued to decline at double-digit rates year-on-year. Due to a methodological change in the reporting of the volume of retail sales, it was difficult to compare the actual rate with those in the preceding months.

[339] The largest decline in real incomes occurred between August and November 1998, real wages plunging by more than 10 per cent. UN/ECE secretariat calculation, based on national statistics.

---

[340] In Latvia, after strong growth during the first two quarters, investment slowed down in the second half of the year (table 3.3.12).

[341] Mostly highways, but also including the construction of the nuclear power station in Mohovce.

TABLE 3.3.12

Investment in selected transition economies, 1995-1998

(Annual percentage change)

	Gross capital formation				Gross fixed capital formation				Investment outlays			
	1995	*1996*	*1997*	*1998* [a]	*1995*	*1996*	*1997*	*1998* [a]	*1995*	*1996*	*1997*	*1998* [b]
Bulgaria	75.4	-53.2	32.8	36.8	16.1	-21.2	-22.1	9.5	..	..	..	..
Czech Republic	23.1	13.0	-2.2	-6.4	21.0	8.7	-4.9	-3.3	30.3	18.1	-9.5	-5.0
Hungary	8.2	12.8	11.0	..	-4.3	6.7	8.8	13.7	-5.3	5.2	8.5	10.2
Poland	24.1	19.5	20.8	..	16.5	19.7	21.7	..	17.1	19.2	22.2	23.9
Romania	-4.2	2.5	-14.4	..	6.9	5.7	-3.0	-18.1	10.7	3.1	-19.0	0.8
Slovakia	29.1	40.8	-4.7	12.0	-0.2	39.8	14.5	10.6	9.4	39.6	11.7	10.3
Slovenia	23.0	4.2	10.1	..	16.8	9.2	11.3	..	..	..	..	..
Yugoslavia	..	..	..	..	..	..	..	..	-3.7	-5.7	..	..
Estonia	4.8	12.5	22.4	7.0	4.0	11.4	12.5	15.6	..	..	..	..
Latvia	-6.6	6.0	10.3	44.8	8.7	22.3	11.1	6.8	8.5	55.5	20.6	2.0
Lithuania	..	10.0	26.6	..	..	10.9	23.5	..	14.3	12.0	14.6	16.8
Armenia	-16.0	7.8	8.6	..	-17.3	10.3	12.4	..	..	..	..	..
Azerbaijan	55.2	111.4	67.0	..	-18.0	111.4	67.0	..	-18.0	110.0	39.0	45.0
Belarus	-28.7	7.2	17.2	..	-29.6	-3.1	23.1	..	-31.0	-4.8	19.5	16.0
Georgia	41.0	..	..	..	64.8	..	..	..	38.0	11.0	36.0	80.0
Kazakhstan	-42.5	-29.5	5.7	..	-37.9	-23.9	3.3	..	-37.0	-39.0	12.0	12.8
Kyrgyzstan	96.3	11.4	0.7	-42.9	60.7	-13.0	-29.6	-14.5	81.7	19.0	-4.0	-53.0
Republic of Moldova	-9.1	0.2	-5.5	-1.0	-3.4	24.9	-4.7	-0.2	-16.0	-8.0	-8.0	-0.2
Russian Federation	-10.8	-17.7	0.3	-12.9	-7.5	-16.9	-4.6	-7.0	-10.0	-18.0	-5.0	-6.7
Turkmenistan	..	..	..	..	..	..	..	..	-45.0	63.0	-53.0	17.0
Ukraine	-46.4	-25.7	-6.5	..	-30.8	-22.7	-6.7	..	-28.5	-22.0	-7.3	5.0
Uzbekistan	..	..	..	..	..	..	..	..	4.0	7.0	17.0	15.0

Source: National statistics; CIS Statistical Committee; direct communications from national statistical offices to UN/ECE secretariat.

Note: "Gross capital formation" and "gross fixed capital formation" are standard categories of the United Nations 1993 SNA (System of National Accounts) and the European Union's 1995 ESA (European System of Accounts). Gross capital formation includes gross fixed capital formation plus changes in inventories and acquisitions less disposal of valuables. "Investment outlays" (also called "capital investment" in transition economies) mainly refers to expenditure on construction and installation works, machinery and equipment. Gross fixed capital formation is usually estimated by adding the following components to "capital investment": net changes in productive livestock, computer software, art originals, the cost of mineral exploration and the value of major renovations and enlargements of buildings and machinery and equipment (which increase the productive capacity or extend the service life of existing fixed assets).

[a] January-September for Bulgaria, the Czech Republic, Hungary and Estonia; January-June for Slovakia and Latvia.

[b] January-September for the Czech Republic, Poland, Slovakia and Latvia; January-June for Romania.

these developments indicate the scale of the problems standing in the way of efforts to achieve a sustainable recovery of economic activity.

As has been repeatedly argued in previous issues of this *Survey*,[342] investment in the manufacturing sector is one of the key factors for success in the whole transformation process. Since most transition economies embarked on the process with over-large industrial sectors and underdeveloped services, it was widely expected that the latter would attract most of the new investment, but in reality things have worked out somewhat differently. The greatest progress in economic restructuring (and in economic transformation in general) has in fact been achieved in the countries where a process of de facto reindustrialization was initiated and where it has advanced most. This process of reindustrialization was based on a combination of large, new (predominantly greenfield) investments, a gradual upgrading of the product mix of manufacturing industry, and a rapid

expansion of exports of manufactured goods to new (mostly west European) markets; in the most successful reformers, this last development was accompanied by an increasing share of products of higher quality and technological content in total exports.

The most recent changes in the transition economies continue to provide evidence in support of this development. It is noteworthy, that both Hungary and Poland – two of the transition economies that have made the most progress in transforming their economies – have done so through such a process of reindustrialization. As already noted in section 3.3(i), since 1993 these two countries have had the highest rates of growth of manufacturing output among the transition economies. The revival of manufacturing, in turn, was based on large-scale new investment in the processing industries: while total investment was growing throughout this period,[343] in both countries there were substantial increases in the share of manufacturing in total

_____

[342] UN/ECE, *Economic Survey of Europe in 1996-1997*, pp. 105-106; *Economic Survey of Europe, 1998 No. 1*, pp. 101-103.

[343] With the exception of Hungary in 1995 when real investment declined (table 3.3.12).

less than 1 per cent in the last quarter of 1997; during 1998, prices rose by only 0.9 per cent for the year as a whole (equivalent to less than 0.1 per cent per month), the lowest rate among the east European and Baltic countries and which is well below the government's year-end target of 16 per cent (equivalent to a monthly rate of 1.2 per cent). However, these rather impressive improvements in macroeconomic stability have been achieved at the cost of a severe depression in aggregate demand and a collapse of output in 1997; there was only a slight recovery of GDP in 1998 while industrial production continued to fall sharply. Furthermore, the very small increase in the unemployment rate[350] suggests that most of the restructuring remains to be done and this will be particularly difficult to undertake without a strong recovery in aggregate demand and output. Therefore to sustain this recent achievement of near price stability in Bulgaria may prove to be costly in terms of overall macroeconomic performance and social cohesion.

Exchange rate targeting and weak demand have also been the crucial factors behind disinflation in 1998 in Albania, Bosnia and Herzegovina and, to a lesser extent, in The former Yugoslav Republic of Macedonia, where there was also a sizeable recovery in measured industrial productivity, due largely to output growth rather than employment contraction, as has been the case in recent years. In the second and third quarters consumer prices in The former Yugoslav Republic of Macedonia in fact fell, largely reflecting the combined effect of the waning of the effect of the July 1997 devaluation of the dinar and a significant increase in wage arrears which further depressed consumer demand.

In the Czech Republic and Slovakia the downward trend in inflation resumed in 1998 after reverses in 1997. In the Czech Republic, despite large increases in controlled prices and the imposition of VAT in January and again in July, consumer price inflation slowed significantly during 1998. The actual "net" inflation rate at the end of the year was 1.7 per cent compared with the central bank's target of 5.5-6.5 per cent.[351] Since the effective devaluation of the Czech koruna in May 1997, the central bank has pursued a very restrictive monetary policy, initially deliberate then, more recently, de facto,[352]

which has significantly dampened domestic demand, thus curbing both the growth of output and of prices. In recent years, in the absence of deep micro-level restructuring and with only slow rates of labour shedding, persistent wage growth in excess of productivity gains has been the major source of inflation in the Czech Republic. Since mid-1997 the factors which have helped to weaken inflationary pressures have come from both the demand and the supply sides. On the demand side, falling real incomes and growing uncertainties on the labour market[353] have led to reduced household expenditure.[354] Other components of domestic demand have also contracted mainly due to very high real lending rates, a problem emanating from the troubled and hesitant banking sector, and the tightening of fiscal policy after the exchange rate crisis of May 1997. On the supply side, cost pressures weakened considerably in 1998 thanks to weaker import prices, in national currency, for raw materials and food. Furthermore, in the first three quarters, there was also a relatively strong growth in labour productivity (5.4 per cent), which exceeded real product wage growth for the first time since the reforms started. However, in the last quarter, industrial production collapsed by 7 per cent and industrial labour cost pressures have started to increase.

In contrast, the expansive stance of fiscal policy continued in Slovakia in 1998, particularly before the September elections. However, as in recent years, the crucial factor behind the combination of relatively low inflation and a high growth rate in 1998 was again the employment of various price controls and a very slow pace of price deregulation. The dampening effect of an artificially strong Slovak koruna on import prices and a relatively tight monetary policy also helped the resumption of disinflation in 1998. However, after the elections, the central bank abolished the 7 per cent fluctuation band in October and allowed the Slovak koruna to float. The subsequent effective devaluation of the currency did not lead to a reversal of the downward trend in Slovak inflation in the closing months of 1998 thanks to a very tight monetary policy, which restrained both real wage growth,[355] and the removal of the import surcharge in October. The austerity package announced in January 1999, however, which includes a significant degree of price deregulation,[356] forecasts a year-on-year inflation rate in December of 10 per cent, up from 5.5 per cent in 1998. In January 1999, monthly inflation jumped to 3 per cent, a rate which may suggest that the government's inflation target is rather ambitious if further major increases in administered prices will be implemented as promised.

---

[350] In Bulgaria, the registered unemployment rate increased from 12.5 per cent at the end of 1996 to 13.7 per cent at the end of 1997 and then fell back to 12.2 per cent in December 1998. In Poland, for example, after seven years of high growth rates, the registered unemployment rate in December 1998 was still only 1.8 percentage points lower than in Bulgaria.

[351] In late 1997 the Czech central bank formulated a new "net" inflation indicator designed to screen out increases in regulated prices. In other words "net" inflation is that part of the price index which can be influenced by monetary policy, and since the beginning of 1998 this has been the measure used for inflation targeting. In July, due to the correction of energy prices and rents, the monthly rate of increase in the CPI was 1.9 per cent, but according to the net inflation index prices fell by 0.2 per cent. During the 12 months to December 1998, regulated prices increased by 20.4 per cent, accounting for 5.1 percentage points of the 6.8 per cent increase in consumer prices. Czech National Bank, *Monthly Bulletin*, No. 12 (Prague), 1998.

[352] On 15 January 1999, the Czech central bank cut interest rates for the eighth time since July 1998 in an attempt to stimulate growth and weaken the koruna.

---

[353] The Czech rate of unemployment, although still the lowest in eastern Europe, increased from 4 per cent in mid-1997 to 7.5 per cent in December 1998 (table 3.5.2).

[354] The volume of retail trade fell by 2 per cent in 1997 and almost 7 per cent in 1998; in 1996 there had been an increase of nearly 10 per cent (table 3.3.11).

[355] The new government lifted wage controls on 15 December 1998.

[356] Electricity prices were raised 30-35 per cent. Other items for which prices were increased include heating, water, sewage and fuels.

In Slovenia, where consumer prices continued to rise at around 9 per cent per annum during 1995-1997, the rate fell rapidly during 1998 and the *ex-ante* target was met, thanks to restrictive income policies, introduced in 1997, which somewhat checked wage increases in spite of strong union resistance.[357] Fiscal discipline was also maintained in 1998, while a strong tolar significantly alleviated external cost pressures and very high real interest rates kept domestic demand subdued.[358] However, as in Slovakia, the deregulation of controlled prices has been rather slow in Slovenia, although it has been precipitated recently in line with the preparations for the pre-accession negotiations with the EU. The introduction of VAT, because of its possible inflationary impact, has been delayed and will only be introduced in July 1999 under pressure from the EU to proceed with tax harmonization.[359] Also, complete price liberalization is due to be implemented by 2000, although the programme is still to be announced. These expected tax increases and the scale of price deregulation in Slovenia are bound to slow the disinflation process in 1999 unless there is a greater moderation in cost increases, and particularly in wage growth which is still increasing rather strongly in real terms in spite of the fact that Slovenian wage levels, in dollar terms, are still very high compared with other countries in the region.

Both in Hungary and Poland, consumer price inflation has been generally higher than in the other early reformers. Disinflation in both countries, however, was not interrupted in 1997 and it has continued in 1998, and even at a more rapid rate, particularly in Hungary where the year-on-year increase in December fell to 10.4 per cent, down from 18.5 per cent in 1997. In Poland the rate fell from 13.2 per cent in 1997 to 8.5 per cent in 1998, the first time it has been in single digits since the start of the reforms. In both countries, but particularly in Hungary, inflation for the year as a whole fell well below the initial targets set in early 1998 (14 per cent in Hungary and 9.5 per cent in Poland for the 12 months to December). In both countries prudent monetary policy and budgetary discipline combined with a carefully designed exchange rate policy and lower import prices all contributed to this favourable price performance. In contrast to most of the other transition economies, disinflation in Hungary and Poland has been achieved without either choking output or demand growth or by further worsening labour market conditions. However, the sustainability of lower inflation rates, supported by progress in reforms and strong growth,

may be more difficult in the near future given the recent weakening of industrial production, particularly in Poland, where economic growth has been one of the major factors behind significantly increased productivity and slower growth in unit labour costs despite slowing but still strong wage growth. In Hungary output growth has held up better than in Poland due to a stronger performance of both exports and domestic demand. In 1998 there was a sharp rise in household consumption, which had fallen precipitously in 1995-1996 and stagnated in 1997.[360] Real wage growth was moderate and real interest rates were high. This upswing in consumer demand can therefore be largely explained by rising consumer confidence emanating from the general improvement in the economic conditions of households, particularly employment.[361] However, a further weakening in exports and therefore of industrial production is likely to lead to a slowdown in measured productivity growth (assuming the usual lag in the employment response) and to an increase in unit labour costs in the short run. Furthermore, if the policy of a moderate depreciation of the real rate of the forint is maintained in 1999, in order to sustain export competitiveness, then the rate of disinflation might slow down unless commodity prices (mainly food and energy) remain weak, which is likely. The Hungarian budget assumes a 10-11 per cent annual average inflation rate in 1999, down from 14.2 per cent in 1998.

In Poland, the gradual slowdown in the economy gained considerable momentum during the last quarter of 1998[362] and the early months of 1999. Domestic demand is subdued, unemployment is rising, world commodity prices seem to remain weak. Furthermore fiscal policy is expected to be tighter and the Monetary Policy Council has adopted direct inflation targeting. Given all these factors, the central bank's inflation target of 8-8.5 per cent for 1999 seems to be easily in reach.

In the *Baltic countries* inflation rates continued to fall in 1998, for the fifth consecutive year. The average monthly rates in Latvia and particularly in Lithuania remain well below those in most of the east European countries and furthermore, in all three countries inflation in 1998 as a whole was well below the initial targets. The crucial factor in Latvia and in Lithuania has been a strong exchange rate which has further lowered both the material costs of production and the prices of imported consumer goods. In Latvia a prudent fiscal policy has also contributed to a subdued inflation rate despite relatively large increases in real wages and household spending.[363] Rapidly growing real wages, far in excess of productivity

---

[357] The Minimum Wage and Adjustment Act was activated in mid-1997 and will remain in force until mid-1999. Among other things, it shifts the indexation of wages from a quarterly to an annual basis, and reduces the compensation to 85 per cent of the annual change in the CPI. Furthermore, the increase in remuneration also takes into account productivity rises.

[358] Retail trade volume increased by 1.9 per cent (year-on-year) in January-December 1998 compared with 5.4 per cent in 1998 (table 3.3.11).

[359] Institute of Macroeconomic Analysis and Development, *Slovenian Economic Mirror*, No. 11, Vol. IV, December 1998.

---

[360] Retail trade fell by 1.4 per cent in 1997 and increased by 7.5 per cent in 1998 (table 3.3.11).

[361] Total employment increased by 2.4 per cent and by 5.1 per cent in industry in the first three quarters of 1998 (table 3.5.1).

[362] Industrial output fell by nearly 3 per cent in the fourth quarter of 1998.

[363] Retail trade volume in 1998 increased by more than 20 per cent (table 3.3.11).

CHART 3.4.1

Consumer prices of food, non-food goods and services in selected transition economies, 1995-1998
(Indices, January 1995=100)

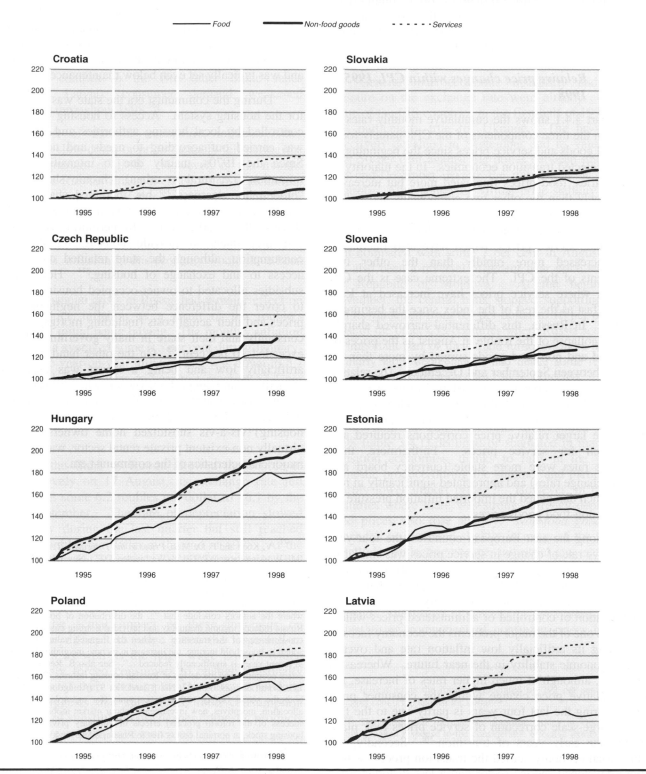

——— Food ———— Non-food goods - - - - - Services

(For source see end of chart.)

CHART 3.4.1 (concluded)

Consumer prices of food, non-food goods and services in selected transition economies, 1995-1998

(Indices, January 1995=100)

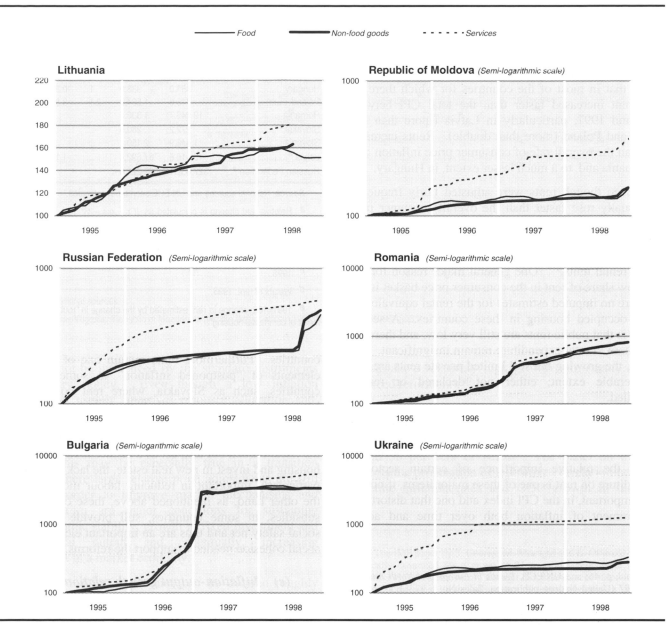

———— Food   ———— Non-food goods   - - - - - Services

Source: National statistics.

After 1989, various market oriented reforms were carried out to transform the housing sector, such as large-scale privatization of public housing (usually by transferring ownership to the occupants and often at nominal fees), the reduction and restructuring of subsidies, etc.[376] The share of owner-occupied housing in some countries increased sharply. In the mid-1990s it reached some 90 per cent or above in Albania, Bulgaria, Croatia, Hungary, Slovenia, Romania and Lithuania.[377] On the other hand, the public or semi-public rental sector

---

[376] For example in Russia, the law "On Privatization of the RSFSR Housing Stock" passed by the Supreme Soviet in June 1991 which mandated the privatization of state owned rental units to registered tenants. However, most tenants refused the offer in order not to be liable for full maintenance and communal service costs, which have in fact increased frequently after 1992. By the end of 1996 about 55 per cent of the total housing stock (including the rural areas) was in private ownership, up from 33 per cent in 1990. R. Struyk, A. Puzanov and L. Lee, "Monitoring Russia's experience with housing allowances", *Urban Studies*, Vol. 34, No.

11 (Abingdon), 1997, pp. 1798-1818. Since early 1997 the Russian government has increasingly focused on housing reform which calls for, *inter alia*, gradual reduction of housing subsidies (for which both owners and tenants of privatized apartments are eligible), "with the goal of 100 per cent cost recovery by 2003 ... cost recovery has increased from less than 2 per cent in 1993 to about 30 per cent by late 1997". A. Guzanova, "The Housing Market in the Russian Federation: Privatization and its Implications for Market Development", World Bank Working Paper Series, No. 1891 (Washington D.C), December 1997.

[377] For example in Hungary, housing subsidies as a percentage of GDP fell from 6 per cent in 1989 to less than 2 per cent in 1994, UN/ECE, *Human Settlement Trends ...*, op. cit, p. 40.

European and Baltic countries.[388] All of these countries have combined relatively uninterrupted rates of output growth and of disinflation during the 1993-1998 period. Furthermore, the higher the average inflation rate, the higher was the average growth in GDP, the main exceptions being Hungary and Slovakia. In Hungary this reflects the sharp slowdown in GDP in 1995-1996 following the launching of the stabilization programme in March 1995. Whereas in Slovakia it reflects mainly the suppressed inflation which has resulted from postponing the deregulation of administered prices.

The right-hand panel in chart 3.4.2 plots the same relationship in the CIS countries: it displays an obviously larger variance but nevertheless it tends to support a negative correlation between the average inflation rate and output growth. In these countries disinflation was generally much faster than in eastern Europe between 1996 and the first half of 1998, and output growth was significantly lower, even declining (except in a few countries where there was significant growth in a few primary commodities such as cotton, metal mining, oil, gas, etc.). This part of the chart, and bearing the above qualifications in mind, shows that although low inflation is generally better for growth, it is not enough to ensure it;[389] on the contrary, a too rapid rate of disinflation may distort the functioning of both the capital and product markets, thus hampering growth and, eventually, macroeconomic stability itself, an outcome which was clearly demonstrated during 1998 by the Russian crisis and its spillover effects in the region.

(iii) Producer prices in industry

The rate of increase in industrial producer prices (PPI) also fell in 1998 (table 3.4.3), in the main reflecting cheaper imported raw materials and intermediate products and a squeeze on profit margins due to intensified competition. Compared with 1997, not only did the deceleration in producer prices gain significant momentum in many of the east European economies in 1998 but it was also much more general (the only exception was Yugoslavia). In the Baltic countries producer prices actually fell markedly in Lithuania. In contrast, in many CIS economies producer price inflation picked up strongly in the second half of 1998 due to falls in productivity and exchange rate depreciation, and the 12-month rate in December was higher than a year earlier.

Producer price inflation, which is a rough indicator of production cost pressures in the economy, was higher

TABLE 3.4.3

Producer prices in industry [a] in the transition economies, 1997-1998
(Percentage change)

	Annual average		December over December	
	1997	1998	1997	1998
Bosnia and Herzegovina	3.2	3.6	9.2	9.0
Bulgaria	888.1	22.8	443.3	4.3
Croatia	3.7	-1.5	2.9	-2.1
Czech Republic	5.1	4.9	5.7	2.2
Hungary	20.9	11.4	19.4	7.1
Poland	12.2	7.2	11.3	4.9
Romania	150.5	33.6	143.8	20.0
Slovakia	4.6	3.3	4.6	1.5
Slovenia	6.1	6.0	6.8	3.6
The former Yugoslav Republic of Macedonia	3.8	4.6	8.5	-0.2
Yugoslavia	20.6	25.9	10.6	41.3
Estonia	8.8	3.8	7.7	-0.3
Latvia	4.3	2.0	3.8	-1.9
Lithuania	6.0	-3.8	0.9	-8.2
Armenia	21.7	4.7	19.2	3.4
Azerbaijan	11.4	-5.5	2.5	-8.4
Belarus	89.4	70.4	90.9	197.7
Georgia	..	2.0	..	3.7
Kazakhstan	15.6	1.0	11.7	-5.2
Kyrgyzstan	27.0	9.4	5.3	26.4
Republic of Moldova	14.9	9.7	13.6	13.6
Russian Federation	15.0	7.3	7.4	23.6
Tajikistan	107.2	28.4	133.2	5.9
Turkmenistan	260.6	-30.5	22.1	6.6
Ukraine	15.1	13.2	5.0	35.4
Uzbekistan	53.9	40.5	37.1	48.9

Source: UN/ECE secretariat estimates, based on national statistics.

[a] Industry = mining + manufacturing + utilities.

than the increase in consumer prices in most of the transition economies in 1997, but in 1998 the pattern was reversed as a result of upward pressure on consumer prices from new taxes and above all by the faster rate of deregulation of controlled prices of services.

(iv) Wages, unit labour costs and profit margins in industry

(a) 1998

Nominal wage growth in industry, which affects both consumer demand and the cost of production, decelerated in the first three quarters of 1998 throughout eastern Europe and the Baltic countries, except Croatia and Yugoslavia (table 3.4.4). However, the rate of increase remained high and in some economies largely outpaced producer price inflation.

Real product wage growth,[390] thus remained high or even accelerated, particularly in Croatia and the three Baltic countries. The main exceptions were the Czech

---

[388] The chart allows for differences in the time at which the reforms, and thus the disinflation process, started.

[389] This has been recently supported by various studies. For example, see L. Valdivieso, *Macroeconomic Developments in the Baltics, Russia and Other Countries of the Former Soviet Union, 1992-1997*, IMF Occasional Paper, No. 175 (Washington, D.C.), 1988. The author emphasizes that to ensure growth these countries must reduce the structural weaknesses (mainly current account and/or fiscal deficits) that underlie their macroeconomic imbalances.

---

[390] Change in average nominal gross wages in industry deflated by the producer price index. *Ceteris paribus,* real product wage growth measures the wage pressure on producer prices.

TABLE 3.4.4

Wages and unit labour costs in industry [a] in the transition economies, 1997-1998

(Annual average percentage change)

	Nominal wages [b]		Real product wages [c]		Labour productivity [d]		Unit labour costs [e]		Real unit labour costs [f]	
	1997	1998 [g]	1997	1998 [g]	1997	1998 [h]	1997	1998	1997	1998
Albania	..	..	..	..	-8.8	..	..	..	..	..
Bosnia and Herzegovina	49.2	34.3	44.6	29.7	11.3	7.7	34.0	24.8	29.9	20.4
Bulgaria	980.9	26.6	9.4	-2.9	-6.4	..	1 054.7	..	16.9	..
Croatia	10.4	13.1	6.5	14.4	11.2	9.2	-0.7	3.6	-4.2	4.8
Czech Republic	12.4	10.3	6.9	5.1	5.6	2.1	6.4	8.0	1.3	2.9
Hungary	21.6	17.0	0.6	4.4	9.3	7.6	11.3	8.7	-7.9	-3.0
Poland	20.0	14.9	7.0	7.2	11.2	5.8	7.9	8.7	-3.8	1.4
Romania	100.1	55.1	-20.1	16.1	-4.9	-12.2	110.3	76.6	-16.0	32.2
Slovakia	9.3	8.7	4.5	5.2	3.7	9.0	5.4	-0.3	0.7	-3.5
Slovenia	12.0	10.8	5.5	4.6	5.5	4.7	6.2	5.8	-	-0.2
The former Yugoslav Republic of Macedonia	2.3	..	-1.8	..	10.0	8.5	-6.9	..	-10.7	..
Yugoslavia	22.0	31.4	1.2	8.6	13.0	6.5	8.0	23.4	-10.5	2.0
Estonia	19.6	17.0	10.0	11.4	20.3	4.1	-0.6	12.4	-8.6	7.0
Latvia	18.7	18.0	13.8	15.7	10.0	1.0	7.9	16.8	3.5	14.6
Lithuania	23.8	13.1	16.8	17.6	3.3	9.7	19.8	3.0	13.0	7.1
Armenia	21.3	36.6	-0.3	27.1	12.4	1.4	7.9	34.7	-11.3	25.4
Azerbaijan	42.5	38.3	27.9	46.4	17.3	13.6	21.5	21.8	9.1	28.9
Belarus	87.5	104.5	-1.0	20.0	18.6	10.5	58.1	85.1	-16.5	8.6
Georgia	..	..	..	..	40.8	..	..	..	..	..
Kazakhstan	25.5	15.2	8.6	12.0	18.0	3.0	6.4	11.9	-7.9	8.8
Kyrgyzstan	27.1	25.0	-	14.3	60.2	5.6	-20.7	18.4	-37.6	8.2
Republic of Moldova	9.4	25.3	-4.8	14.3	2.4	-9.6	6.9	38.6	-7.0	26.5
Russian Federation	19.8	13.6	4.2	5.9	12.1	-3.9	6.9	18.2	-7.1	10.2
Tajikistan	76.3	79.5	-14.9	39.7	13.0	9.8	56.0	63.4	-24.7	27.2
Turkmenistan	214.5	47.7	-12.8	112.5	-38.1	..	408.0	..	40.9	..
Ukraine	16.5	7.6	1.2	-4.9	8.9	2.9	6.9	4.6	-7.1	-7.6
Uzbekistan	69.3	47.3	10.0	7.1	3.9	4.9	62.9	40.3	5.9	2.1

Source: UN/ECE secretariat estimates, based on national statistics and direct communications from national statistical offices.

[a] Industry = mining + manufacturing + utilities.

[b] Average gross wages in industry except in Bosnia and Herzegovina and The former Yugoslav Republic of Macedonia: net wages in industry; in Bulgaria. Estonia and all the CIS economies: gross wages in total economy; in Yugoslavia: net wages in total economy.

[c] Nominal wages deflated by producer price index.

[d] Gross industrial output deflated by industrial employment.

[e] Nominal wages deflated by productivity.

[f] Real product wages deflated by productivity.

[g] January-September 1998 over January-September 1997, except in Poland, Romania, Slovakia, Lithuania, Belarus, Kyrgyzstan and the Russian Federation.

[h] Estimated on the basis of January-December output data and January-September employment data.

Republic and Slovenia where the downward trend that started in 1997 accelerated, and Bulgaria where they actually fell by nearly 3 per cent. In the Czech Republic the deceleration both in nominal and real wage growth in 1998 was a consequence of tighter monetary policy and the wage freeze in the government sector. In Slovenia, restrictive income policies, introduced in 1997, kept nominal and particularly real wage growth subdued.

Real product wage growth in 1998, as in 1997, remained in double digits in all three Baltic economies and remains a major domestic source of inflationary pressure in these economies. It is not only damaging their export competitiveness during a period of already faltering demand, but also their enterprise profitability,

which in the medium term can lead to a sharply lower growth of investment and thus hinder restructuring.

In most of the CIS countries, compared to the majority of east European and Baltic economies, nominal wage growth in 1998 remained considerably higher, or even accelerated, compared with 1997 (except in Kazakhstan, the Russian Federation and Ukraine). Furthermore, given the significant fall in producer price inflation, real product wages, which had still been declining in 1997 in many of these countries, generally rose sharply; the exceptions are Ukraine where they actually fell and Russia and Uzbekistan where the rate remained in single digits. However, given the huge wage arrears in most of the CIS economies, these data should

BOX 3.5.1

Goskomstat revision of Russian unemployment

Further revisions to the series for Russian monthly unemployment – known as "unemployment according to ILO methodology" – were issued by the Russian State Statistical Committee (Goskomstat) in January 1999.[1] The need for a revision to the series arose from the initial results of Goskomstat's October 1998 labour force survey. (The previous survey had been conducted in October 1997.) The table below shows the new and old Goskomstat series for the entire period covered by the revision, November 1997 to December 1998. The magnitude of the change is shown by the revision for October 1998, from 11.6 per cent of the labour force to 12.3 per cent. The movement of the two series was rather similar until May but, as the chart clearly illustrates, they then diverge strikingly, particularly after the August crisis.

Russian unemployment: old and revised data for 1997-1998
(Per cent of labour force)

	January	February	March	April	May	June	July	August	September	October	November	December
1997												
Old data										11.1	11.2	11.3
Revised data										11.1	11.2	11.2
1998												
Old data	11.3	11.4	11.4	11.6	11.5	11.5	11.5	11.5	11.5	11.6	11.7	11.8
Revised data	11.4	11.6	11.7	11.7	11.5	11.3	11.3	11.6	11.9	12.3	12.3	12.4

Russian unemployment, 1997-1998
(Per cent of labour force)

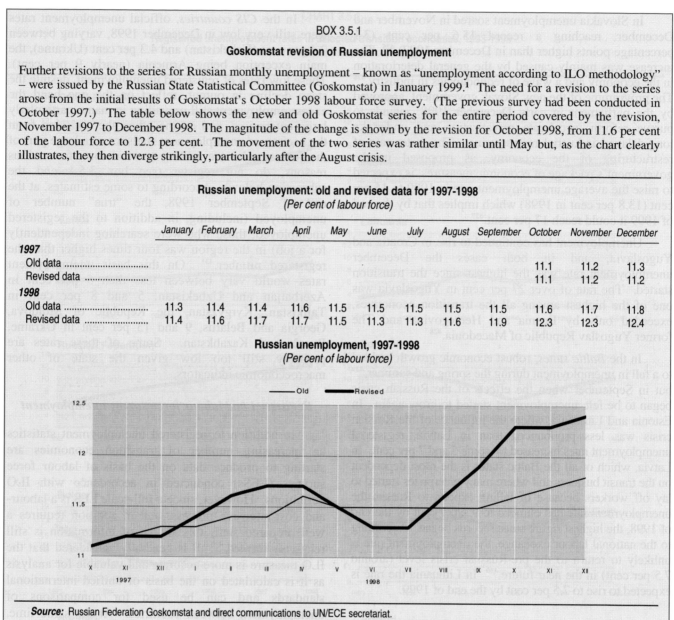

Source: Russian Federation Goskomstat and direct communications to UN/ECE secretariat.

Although the revision raises the unemployment rate the rise in unemployment was unexpectedly small given the financial turmoil in August 1998 and the subsequent sharp economic downturn.[2] The unemployment rate stood at 12.4 per cent in December 1998, only 1.2 percentage points higher than a year earlier, and 1.1 percentage points over the pre-crisis month of July 1998 (the old series suggested increases of only 0.5 and 0.3 percentage points, respectively). One reason for this mild reaction is the traditional and continuing reluctance of managers and local authorities to encourage large-scale redundancies, a reluctance which leads to increased hidden unemployment, widespread unpaid administrative leave and part-time employment, and a high level of wage arrears. However, another reason is the marked decline in real wages as a result of the post-August inflation and the absence of any significant degree of wage indexation.[3] Under these conditions it is easier for management to pay low wages (or in many cases not to pay them at all) than to undertake the politically and socially unpopular move of releasing workers. The indexation of public sector salaries, planned for 1 April 1999, may change this situation.

When commenting on the Russian monthly "ILO" unemployment data it should be borne in mind that they are always estimates of what the situation would have been if a survey had been conducted at the relevant time. In 1999, Goskomstat plans to start conducting quarterly labour force surveys. The first was already conducted at the end of February and the results, which are expected in May, should better reflect the real situation on the Russian labour market.

[1] Direct communication to UN/ECE secretariat. For a more detailed discussion of the content and some of the peculiarities of the Russian monthly "ILO" series see UN/ECE, *Economic Survey of Europe, 1998 No. 3*, pp. 68-69. That discussion refers to the revisions published by Goskomstat in June 1998.

[2] Industrial output declined by nearly 15 per cent in September and by some 11, 9 and 7 per cent in October, November and December respectively; GDP fell by 4.6 per cent in 1998.

[3] In the 12 months to December 1998, real wages declined by some 40 per cent in rouble terms and by more than 60 per cent in dollar terms.

In the second quarter of 1998, in the majority of east European countries for which both sets of data are available, the rates of unemployment based on registration tended to give similar results to those based on LFS data (chart 3.5.2). Surprisingly, in Croatia, Romania and Slovenia registered unemployment rates were substantially higher than those obtained from the labour force surveys. In contrast, in all the Baltic states, Ukraine and particularly in Russia the registration data are much lower than the survey-based unemployment rates. The comparison in individual countries becomes more evident when the relationship between the two measures is expressed in relative terms (chart 3.5.3). In Croatia, Romania and Slovenia registered unemployment rates exceeded those of the LFSs by some 60 to 90 per cent, while in the other countries of eastern Europe they tend to be rather close to the LFS figures (particularly in Bulgaria, the Czech Republic and Poland). In all the Baltic states, a very similar pattern prevails: the registered unemployment rates are less than half the rates derived from the LFSs. In Ukraine the proportion is about 36 per cent; in Russia, the registered measure is virtually useless as it is only just above 20 per cent of the rate estimated on the basis of the ILO definition. These large differences between the two measures in the Baltic states, Ukraine and Russia on the one hand (the registered unemployment rates are considerably lower) and Croatia, Romania and Slovenia on the other (where they are substantially higher) can probably only be explained by the specific characteristics of the statistics prevailing in the individual countries.[433]

As was already mentioned, LFS unemployment rates, being calculated on the basis of unified international standards, can provide a good basis for intercountry comparisons. The picture changes radically when, instead of registered unemployment, LFS data are used for analysis. LFS unemployment rates in the countries under review varied in the second quarter of 1998, between some 6 and 8 per cent of the labour force in Romania, the Czech Republic, Slovenia and Hungary; some 10 and 12 per cent in Estonia, Poland, Croatia, Bulgaria, Ukraine, Russia and Slovakia; and they exceeded 14 per cent in Latvia and Lithuania whereas, according to the registration data, the Baltic states, Ukraine and Russia belong to the group of countries with a low unemployment rate.

Structure of unemployment

In the third quarter of 1998, *the share of women in total unemployment* remained very high in the Czech Republic and Poland, exceeding 55 per cent, whereas it was lower in Hungary (less than 40 per cent) (chart

3.5.4). In all other countries the female share fell within the range of 44 to 47 per cent. The proportion of women among the unemployed has tended to fall in all the countries under review.[434]

A worrying trend is the very high proportion of *youth unemployment* in the total. The available data suggest that young persons under 25 years old, given their share in the total labour force, are disproportionately represented among the unemployed. In the third quarter of 1998, young people accounted for more than 40 per cent of total unemployment in Romania, and one third or more in the Czech Republic, Slovakia and Slovenia, and for around one fourth in the other countries in chart 3.5.4. Moreover, youth unemployment is continuing to increase in most countries and has become one of the most pressing social problems in all the transition economies.

In spite of a relatively short history of open unemployment, most of the transition economies are facing the increasingly serious problem of *long-term unemployment*. In the third quarter of 1998, the share of the long-term unemployed in total unemployment varied between some 31 and 37 per cent in the Czech Republic and Poland, but it was more than 40 per cent everywhere else, and close to 60 per cent in Bulgaria and Slovenia (chart 3.5.4). A striking feature of the development of long-term unemployment is that between the third quarters of 1996 and 1998, there had been a notable decline in its share of the total in all the east European countries except Slovenia, where it increased from 52 to nearly 57 per cent. In contrast, in the Baltic states and Russia the share of long-term unemployed increased considerably in a very short period, in Latvia and Lithuania reaching a very high 55 per cent, a level exceeded only by Bulgaria and Slovenia.

Long-term unemployment is not only very painful for individuals and a potential source of social instability, but it also creates serious obstacles for the market-clearing mechanism. The experience of west European countries since the 1980s demonstrates that reducing unemployment during a recovery is much more difficult when there is a high incidence of long-term unemployment. It seems that it is also true for the transition economies. The case of Slovenia is illustrative: although a relatively strong recovery in output was already in its sixth year and employment began to increase, a very high and persistent unemployment rate (above 14.5 per cent) prevailed through 1997-1998.

---

[433] For a more detailed discussion see UN/ECE, *Economic Survey of Europe in 1995-1996*, p. 89.

[434] In the same period of 1996, it was only in Hungary and Slovenia that the female share was less than 50 per cent. See UN/ECE, *Economic Survey of Europe in 1996-1997*, p. 118. For a more detailed discussion of women's position in labour markets in the transition economies see the next subsection.

CHART 3.5.2

Registered and labour force survey unemployment rates in selected transition economies, 1998-QII
(Per cent of labour force)

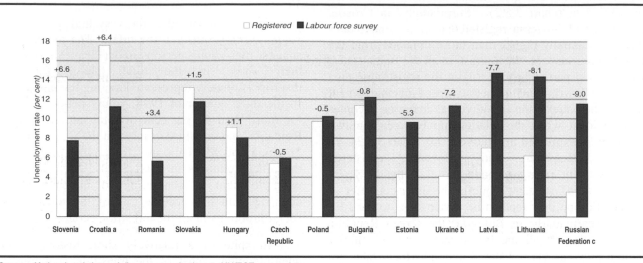

Source: National statistics and direct communications to UN/ECE secretariat.

Note: Countries are ranked by the absolute deviation between the two measures.

a Average for the first half of the year.

b November 1998.

c Based on Russian Federation Goskomstat estimates according to the ILO definition.

CHART 3.5.3

Relationship between registered and survey-based unemployment rates in selected transition economies, 1998-QII
(Labour force survey unemployment rate =100)

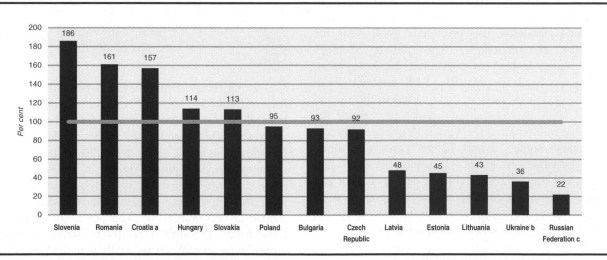

Source: National statistics and direct communications to UN/ECE secretariat.

Note: Countries are ranked by the relative deviation between the two measures.

a Average for the first half of the year.

b November 1998.

c Based on Russian Federation Goskomstat estimates according to the ILO definition.

CHART 3.5.4

Unemployment rate, share of women, youth and long-term unemployed in total unemployment in selected transition economies, 1998-QIII
(Percentages)

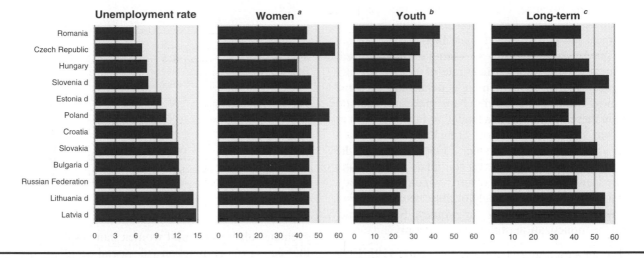

Source: National statistics and direct communications from national statistical offices to UN/ECE secretariat.

Note: Data refer to labour force survey results.

a Share of women in total unemployment.

b Share of persons less than 25 years old in total unemployment.

c Share of persons who have been unemployed for more than 12 months in total unemployment.

d Second quarter.

(ii) Effects of transition on the labour force and employment from a gender perspective, 1985-1997

(a) Introduction

One of the major transformation shocks in the former centrally planned economies at the start of their reform process was the severe decline in employment and the emergence of open unemployment, a phenomenon which was generally unknown in the communist era. Unemployment benefits, which were initially rather generous, have been cut gradually in real terms (in the CIS falling well below the minimum subsistence levels) and entitlement has been subject to tighter conditions. Large numbers of the unemployed have thus stopped registering and some have also stopped looking for work (the discouraged worker effect). Both men and women were affected by the closure of plants, restructuring and the overall fiscal squeeze. However, women were disproportionately affected by the transition from a centrally planned to a market economy; not only did a large number of them lose their jobs and their wages, just as men did, but those who kept their jobs lost their social benefits and services which, in addition to the loss of a large part of their money wages in real terms, rendered their employment uneconomical. Therefore they left their jobs and withdrew from the labour force altogether, changing their role in society, from second bread winner to that of full-time mother or to take care of ailing parents.

Policies towards women's employment in the centrally planned economies was more progressive than in the west in the sense that it facilitated the combination of women's productive and reproductive roles, the "double burden". By the 1980s, women accounted for nearly half of the labour force in these economies and also, in the absence of open unemployment, of employment. Measures such as free childcare facilities, extended maternity and sick child leave, etc., were part of the labour codes and were provided by the enterprises which, in turn, were supported by generous subsidies from the government. With the squeeze on government budgets and the removal of subsidies, these social welfare measures in favour of the female labour force were dramatically reduced de facto, but to a large extent remained on the statute books in most of the transition economies. Women therefore not only lost most of their privileges, in fact, as workers, but they were also considered overpriced in terms of the remaining welfare codes even if these were usually ignored.[435]

The various labour market indicators discussed below demonstrate that in fact women are disproportionately affected in general by the transition from a centrally planned to a market economy. The main findings of the analysis show that the transition process has involved large job losses both for men and women.

---

[435] V. Einhorn, "Gender issues in transition: the east and central European experience", *The European Journal of Development Research*, Vol. 6(4), December 1994.

However female employment fell more than male employment due to the large cuts in public sector service jobs which were (and still are) predominantly held by women. Furthermore, as mentioned above, there were women who could have kept their jobs but preferred to give them up because they were no longer paid an economic wage. This last reason for declining female employment led to a smaller female labour force but not to a much larger pool of female unemployed. Consequently, the unemployment rate of women was not significantly higher than men in general, and in some economies it was even lower. Nevertheless, structural change in these economies has tended to favour growth in a number of service sector branches where again women's occupations are rising. Furthermore, if the pattern in the western economies is a guide to the future, then the new social infrastructure, which has already started to be constructed in many of these economies, will create new job opportunities for women, for example, through the monetization of the "care economy".

The data used in this note for the period 1992-1997 are mostly taken from the national labour force surveys conducted in seven east European, three Baltic countries and Russia, according to the ILO's methodology.

(b) Labour force

Growth, 1985-1997

The female labour force shrank in all eight countries, for which there are data, between 1985 and 1997 (table 3.5.3). It declined even in those countries where the male labour force remained fairly stable (Poland, Estonia, Latvia) or even increased (Czech Republic, Lithuania, Russia). In Hungary, the female labour force in 1997 was more than a third smaller than in 1985; however, the male labour force also fell strongly, by more than one fifth. In Estonia and Latvia female labour force fell by nearly one fourth between 1985 and 1997. In Estonia, much of this decline can be explained by demographic changes,[436] but in Latvia it was mainly due to a fall in activity rates.

Activity rates and labour force population ratios

Female activity rates[437] were lower than in 1985 in all the countries for which there are data (table 3.5.4). The large fall in some countries is partly due to the early retirement schemes promoted at the onset of the reforms (for example, in the Czech Republic). These schemes also affected the male rates, but the fiscal squeeze and

TABLE 3.5.3

Growth rates of labour force and employment in selected transition economies, by sex, 1985-1997

(Cumulative, percentages)

	Labour force		Employment	
	Male	*Female*	*Male*	*Female*
Czech Republic	2.9	-5.5	-1.2	-11.8
Hungary	-22.5	-35.1	-29.8	-40.1
Poland	0.4	-1.6	-8.3	-13.4
Slovenia	-9.2	-9.7	-15.6	-16.2
Estonia	0.5	-23.5	-10.8	-30.9
Latvia	-0.9	-22.5	-16.4	-33.3
Lithuania	7.8	-11.2	-7.4	-23.7
Russian Federation	5.6	-11.1	-6.4	-20.6

Source: UN/ECE secretariat estimates, based on national labour force surveys, statistical yearbooks and direct communications from national statistical offices.

eventual subsidy cuts hurt women more as these included the de facto elimination of social entitlements and services, cuts which remained in place even after growth resumed. The female activity rates fell significantly (by about one fifth) in Hungary, Slovenia and Latvia. However, in Hungary and Slovenia male rates also fell by as much, while in Latvia they remained stable. In Estonia and Lithuania male activity rates were even higher in 1997 than in 1985 while the female rates, which were nearly as high as male rates in 1985, fell by 10 percentage points in both countries during 1985-1997. Nevertheless, the Baltic countries had the highest female activity rates of all the 11 transition economies in 1997. Female activity rates in 1997 were also high in Romania, largely because of the high share of agriculture in the economy where women farmers, although decreasing, remain in a slight majority (see below). The lowest female rate in 1985 was in Poland (some 55 per cent), but the smallest decline was also in Poland, probably because of the relatively earlier recovery in economic growth which started in 1992 and accelerated thereafter. However, the female activity rate of 50 per cent in 1997 in Poland was again relatively low compared with most of the other transition economies; the exceptions were Hungary and Bulgaria where the rates fell to just below 43 per cent and 47 per cent, respectively.

As activity rates can vary among countries because of differences in the definition of working age, it is sometimes more appropriate to use labour force population ratios which can be defined as crude activity rates. These crude rates also show that female labour force participation declined everywhere and faster than male rates.

Share of women in the labour force

In 1985, women were a majority of the labour force in the Baltic countries and Russia (table 3.5.5). In the four east European countries, for which there are data, the female share was relatively smaller but still very high by western standards, varying between 46 and 48 per cent.

---

[436] In Estonia, between 1985 and 1997, the female population of working age declined by 16 per cent against 7 per cent for males.

[437] Activity rates show the share of the working-age population participating in the labour force (i.e. employed plus unemployed). These activity rates are lower than those reported by the countries as the upper age limit differs among countries, over time, and in some also between males and females. In order to have more comparable rates, the working age population is taken here as 15 years of age and over for both sexes throughout the period 1985-1997.

TABLE 3.5.4

Gender specific labour market indicators in selected transition economies, 1985 and 1997

(Percentages)

	Activity rates [a]		Unemployment rates		Labour force-population ratio		Employment-population ratio	
	1985	*1997*	*1985*	*1997*	*1985*	*1997*	*1985*	*1997*
Bulgaria								
Male	..	56.8	–	14.7	..	46.8	..	40.0
Female	..	46.9	–	15.3	..	39.4	..	33.4
Czech Republic								
Male	75.1	71.3	–	4.0	56.5	58.2	56.5	55.9
Female	59.3	52.1	–	6.7	46.0	43.5	46.0	40.6
Hungary								
Male	73.9	60.4	–	9.5	57.1	46.4	57.1	42.0
Female	61.3	42.8	–	7.8	48.9	32.7	48.9	30.2
Poland								
Male	69.5	65.5	–	8.7	50.9	49.3	50.9	45.0
Female	54.9	50.0	–	12.0	41.5	39.2	41.5	34.5
Romania								
Male	..	72.3	–	5.7	..	57.7	..	54.4
Female	..	57.5	–	6.4	..	46.8	..	43.9
Slovakia								
Male	..	66.2	–	10.8	..	51.6	..	46.0
Female	..	51.0	–	12.5	..	40.8	..	35.7
Slovenia								
Male	82.3	65.7	–	7.0	62.5	53.5	62.5	49.8
Female	65.2	53.0	–	7.2	51.3	44.0	51.3	40.9
Estonia								
Male	68.4	71.5	–	11.2	51.4	54.1	51.4	48.1
Female	67.7	57.7	–	9.6	53.9	43.4	53.9	39.2
Latvia								
Male	69.4	69.8	–	14.1	53.2	54.5	53.2	46.0
Female	68.4	54.3	–	14.0	55.2	44.5	55.2	38.2
Lithuania								
Male	70.1	72.4	–	14.1	52.6	54.8	52.6	47.1
Female	65.1	55.6	–	14.0	51.2	44.0	51.2	37.8
Russian Federation								
Male	72.6	70.9	–	11.4	55.0	55.3	55.0	50.0
Female	63.5	53.6	–	10.7	50.0	43.7	50.0	39.8

Source: UN/ECE secretariat estimates, based on national labour force surveys, statistical yearbooks and direct communications from national statistical offices.

Note: Working age population used to calculate activity rates is: 15 and over except for Hungary and Estonia: 15-74.

[a] Labour force ÷ working age population.

However, as female activity rates fell faster than male rates during 1985-1997, even when the male rates remained stable or increased, the female share of the labour force declined rapidly, particularly in the Baltics and Russia although they still remained high in 1997, between 47-49 per cent. The lowest proportions of females in the labour force in 1997 were in Hungary (43.5 per cent, down from some 48 per cent in 1985) and the Czech Republic (some 44 per cent).

(c) *Employment*

Growth, 1985-1997

One of the major consequences of the reforms and the accompanying structural adjustments was the general decline in employment during the 1990s, even in those economies where the recovery in output occurred relatively quickly. Both male and female employment fell, but, the decline in female employment was considerably sharper because of the fiscal squeeze and loss of jobs in the public sector.

In Hungary, female employment fell by 40 per cent, while for males by 30 per cent, the largest rates of decline in all eight countries. Female employment fell more than 30 per cent in both Estonia and Latvia, considerably more than the fall in male employment. Even the smallest cut in female employment, in the Czech Republic (less than 12 per cent), was nearly 10 times larger than that for male employment. Only in Slovenia did male and female employment shrink at the same rate between 1985 and 1987.

Female employment not only fell more than male employment, but also more than the decline in the female labour force, a fact which is reflected in soaring female (open) unemployment, much of it remaining unemployed for more than one year.

TABLE 3.5.5

Share of women in labour market indicators in selected transition economies, 1985 and 1997

(Percentages)

	Labour force		Employment		Unemployment	Long-term unemployment [a]
	1985	1997	1985	1997	1997	1997
Bulgaria	..	46.8	..	46.7	47.8	47.6
Czech Republic	46.2	44.1	46.2	43.4	57.0	53.9
Hungary	47.9	43.5	47.9	44.0	38.6	35.8
Poland	46.2	45.7	46.2	44.7	53.8	59.7
Romania	..	45.8	..	45.7	48.4	52.4
Slovakia	..	45.4	..	45.0	49.0	50.6
Slovenia	46.5	46.4	46.5	46.3	47.0	43.2
Estonia	54.7	47.9	54.7	48.4	44.1	..
Latvia	54.8	48.6	54.8	49.1	46.0	48.8
Lithuania	52.2	47.3	52.2	47.4	47.1	..
Russian Federation	51.5	47.3	51.5	47.4	45.8	48.9

Source: UN/ECE secretariat estimates, based on national labour force surveys, statistical yearbooks and direct communications from national statistical offices.

[a] Unemployed for more than one year.

Employment-population ratio

The employment-population ratio is a better basis for comparison among countries of the changes in the employment opportunities as it is neither affected by different definitions of working age population (as in the case of conventional activity rates) nor by differences in the coverage of the unemployed (as in the case of the labour force). It also measures (inversely) the dependency rate (sex-specific in this case) in an economy. The only bias which may arise is from the shadow (grey) economy which is unfortunate because this is important in these countries and its size probably varies greatly not only between countries but also by gender. However, this is a bias which is embodied, directly or indirectly, in all the labour market indicators.

The employment-population ratio fell in all eight countries for both men and women between 1985 and 1997, although, the female ratio fell much more. In the Czech Republic the male ratio fell less than 1 percentage point while the female ratio fell more than 5 percentage points. Nevertheless, the largest fall was again in Hungary, from 49 per cent in 1985 to 30 per cent in 1997, the lowest rate in the region; in other words, in 1985, one out of two Hungarian women (regardless of age) was employed; in 1997 this ratio was less than one out of three. The employment-population ratio in 1997 was also very low in Bulgaria, Slovakia and Poland but the latter country had the lowest ratio among the eight countries already in 1985 (41.5 per cent). In Estonia and Latvia, the ratio fell considerably, from some 55 per cent in 1985 in both – higher than for men – to less than 40 per cent in 1997 – nearly 10 percentage points lower than men. In 1997 the ratio remained above 40 per cent in the Czech Republic, Romania and Slovenia.

Share of women in employment

Not only did the proportion of women in the labour force fall everywhere between 1985 and 1997, but so did their share in employment (except in Slovenia where it remained stable). It nevertheless remained high in the Baltics and Russia (between 47.5-49 per cent), where women were in a majority in 1985. In the Czech Republic, Hungary and Poland it fell below 45 per cent. However these rates are still high by western standards.

The massive decline in employment, both for men and women, during the transition process has been accompanied by considerable changes in the industrial distribution of employment. The share of goods producing sectors (i.e. agriculture, industry and construction) in total employment has declined while the share of services has increased in general. This structural change in employment affected both men and women but was more pronounced for women. Chart 3.5.5 shows the rate of change in employment in a given industry[438] relative to the rate of change in total employment,[439] where employment, both in industry and total economy, is gender specific. Both male and female agricultural employment declined faster than total employment in the majority of countries, but for women, the relative fall was generally much greater than for men. There was a similar development in industry except in Poland, where there was an increased share of women workers in certain labour intensive branches such as textiles, and utilities.

In contrast, employment growth in the service sector in all 10 economies was greater than in the rest of the economy, both for men and women, although relatively better for men, in general. The sectors where the shares of total female employment generally fell were transport and communications, but they did significantly better in financial, real estate and business services, as well as public administration. However in many countries the shares of total male employment in these branches increased even more than those for women (the main exceptions being the Czech Republic, Poland and Slovenia).

These structural changes in male and female employment rates are, of course, reflected in the gender composition of employment in each sector (table 3.5.6). While the female share in agriculture, industry and construction generally has fallen during the transition (except in agriculture in Slovenia, Estonia and Latvia and industry in Poland), it increased in many service sectors where females were already in a large majority in the early 1990s.

However, in the service sector as a whole the female share of total employment has fallen, albeit by much less than in the goods producing sectors. Furthermore, the women's share in the majority of services was still larger than that of men in 1997, varying between some 53 per cent in Hungary and 63 per cent in Lithuania.

---

[438] NACE classification as given in the national labour force surveys.

[439] Here the size of the sector in the initial period is an important factor while interpreting the relative growth rates. Furthermore, the initial period differs among countries which is dictated by data availability. This does not affect cross sectoral analysis but should be borne in mind when the comparison is done across countries.

CHART 3.5.5

Relative total and gender specific employment growth index [a] by sectors in selected transition countries, 1992-1997
(Percentages)

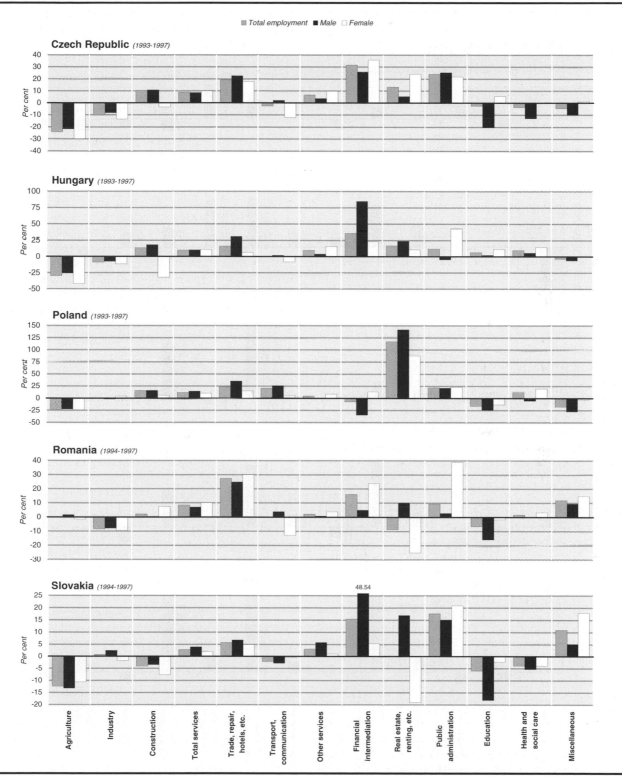

(For source and notes see end of chart.)

CHART 3.5.5 (concluded)

Relative total and gender specific employment growth index [a] **by sectors in selected transition countries, 1992-1997**
(Percentages)

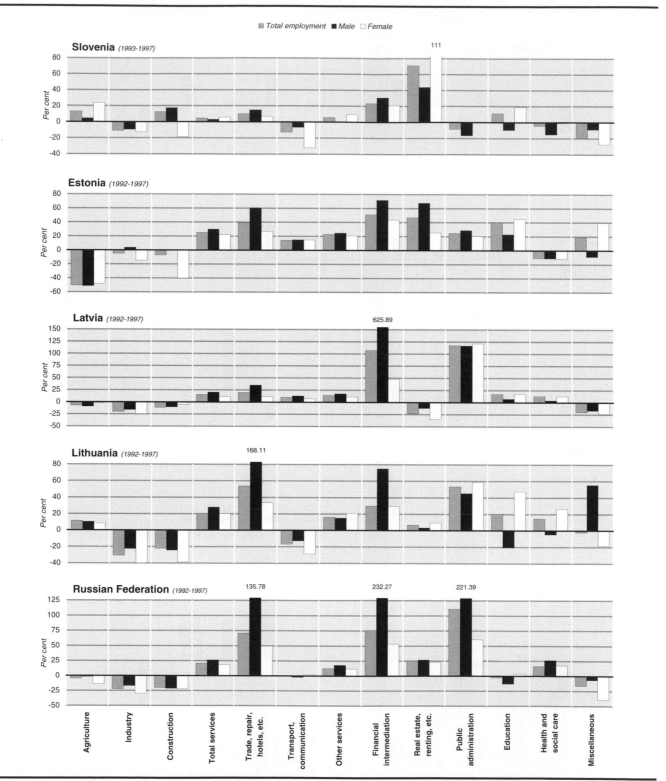

Source: UN/ECE secretariat estimates, based on national labour force surveys and direct communications from national statistical offices.

a The zero-line is the cumulative per cent change in total employment (i.e. total, total male, total female). Each sector's relative employment change is calculated as the following: [(Ij ÷ It)-1] * 100; where I is the employment indice in 1997 with 1992=100, j is the sector and t, the total (i.e. total, total male, total female).

TABLE 3.5.6

Share of women in total employment by industry in selected transition economies, 1992-1997

(Per cent)

	Czech Republic		Hungary		Poland		Romania		Slovakia	
	1993	1997	1992	1996	1993	1997	1994	1997	1994	1997
Total	100.0	100.0	100.0	100.0	100.0	100.0	100.0	100.0	100.0	100.0
Female	44.1	43.4	45.7	44.0	45.2	44.7	46.2	45.7	44.3	45.0
Agriculture	35.7	32.7	31.2	24.8	45.6	44.5	52.1	50.8	31.1	31.3
Industry	39.5	37.5	41.3	38.6	33.9	34.8	40.6	39.6	39.0	38.2
Mining and quarrying	16.0	16.9	13.7	12.1	13.1	8.6	14.8	15.5	17.2	15.8
Manufacturing	42.1	39.8	43.9	40.8	37.0	39.3	44.3	43.3	42.0	41.5
Electricity, gas, etc.	26.7	23.6	29.1	25.9	20.8	22.3	23.3	23.8	19.8	18.7
Construction	10.3	8.9	15.0	8.6	10.4	9.4	13.5	14.1	10.1	8.6
Total services	54.8	54.4	54.2	52.6	56.4	55.0	48.6	48.7	56.5	57.3
Trade, repair, hotels, etc.	56.9	55.2	58.2	51.3	57.9	53.5	55.6	56.1	57.9	58.9
Trade and repair	57.0	55.1	58.2	51.4	56.9	52.2	53.9	54.5	56.2	57.7
Hotels and restaurants	56.7	55.8	57.9	50.7	70.4	67.7	63.5	64.7	64.7	64.0
Transport, communication	35.0	31.1	29.8	26.3	28.6	24.9	26.2	22.6	30.4	30.6
Other services	59.4	60.1	59.0	59.9	61.2	62.7	52.4	52.6	62.6	63.1
Financial intermediation	66.8	67.8	76.0	66.3	58.2	70.3	61.9	65.3	77.0	72.5
Real estate, renting, etc.	43.7	47.1	51.2	46.8	45.5	38.9	53.4	43.3	46.2	41.8
Public administration	38.8	37.5	34.7	42.7	42.0	42.0	16.7	21.0	44.0	46.9
Education	72.1	76.9	75.8	76.1	73.8	76.1	69.0	71.8	75.1	79.5
Health and social care	79.3	81.1	75.1	75.3	79.5	82.8	76.9	77.1	80.6	79.9
Miscellaneous	51.6	53.8	49.0	48.8	40.1	46.7	47.6	48.3	44.7	48.3
Private sector	..	..	..	..	43.6	41.7	54.4	50.7	24.0	26.6

	Slovenia		Estonia		Latvia		Lithuania		Russian Federation	
	1993	1997	1992	1996	1992	1997	1992	1997	1992	1997
Total	100.0	100.0	100.0	100.0	100.0	100.0	100.0	100.0	100.0	100.0
Female	46.7	46.3	47.2	48.4	47.8	49.1	52.9	49.2	49.2	47.4
Agriculture	44.4	48.1	36.6	37.5	34.2	37.3	41.2	37.2	36.0	31.5
Industry	40.7	39.4	45.7	40.9	46.4	45.1	51.7	41.8	45.1	39.3
Mining and quarrying	..	14.3	20.5	12.7	38.5	26.1	35.0	30.3	..	..
Manufacturing	42.2	41.0	48.8	43.6	47.2	47.6	53.2	45.0	..	..
Electricity, gas, etc.	25.0	15.4	31.8	29.6	31.6	23.5	30.2	20.0	..	..
Construction	15.2	10.9	16.5	12.9	12.4	13.7	15.0	11.0	25.0	23.5
Total services	55.8	56.0	59.2	57.5	59.0	58.2	67.3	62.5	61.9	58.7
Trade, repair, hotels, etc.	58.1	55.9	63.4	59.9	66.6	63.4	82.1	66.3	73.0	61.5
Trade and repair	56.3	52.3	61.2	57.3	65.2	61.9	81.7	65.8	..	..
Hotels and restaurants	64.3	65.8	72.7	73.9	70.8	74.6	85.5	71.6	..	..
Transport, communication	25.5	19.6	27.9	33.4	33.5	33.5	39.3	31.3	32.5	31.9
Other services	62.6	64.3	67.3	63.7	62.5	62.4	68.5	66.4	66.8	64.0
Financial intermediation	68.8	66.7	76.3	68.2	90.1	66.2	86.1	79.8	85.8	72.2
Real estate, renting, etc.	40.9	50.0	48.6	43.8	49.3	43.3	49.1	46.8	48.0	45.5
Public administration	48.6	52.8	48.1	40.1	39.8	41.5	37.1	35.8	68.3	50.0
Education	73.9	78.5	74.0	79.0	77.8	80.1	67.2	76.6	71.9	74.0
Health and social care	78.9	81.1	86.5	82.1	81.7	83.6	82.4	84.2	83.0	80.9
Miscellaneous	56.1	50.0	61.0	60.4	42.5	41.7	76.1	59.0	34.7	24.3
Private sector	..	..	..	..	..	..	..	..	..	..

Source: UN/ECE secretariat estimates, based on national labour force surveys and direct communications from national statistical offices.

(d) Unemployment

Share of women in unemployment

Even though the women's share of total employment fell everywhere between 1985 and 1997 (except in Slovenia), their share in unemployment in 1997 was generally smaller than that of men. This largely reflects their departure from the labour market, encouraged by the loss of benefits which supported their employment,[440] as discussed above. For example, in Hungary the female share in total unemployed was less than 40 per cent, the lowest share of all the 11 transition economies. Between 1985 and 1997 female employment fell by more than 1 million while the number of women

_____

[440] Hidden unemployment, i.e. unemployed but not registered, is not an issue here due to the use of the comprehensive definition (ILO) of the unemployed in the national labour force surveys.

TABLE 3.6.1

Trade performance and external balances in the east European and Baltic countries, 1998 [a]

(Value in million dollars, growth rates in per cent)

	Exports growth rates		Imports growth rates		Trade balances	
	Oct.-Dec.	Jan.-Dec.	Oct.-Dec.	Jan.-Dec.	Oct.-Dec.	Jan.-Dec.
Eastern Europe	7.2	9.4	6.9	8.5	-11 532	-40 548
Albania	19.9	34.5	-23.4	25.8	-153	-590
Bosnia and Herzegovina [b] .	..	56.9	..	-32.5	..	-879
Bulgaria [b]	..	-12.5	..	-1.0	..	-540
Croatia	15.7	8.9	-21.7	-7.9	-946	-3 842
Czech Republic	12.3	15.7	8.7	4.6	-1 033	-2 464
Hungary	15.8	20.5	19.3	21.0	-722	-2 690
Poland [c]	-10.3	2.2	6.4	12.2	-6 210	-21 174
Romania	3.7	-1.6	-1.5	-4.9	-1 094	-2 436
Slovakia	14.8	10.7	21.3	11.0	-735	-2 292
Slovenia	10.1	8.1	13.8	7.9	-306	-1 049
The former Yugoslav						
Republic of Macedonia [b] .	..	11.0	..	9.0	..	-602
Yugoslavia	43.0	20.3	-20.0	1.0	-333	-1 990
Baltic states	-9.6	3.3	-9.4	7.3	-1 274	-5 005
Estonia	1.2	9.7	-13.0	7.1	-281	-1 545
Latvia	-3.8	8.4	5.0	17.1	-418	-1 377
Lithuania	-20.7	-3.8	-13.6	2.7	-575	-2 084
Total above	5.9	9.0	5.4	7.8	-12 807	-45 553

Source: National statistics and direct communications from national statistical offices to UN/ECE secretariat.

[a] Preliminary data.

[b] Annual rates and trade balances based on reported January-October growth rates.

[c] Annual rates and trade balances based on reported January-November growth rates. October-November 1998 over same period in 1997 instead of October-December data.

current dollar values) after increasing by 13 per cent in January-June (for quarterly year-on-year changes see chart 3.6.2).[443]

Among individual countries, only in Croatia, Slovakia and Slovenia was there a continued expansion of export value in the second half of the year.[444] Slovenia's exports, concentrating increasingly in a few manufacturing sectors, were gradually gathering momentum throughout the year, helped by sustained import demand in some of its

major western markets – Italy and lately also France (the latter reflecting the increasing activity of a Renault subsidiary in Slovenia). The further liberalization of trade within CEFTA and its low exposure to the Russian and other CIS markets were also favourable factors for Slovenia. The 9 per cent rise in the value of Croatian exports in 1998 was entirely generated in the second half of the year (up 18 per cent, year-on-year, after zero growth in January-June), and reflected a more than doubling of the dollar value of exports in the machinery and transport equipment sector, whereas exports of all other commodity categories fell or stagnated during 1998.[445] Slovakia's export growth was also generated exclusively in the transport equipment sector, which posted a 45 per cent rise in export sales in 1998, due mainly to capacity expansion in the Bratislava plant of Volkswagen,[446] while exports from all other economic sectors declined in dollar value.

Although export growth moderated somewhat in the south-east European transition economies, increases remained above 20 per cent in Albania and Bosnia and Herzegovina and Yugoslavia and was in two digits in The former Yugoslav Republic of Macedonia. The continuing economic recession in Bulgaria and crisis in Romania, in addition to the unfavourable external environment, strongly affected their export performance: Bulgaria's exports shrank by nearly 13 per cent in January-September 1998, compared with the same period of 1997, while Romania's declined by 2 per cent in 1998 according to preliminary data for the full year.[447]

East European import growth tended to strengthen slightly in the first three quarters of 1998, but later in the year, with domestic demand cooling down throughout the region (section 3.3 above) and world commodity prices sinking even deeper in October-December,[448] there was a sharp loss of momentum: the value of imports in January-September was some 9 per cent higher than a year earlier but in October-December the rate was below 7 per cent (table 3.6.1). Nevertheless, there was still rapid import growth (19 per cent) in Hungary for the second consecutive year and in Poland, it remained in two digits, although it decelerated somewhat in the last quarter.

---

[443] For comparisons of individual country performance, see table 3.6.1 above and tables 2.3.6, 3.2.1-3.2.3 in the previous issue of this *Survey*. Note that the Statistical Office of the Czech Republic, after discovering some methodological biases, has recently revised the export and import values series back to 1994; the final complete series after revision are to be published in the second half of 1999. In tables 3.1.2. and 3.6.1, export and import growth rates and the merchandise trade deficit to GDP ratios are based on the preliminary revised figures kindly made available by the Czech Statistical Office to the UN/ECE secretariat in March 1999. For the revised values of Czech trade flows see appendix tables B.10-B.12 of this *Survey*. There was also a recent downward revision of 1998 quarterly data for Lithuania.

[444] The apparent strong export gains in the last two quarters of 1998 in Slovakia's trade, however, raise some doubts as to the reliability of the data. There are many deficiencies in the recently revised (according to a new methodology) monthly and quarterly figures for the base year 1997. Note, for instance, the very different year-on-year growth rates of monthly exports and imports in 1998 shown in the last two issues of Slovakia Statistical Office, *Economic Bulletin,* both claiming to be based on the definitive data for 1997.

[445] The main factor behind this development of exports were discontinuities in export deliveries from Croatia's shipbuilding sector: in 1997 the sector's exports were rather sluggish, but in the second half of 1998 it delivered several oil tankers. At least two oil tankers, with a carrying capacity of over 47,000 tons, were launched and delivered in September and October 1998 to the Liberian Shipping Company and a Moscow-based shipping company. *Reuters Business Briefing*, 8 and 17 October 1998.

[446] In 1998, Volkswagen of Germany employed an extra 1,500 workers in its Bratislava plant and raised its production of VW Golf and Bora family cars to 125,000 units from 40,000 in 1997. VW also assembles gearboxes in Bratislava, output of which increased from 280,000 in 1997 to 328,000 units in 1998, while at the same time the gearbox components output was raised from 6 million to 8 million units. The bulk of the output is distributed outside Slovakia via the VW distribution network. *Financial Times*, 21 January 1999.

[447] For more details on recent developments in the Romanian economy, see sect. 3.2(iii) above.

[448] In the last quarter of 1998 world commodity prices contracted by 27 per cent on average on a year-on-year basis, and by 6 per cent against the previous quarter. For details see chap. 2.1(i) above.

TABLE 3.6.2

Foreign trade of the ECE transition economies by direction, 1996-1998

(Value in billion dollars, growth rates in per cent) [a]

	Exports				Imports			
	Value	Growth rates			Value	Growth rates		
Country or country group [b]	1997	1996	1997	1998 [c]	1997	1996	1997	1998 [c]
Eastern Europe, to and from:								
World	102.5	2.1	5.8	9.9	136.2	13.1	5.8	9.3
ECE transition economies	27.5	6.1	6.7	1.0	29.7	9.4	0.1	-2.6
CIS	9.3	8.3	17.4	-8.9	14.0	12.2	-2.6	-14.1
Baltic states	0.9	37.6	26.8	30.5	0.2	22.0	0.8	11.9
Eastern Europe [d]	17.3	4.2	0.8	4.6	15.5	6.8	2.7	7.8
Developed market economies	67.7	–	7.6	15.7	93.4	13.1	7.4	13.1
European Union	62.1	-0.1	7.3	16.0	80.9	13.0	6.5	13.8
Developing economies	7.3	5.7	-10.5	-10.4	13.1	23.1	7.9	9.5
Baltic states, to and from:								
World	8.5	17.6	23.0	8.3	12.8	26.6	26.7	14.1
ECE transition economies	4.3	24.3	19.0	-2.6	4.6	14.7	17.6	4.6
CIS	3.1	21.8	19.3	-10.0	3.0	4.5	12.4	-8.6
Baltic states	1.1	43.4	25.1	16.3	0.8	38.1	25.7	29.2
Developed market economies	3.9	9.0	26.5	20.1	7.6	32.0	31.1	21.4
European Union	3.5	9.9	24.5	17.8	6.7	30.8	29.7	20.3
Developing economies	0.3	55.4	44.9	9.5	0.6	88.8	53.4	-2.0
Russian Federation, to and from:								
World	85.0	8.8	-0.1	-14.5	52.9	-1.4	14.9	-2.5
Intra-CIS	16.6	9.4	4.3	-12.8	14.1	7.0	-3.2	-8.8
Non-CIS economies	68.4	8.7	-1.2	-14.9	38.8	-4.9	23.3	-0.2
ECE transition economies	13.3	17.9	6.0	-19.8	5.3	-22.7	34.4	-1.6
Baltic states	3.1	16.4	17.4	-26.7	1.0	-38.8	61.9	-17.6
Eastern Europe	10.2	18.3	3.0	-17.8	4.3	-18.6	29.2	-5.1
Developed market economies	40.1	4.1	-0.2	-12.3	26.5	-7.2	24.0	-0.1
European Union	28.0	4.0	2.4	-16.4	19.5	-11.6	23.2	-2.2
Developing economies	15.0	14.1	-9.0	-17.3	7.0	24.2	13.5	4.8
Other CIS economies, to and from: [e]								
World	32.1	10.5	4.1	-11.4	36.6	16.8	4.0	-8.3
Intra-CIS	16.1	13.6	-7.1	-14.1	21.2	12.0	-1.3	-13.9
Russian Federation	11.7	9.3	-2.8	..	15.8	12.8	-0.2	..
Non-CIS economies	16.0	6.7	18.5	-8.9	15.4	25.1	12.3	-1.5
ECE transition economies	2.8	7.2	-8.2	..	3.3	12.9	14.5	..
Baltic states	0.6	-0.5	-27.6	..	0.8	17.4	28.7	..
Eastern Europe	2.2	10.4	-1.0	..	2.5	11.7	10.7	..
Developed market economies	6.3	5.5	18.6	..	9.1	30.3	16.6	..
European Union	4.6	31.0	21.9	..	6.7	21.9	22.9	..
Developing economies	6.9	7.6	34.2	..	2.9	25.3	-1.3	..
ECE transition economies, to and from:								
World	231.7	7.2	4.0	-2.0	246.6	12.5	8.6	3.9

Source: National statistics and direct communications from national statistical offices to UN/ECE secretariat; for the Russian Federation, State Customs Committee data; for other CIS economies, CIS Interstate Statistical Committee data.

Note: There were changes in the methodology of foreign trade reporting in several economies in transition in 1996-1998. Starting 1998, Slovakia reports foreign trade flows according to the new methodology (including imports for inward processing and exports after processing). The Czech Republic has recently revised its export and import figures back to 1994. However, these revisions are not reflected in the eastern Europe aggregate above because revised data by destination are not yet available. For details on prior-1998 changes see UN/ECE, *Economic Bulletin for Europe,* Vol. 48 (1996) and Vol. 49 (1997).

[a] Growth rates are calculated on dollar values.

[b] "Eastern Europe" refers to Albania, Bulgaria, Croatia, the Czech Republic, Hungary, Poland, Romania, Slovakia and Slovenia. For lack of adequate data, the trade of Bosnia and Herzegovina, The former Yugoslav Republic of Macedonia and Yugoslavia is not covered. The partner country grouping has been revised recently (subsequent changes back to 1980 were made also in appendix table B.13) following the changes in the national statistical sources. Thus, the earlier reported "Transition economies" group is now replaced by "ECE transition economies", which covers the east European countries, including the successor states of the former SFR of Yugoslavia, the Baltic states and the CIS. "Developed market economies" excludes Turkey and includes Australia, New Zealand and South Africa.

[c] January-September over same period of 1997. For Slovakia data are derived from export and import data reported according to the new methodology.

[d] Including Bosnia and Herzegovina, The former Yugoslav Republic of Macedonia and Yugoslavia.

[e] Aggregate values and growth rates do not include Uzbekistan.

TABLE 3.6.3

Trade balances of the ECE transition economies, 1993-1998
(Billion dollars)

	1993	1994	1995	1996	1997	January-September	
						1997	1998
Eastern Europe [a]							
World	-13.6	-12.5	-19.7	-31.9	-33.7	-23.8	-25.6
ECE transition economies	-3.8	-2.1	-3.2	-3.9	-2.2	-1.9	-1.2
Developed market economies	-10.5	-10.2	-15.1	-24.1	-25.7	-17.9	-18.9
European Union	-5.6	-6.1	-10.6	-18.0	-18.8	-13.0	-13.8
Developing economies	0.7	-0.2	-1.4	-3.9	-5.7	-4.0	-5.5
Baltic states [b]							
World	-0.3	-0.9	-2.2	-3.2	-4.3	-2.9	-3.7
ECE transition economies	0.1	–	-0.5	-0.3	-0.3	-0.2	-0.4
Developed market economies	-0.3	-0.8	-1.6	-2.7	-3.7	-2.5	-3.1
European Union	-0.1	-0.4	-1.4	-2.4	-3.2	-2.1	-2.6
Developing economies	-0.1	-0.1	-0.1	-0.2	-0.3	-0.3	-0.2
Russian Federation [c]							
World	17.5	24.6	31.5	39.1	32.1	23.6	15.7
Intra-CIS	..	3.8	0.9	1.3	2.5	1.6	1.0
Non-CIS economies	17.5	20.9	30.6	37.7	29.6	22.0	14.7
ECE transition economies	5.3	4.3	5.5	8.6	8.0	6.1	4.4
Eastern Europe [d]	4.6	3.3	4.3	6.6	5.9	4.5	3.4
Developed market economies	10.2	12.8	15.6	18.8	13.6	10.2	6.8
European Union	8.4	6.9	8.4	11.5	8.5	6.7	3.7
Developing economies	2.0	3.8	9.4	10.3	8.0	5.7	3.5
Other CIS economies [e]							
World	..	-1.3	-2.1	-4.3	-4.4	-3.7	-4.2
Intra-CIS	..	-2.6	-4.0	-4.2	-5.1	-3.8	-3.3
Non-CIS economies	1.7	1.3	1.8	-0.1	0.7	0.1	-0.9
ECE transition economies	..	0.4	0.1	0.1	-0.5	..	..
Eastern Europe	..	0.2	-0.2	-0.1	-0.3	..	..
Developed market economies	..	-0.6	-0.7	-2.5	-2.8	..	..
European Union	..	-0.3	-0.6	-1.7	-2.2	..	..
Developing economies	..	1.5	2.4	2.2	4.0	..	..

Source: National statistics and direct communications from national statistical offices to UN/ECE secretariat.

Note: There were changes in the methodology of foreign trade reporting in several economies in transition in 1996-1998. Starting in 1998, Slovakia reports foreign trade flows according to the new methodology (including imports for inward processing and exports after processing). The Czech Republic has recently revised its export and import figures back to 1994. However, these revisions are not reflected in the eastern Europe aggregate above because revised data by destination are not yet available. For details on prior-1998 changes see UN/ECE, *Economic Bulletin for Europe*, Vol. 48 (1996) and Vol. 49 (1997).

[a] Trade balances as from 1996 are derived from export and import data reported by Hungary according to the new methodology and those for January-June 1998 are derived from export and import data reported by Slovakia according to the new methodology.

[b] Trade balances as from 1995 are derived from export and import data reported by Lithuania according to the new methodology.

[c] For the Russian Federation: Goskomstat data for 1993; State Customs Committee data for 1994-1998. The two series are not fully comparable.

[d] Excludes the former SFR of Yugoslavia in 1993.

[e] Trade balances for 1996, 1997 and first half of 1998 do not include Uzbekistan.

There was a strong pick-up of imports, partly boosted by favourable changes in the terms of trade and the increased demand of exporting sectors for imported inputs, in the Czech Republic, Slovakia and Slovenia, following declines in 1997. Everywhere else in eastern Europe, imports stagnated or declined in 1998 – most strongly in Croatia, where they fell by 8 per cent in dollar value after rapid growth in the three preceding years. The latter slump resulted from depressed domestic demand, due mainly to the very tight fiscal stance adopted earlier in the year, coupled with measures introduced in April by the Croatian national bank to discourage domestic banks from borrowing abroad.

In the Baltic countries changes in imports were in line with those for exports: a steady deceleration in value growth from early on in 1998, turned into an 9 per cent fall (year-on-year) in the last quarter of 1998 (table 3.6.1). The growth of imports slowed most steeply in Estonia, from an average annual rate of nearly 40 per cent in 1995-1997 to just above 7 per cent in 1998. There was also a dramatic deceleration in growth in Lithuania as well, although in Latvia it remained in two digits. Falling world commodity prices certainly played a role in slowing growth in the value of imports, but the cooling of domestic demand, due mainly to the collapse of export earnings from the Russian and other CIS markets, as well

TABLE 3.6.4

Changes in the volume of foreign trade in selected transition economies, 1995-1998

(Per cent)

	Exports						Imports					
				1998 [a]						1998 [a]		
	1995	*1996*	*1997*	*Jan.-Mar.*	*Jan.-Jun.*	*Jan.-Oct.*	*1995*	*1996*	*1997*	*Jan.-Mar.*	*Jan.-Jun.*	*Jan.-Oct.*
Czech Republic	5.7	2.7	14.2	29.1	20.4	16.0	23.7	10.7	7.6	11.2	7.7	7.6
Hungary	8.4	4.6	29.9	32.8	29.5	24.0	-3.9	5.5	26.4	28.1	27.4	26.6
Transition economies	20.2	-0.2	25.2	23.4	20.2	8.3	-4.1	2.8	5.3	6.0	9.9	11.5
European Union	5.1	5.7	33.6	36.2	29.9	25.6	-2.7	4.0	29.7	29.3	27.8	26.6
Poland	16.7	9.7	13.7	18.1	10.0	3.8	20.5	28.0	22.0	20.1	16.7	16.2
Transition economies	46.5	29.0	35.8	31.2	19.2	0.8	25.1	19.3	13.5	14.2	13.8	15.9
European Union	17.1	5.7	11.9	19.3	11.8	8.1	19.6	27.3	25.2	20.5	18.3	17.4
Slovenia [b]	7.5	3.1	11.3	15.9	10.0	9.0	15.5	-	9.6	18.1	10.1	9.3
Estonia	8.1	6.7	51.1	27.0	23.0	14.7	..	..	..	..	..	..
Latvia [c]	7.1	8.8	20.1	33.1	24.5	16.7	..	..	..	..	..	..
Russian Federation [c]	..	0.1	1.8	0.1	0.4	1.4	..	-1.9	21.1	24.1	17.5	4.8
Non-CIS	6.4	3.6	1.8	-2.6	-1.4	0.4	-3.2	-0.1	31.7	32.4	24.3	9.9
CIS	..	-15.6	1.9	10.6	7.7	5.3	..	-6.2	-1.8	2.9	0.1	-8.8

Source: UN/ECE secretariat calculations, based on national foreign trade statistics.

a Over same period of 1997.

b Volume indices for Slovenia as reported by IMAD, *Slovenian Economic Mirror*, Vol. III, 1997; Vol. IV, 1998 and *Spring Report*, 1998. January-July instead of January-June in 1998.

c Volume indices for January-September instead of January-October 1998.

as unfavourable developments in the conditions for import credit in the Baltic countries, were also important.

Lower import growth in the last months of 1998 allowed a few countries to contain their trade deficits (Croatia, Estonia and Romania), but, in general, they increased, and, in some countries, quite considerably. In January-September 1998 the aggregate trade deficit of eastern Europe and the Baltic states, on the basis of the customs data, widened by some $2.7 billion, to $29.4 billion (table 3.6.3), but for the year as a whole it may well have risen to over $42 billion.[449] The sharpest absolute deterioration again was in Poland, where the trade deficit rose from almost $17 billion in 1997 to over $21 billion in 1998. Deficits widened notably in Bulgaria and Hungary, by some $0.6 billion in each, while in Latvia, Lithuania, Slovakia and Slovenia the increases were less pronounced ($0.1 billion-$0.3 billion). The considerable narrowing of the trade deficit (by nearly $2 billion) in the Czech Republic resulted mainly from increased export earnings, particularly in the early months of the year. In relation to GDP, trade deficits remained very high in Croatia, Estonia, Latvia and Lithuania, near or above 20 per cent. The ratio was also high in Poland, at 12.5 per cent in January-September 1998 (table 3.1.2). Balance of payments data, however show much smaller deficits on the merchandise trade

account for some countries, reflecting differences and lags in the coverage of trade flows between the two data sets (section 3.7 below).

(b) Effect of Russia's market collapse

The crisis that unfolded in Russia in late summer 1998 and its repercussions on other CIS countries had a strong immediate effect on export performance and, less directly, on import growth throughout the east European and Baltic region. Although the region's reliance on the Russian and other CIS markets had already been considerably reduced by mid-1998 – CIS partners including Russia accounted for some 10 per cent of the region's total exports and imports in January-June 1998, as against 20-22 per cent in 1991 – for some important east European and Baltic export products, such as foods, beverages, and other consumer goods and, in some cases, machinery and equipment, these countries still remained major export markets.[450]

Trade with Russia and many other CIS member-countries had plummeted in August-October 1998 as the result of hard currency shortages and the collapse of the payments system in Russia. The attempts of exporters in the east European and Baltic countries to resort to barter deals or to arrange state-to-state export sales have not so far been very successful. For several countries their export earnings from Russia during these three months declined by 50-70 per cent, as compared with the same

---

[449] In tables 3.6.2 and 3.6.3 the aggregate figures for eastern Europe do not include data for Bosnia and Herzegovina, The former Yugoslav Republic of Macedonia and Yugoslavia (see notes to the tables). If estimates for these countries are taken into account (as is done in table 3.6.1), the full-year 1998 trade deficit of the region might be nearly $45.5 billion.

[450] For further details see UN/ECE, "Outlook for trade in the wake of Russian and global financial turmoil", *Economic Survey of Europe, 1998 No. 3*, pp. 85-88.

CHART 3.6.2

Quarterly changes in east European and Baltic exports and imports, 1997-1998
(Index over same quarter of the preceding year)

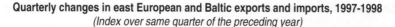

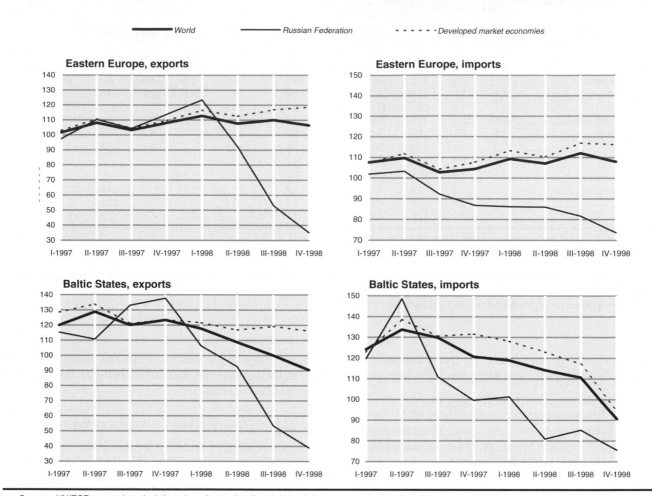

Source: UN/ECE secretariat calculations, based on national statistics and direct communications from national statistical offices.

period in 1997; in addition there were losses of 25-45 per cent in trade with Ukraine and probably of a similar order of magnitude in trade with other CIS countries (table 3.6.5). Based on the three different scenarios, presented in table 3.6.5, the secretariat estimates that the losses by the end of October 1998 ranged from some $90 million to $220 million in the Czech Republic, Estonia and Latvia, from $230 to $420 million in Hungary and Lithuania, and from $550 million to $1.3 billion in Poland.

The data in table 3.6.5 indicate that none of these countries except Hungary managed to offset these losses with exports to other markets, including intraregional ones. The cumulative effect of these losses on total export performance was largest in Poland and the three Baltic countries, where in the second half of the year previously strong growth was cut short and exports declined (chart 3.6.2).

In relative terms, the share of the Russian market in east European exports declined by some 1-3 percentage points in January-October 1998, while for the Baltic countries the reduction was 5-6 percentage points, to 13-

14 per cent of exports from Estonia and Latvia and under 19 per cent for Lithuania. The share of the CIS in total east European and Baltic exports may have declined by some 1.5-2 percentage points in 1998. The share of their exports going to western market economies more than offset this decline; exports to developing country markets also fell, while growth in intraregional trade was relatively sluggish.

As mentioned above, individual commodity categories were differently affected by the collapse of trade with Russia and other CIS countries. In the third quarter of 1998, there was a 12-18 per cent fall in the dollar value of total exports of foods and beverages (SITC 0, 1) in Poland and the three Baltic states, and there was also a decline in their exports of chemical products (SITC 5) and some manufactured goods (SITC 6). Exports of these commodities were also noticeably depressed in the Czech Republic, Croatia, Hungary and Slovakia in the last two quarters of 1998. Sales of machinery and equipment (SITC 7) only appear to have been hit in the three Baltic countries (down by 2-5 per

TABLE 3.6.5

Effect of Russia's August 1998 market collapse on export performance in selected east European and Baltic countries

(Growth rates in per cent, value in million dollars)

	Growth rates[a]		Value of hypothetical loss in January-October 1998[b]		
	Jan.-Oct. 1998	Aug.-Oct. 1998	Scenario A	Scenario B	Scenario C
Czech Republic					
Total exports	16.2	14.0	171.2	85.4	206.7
of which:					
Russian Federation	-9.3	-51.3	167.5	80.2	205.7
Ukraine	14.9	-6.0	3.7	5.2	1.0
Rest of the world	17.1	17.1	–	–	–
Estonia					
Total exports	11.4	0.7	169.3	225.6	152.4
of which:					
Russian Federation	-19.4	-47.2	169.7	185.3	109.1
Ukraine	19.0	-24.8	-0.4	40.4	43.4
Rest of the world	18.6	16.7	–	–	–
Hungary					
Total exports	21.4	20.5	418.7	251.0	364.6
of which:					
Russian Federation	-22.9	-71.3	362.0	225.7	305.7
Ukraine	-4.5	-46.4	56.7	25.3	58.9
Rest of the world	24.1	26.5	–	–	–
Latvia					
Total exports	10.6	-5.7	171.8	118.7	120.6
of which:					
Russian Federation	-30.0	-71.4	149.4	106.8	113.9
Ukraine	-17.8	-39.5	22.4	11.9	6.7
Rest of the world	23.2	15.3	–	–	–
Lithuania					
Total exports	–	-13.5	233.9	405.9	308.6
of which:					
Russian Federation	-21.7	-59.7	218.5	298.8	213.3
Ukraine	2.0	-43.5	15.4	107.1	95.4
Rest of the world	7.5	7.2	–	–	–
Poland					
Total exports	3.6	-8.5	546.1	1 313.1	1 157.1
of which:					
Russian Federation	-18.2	-69.7	415.3	856.2	939.5
Ukraine	-7.0	-38.4	130.7	456.8	217.5
Rest of the world	6.2	-0.4	–	–	–

Source: UN/ECE secretariat calculations, based on national statistics.

a As compared with the same period of 1997.

b Difference between actual export value in January-October 1998 and the hypothetical export value for the same period, as derived from the following three scenarios. Scenario A: the actual export growth rate to the rest of the world is applied across the board (constant shares). Scenario B: hypothetical values of exports to Russia and Ukraine are based on the average annual rate of their growth in 1995-1997, while for the rest of the world actual export value of January-October 1998 is used. Scenario C: hypothetical values of exports to Russia and Ukraine are based on the January-March 1998 growth rates while for the rest of the world actual export value of January-October 1998 is used.

cent in the third quarter of 1998) (chart 3.6.3). In eastern Europe, in contrast to the Baltic countries, this sector is widely engaged in vertically integrated production processes organized by EU and United States multinational companies, a development which improves the stability of export orders and, in 1998, was behind the relatively strong export performance of several countries of the region.

(c) Trade prospects in 1999

As already noted, the weakening of export growth became more pronounced after Russia's default in August, but the data in chart 3.6.2 show that exports had begun to falter several months earlier, particularly from the Baltic states. The virtual disappearance of the Russian export market in the last months of 1998, and the difficulties encountered by the east European and Baltic exporters in their attempts to revive trade on the basis of barter deals or export credits from state agencies or commercial entities, suggest that the prospects for a full export recovery in the short- or even medium-run are rather poor.[451] In addition, the steep devaluation of the Russian rouble, and its impact on the currencies of other CIS countries, have sharply raised the rouble cost of imports from eastern Europe and the Baltic countries (even when subsidized by the exporting countries), which in turn has prompted widespread import substitution by domestically produced goods (or goods received on a non-commercial basis from the EU and the United States) in an environment of depressed consumer demand.

The recent signs of a noticeable weakening of demand in western Europe also weigh on the prospects for east European and Baltic exports, including those areas where they had acquired some competitive advantage in recent years thanks to their integration into the production networks of multinational companies (transport equipment, machinery and especially engineering; see chart 3.6.3). The forecasts of estimated western import demand for east European and Baltic exports point to a strong deceleration in 1999 (chart 3.6.1). The negative effect of this development on transition economies' exports may be still stronger, bearing in mind the current high income and price elasticities of western imports from these countries. According to ECE estimates, the income elasticity coefficient for total west European imports in 1990-1996 was 2.42, with a price elasticity of -0.526; but for west European imports from Poland and Hungary the income (price) elasticity coefficients ranged from 5.68 (-2.34) to 7.36 (-1.98), respectively.[452]

---

[451] At the time of writing this *Survey* there had been announcements of only two barter deals concluded with Russia, by Bulgaria and Hungary. For details see *BBC Monitoring Service: Central Europe and Balkans*, 31 December 1998. On 20 January 1999, the Hungarian Economics Minister told journalists, after a meeting in Moscow with the Russian Deputy Prime Minister and Foreign Trade Minister, that the Russian partners did not show any particular interest in the offer of a Hungarian credit of $200-$250 million annually (with a one-year grace period, repayment over three years and interest at 4-6 percentage points above LIBOR), as both the United States and the EU had offered credits with very preferential terms. *Reuters*, 22 January 1999.

[452] Of course these very high elasticity coefficients reflect the major changes in trade regimes since transition started and cannot be expected to last in this order in a longer run. One also has to be cautious interpreting these short-run elasticities as they are prone to several shortcomings as compared with the long-run results (see for instance, P. Hooper, K. Johnson and J. Marquez, "Trade elasticities for G-7 countries", Board of Governors of the Federal Reserve System, *International Finance Discussion Papers*, No. 609, April 1998). Income and price elasticities above were estimated from the conventional trade equation: $M(t)=a+b*GDP(t)+c*(Pm(t)/P(t))+u(t)$, where $M(t)$ denotes imports of west European countries (EU+EFTA) in volume terms. For imports in volume terms from transition economies, data on quarterly western imports in current dollar values were deflated by German import unit values for east European goods.

CHART 3.6.3

Changes in east European and Baltic exports by commodity, 1993-1998

(Structure and growth rates, per cent)

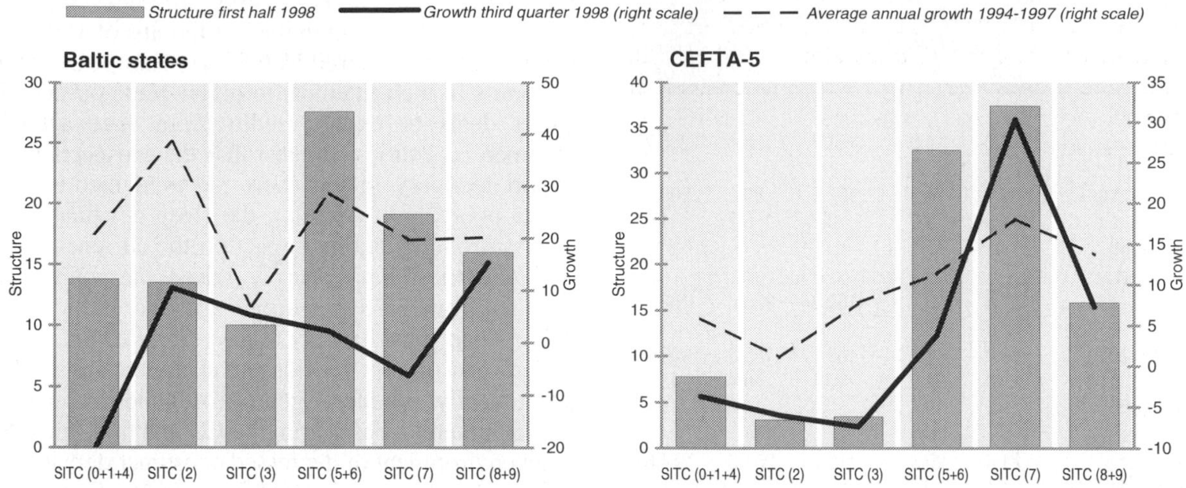

Baltic states

CEFTA-5

Source: UN/ECE secretariat calculations, based on United Nations COMTRADE Database; national statistics and direct communications from national statistical offices.

Note: Commodity groups are Sections of the United Nations Standard International Trade Classification (SITC Rev. 3): (0+1+4) – Food, beverages, agricultural products; (2) – Raw materials except fuel; (3) – Mineral fuels; (5+6) – Chemical products and intermediates; (7) – Machinery and transport equipment; (8+9) – Other manufactured goods. Growth rates (year-on-year basis) are calculated on dollar values of exports. CEFTA-5 includes the Czech Republic, Hungary, Poland, Slovakia and Slovenia.

Moreover, the increasing competitive pressure on these markets, in particular from Asian exporters, narrows the possibility of redirecting exports from CIS markets to the west, since they tend to consist mainly of low value-added products. Nor are the east European markets themselves ready to absorb these goods. The duality of the commodity structure of east European and Baltic exports, where the higher value added goods are traded with western countries and lower value exports with the east, is now a problem because the possibility of substituting western for eastern markets is constrained by the competitiveness of the cheaper Asian producers. The competitiveness of east European and, in particular, Baltic exports is also burdened by the real appreciation of domestic currencies in many countries of the region. In recent years, east European and Baltic export growth has tended to react in general to shifts in the valuation of the domestic currency, with a one-quarter lag (with the exception of the strong pick-up in Czech exports in the third quarter of 1997 after the devaluation of the koruna in May). The effect of changes in the exchange rate policies implemented at the beginning of 1999 in some of these countries (see above section 3.2(ii)) are therefore likely to be seen in the second or third quarter.

(d) Rising protectionist sentiments

Competitive pressures and the necessity of finding alternative export markets to the CIS have prompted protectionist pressures throughout the region. The strongest and in many cases successful appeals have come from the agricultural and food sectors. Demands to

strengthen protection of domestic producers have also been common in other traditional sectors (textiles and clothing, footwear, steel and coal, etc.).[453]

Starting in October 1998, a number of countries have not only intensified the surveillance of imports but have also increased export subsidies and/or raised customs (including preferential) tariffs on meat and other agricultural products.[454] In January 1999, the Czech Republic amended its agricultural law to allow the use of special tariffs and quotas and minimum intervention prices. At about the same time the Polish government, in

---

[453] Poland, for instance, instead of lifting duties on textiles and leather products imported from Turkey in January 1999, as expected, decided to maintain tariff protection until 2001 or 2002. Higher tariffs (16.6 per cent) have also been levied, for three years, on shoes imported from China. *BBC Monitoring Service: Central Europe and Balkans*, 31 October 1998; *Rzeczpospolita*, 7 January 1999.

[454] In Poland, export subsidies were raised and, as from 22 October 1998, duties on pork imports were increased by 20 percentage points to 80 per cent, with preferential rates of 45 per cent on imports from CEFTA and 50 per cent on imports from Lithuania. *Prawo i Gospodarka*, 22 October 1998; *Rzeczpospolita*, 20 October 1998. Also in October, Croatia increased its import duty on wheat from 400 to 520 kuna per tonne, while the Latvian parliament approved an increase of the basic import duty on margarine to 20 per cent (from 1 per cent). *MTI-Econews*, 2 October 1998; *Baltic Business Daily*, 16 October 1998. In November, the import tariffs on pork were also raised in Croatia. In the same month, Lithuania introduced new, higher customs tariffs on various commodities imported from countries with which it does not have free trade agreements, and in February 1999 it raised import duties for agricultural products from the EU. *BBC Monitoring Service: Central Europe and Balkans*, 12 November 1998; *ITAR-TASS World Service*, 1 November 1998; *ELTA*, 1 March 1999.

addition to the measures taken in October 1998 and in response to farmers' protests which had led to roads being blocked for several days in January, increased minimum intervention prices for pork and moved to amend the 1999 budget to provide extra funds to subsidize those purchases.[455] These measures, more often than not, have resulted from increased tension between the EU and east European countries after the EU, in an attempt to protect its own farmers with higher support prices for pork, boosted export subsidies by 30 per cent in mid-October 1998. The EU arrangement for agricultural exports to Russia under very favourable terms, together with a similar arrangement by the United States government, also played a role here, as east European and Baltic exporters saw little chance of regaining their export markets in Russia in the near future.[456]

Trade frictions among CEFTA and Baltic Free Trade Agreement (BAFTA) countries were also on the rise during the last months of 1998 and in some cases have resulted in complaints being lodged at the WTO. The Czech Republic, for instance, has filed a complaint to the WTO about Hungary's imposition in December of a quota on imports of Czech steel.[457] Hungary, in its turn, claimed that the quota was imposed in response to restrictions introduced earlier on its wheat exports to the Czech Republic.[458] A dispute among members of the Baltic Free Trade Agreement on quotas for pork (approved by Latvia's parliament in late 1998 for introduction in January 1999) was resolved before the quotas took effect when Latvia revoked the bill under the threat of countermeasures by Estonia and Lithuania. At the same time another dispute arose as the Lithuanian government increased reference border prices for imported foodstuffs and some other agricultural products.[459]

Against a background of excess capacity and falling prices for many traded products, a new wave of anti-dumping complaints against east European and Baltic producers were filed in the second half of 1998 and in the first few months of 1999. Provisional duties on steel and iron products, fertilizers, hardboard and some other products were imposed by the EU and the United States, as well as by Australia and India.[460] In a few cases, price commitments made by Czech, Hungarian, Latvian and Polish producers were accepted and the provisional duties were removed or lowered.[461] In their turn, east European and Baltic countries also tried to protect their own local steel and chemical markets by resorting to quotas, surcharges or the postponement of scheduled reductions of tariffs.[462] These measures most strongly affected Russian and other CIS producers, but they have also had an impact on intraregional trade as in the case of the above-mentioned Czech-Hungarian dispute.

Nevertheless, there have been no major trade policy reversals in the east European and Baltic region, as most of the measures undertaken had been provided for in the existing bilateral or multilateral agreements, and those which were disputed were quickly abandoned. Moreover, the general tendency remains for a further liberalization of tariffs in 1999. Tariffs on the region's trade with the EU, as well as within CEFTA and BAFTA, are expected to be reduced according to existing schedules. Romania is expected to catch up with its obligations as a CEFTA member. Bulgaria, too, after joining CEFTA on 1 January 1999 and abolishing tariffs on most industrial goods, should soon begin to reduce its tariff barriers to trade in agricultural products within this area. The three Baltic countries have now signed bilateral free trade agreements with all the CEFTA founding countries including Slovenia, and a number of these agreements (for instance with Hungary) are expected to take effect in 1999. Croatia is also attempting to enter CEFTA by signing bilateral free trade agreements with the existing members; however, so far there have only been outline discussions with Bulgaria and the Czech Republic, while the recent confirmation by Hungary to start free trade agreement negotiations with Croatia has prompted a rather negative reaction on the part of the EU.[463]

Estonia and Lithuania have intensified WTO accession negotiations after Latvia became a member on 10 February 1999, the two hoping to join WTO before the end of 1999. Croatia, too, intensified its WTO

---

[455] *Prawo i Gospodarka*, 2 February 1999.

[456] *Reuters News Service*, 5 December 1998; *Rzeczpospolita*, 23 February 1999.

[457] Hungary introduced a quota of 45,000 tons a year for seven groups of metallurgic products from the Czech Republic for four years in response to the Czech restrictions on Hungarian wheat. *Financial Times*, 27 January 1999.

[458] The restrictions imposed on Hungarian wheat exports are to be removed in the Czech Republic from 1 April 1999 and in Slovakia from 1 May 1999. Hungary also held talks with Slovenia in order to remove its market protection measures against Hungarian wheat. An agreement on the same issue was reached with Poland early in January 1999. *BBC Monitoring Service: Central Europe and Balkans*, 31 December 1998; *MTI-Econews*, 26 January 1999.

[459] The Lithuanian imposition of reference border prices for imported foodstuffs and other agricultural products is to remain in force until 1 January 2000 or until Lithuania is accepted into WTO. *ELTA*, 2 February 1999.

[460] For instance, in January 1999, definitive anti-dumping duties were imposed on EU imports of hardboard originating in Bulgaria, Estonia, Latvia, Lithuania, Poland and Russia, while in February the EU imposed provisional anti-dumping duties on imports of steel ropes and cables from seven countries including Hungary and Poland. Several anti-dumping complaints against such imports were filed by steelmakers with the United States International Trade Commission. *Reuters News Service*, 29 January 1999 and 3, 12 and 17 February 1999.

[461] *Agence Europe* (Brussels), 15 December 1998; *Timber Trades Journal*, 13 February 1999.

[462] In December 1998, Hungary, for instance, imposed an import duty surcharge on nitrogen-based fertilizers from Russia and Ukraine, while Poland decided to reduce import tariffs on EU steel products from 4 to 3 per cent instead of eliminating them altogether. *BBC Monitoring Service: Central Europe and Balkans*, 31 December 1998; *Rzeczpospolita*, 16 December 1998.

[463] *Financial Times*, 3 February 1999.

accession negotiations in January 1999 when it emerged that if it did not join before November 1999, it might have to wait for three years because of the planned reorganization of the WTO.

(iii) Trade of the CIS countries

In the first nine months of 1998, the dollar value of total merchandise *exports* from CIS countries declined by 14 per cent (table 3.6.6). Only in Armenia and Belarus, was there an increase in total exports; in all the others, including Russia, exports fell, from 10 per cent in Kazakhstan to 36 per cent in Azerbaijan. As most CIS countries are dependent on exports of natural resources, the poor export performance was, to a large extent, the result of falling commodity prices. On the *import* side, the dollar value of total CIS merchandise imports decreased by 5 per cent. Only in Azerbaijan and Kyrgyzstan were there significant year-on-year increases, a result of rising imports of machinery and equipment by the oil sector in Azerbaijan and the gold mining sector in Kyrgyzstan. The imports of other CIS countries were either stagnant (Armenia, Georgia, Kazakhstan, the Republic of Moldova and Tajikistan) or declining (Turkmenistan, Ukraine and Uzbekistan). In Turkmenistan and Uzbekistan, where international trade is still state-controlled, the falls in imports reflected current account difficulties exacerbated by low merchandise exports.[464] In Ukraine, the fall in imports was the result of balance of payments concerns and the country's continued weak trade performance with its principal trading partner, Russia. The CIS region's aggregate *trade surplus* decreased by over 40 per cent, mainly due to the decline in the Russian surplus, but there was also a worsening in the trade deficits of most other CIS countries. Russia and Kazakhstan were the only CIS members with a merchandise trade surplus. The financial crisis in Russia was already contributing to the region's overall trade decline in the first nine months of 1998, but its effects are likely to be much more visible in the data for the fourth quarter.

The *volume* of Russia's exports was slightly higher while the volume of imports increased by 5 per cent in the January-September period (table 3.6.4). The third-quarter export volumes were up by 3 per cent (year-on-year), chiefly the result of exporters attempting to counteract falling commodity prices. The third quarter's import volumes fell by 16 per cent, a dramatic reversal of the 24 and 12 per cent (year-on-year) increases in the first and second quarters, respectively. Estimates of trade volumes for other CIS countries are not available.

Russia and the other CIS countries are not expected to show any significant improvement in their international trade performance in the immediate future. Their short-term export performance is largely determined by commodity prices and these are unlikely to recover in

1999, thus continuing to have a negative effect on foreign exchange receipts. The price of *crude oil*, the key export commodity in Russia, Azerbaijan and Kazakhstan fell by some 35 per cent in 1998 and the slowing global economy is unlikely to absorb the excess oil supply in the near future. In mid-March 1999, oil prices were about 25 per cent higher than in December 1998 following a production cuts agreement among leading exporters. Nevertheless, many remain sceptical that any price turnround can be long-lasting given the weak demand conditions. Similarly – and partly as a result of the Asian crisis and the continued underperformance of the Japanese economy – the world's *base metal* production needs to be reduced to match the lower global demand. Future improvements in the demand for base metals such as copper, nickel and aluminium are dependent, to a large degree, on the resurgence of interest in large-scale capital investment projects, particularly in Asia. Until then, the export performance of Tajikistan, Kazakhstan and, to a lesser degree Russia, is not expected to improve. With respect to *ferrous metals*, cheap Russian and Ukrainian steel exports are facing numerous anti-dumping actions throughout the world, most recently in North America, and the use of this largely protectionist trade device is not expected to abate.[465] The price of gold, of particular importance to Kyrgyzstan and Uzbekistan, has been relatively steady but low. Cotton prices have fallen by 17 per cent in 1998, negatively affecting the exports of the CIS countries of central Asia and Azerbaijan.

Another unfavourable development affecting Russian exporters is the reintroduction of *export duties*. The duties, applicable only to non-CIS exports, are aimed at increasing federal revenues.[466] The new export tariffs coupled with a mandatory 75 per cent surrender requirement on foreign exchange earnings have clearly reduced incentives to export. They have also diminished the windfall devaluation gains accruing to the hard-pressed Russian oil and metal producers. Russian commodity exporters, however, are unlikely to redirect their exports towards the domestic or CIS market as they are facing extremely weak domestic demand and non-paying customers in the CIS.[467]

---

[465] In February 1999, rather than face punitive tariffs, Russia agreed to an annual quota and a minimum price for its steel exports to the United States.

[466] The duties will apply to crude oil exports at the level of 2.5 euros per tonne if the price falls between $9.8 and $12.3 a barrel. The duty will double if the price is higher and will not be charged if it falls below the limit. Duties of 5 per cent will apply to exports of oil products, natural gas (reportedly rescinded six days after its introduction), coal, copper and nickel. Export duties of 10 per cent (with lower limits denominated in euros) will be levied on scrap metals, selected lumber products and various agricultural products such as soya beans, seeds, animals and leather. All export duties will be in effect for a period of six months.

[467] While the government often resorts to limiting access to export pipelines to oil producers who "fail" to supply domestic refineries, the oil producers are not likely to increase their domestic shipments voluntarily. Similarly, in the natural gas sector, the government generally prohibits cutting off gas deliveries to non-paying customers, but only about 12 per cent of Russian gas consumers pay in cash, and many pay nothing at all. In September 1998, Gazprom was owed about $13 billion in consumer debt. *Petroleum Economist*, September 1998, p. 8.

---

[464] Both countries have also tightened their foreign exchange regulations. In Turkmenistan, the government suspended hard currency conversion, while in Uzbekistan the foreign exchange surrender requirement was raised to 50 per cent.

TABLE 3.6.6

CIS countries' total trade, 1996-1998

(Value in million dollars, growth rates in per cent)

	Exports			Imports			Trade balances			
	Value	Growth rates		Value	Growth rates				January-September	
	1996	1997	1998 [a]	1996	1997	1998 [a]	1996	1997	1997	1998
Armenia	290	-19.9	12.9	856	4.3	0.4	-566	-660	-474	-457
Azerbaijan	631	23.8	-35.8	961	-17.3	33.5	-329	-13	-1	-398
Belarus	5 652	29.2	4.1	6 939	25.2	5.4	-1 288	-1 388	-1 087	-1 211
Georgia	199	20.5	-13.6	687	36.9	-1.6	-488	-701	-517	-528
Kazakhstan	5 911	7.7	-10.0	4 241	0.8	2.3	1 670	2 091	1 622	1 085
Kyrgyzstan	505	19.5	-12.0	838	-15.3	22.9	-332	-106	-37	-198
Republic of Moldova	795	10.0	-16.1	1 072	9.3	-1.9	-277	-297	-256	-336
Tajikistan	770	-3.2	-19.8	668	12.3	-2.9	102	-5	-85	-171
Turkmenistan [b]	1 693	-55.6	-28.8	1 314	-6.5	-16.1	379	-476	-257	-292
Ukraine	14 401	-1.2	-14.1	17 603	-2.7	-16.1	-3 203	-2 896	-2 270	-1 704
Uzbekistan [c]	4 211	-0.4	-21.3	4 712	-3.8	-30.2	-501	-340	-362	-2
Total above	35 058	3.6	-11.4	39 890	3.1	-8.3	-4 833	-4 790	-3 724	-4 213
Russian Federation	85 107	-0.1	-14.5	46 034	14.9	-2.5	39 073	32 110	23 594	15 713
CIS total	120 165	1.0	-13.6	85 924	9.4	-5.1	34 241	27 320	19 870	11 500
Memorandum item:										
Russian Federation [d]	89 100	-1.9	-14.4	62 300	8.5	-4.6	26 800	19 800	11 200	4 500

Source: CIS Statistical Committee; direct communications to UN/ECE secretariat; CIS Statistical Committee, *CIS Statistical Bulletin, 22 (206)*, November 1998; for the Russian Federation, State Customs Committee data.

[a] January-September over same period of 1997.

[b] For 1998, Turkmenistan's State Statistics Committee as reported by *Reuters News Service*, 18 November 1998.

[c] CIS Statistical Committee estimates for 1996 and 1997. For 1998, TACIS, *Uzbekistan Economic Trends*, Third Quarter 1998 and UN/ECE secretariat calculations.

[d] Adjusted for non-registered trade; for 1996 and 1997, Russian Federation Goskomstat, *Sotsial'no-ekonomicheskoe polozhenie Rossii*, No. 1 (Moscow), 1998. For 1998, *Sotsial'no-ekonomicheskoe polozhenie Rossii* (Moscow), October 1998. Note that the two series may not be directly comparable as the 1998 statistics are revised to be compatible with balance of payments data.

Nevertheless, the new export duties and surrender requirement create an incentive for Russian exporters to find ways to lower their non-CIS export receipts in order to minimize their tax burden.[468]

Russia's *imports* will remain depressed reflecting the country's current banking crisis and stalled foreign investment, as well as falling GDP and currency devaluation. While the rouble's real depreciation was spectacular – the currency lost about half of its value against the dollar between August and December 1998 – the future course of the real exchange rate (and consequently of imports) will depend on the scale of money emission. The currency devaluation will continue to affect imports of foodstuffs and consumer products as well as those sectors of manufacturing that depend on foreign intermediate inputs. Moreover, the country's fiscal requirements will continue to influence the country's import policies, just as they have already affected export policies. The early 1999 postponement of the deadline for the reduction of import duties from 30 to

20 per cent on some goods is perhaps a harbinger of the future direction of import policies.

In other CIS countries, the Russian financial crisis, aside from its immediate effects in reducing the demand for CIS goods and services, has triggered a series of *currency devaluations*. While these realignments are still underway, the initial currency movements have caused some "traditional" trade flows, especially of foodstuffs and consumer goods, to be redirected, bringing about local shortages in exporting countries and a backlash of producers against cheap imports in importing countries. Kazakhstan, for example, imposed 200 per cent tariffs on selected products from Kyrgyzstan and Uzbekistan in February 1999, following an earlier ban on imports of Russian food products. The appearance of these regional "trade shocks" have resulted in calls for trade measures to protect domestic enterprises, accusations of trade blockades, and even prospects of a trade war among the CIS countries of central Asia.[469]

Finally, low commodity prices, which have hit Russia's and other CIS countries' natural resource exports, have lowered the cost of *food imports*. New

_____

[468] The State Customs Committee has already claimed that Russian exporters are evading the 75 per cent surrender requirement and export duties by signing rouble contracts with agents from other CIS countries to re-export their products outside the CIS. *ITAR-TASS News Agency* (Moscow) as reported by *BBC Monitoring Summary of World Broadcasts*, 12 February 1999.

_____

[469] "Central Asia tariff war beckons", *Financial Times*, 12 February 1999 and "Kyrgyz President accuses neighbors of trade blockade", *Russia Today*, 11 February 1999 (internet website).

TABLE 3.6.8

Russian Federation's merchandise trade, July-November 1998

(Billion dollars and per cent)

	July		August		September		October		November	
	Value	Change	Value	Change	Value	Change	Value	Change	Value	Change
Non-CIS										
Exports	4.7	-20	4.9	-17	4.8	-12	4.9	-24	4.6	-28
Imports	4.4	-7	3.9	-18	2.5	-50	2.2	-60	2.2	-53
Machinery and equipment *(million dollars)* 1184.0		-20	1 255.7	1	132.3	-29	746.5	-42	684.5	-48
Furniture *(million dollars)*	23.4	-41	19.5	-48	15.6	-68	13.7	-76	15.0	-68
Clothing *(million dollars)*	17.0	-11	18.9	-25	9.4	-70	10.9	-70	15.6	-45
Pharmaceuticals *(million dollars)*	101.8	-35	92.7	-10	33.5	-74	31.6	-84	42.6	-70
Meat *(thousand tonnes)*	77.8	–	41.2	-38	19.3	-64	8.2	-87	20.2	-61
Poultry *(thousand tonnes)*	103.7	-9	57.7	-54	20.4	-78	22.2	-80	31.8	-68
Citrus fruit *(thousand tonnes)*	22.7	32	11.1	-17	9.2	-67	12.9	-65	29.7	-41
Trade balance	0.3	..	1.0	..	2.3	..	2.7	..	2.4	..
CIS										
Exports	1.3	6	1.0	-30	0.8	-47	1.1	-35	1.3	-24
Imports	1.2	-21	1.3	-18	0.7	-55	0.8	-55	0.8	-43
Trade balance	0.1	..	-0.3	..	0.1	..	0.3	..	0.5	..

Source: Russian Federation Goskomstat, *Sotsial'no-ekonomicheskoe polozhenie Rossii* (Moscow), various issues.

Note: Non-registered trade is only included in total exports and imports. Change is percentage change over same month of 1997.

Low demand for steel, caused by the diminished Asian demand and the threat of anti-dumping measures in many Asian countries, has forced the Russian steel exporters to redirect their shipments to other markets.[477] A subsequent influx of steel imports from Russia and other CIS countries to North America has prompted domestic steel producers there to initiate anti-dumping proceedings. In contrast to the third quarter performance of Russian non-CIS exports, which was generally in line with the first half of 1998, third quarter *imports* were drastically lower. The August devaluation, debt default and, most importantly, paralysis in the banking sector caused large import declines in August and September (food, consumer products, textiles). Imports of machinery and equipment and chemicals also fell reflecting the immediate currency and banking crisis and the continuing poor industrial performance.

Determinants of trade performance

Russia's overall export performance is closely related to fluctuations in world commodity prices. As prices of virtually all commodities continued to fall in 1998, Russia's export performance suffered correspondingly. While Russian producers have attempted, in some sectors, to boost export volumes to make up for the falling prices, it appears, in general, that the limits of production capacity have been reached for many natural resources. Moreover, transport bottlenecks are likely to prevent any significant increase in exports in the near future.[478] In addition to falling commodity prices, the August devaluation of the

Russian rouble has also had a significant impact on trade. The central bank also implemented administrative controls to prevent capital flight and to slow down the rate of nominal depreciation.[479] All of these measures have had a direct impact on Russian trade, imports in particular. While the immediate dramatic fall in *imports* was caused mainly by the banking crisis that accompanied the devaluation, the currency devaluation raised the rouble prices of imported goods, drastically curtailing the demand for many imports. The combined effect of the payments crisis, paralyzing the activities of many importers, and the subsequent fall in the rouble have caused a sharp drop in import demand and the collapse of imports since August (table 3.6.8).

(b) Other CIS countries: trade with non-CIS countries

Trade performance

In the first three quarters of 1998, the value of *exports* from CIS countries other than Russia to the rest of the world declined by 9 per cent (table 3.6.7). Only in Armenia and Kyrgyzstan were there increases while declines in the remaining countries ranged between 3 per cent in Kazakhstan to 40 per cent in Azerbaijan. Aggregate *imports* from the non-CIS area were down 2 per cent, largely as a result of declines in Ukraine, Uzbekistan and, to a lesser extent, Turkmenistan and Tajikistan. All other CIS countries registered double-digit import increases, although in most cases there was a considerable deceleration in the second half of 1998. The

---

[477] In 1998, the United States share of Russian steel exports was about 50 per cent, up from 30 per cent in 1996.

[478] Preliminary data indicate that crude oil production fell by 0.6 per cent, but natural gas was up by 3.5 per cent in 1998.

[479] The partial re-regulation of the foreign exchange market includes a mandatory 75 per cent surrender of export receipts and a dual exchange rate regime.

TABLE 3.6.9

Non-CIS trade of the Russian Federation by selected commodities, 1994-1998

(Shares and growth rates in per cent)

	Exports					Imports				
	Share			Growth rates		Share			Growth rates	
	1994	1997[a]	1998[a]	1997	1998[b]	1994	1997[a]	1998[a]	1997	1998[b]
Agricultural products (I-III)	1.2	0.6	1.1	-5.4	43.7	13.4	14.2	13.7	30.6	-4.9
Food, beverages and tobacco (IV)	0.6	0.4	0.2	-30.7	-64.3	17.0	12.8	14.5	28.7	11.2
Mineral products (V)	41.5	49.1	43.2	-1.0	-28.0	2.9	2.8	2.4	21.4	-13.6
Chemical or allied products (VI)	7.3	6.8	7.7	-3.3	-8.3	8.8	12.5	12.3	24.0	-3.2
Textiles and textile articles (XI)	1.8	0.9	1.0	-3.0	-4.5	5.3	2.5	2.3	8.9	-9.5
Precious metals and stones (XIV)	12.7	2.8	3.2	-16.4	-6.8	0.1	0.3	–	-75.3	-85.0
Base metals and articles (XV)	20.8	24.1	26.5	5.1	-10.3	3.9	4.4	4.3	7.4	-3.3
Machinery and equipment (XVI)	2.9	3.1	3.6	12.8	-5.8	27.6	24.7	23.1	19.8	-8.0
Vehicles, transport equipment (XVII)	3.3	4.4	4.8	-5.6	-9.7	4.7	9.4	10.8	95.4	13.6
Precision and optical equipment (XVIII)	0.2	0.3	0.6	12.7	54.7	5.4	3.9	4.3	1.1	9.2
Arms and ammunition (XIX)	0.9	0.5	0.3	-56.7	-45.8	–	–	–	50.0	10.4
Total above	93.4	93.2	92.3	-1.4	-18.9	89.2	87.6	88.0	24.7	-1.2
Total	100.0	100.0	100.0	-1.2	-14.9	100.0	100.0	100.0	23.2	-0.2

Source: Russian Federation State Customs Committee, *Tamozhennaya statistika vneshnei torgovli Rossiiskoi Federatsii* (Moscow), various issues. Commodity groups are Sections of the Harmonized Commodity Description and Coding System (HS).

[a] January-September.

[b] January-September over same period of 1997.

aggregate merchandise *trade deficit* was $900 million with only Kazakhstan, Tajikistan, Ukraine and Uzbekistan running trade surpluses.

Determinants of trade performance

The decline in the value of exports to non-CIS countries was closely related to the drop in prices for the major export commodities. The declines in value occurred in spite of, in many cases, increased volumes. For example, in Kazakhstan crude oil exports were up by 31 per cent in volume but remained flat in value. Similarly, copper and zinc exports were over 10 per cent higher in volume but revenues were almost 20 per cent lower. Shrinking demand for ferrous metals also affected Kazakh and Ukrainian exports. Non-CIS exports of iron ores and ferrous metals fell by 60 and 14 per cent in volume, respectively. In other commodity exporting countries, lower prices, fluctuating volumes and production difficulties played variable roles in determining performance. In Azerbaijan, exports of oil products decreased by 22 per cent in volume. The decline was related to drastically lower shipments to Iran, traditionally a major purchaser of Azerbaijani oil products, which apparently has found alternative and cheaper sources of supply. Despite lower oil prices, Turkmenistan has continued to increase crude oil extraction and refining in an attempt to offset the revenue lost because of the country's inability to export natural gas (natural gas exports to Ukraine resumed in early 1999). Tajikistan's aluminium exports, representing over half of the country's exports to non-CIS countries, increased marginally but revenues were down by 8 per cent. Despite the improved cotton harvest, exports of cotton fibre, contributing about 40 per cent of total non-CIS exports, decreased by a third in value.

On the *import* side, CIS countries buy non-CIS products such as foodstuffs, machinery and equipment and, in some cases, raw materials. A slowdown in imports of food suggests reduced consumption levels following the Russian crisis and subsequent currency devaluations in many CIS countries (e.g. Georgia and the Republic of Moldova). The persistent pressures on many regional currencies are expected to have a significant impact on non-CIS trade flows in 1999. In recent years, substantial imports of machinery and equipment have been associated with the industrialization and modernization of CIS economies. While foreign investment continues to play an important role in Azerbaijan, Kazakhstan and Kyrgyzstan, the unfavourable conditions and outlook in the oil sector are affecting imports of machinery and equipment in Kazakhstan. In contrast, in the third quarter, the rate of increase of Azerbaijan's imports rose on account of continued vigorous activity in the country's oil industry, but it slowed down in Kyrgyzstan due to the completion of the import-intensive Kumtor gold mine. In Turkmenistan, Ukraine and Uzbekistan, balance of payments problems will continue to limit their ability to import from non-CIS countries.

(c) Intra-CIS trade

Trade performance

In the first nine months of 1998, the value of intra-CIS trade decreased, with the decline rapidly accelerating in the third quarter. Russian and other CIS countries' *exports (imports)* fell by 14 per cent (table 3.6.7). The only two countries that increased their exports to other CIS countries were Armenia and Belarus, but the rates of increase were less than half those in the first half of 1998.

"voluntary" export quota and agreement to maintain a minimum price.)[489] Third, the WTO as an international body collects and disseminates trade-related information, which members often find invaluable.[490] Transition economies could use WTO trade policy reviews to critically assess their own trade policies and scrutinize the trade regimes of their trading partners. Finally, WTO membership puts at new members' disposal a contractually binding dispute settlement mechanism: small economies – such as the CIS countries – are most likely to benefit from access to an impartial and binding dispute settlement.

In addition to the above-mentioned benefits, the WTO accession process can provide some impetus for further development of the institutional framework in CIS countries. It is important to note that the former republics of the Soviet Union had no borders, no national currencies, no customs infrastructure and no trade policies of their own. The accession process helps CIS countries in institution-building through encouraging improvements in the quality and transparency of government policies; in supporting market-oriented reforms and encouraging governments' resistance to protectionist or anti-reform pressures; and improving fiscal discipline by hardening budget constraints through the introduction of bankruptcy procedures and the lowering of subsidies.

While the potential benefits of WTO membership are extensive, the immediate costs of meeting the accession requirements, and the (post-accession) adjustments costs arising from opening up the national economy, cannot be ignored.[491] On the one hand, international trade rules assume the existence of an economic system largely based on market transactions and because market-oriented reforms are far from complete in the CIS area, a large part of *pre-accession* costs is incurred in designing, developing and implementing market-supporting institutions.[492] On the other hand, the *post-accession* adjustment costs, which, it is assumed, are likely to be outweighed by the benefits of being part of a large and competitive marketplace,

usually involve politically sensitive short-term costs such as increased bankruptcies and higher unemployment. However, if these adjustment costs are ignored, or if the process of liberalization is too rapid for the rate of adjustment to cope, then there is likely to be increasing resistance to the entire process.

In part because of these potentially high costs, there has been some delay and hesitation on the part of most CIS countries in making commitments to and implementing comprehensive trade liberalization. However, the reasons for delay in CIS countries are many. In some cases, they reflect a weak commitment to market-oriented economic principles, in others, the lack of capacity to negotiate at the bilateral and multilateral level or to put the necessary legislative and administrative infrastructure in place.[493] Other factors, beyond the CIS countries' control, also affect the pace of accession. The relatively new WTO now has a "jurisdiction" which extends from goods to services to government procurement to intellectual property, in effect, covering many sectors of the national economy. As a result, WTO accessions have become more complex and, as the experience of recent accessions shows, the terms of membership have become more demanding.[494] Nevertheless, at present, it does not appear that CIS countries, on average, will take much longer to join the WTO than four recent new members (Bulgaria, Equador, Mongolia and Panama, for which the negotiations lasted about six years each).[495] In fact, the two first accessions from countries of the former Soviet Union – Kyrgyzstan and Latvia – took rather less time to complete (roughly three and five years, respectively).

While Kyrgyzstan's accession proceeded relatively rapidly, other CIS applicants are advancing at different rates (table 3.6.11). Armenia is the most advanced – its bilateral market access negotiations in the goods and services sectors are near completion and a draft report describing the terms of entry has been discussed. Similarly, the first draft of Georgia's accession conditions was discussed in October 1998. The Georgian negotiations covering the goods sector have been concluded and rapid progress is reported in all the remaining areas. Georgian officials hope to join the WTO in 1999, subject to the introduction of the required domestic legislation, especially in the areas of patents and trademarks. The Republic of Moldova's bilateral market

---

[489] "U.S. set to be lenient on Russian steel imports", *International Herald Tribune*, 12-13 December 1998.

[490] J. Pietras, "The role of the WTO for economies in transition", in A. Krueger (ed.), *The WTO as an International Organization* (Chicago, The University of Chicago Press, 1998), p. 356,

[491] These costs, in particular pre-accession costs, should be seen as one-off investments necessary to modernize and advance the CIS national economies. K. Dziewulski, "Korzysci z uczestnictwa Polski w WTO", *Gospodarka Narodowa*, No. 3, 1996, p. 28.

[492] Despite the onus on the potential entrants, the WTO accession process does take into consideration the legacy of central planning and the fact that the transition process does not entail marginal changes. Accordingly, "the overall guiding principle [of the accession process] is to achieve the right balance in determining the terms of entry, keeping in view the capacities of individual acceding governments and the need to maintain the credibility of the WTO system." WTO, "Note by the secretariat", Document WT/GC/W/100, 30 September 1998 (internet website).

[493] The existence of an "institutional infrastructure" is essential to ensure that a new member is able to participate effectively in the WTO framework of rights and obligations and the infrastructure must be transparent to be verifiable for compliance with international trade liberalization commitments.

[494] Z. Drabek and S. Laird, "The new liberalism: trade policy developments in emerging markets, *World Trade Organization Staff Working Paper*, ERAD-97-007, January 1997, p. 14.

[495] C. Michalopoulos, "WTO accession for countries in transition", *World Bank Policy Research Paper*, No. 1934 (Washington, D.C.), June 1998.

TABLE 3.6.11

Status of World Trade Organization accession and major outstanding bilateral issues, as of 30 September 1998

	Armenia	Belarus	Georgia	Kazakhstan	Republic of Moldova	Russian Federation	Ukraine	Uzbekistan [a]
Agriculture	X	X	X	X	X	X	X	
Customs system	X	X	X	X	X	X	X	
Industrial subsidies	X	X	X	X	X	X	X	
State trading	X	X	X		X		X	
SPS and TBT	X	X	X	X	X	X		
Trade-related Aspects of Intellectual Property	X	X	X	X	X	X	X	
Barter trade		X						
Institutional transparency		X	X	X	X		X	
Price controls				X				
Import licensing or non-tariff barriers				X	X	X	X	
Taxation and national treatment					X	X	X	
Trade-related investment measures						X		
Services					X	X	X	
Status of market access negotiations	Near completion (in goods and services)	Have begun (in goods)	Actively engaged (in goods and services)	Ongoing (in goods and services)	Actively engaged (in goods and services)	Have begun (in goods)	Ongoing (in goods and services)	Initiated

Source: The World Trade Organization.

Note: SPS: Sanitary and phytosanitary measures; TBT: Technical barriers to trade. Azerbaijan has not submitted a Memorandum on the Foreign Trade Regime yet. Kyrgyzstan is a member since December 1998. Tajikistan and Turkmenistan have not applied for membership. X denotes topics under discussion in the Working Groups.

[a] Submitted a Memorandum on the Foreign Trade Regime in September 1998.

access negotiations, covering both goods and services, are underway but the Working Party has not produced a draft report yet. The country recently introduced a new 5 per cent tax on all imports to protect local producers and to stabilize the domestic situation in the wake of the Russian financial crisis. While these measures run counter to a possible agreement with WTO members, the government argued that international economic conditions were exceptionally damaging. The market access negotiations with Kazakhstan and Ukraine are continuing in the goods and services sectors based on a revised goods offer by Kazakhstan and a revised services offer by Ukraine. Kazakhstan is scheduled to submit draft domestic legislation designed to comply with WTO accession requirements in early 1999. The Ukraine accession process, however, appears to have stalled. At its last Working Party meeting, the country was criticized for raising import duties on hundreds of goods, for introducing restrictive import quotas on agricultural products, for maintaining various non-tariff barriers to trade and for its foreign investment policy.[496] Russia and Belarus have begun bilateral negotiations in the goods sector. Russia has yet to provide a service sector offer and has recently come under pressure to release more up-to-date information concerning its agricultural sector. Continued bilateral negotiations coupled with a very gradual and moderate opening of the Russian economy appear to remain central to the overall Russian policy stance with respect to WTO membership. Finally, the

government of Azerbaijan is actively seeking accession to the WTO, but the process remains at a very early stage. As part of the country's unilateral trade liberalization, the authorities intend to reduce the general import tariff rate from 15 per cent to 10 per cent by the year 2001, but earlier plans to cut the rate to 12 per cent in 1999 have been postponed.[497]

Most of the CIS countries also face difficulties in improving the institutional aspects of their trade regimes. Many of these difficulties reflect the broader problems of reforming systems of public administration and practice that were designed for a relatively closed centrally planned economy, not a market economy operating in an open, international environment. Nevertheless, they impinge on the trading system in many ways that complicate the accession negotiated with WTO. Certification requirements for consumer goods, import licensing procedures, and customs clearance, are just three examples of areas where the rules are frequently obscure and complex and where bureaucratic process is characterized by inordinate delay and unpredictability. Complying with the accession conditions demanded by the existing WTO members, however, is closely connected to the transition process as a whole and especially with its dimension of building the institutional infrastructure for a market economy.

Agriculture, industrial subsidies and state trading also appear to be issues that are characteristically difficult

---

[496] "WTO scolds Ukraine on protectionist trade policies", *Journal of Commerce*, as quoted by *Reuters New Service*, 12 June 1998.

[497] *IMF*, "Azerbaijan: enhanced structural adjustment facility, 1999-2001, *Policy Framework Paper,* 8 January 1999 (internet website).

to settle. First, most transition economies have found the negotiations on agriculture very difficult as, in general, they are trying to retain the right to subsidize agricultural exports. Moreover, demands by WTO members to bind domestic agricultural support at low levels appear to be particularly stringent when compared with the agricultural policies of some OECD countries.[498] Second, also in the industrial sector, many countries are resisting the elimination of subsidies to producers which are viewed by WTO members as inherently trade distorting.[499] Third, state trading – defined by the WTO as trading by an enterprise that has special trading privileges and is not necessarily a state owned enterprise – also represents a typical impediment to WTO accession. While the "size" of state involvement is not as important an issue as that of transparency between the state and exporters, in Russia, for example, the state nevertheless controls an estimated 10-20 per cent of the country's international trade.[500] Reducing the role of monopolies, introducing more transparency between the state and the private sector, and terminating the state trading aspects of intergovernmental (intra-CIS) agreements appears to be key in advancing the applications of Russia and other CIS countries for WTO membership. Finally, progress in privatization in transition economies is also considered very important by the existing WTO members; in fact, privatization has become a proxy for the transformation of economic institutions in general.

The "entry fee" for joining the WTO is a negotiated one; it is tailored to each applicant and it is represented by the entire package of trade liberalization commitments with flexibility in one area likely offsetting more rigorous demands in others.[501] The entry fee is considered by CIS governments to be worth paying not only to enhance the credibility of their policies and to make transition economies more attractive destinations for foreign investment, but also to encourage structural change and to anchor their economies to market-based principles.[502]

[498] M. Lucke, "Accession of the CIS countries to the World Trade Organization", *German Yearbook of International Law*, Vol. 39, 1996, p. 146.

[499] P. Milthorp, "Integration of FSU/economies in transition into the World Trade Organization", *Economics of Transition*, Vol. 5, No. 1 (Oxford), 1997, pp. 220-221.

[500] C. Michalopoulos and V. Drebentsov, "Observations on state trading in the Russian economy", *Post-Soviet Geography and Economics*, Volume XXXVIII, No. 5, pp. 273-274.

[501] P. Milthorp, op. cit., p. 223.

[502] This could be accomplished through the reduction in direct state economic intervention, the creation of a viable private sector, economic autonomy for state owned enterprises, the establishment of linkage between domestic and world prices (and a unified and undistorted exchange rate) and exposing domestic producers to external competition. OECD, *Integrating Emerging Market Economies into the International Trading System* (Paris), 1994, pp. 22-23.

3.7 Balance of payments and external finance

(i) Introduction

The turmoil in international markets was already putting pressure on the current account balances of the transition economies in the first half of 1998 as the continuing Asian crisis weakened economic activity in an increasing number of major foreign markets. The collapse of Russian and CIS import demand intensified these pressures, although falling commodity prices provided some relief for many countries. The "flight to quality" in the financial markets in October 1997 had an immediate and long-lasting impact, affecting all types of capital flows into the transition economies. Moreover, contagion effects occasionally triggered the flight of short-term funds, drove down exchange rates and in some cases led to the loss of official reserves. Despite all this, capital flows into eastern Europe and the Baltic states increased again in 1998. The few countries seriously affected by the financial shocks were vulnerable not only because of their weak external positions, but also because of inconsistent macroeconomic policies and the slow pace of structural reform.

The outlook for increasing current account deficits, large scheduled repayments of debt (in several cases), continuing constraints on access to international finance, and uncertainty about FDI flows raise concerns about the sustainability of several European transition economies' financial positions. This is particularly true of those countries which are rated subinvestment grade risks. Their plans for external financing typically count on privatization revenues, multilateral funding and some borrowing in international markets, but their room for manoeuvre is limited especially as official reserves tend to be low. In these cases, failure to reach agreement with the IMF, delays in privatization or further upheavals in the international financial markets could require a tightening macroeconomic policy and/or precipitate a crisis.

(ii) Current account developments

(a) Eastern Europe and the Baltic states

The aggregate current account deficit of eastern Europe continued to grow in 1998 (table 3.7.1), to an estimated $17 billion (4.5 per cent of GDP). In most countries current account imbalances worsened throughout the year, accelerating in the last quarter as the full impact of slowing western demand, falling imports into Russia (and certain other CIS) and, often, appreciating real exchange rates, began to be felt. In virtually all cases, the current account deficits being reported in the last months of 1998 were larger than had been expected, even under the more pessimistic projections made earlier in the year. The imbalances would have been even greater but for the considerable drop in the import prices of commodities and intermediate goods (section 3.6). In several countries, current account deficits were constrained by the tight international financing conditions affecting all emerging market economies.

TABLE 3.7.1

Current account balances of eastern Europe, the Baltic countries and European members of the CIS, 1996-1998

(Million dollars and per cent)

			January-September			Per cent of GDP		
	1996	1997	1997	1998	1998	1996	1997	1998[a]
Eastern Europe [b]	-13 189	-14 662	-10 269	-10 139	-16 974	-3.7	-4.2	-4.5
Albania	-107	-271	-121	-21	-50*	-4.0	-12.0	-1.7*
Bosnia and Herzegovina	-748	-1 046	..	..	..	..	..	..
Bulgaria	16	427	380	-91	-273	0.2	4.2	-2.1
Croatia	-858	-2 434	-1 085	-862	-1 554	-4.3	-12.1	-7.3
Czech Republic	-4 292	-3 211	-2 564	-481	-800*	-7.6	-6.2	-1.5
Hungary	-1 678	-981	-686	-1 337	-2 298	-3.7	-2.1	-4.8*
Poland	-1 352[c]	-4 268[c]	-3 638[c]	-3 846	-6 810	-0.9	-3.0	-4.3
Romania	-2 571	-2 338	-1 277	-1 849	-2 633[d]	-7.3	-6.7	-6.9
Slovakia	-2 098	-1 347	-1 102	-1 542	-2 300*	-11.2	-6.9	-11.3*
Slovenia	39	37	-16	58	-6	0.2	0.2	–
The former Yugoslav Republic of Macedonia	-288	-275	-161	-168	-250*	-6.5	-7.4	-7.1
Baltic states	-1 425	-1 889	-1 145	-1 854	..	-8.2	-9.5	-11.3
Estonia	-423	-563	-349	-370	..	-9.7	-12.0	-9.7
Latvia	-279	-345	-222	-456	..	-5.4	-6.2	-9.7
Lithuania	-723	-981	-574	-1028	..	-9.2	-10.2	-13.0
CIS	10 207	934	1 096	-8 012	..	2.1	0.2	-3.2
Belarus	-516	-799	-525	-797	..	-3.8	-6.0	-7.4
Republic of Moldova	-188	-267	-208	-280	..	-11.1	-13.9	-23.3
Russian Federation	12 096	3 335	3 011	-5 625	..	2.8	0.8	-2.7
Ukraine	-1 185	-1 335	-1 181	-1 310	..	-2.7	-2.7	-4.1
Total above	-4 408	-15 617	-10 318	-20 005	..	-0.5	-1.8	..

Source: National balance of payments statistics; press reports; UN/ECE secretariat estimates.

[a] Full year except for Baltic states and CIS which are January-September.

[b] Eastern Europe aggregate excludes Bosnia and Herzegovina.

[c] Convertible currencies.

[d] Official forecasts.

The growth of east European trade in goods[503] and services quickened slightly in the first three quarters of 1998 (table 3.7.2). The dollar value of exports increased by 8 per cent (perhaps 11-12 per cent in terms of volume), although service exports ceased to grow. Fragmentary statistics for merchandise trade in the last months of the year indicate a sharp fall of export growth as the international environment deteriorated (section 3.6). Imports of goods and services rose by 9 per cent (some 12-13 per cent in volume) in the first nine months of 1998 with service imports tending to rise strongly.

The development of trade in services indicates that the deterioration in merchandise trade (reflecting the external environment) was not uniquely responsible for the worsening of current account balances. In fact, domestic factors seem to explain some of the $1 billion decline in eastern Europe's surplus on services in 1998. This had increased since the beginning of the decade, helping to offset the steady growth in the merchandise trade deficit. The recent change mainly reflects a stagnation of receipts from services (including tourism) and a further expansion of imports of business services (associated with the

development of a market economy). If the demand for foreign business services continues to grow quickly, the negative trend in the overall services balance may be difficult to reverse. Most countries reported larger net inward transfers, mainly remittances from nationals working abroad. Net income payments were largely unchanged, smaller interest payments (due to declining international interest rates) being offset by larger outflows of other income, including, increasingly, foreign investment income.

Among the central European countries, exports of goods and services expanded at a rapid pace (although growth rates slowed as the year progressed). However, current account balances deteriorated in Hungary, Poland and Slovakia, all of which experienced strong GDP growth. In *Hungary* the improvement in the current account, underway since the launching of the 1995 stabilization programme, ceased in the first half of 1998. Although monetary and fiscal policies remained prudent and the real exchange rate was kept roughly constant (chart 3.7.1), the current account deficit more than doubled.[504]

[503] This section is based on balance of payments statistics, which may show a different development of merchandise trade than the customs statistics used in sect. 3.6.

[504] Attention is drawn to the difference between the growth rates of merchandise trade in table 3.7.2 (based on the balance of payments) and the much higher rates calculated from customs statistics (table 3.6.1). Attempts to reconcile the two have been made, but large differences remain unexplained. OECD, *Economic Surveys: Hungary* (Paris), 1999, pp. 144-145.

TABLE 3.7.2

Foreign trade in goods and non-factor services of eastern Europe, the Baltic countries and European members of the CIS, 1996-1998

(Per cent)

| | Growth rates | | | | | | | Growth rates | | | | | |
| | Exports | | | Imports | | | | Exports | | | Imports | | |
	1996	1997	Jan.-Sept. 1998[a]	1996	1997	Jan.-Sept. 1998[a]		1996	1997	Jan.-Sept. 1998[a]	1996	1997	Jan.-Sept. 1998[a]
Eastern Europe							**The former Yugoslav Republic of Macedonia**						
Goods and services [b,c] .	5	7	8	14	7	9	Goods and services ...	-6	2	9	-2	5	10
Goods	3	10	10	14	8	9	Goods	-5	5	10	3	9	10
Services	13	-2	–	13	-3	6	Services	-17	-17	–	-20	-12	13
Albania							**Baltic states**						
Goods and services ...	24	-40	20	33	-27	36	Goods and services ...	21	20	10	25	20	16
Goods	19	-35	23	36	-25	33	Goods	13	24	12	19	21	17
Services	33	-49	14	21	-38	52	Services	46	12	8	62	14	15
Bulgaria							**Estonia**						
Goods and services ...	-8	–	-10	-9	-4	1	Goods and services ...	6	25	19	12	21	19
Goods	-9	1	-12	-10	-3	3	Goods	-4	28	21	11	21	19
Services	-5	-2	-2	-3	-6	-7	Services	27	19	15	19	23	20
Croatia							**Latvia**						
Goods and services ...	11	2	2	7	15	-3	Goods and services ...	25	10	9	38	11	18
Goods	-2	-7	7	4	15	-2	Goods	9	24	14	17	18	22
Services	33	15	-3	21	15	-4	Services	56	-8	-1	202	-11	3
Czech Republic							**Lithuania**						
Goods and services ...	6	–	14	13	-3	4	Goods and services ...	32	24	6	28	25	14
Goods	1	5	17	10	-1	5	Goods	26	23	6	27	24	12
Services	22	-12	4	28	-14	-1	Services	64	29	6	36	33	20
Hungary [b]							**3 European CIS**						
Goods and services ...	12	..	3	8	..	5	Goods and services ...	21	6	-9	20	8	-8
Goods	11	..	4	10	..	4	Goods	13	7	-9	20	6	-10
Services	18	..	-1	-1	..	10	Services	68	3	-11	17	33	19
Poland							**Belarus**						
Goods and services [c]	7	11	14	30	16	15	Goods and services ...	30	24	2	27	25	6
Goods	7	12	16	32	18	15	Goods	23	28	2	27	26	5
Services	6	10	1	18	-5	17	Services	95	2	1	18	15	34
Romania							**Republic of Moldova**						
Goods and services ...	3	2	-3	11	–	9	Goods and services ...	6	9	-14	23	14	-2
Goods	2	4	-3	11	-1	8	Goods	11	8	-16	33	15	-3
Services	5	-9	-1	7	5	16	Services	-22	18	-2	-14	10	10
Slovakia							**Ukraine**						
Goods and services ...	–	1	16	27	-6	20	Goods and services ...	19	–	-13	17	2	-14
Goods	3	–	19	31	-8	21	Goods	9	-1	-14	17	-1	-17
Services	-13	5	3	11	3	12	Services	69	3	-13	22	40	18
Slovenia							**Russian Federation**						
Goods and services ...	1	–	6	–	–	5	Goods and services ...	11	-1	-13	5	5	-5
Goods	–	–	7	-1	-1	5	Goods	9	-2	-14	9	6	-5
Services	5	-4	-1	2	2	5	Services	23	7	-6	-7	2	-7

Source: UN/ECE secretariat, based on national balance of payments statistics.

[a] Over same period of 1997.

[b] 1997 Hungarian data are estimated.

[c] Excludes "non-classified current transactions" reported by Poland.

The doubling of outflows of net investment income, associated with foreign direct investment, to almost $1 billion was an important factor in this regard. In *Poland* a loss of competitiveness (reflected in the appreciation of the real exchange rate) contributed to the deterioration of the trade and current account balances (although exports remained buoyant for much of the year). Following the Russian devaluation, there was a marked fall in net receipts from unclassified trade in goods and services (which includes cross-border trade with Russia and Ukraine).[505] In *Slovakia*, the already high current account deficit was exacerbated by a lax fiscal stance, setting the stage for the abandonment of

[505] These exchanges are not recorded in the customs statistics. Net receipts fell by about $140 million a month (or to $1.7 billion at an annual rate) following the Russian crisis.

the currency band (October 1) in the wake of the Russian devaluation. In the *Czech Republic*, the lagged effect of the devaluation of 1997 and tight monetary policies compressed domestic demand, helping to boost export growth. However, this expansion eventually slowed as the real exchange rate appreciated strongly and external demand weakened. Nonetheless, the current account imbalance improved in 1998, by almost 5 per cent of GDP. In contrast to most transition economies, the Czech Republic's surplus on services improved, mainly because of tourism.

In south-east Europe, the pace of trade in goods and services of the republics of the former SFR of Yugoslavia tended to pick up in 1998. In *Slovenia* this followed two years in which the value of these exchanges stagnated. A decline in competitiveness may have contributed to the worsening of the current account, which nonetheless remained roughly balanced. *The former Yugoslav Republic of Macedonia* posted its fastest growth of trade in goods and services since 1995, due in part to the shift in trade toward western Europe. However, there was little change in its large current account deficit. Trimming the large current account deficit was a key policy objective in *Croatia* in 1998. The tightening of fiscal and monetary policies (in part prompted by limited access to international funds) and some depreciation of the real exchange rate had the desired effect. However, exports of services stagnated as the anticipated surge in tourism receipts failed to materialize (they rose by only 5 per cent). The balance of payments data which have recently become available for *Bosnia and Herzegovina*, indicate the persistence of a large current account deficit, despite substantial official transfers. After a hiatus of five years, the central bank of Yugoslavia began to publish the balance of payments. They show that in 1997 the country ran a current account deficit of $1.3 billion, consisting of a $1.9 billion trade deficit and a $0.6 billion surplus on the services account.[506]

In *Albania*, trade in goods and services recovered from the economic crisis of 1997, the upturn being stronger on the side of imports. Also, private transfers (workers' remittances) recovered, significantly improving the current account. The export performance of Bulgaria and Romania deteriorated in 1998. In addition to the negative external environment, the explanation in *Bulgaria* seems to be an appreciating real exchange rate (section 3.7(iv)), which caused a shift of over 8 per cent of GDP in the current account. The growth of the current account imbalance in *Romania* appears to be due primarily to a large loss of competitiveness and other supply side factors.[507] Tight monetary policy has kept consumption in check and external borrowing was restricted (causing a drawdown of official reserves).

The impact of the collapse of Russian trade on the *Baltic states'* trade in goods and services was greater than in eastern Europe. Moreover, real exchange rates appreciated in all three countries, which probably contributed to the slowdown in the (high) growth of exports of goods and services. Consumption continued to expand strongly in Latvia and Lithuania, contributing to the near doubling of their current account deficits in the first three quarters of 1998. The tightening of monetary policy, weakening consumer demand, and higher net receipts from tourism[508] seem to have slowed the deterioration of the current account in Estonia. Nonetheless the external imbalances of all three countries remain very high.

(b) European CIS

A further decline in Russia's merchandise exports and buoyant imports in the early part of the year, together with a sizeable increase in interest obligations (on both internal and external debt), shifted the current account into deficit ($5.6 billion) in the January-September period. In the third quarter of the year, the combination of a banking crisis, the loss of external financing and the devaluation of the rouble caused imports to fall sharply, and the current account reverted to surplus. Large merchandise trade surpluses in the last months of the year point to a positive current account balance for all of 1998.

Despite severe limits on new financing, the current account deficits of the other European CIS increased in the first three quarters of 1998. In Ukraine, financial constraints contributed to the contraction of the merchandise trade deficit, but the other components of the current account deteriorated, led by a $1.3 billion loss of net transport revenues (mainly from natural gas pipelines). Economic policies did little to curb the growth of the large external imbalance in the Republic of Moldova which left the country vulnerable to contagion from Russia's financial problems. Expansionary monetary and fiscal policies in Belarus placed pressure on the current account, but it was the only European member of the CIS in which trade in goods and services expanded.

(iii) External financing and FDI

(a) Funds raised on the international markets

The Asian crisis and the following period of market turbulence has led to a major setback in the international borrowing activities of the transition economies, reversing years of progress toward greater market access. In October 1997, the profound shift in investor sentiment away from emerging markets caused the premia on secondary market debt to rise (chart 3.7.2) and substantially increased the cost of new funds. In consequence, many countries shelved or cancelled their plans to borrow or issue equities. Even short-term trade credits, previously available to many CIS countries, appear to have dried up.[509]

---

[506] *Trziste Novac Kapital* (Belgrade) July-September 1998. The reported trade balance of $1.9 billion has been adjusted to incorporate exports of processed goods lowering it to $1 billion.

[507] The closure of some loss-making enterprises has adversely affected exports.

[508] Tourism reflects some unrecorded cross-border trade, including important links with Finland.

[509] The loss of access to trade credits has prompted the EBRD to launch a programme of trade finance for the affected countries.

CHART 3.7.1

Real exchange rates based on unit labour costs [a] for selected transition economies, 1994-1998

(1994 QI=100)

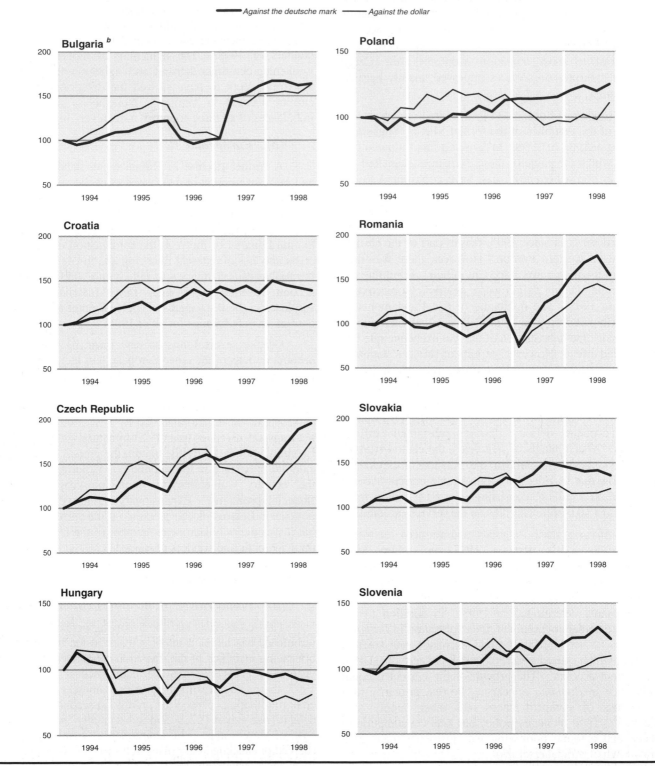

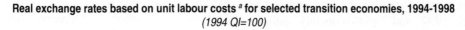

(For source and notes see end of chart.)

CHART 3.7.1 (concluded)

Real exchange rates based on unit labour costs [a] **for selected transition economies, 1994-1998**
(1994 QI=100)

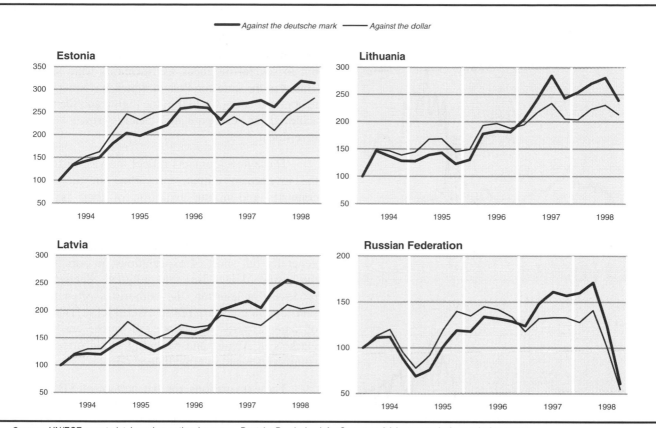

Source: UN/ECE secretariat, based on national sources. Deutche Bundesbank for German unit labour costs in the producing sector.

Note: An increase in the index indicates an appreciation of the real exchange rate. Indices of real deutsche mark and dollar exchange rates have been calculated as the ratio of indices of domestic unit labour costs in marks (and dollars) and unit labour costs in Germany (and the United States). Gross wages and labour productivity are for industry except in Estonia for which gross wages in the whole economy were used. Unit labour costs for Germany are for the producing sector (manufacturing and mining and quarrying), but for the United States they reflect the whole economy. The indices are not adjusted for seasonal variation.

[a] Based on unit labour costs in industry.

[b] Based on consumer price indices.

In March 1998, conditions eased as the markets began to believe that the worst of the global crisis was over. Terms improved (although premia remained above their pre-October 1997 levels), prompting Croatia, Hungary, Slovakia and Slovenia (all investment grade risks) to arrange new funds. Substantial funds were raised by Russia ($7.3 billion) and Ukraine ($1.1 billion), the latter, however, having to borrow at particularly unfavourable terms. However, global market conditions deteriorated again in mid-year and in August Russia devalued. Premia on emerging market debt skyrocketed (chart 3.7.2), and lending virtually ceased. In the remainder of the year, the transition economies issued only two bonds, DM 500 million by Hungary and $1 billion by Poland's Poltelecom (shortly after its privatization). Due to these unfavourable conditions and the downgrading of the credit ratings of several countries, the volume of medium- and long-term funds obtained by the transition economies fell to about $22 billion in 1998,[510] compared with nearly

$30 billion in 1997. Bank lending has held up better than bond issues and sovereign borrowing better than that of the corporate and financial sectors.

In early January 1999, the Brazilian crisis unsettled the markets once again, which may help to explain why only Hungary and Croatia issued bonds (of €500 million and €300 million, respectively) in the first two months of the year.

Despite the upheavals in 1998, most countries maintained their sovereign *international credit ratings* (table 3.7.3). In fact, Hungary was raised a notch by Moody's in May and Poland by Fitch IBCA in November. In the same month, Bulgaria received a rating from Standard & Poor's. The downgrades were concentrated among the countries in the speculative category, although Slovakia lost its investment grade rating. The reasons for these latter changes include domestic financial instability, losses in the terms of trade, inconsistent macroeconomic policies, the slow progress of economic reforms, and a weakened financial position

_____

[510] Some $19 billion of this was raised in January-October. UN/ECE, *Economic Survey of Europe, 1998 No. 3*, table 4.3.4.

CHART 3.7.2

**Premia on selected transition economy bonds,
September 1997-February 1999**
(Percentage points)

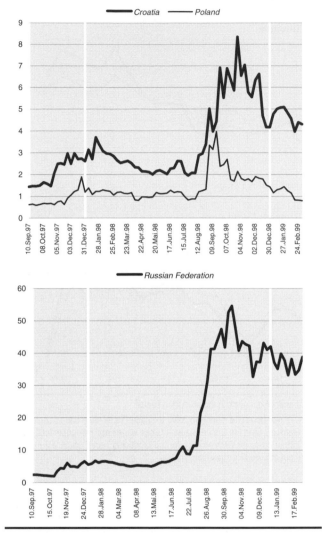

Source: *Financial Times*, various issues.

Note: The premia are over United States treasury bonds.

after contagion from the Russian crisis. In general, investors have differentiated between eastern borrowers. For example, Hungary has retained market access and during an unpropitious period (January 1998) was able to issue a bond on the best terms it has ever obtained (37.5 basis points over LIBOR). Other countries, when they were able to borrow, had to pay much more (Croatia paying 375 basis points over LIBOR) and the premia on the secondary market debt of many countries have remained high.[511]

---

[511] For example, the spread on Slovakia's benchmark eurobond was over 500 basis points in February 1999.

(b) Foreign investment

There was a modest increase in the total volume of FDI flows into the European transition economies in the first three quarters of 1998. Fragmentary data, mostly for eastern Europe, indicate that FDI inflows for the whole year will be little changed from 1997 (table 3.7.4).[512] Only about half of the countries reported larger inflows, but in several instances the increases were significant. This was the case for Poland which has emerged as the major destination for FDI in the region and seems to have achieved an exceptionally steady growth of inward investment.

These developments reflect the vast differences in the investment climate prevailing in the individual countries and in the evolution of their privatization programmes. The programmes are in different stages, ranging from near completion (in Hungary) to those just getting underway. Actual sales of state assets in 1998 generally fell short of expectations, in part because of the usual delays in the political decision-making process. In addition, the authorities often postponed sales due to the sharp fall in asset prices. The valuation of state property was depressed by the crash of stock markets in August and declining world prices of basic commodities and intermediate goods.

The explanations for the pattern of FDI flows in 1998 are complex. Only in Poland did favourable growth prospects (at least, until recently), candidacy for EU membership and privatization – all viewed as important influences on foreign investment decisions – all seem to move together to boost FDI. Among the other EU candidate countries, only the Czech Republic and Estonia reported higher inflows; in Estonia they were heavily influenced by the privatization of two banks in the summer, but thereafter other sales were postponed. The absence of large privatizations seems to explain the decline of FDI in Hungary (since 1995), but flows to the Czech Republic rose markedly although there were no sales of large state assets.[513] Neither are changes in FDI flows explained by economic prospects. Those of the Czech Republic were rather subdued in late 1997 and early 1998 while Hungary was looking forward to another year of high growth.

---

[512] Recent estimates suggest that foreign direct investment into all emerging market economies declined from $117 billion in 1997 to $111 billion in 1998. Due to the subdued outlook for growth, a further decline has been forecast for 1999. Institute of International Finance, Inc. (IIF), *Capital Flows to Emerging Market Economies* (Washington, D.C.), 27 January 1999.

[513] In the Czech Republic, the adoption of a state incentive scheme to support foreign investment in late April 1998 seems to have had the desired effect. In the first half of 1998 at least, FDI inflows reflected the establishment of new joint ventures and injections of additional capital into existing financial institutions and businesses under partial foreign ownership. Czech National Bank, *Monthly Bulletin*, No. 7, 1998.

TABLE 3.7.3

International credit ratings of eastern Europe, the Baltic countries and the CIS

Moody's			Standard & Poor's			Fitch-IBCA	
Rating	Country	Date received	Rating	Country	Date received	Rating	Country
Investment grades							
Aaa-Aa			AAA-AA			AAA-AA	
A2			A	Slovenia	May 1996	A	
A3	Slovenia	May 1996	A-	Czech Republic	November 1998 [a]	A-	Slovenia
Baa1	Czech Republic	September 1995	BBB+	Estonia	December 1997	BBB+	Czech Republic
	Estonia	September 1997					Poland [b]
Baa2	Latvia	December 1997	BBB	Latvia	January 1997	BBB	Hungary
	Hungary	May 1998 [b]		Hungary	1998		Estonia
Baa3	Croatia	January 1997	BBB-	Croatia	January 1997	BBB-	Croatia
	Poland	June 1995		Lithuania	June 1997		
				Poland	April 1996 [b]		
Sub-investment (speculative) grades							
Ba1	Lithuania	December 1997 [b]	BB+	Slovakia	April 1996	BB+	Lithuania
	Slovakia	September 1998 [a]					Slovakia
Ba2			BB			BB	Kazakhstan
Ba3			BB-			BB-	
B1	Kazakhstan	September 1998 [a]	B+	Kazakhstan	September 1998 [a]	B+	Bulgaria
B2	Bulgaria	December 1997 [b]	B	Bulgaria	November 1998	B	Republic of Moldova
	Turkmenistan	November 1997					
	Republic of Moldova	July 1998 [a]					
B3	Russian Federation	August 1998 [a]	B-	Romania	October 1998 [a]	B-	Romania [a]
	Ukraine	September 1998					
	Romania	November 1998 [a]					
			CCC+			CCC+	
			CCC			CCC	Russian Federation [a]
			CCC-	Russian Federation	September 1998 [a]	CCC-	

Source: Press reports.

Note: Foreign currency, long-term, sovereign debt ratings.

[a] Indicates a downgrade.

[b] Indicates an upgrade.

Toward the end of 1998 and early 1999, privatization picked up in a number of countries. The improvement in world market conditions raised valuations somewhat, making sales more attractive to governments. However, constraints on capital market borrowing and the need for funds was the prime motivation in Romania[514] and Russia.[515] Foreign investors, on the other hand, benefited from asset prices which were still lower than in the first half of 1998.[516]

Also arranged at this time (but not because cash was needed) was the initial public offering (IPO) of equity by the TPSA (Polish Telecommunications) which yielded $622 million (the largest IPO in the region).[517] Despite this large deal, the total value of equity issued by the transition economies fell from $3 billion in 1997 to around $2 billion in 1998.[518]

Although FDI investors are assumed to take the long view, the persistent turmoil in international markets, declining commodities prices, the Russian crisis and steadily worsening global economic prospects raised concerns in 1998 about future FDI flows. In fact, scattered data for the last few months of the year indicate that at least some projects in the pipeline did go ahead.[519] FDI flows into Poland actually accelerated during the year and Romania completed several key deals in November-December. However, the turmoil in Russia

[514] In Romania, foreign investors bought stakes in RomTelecom, the Romanian Development Bank and, in early 1999, in Petromidia ($740 million).

[515] In December the Russian authorities sold a 2.5 per cent share of Gazprom for $660 million. The funds were intended to cover part of the federal budget deficit.

[516] For example, it has been reported that the sales price of Poltelcom, the Polish telecommunications company, was two thirds of what it would have fetched earlier in the year (see below).

[517] This represents only the part of the IPO allocated to foreign institutional investors.

[518] International equity issues of the transition economies are presented in UN/ECE, *Economic Survey of Europe, 1998 No. 3*, table 4.3.6.

[519] The lumpiness of FDI flows caused by large privatizations might make any crises-induced changes in FDI trends difficult to identify.

deteriorated.[563] In western Europe, the main source of FDI and the major goods market for many transition economies, growth prospects are subdued and the outlook in most transition economies themselves is also weakening. Concerns about global overcapacity in many industries may adversely affect greenfield projects and follow-on investments in foreign investment enterprises (i.e. non-privatization related investments).

(b) Prospects for individual countries

The prospects for sustaining current account deficits in the European transition economies vary considerably. By virtue of their adequate official reserves, international investment grade ratings and generally large FDI inflows, the projected financial needs of the leading reforming countries appear manageable.[564] Nonetheless, given the prospects for larger current account deficits in the Czech Republic, Hungary and Poland, authorities have announced that their evolution will be carefully monitored with a view to making any necessary policy corrections. In *Hungary*, a deficit of $2.5-$2.7 billion (nearly 6 per cent of GDP) and repayments of around $2 billion are expected in 1999. The success of a €500 million bond issue in January suggests that the national bank will not have difficulty in meeting its borrowing requirement for the year.[565] The government is also examining the possibility of further sales of state assets and measures to encourage the reinvestment of profits (and thus reduce repatriation). The financing requirement of *Poland* in 1998 amounts to some $7-$8 billion. Several large privatizations should buoy already large inflows of foreign investment, and foreign currency reserves of some $26 billion can be tapped. In the *Czech Republic*, a small current account deficit is not likely to increase significantly given the modest growth prospects. However, there is concern about the impact of rapidly rising unit labour costs on export competitiveness and domestic consumption.

The Baltic states hope to continue to finance large current account deficits with FDI – more privatization of large assets is planned – and through medium and long-term borrowing, since debt levels are low. The credits associated with the IMF stand-by arrangements of Estonia[566] and Latvia remained unused at the beginning of the year and thus offer a potential source of finance. However, unless these countries can curb the growth of unit labour costs (Lithuania was relatively successful in this regard in 1998), pressures on their current account balances will persist.

Bulgaria will have to rely heavily on official funding to meet its financial obligations in 1999. This includes EU macroeconomic funds and IMF (EFF) resources, disbursements from both facilities being subject to various conditions. The agreement with the IMF foresees an acceleration of the privatization programme (involving sales of Bulgarian Telecom, the Neftochim refinery and Bulbank, among others). A modest bond issue is planned for the second half of the year. In the longer term, the apparent loss of competitiveness under the currency board may become more of an issue.

Most other European transition economies face more serious external financing constraints and, as a result, the sustainability of the current account is the major problem confronting policymakers. In these cases the challenge is to adjust policies to achieve a current account balance consistent with available financing and the desired (or minimum tolerable) level of official reserves. Even without further turmoil in the global markets, considerable uncertainty surrounds the financial possibilities of some of these economies and several risk an external financing crisis.

Although the Croat and Slovak governments are aiming to reduce their current account deficits in 1999, both are faced with limited borrowing possibilities and significant financing requirements (including repayments of long-term debt): $2.2-$2.4 billion in Croatia and $3 billion in Slovakia. Croatia's programme started well with a €300 million bond issue in February, but it also depends on an ambitious privatization programme (involving the telecommunications company (HPT), three banks and possibly the state oil company (INA)) moving ahead. Most of the funds associated with the IMF EFF (SDR 353 million) were still available at the beginning of 1998. Foreign investment in Slovakia remains low and its growth will largely depend on the privatization programme currently under consideration. In downgrading Slovakia's credit rating in October 1998, Fitch-IBCA cited the external large financial requirements and the loss of investor confidence as risks which could force the country into an external financing crisis. Slovakia does not have an IMF programme at this time.

A host of countries in deficit on current account and possessing only meagre foreign currency reserves have virtually no possibility of gaining access to the international capital markets. Financing constraints have already lead to cutbacks of energy imports by the Republic of Moldova, Belarus[567] and Ukraine and to

---

[563] These issues, including the possible repercussions of the troubled Russian economy on FDI in other transition economies, are discussed in UN/ECE, *Economic Survey of Europe, 1998 No. 3*, pp. 128-129.

[564] The current account of Slovenia has remained in virtual balance.

[565] The national bank has announced a borrowing requirement of $1.7 billion for 1999.

[566] In January 1999, Eesti Telecom was privatized yielding some $200 million, of which $100 million was deposited abroad.

---

[567] In October Belarus applied to the IMF for assistance under the Compensatory and Contingency Financing Facility (CCFF), under which it could receive financial assistance (up to $100 million) to compensate for its losses of export earnings (related with the Russian import compression) and increases in import expenditures (due to a poor harvest). However, it does not appear that the authorities are willing to meet the condition of significant monetary tightening. *Belarus Economic Trends*, November 1998.

increased payments arrears. Negotiations with the IMF have so far been inconclusive although its resources are indispensable. Only Romania has plans to acquire sizeable funds through privatization.

The $2 billion target current account deficit and repayment obligations of *Romania* in 1999 total nearly $3 billion. The government hopes to finalize an agreement with the IMF (which it failed to do in February) and conclude the sale of several large assets to strategic investors (including BancPost and Dacia, the automobile maker) to help meet its $1.3 billion FDI target. The sharp downgrading of the country's credit rating last year (in part because of the bleak financing prospects) will make planned medium- and long-term borrowing very expensive. Fiscal and current account deficits are to be curbed with a 6 per cent surcharge on imports.[568] However, the financial conditions involved in the settlement of the miners strike are likely to make this more difficult. The balance of payments of *The former Yugoslav Republic of Macedonia* also remains fragile. The current account deficit is expected to remain large, financed largely from official sources. The completion of several large privatizations, including the state telecommunications company, is being counted upon to ease funding pressures. Plans to obtain a credit rating were derailed by the Asian crisis.

Steep falls in the value of the leu are expected to curb imports and reduce the current account deficit in the *Republic of Moldova*. Large arrears on payments due in 1998 and 1999 have led to rescheduling negotiations which are necessary even with the help of multilateral financing. Privatization plans, including Moldtelecom, have been set back by depressed asset values. *Ukraine* faces a major challenge in 1999 in financing a current account deficit (estimates range from $400-$900 million), debt repayments of $1.5-$1.6 billion (increasing to $2.6 billion in 2000), and arranging natural gas financing with Russia (Gazprom) and Turkmenistan. Without IMF and other multilateral sources of funds Ukraine may not be able to avoid defaulting on some of its financial obligations.[569]

Assuming that imports remain at their current depressed level, *Russia* could generate a large current account surplus in 1999 (in January the merchandise trade surplus rose to $2.1 billion). This surplus could help the federal government meet a large share of its external debt servicing obligations in 1999 ($17.5 billion in principal and interest). However, capital flight remains

a major threat to its debt servicing capacity.[570] Russia is effectively excluded from the new funds market and, according to official estimates, FDI will amount to only $2-$2.5 billion. Thus a great deal hinges on reaching agreement with the IMF, which can provide access to $7 billion in multilateral and bilateral funds. At the time of writing, the government has committed itself to servicing that part of the debt incurred by the Russian Federation (the so-called new Russian debt). However, Russia has already missed payments on the debt of the former Soviet Union, which was already rescheduled several years ago.[571]

The risks involved in the current outlook are mostly on the downside. Given the unexpectedly poor end-year current account results reported by several countries, pressures on the external balances may be greater than those reflected in current forecasts. One risk is the apparent acceleration of unit labour costs at the end of 1998 (important for price-sensitive exports). Even in countries where the nominal exchange rate has recently depreciated, it is uncertain whether it has been sufficient to prevent a further decline in competitiveness. Second, new shocks could once again curb access to the international financial markets. Third, FDI flows could fall short of expectations if the investment climate worsens or because planned privatizations do not go ahead. The risks are greatest for the most financially constrained countries, several of which could default on their external obligations. Needless to say, the failure of several countries to obtain adequate financing could have a further contractionary impact on the region as a whole.

(v) Short-term funds, macroeconomic instability and sustainability

Although capital inflows are essential to sustain a current account deficit, they can themselves threaten the sustainability of a country's financial position. Large capital inflows can boost domestic demand and the real exchange rate, causing the current account balance to worsen. This has been the experience of several transition economies since they started the reform process and liberalized the foreign sector.[572] In the first half of 1998, Poland, the Czech Republic, Hungary and the Baltic states all attracted relatively large inflows of short-term capital (often exceeding the FDI inflows; chart 3.7.2) which placed upward pressure on real exchange rates (chart 3.7.1) and current account deficits.

---

[568] The surcharge, which covers about 60 per cent of imports, was put into place in early October 1998. It is to be gradually reduced and fully eliminated by the end of 2000. The action appears to be in response to an IMF warning in October that current fiscal and monetary policies were unsustainable.

[569] Ukraine has failed to meet the IMF's conditions for disbursements of three monthly tranches.

[570] Although large trade surpluses emerged after the devaluation of the rouble in August 1998 and surrender requirements on export receipts were tightened, official reserves have barely changed, remaining below $12 billion (including $4 billion in gold).

[571] Some payments to the Paris Club of official creditors were missed in October and parts of the commercial debt (London Club) are technically in default.

[572] "Capital surges into the transition economies, 1990-1997", UN/ECE, *Economic Bulletin for Europe*, Vol. 49 (1998).

Subsequently, the devaluation in Russia triggered short-term capital outflows which caused sharp declines in exchange rates and/or losses of official reserves. Although some currency depreciation was welcome – the Czech, Hungarian and Polish authorities had been concerned about the impact of appreciating exchange rates on export growth – the correction occurred under crisis conditions and cost Hungary, for example, about $2 billion in reserves. With the easing of tensions in the international markets in the last months of 1998, short-term flows returned to these countries, again pushing up exchange rates, often to pre-crisis levels. The appreciation was not welcome by the authorities since the growth of exports and output had faltered and current account deficits were widening. This appears to have been yet another example of short-term capital inflows, driven largely by financial factors, moving real exchange rates in the opposite direction to that required for external adjustment. In fact, economic fundamentals pointed to the need for a real depreciation.[573] This was the position taken by Czech and Polish officials in the final months of 1998 and early 1999 when they argued for lower interest rates (and thus some currency depreciation) to give exporters a boost. In Hungary, where exchange rate movements have been constrained by the ±2.25 intervention band, exports have continued to grow at a high rate.

The potential adverse impact of capital surges on exchange rates, export competitiveness and current account balances are a source of concern to policy makers the world over. The phenomenon may be especially important for most transition economies since they appear to be facing relatively large price elasticities of demand for their exports.[574] This implies that a given appreciation of the real exchange rate has a greater negative impact on their export growth than for countries with lower elasticities. If this is correct, exports and the current account balances of the transition economies are particularly vulnerable to capital surges. Moreover, as their economic growth so far has been predominantly export-led (section 3.2), their overall macroeconomic performance would also be sensitive to capital surges.

Other adverse consequences of recent short-term capital flows and exchange rate appreciation have been the erosion of profitability, and in some cases, large sterilization costs in relation to GDP. In a number of cases, interest rates were raised to protect exchange rates when short-term funds were withdrawn from following the rouble devaluation in August (section 3.2(ii)). In Hungary, at least, domestic interest rates have been kept higher than might be justified purely by macroeconomic conditions in order to deter speculative attacks on the currency.[575] (Conversely, the recent narrowing of interest rate differentials may make these countries even more vulnerable to currency speculation). More generally, there is considerable risk involved in financing persistent current account deficits with short-term credits, as several transition economies are doing. Thus while certain types of foreign short-term capital are essential for the functioning of a market system, in financing merchandise trade, for example, the economic usefulness of large volumes of short-term flows across borders is highly questionable.[576]

Given the apparent costs and risks to the transition economies, an important issue is how to respond to large short-term capital inflows. Cuts in domestic interest rates (when this has been made possible by falls in inflation) have not always helped to diminish inflows (and such a policy can anyway exacerbate current account deficits). Nor did the widening of the exchange rate corridor in Poland seem to be successful in this respect, although it is a widely recommended policy prescription. This apparent impotence suggests the need for additional instruments (preferably market-based) to control short-term capital. However, if market-based means are ineffective – as they have proved to be in other emerging markets – the case for considering direct controls on short-term capital, as a means of preserving macroeconomic stability and promoting economic growth, becomes very strong.

---

[573] This recalls the Czech experience in early 1997, several months prior to the abandonment of the koruna band. Heavy demand for euro-koruna bonds drove up the exchange rate while export growth was coming to a standstill and the current account deficit was growing rapidly.

[574] See the price elasticity estimates in sect. 3.6. There would appear to be several reasons for high export price elasticities, all associated with the particular economic development of the former centrally planned economies. The quality of goods was generally lower than in the west (this was reflected in relatively low export unit values) and the export commodity structures of the transition economies were broadly similar, implying keen competition between them. Also the share of foods, raw materials and semi-finished goods in their exports – products facing higher price elasticities than high value added manufactured goods – is relatively large. Export price elasticities have probably declined during the transition process (but not necessarily in all countries) due to restructuring, FDI, and other factors, but they may still appear to be higher than in other countries. For various reasons, the import elasticities of demand in the transition economies are generally assumed to be lower than those of exports which would imply that an appreciation of the exchange rate could curb exports more than imports.

[575] Gy. Suranyi, President of the National Bank of Hungary. He added that real interest rates would also be kept high to curb domestic demand. *The Wall Street Journal Europe*, 17 December 1998. The recent Hungarian and Polish experiences show that even countries with good economic fundamentals are not immune to contagion. Paradoxically, the great strides they have made in developing highly liquid domestic securities markets have actually made them more vulnerable to changes in investor sentiment.

[576] This is a view which is increasingly shared even by members of the private financial sector. For example, see the comments of D. Lachman, Managing Director of Emerging Markets Economic Research at Salomon Smith Barney, to the IMF Economic Forum, "Financial markets: coping with turbulence", *IMF Survey* (Washington, D.C.), 14 December 1998.

CHAPTER 4

FERTILITY DECLINE IN THE TRANSITION ECONOMIES, 1982-1997: POLITICAL, ECONOMIC AND SOCIAL FACTORS

4.1 Introduction

The change of regimes in central and eastern Europe a decade ago and the political and economic transition that ensued have been accompanied by major, often complex, demographic developments. After a few decades of gradual demographic change the populations of this region entered a period of demographic turbulence centred on 1990. International migration, which had been tightly controlled by the State almost everywhere except in the former SFR of Yugoslavia, re-emerged on a scale that rendered some of the newly created states, such as the Russian Federation, major immigration or emigration countries. Mortality took on highly complex patterns of change, declining at an accelerated pace in the majority of central European countries, rising in the Soviet successor states as well as in some countries in the Balkans and mainly stagnating elsewhere. Fertility, which in the 1980s has been generally close to the levels conducive to the long-term replacement of population fell steeply; this was the case everywhere except in a few countries, including Slovenia and Croatia, where the fall already underway since the beginning of the decade did not accelerate into the 1990s. The result of these changes is a new demographic landscape in central and eastern Europe, which is in stark contrast with the demographic situation of a decade and a half ago. One of its defining features, an outcome of these shifts, is population decline, a development unknown in peacetime to the world during the modern era. Another characteristic, primarily a consequence of the recent fertility decline is an acceleration of shifts in the age distribution of the population, in particular population ageing.

The fertility decline, particularly its speed and magnitude has taken by surprise the governments and policy makers in the transition economies; the same is true of population scholars and observers in this part of Europe and elsewhere. Many governments view the resultant low fertility levels with concern. All the European countries with transition economies that responded to the recent Eighth United Nations Inquiry Among Governments on Population and Development indicated that they consider their fertility levels overly low. Several countries, particularly the countries of the Commonwealth of Independent States (CIS), appear to be seriously concerned by their demographic present and

future. To a considerable extent the concern has been caused by the fall in fertility to unprecedentedly low levels and the fact that there are no signs of an imminent recovery. Population analysts and scholars, including those in countries with transition economies rightly perceive the new development as a radical break with the fertility behaviour of the communist era. However, writing about the development in different national settings, they disagree about the causes of the shift to lower fertility. This is partly a consequence of the fact that causes indeed may differ across the region where demographic behaviour, including family and reproductive behaviour, grew increasingly diverse during the 1990s.

The theme of this chapter is the fertility decline in the European countries with transition economies since the time when they broke away from their communist past.[577] The various features of the decline – the timing of its onset as well as its speed and magnitude – are analysed. Other aspects of the fertility transition, from replacement levels in the 1980s to some of the lowest levels on record, are also considered. These include shifts in the age structure of fertility, which often signify changes in the timing of childbearing, as well as the spread of out-of-wedlock fertility, which is usually lower than marital fertility, a major trend permeating the region. The various facets of the recent fertility changes are analysed in a broader temporal and geographic perspective; the analysis starts with the early 1980s and contrasts the transition economies with the European countries with market economies.[578] As the analysis straddles the time when the former republics of the now defunct socialist federal states became independent countries, those republics and their successor states are units of analysis along with the countries that remained intact. Included in the analysis, as a separate entity, is eastern Germany (the former German Democratic

---

[577] The countries included in the analysis are all the European countries with transition economies except Albania and Bosnia and Herzegovina, for which the requisite data are not available.

[578] The chapter expands an earlier analysis on the recent fertility decline in central and eastern Europe by M. Macura, "Fertility and nuptiality changes in central and eastern Europe: 1982-1993", *Studia Demograficzne*, Vol. 4, No. 122, 1995.

Republic (GDR)), which deserves to be studied along with the countries with transition economies. The chapter also seeks to explore, however, in a tentative and speculative manner, the causes of the complex fertility changes. Answers to questions, such as the following are sought: was the onset of the decline brought about by uncertainties of what might have been perceived at the time as an oncoming political instability or perhaps as an imminent fall of communism? Were the pace and magnitude of the fertility decline influenced by the intensity and the duration of the economic downturn? Was the decline caused by the spread of western family and fertility behaviour into this part of Europe, which since the 1960s has brought fertility in European countries with market economies to moderate or low sub-replacement levels. Did a combination of these developments play a role in the various countries with transition economies?

4.2 Fertility decline to the lowest levels yet observed

By the early 1980s, the fertility trends in central and eastern Europe had brought about a remarkable convergence towards of replacement levels. Over two thirds of what today are the European countries with transition economies (all except Albania and Bosnia and Herzegovina) had total fertility rates (TFRs)[579] in 1982 within a very narrow range – between 1.9 and 2.3 – centred on replacement, or 2.1 children per woman.[580] The transition to about replacement fertility was completed by this time in all of these countries, except in the Republic of Moldova and The former Yugoslav Republic of Macedonia, comprising 98 per cent of the combined population of the countries analysed here. By European standards, these fertility levels were high and tightly clustered; the mean and the standard deviation of TFRs for the present-day countries with transition economies (and eastern Germany) were 2.07 and 0.18, those for 16 European countries with market economies and populations of over a million in 1982 were 1.78 and 0.37, respectively.[581] The rates in more than half of the

countries with transition economies that had sub-replacement fertility were similar to those of France, Greece, Portugal and Spain, countries with market economies with the highest fertility rates at the time.[582]

Judging by the west European experience, fertility in central and eastern Europe had substantial room for a further decline and it did in fact decline and at a speed that was faster than anywhere else in postwar Europe. In each and every one of these countries fertility in the middle of the 1990s was lower than in the early 1980s (chart 4.2.1). By the middle of the 1990s, in more than two thirds of the countries with transition economies, the decline that had begun in some countries as early as the late 1980s resulted in TFRs below 1.5 children per woman (chart 4.2.2). In 1996, 83 per cent of the combined population of the countries included in this analysis lived in a setting where, only a few years earlier, fertility levels would have been considered exceptionally low. That same year the population of eastern Germany had the lowest TFR (0.95) among all the former socialist countries or their constituent republics. In 1997, the year for which the Council of Europe provides the latest statistics, five out of seven European countries with total fertility rates below 1.25 were countries with economies in transition.[583] The overall picture for this part of Europe was one of grossly depressed fertility; the mean TFR for countries with economies in transition in 1996 was 1.35, that for countries with market economies 1.53. The former countries now constitute a group with the lowest fertility in Europe, and in the world.

The very low fertility levels recently attained are the consequence of rather complex patterns of change since the beginning of the 1980s. The data reveal two broad patterns, one prevailing in the Baltic states and the European CIS countries and the other in central and south-eastern Europe. The fertility shifts in the former Soviet republics and their successor states displayed remarkable similarities, those in the other parts of the region, a fairly large degree of diversity.

For several years after 1982 the Baltic states and the Slavic republics of the former Soviet Union, along with the Republic of Moldova, experienced a modest gradual increase in fertility at levels higher than two children per women (chart 4.2.3). This fertility revival, a prelude to a subsequent decline, occurred throughout the former Soviet Union in response to the family policy measures announced at the 26th Party Congress held in 1981 and introduced during the period 1981-1983. Within a few years the effects of more generous child allowances and longer maternity leave wore off, a typical outcome of the

---

[579] Total fertility rate is the average number of children that would be born per woman if all women lived to the end of their childbearing years and bore children according to a given set of age-specific fertility rates. Age-specific fertility rate is the number of births occurring during a specified period to women of a specified age or age group, divided by the number of person-years-lived during that period by women of that age or age group.

[580] Replacement is the level of fertility that in the long run ensures the replacement of generations. In low-mortality populations replacement fertility is slightly over two children per woman. Given generally low mortality in Europe, fertility analyses pertaining to these countries typically assume that 2.1 children per woman is a good approximation for replacement fertility in these populations.

[581] The 16 countries are as follows: Austria, Belgium, Denmark, Finland, France, western Germany (i.e. the territory of the Federal Republic prior to unification), Greece, Ireland, Italy, Netherlands, Norway, Portugal, Spain, Sweden, Switzerland and the United Kingdom. It is these countries with market economies, all having populations over 1 million in the 1990s, that are contrasted with countries with transition economies throughout the chapter.

[582] Total fertility rates in the other market economies varied between the rate of western Germany, 1.41, the lowest on record at the time, and the United Kingdom rate, 1.79. Ireland's TFR (2.96), the highest in western Europe, was the only exception.

[583] In this group were Bulgaria (1.09), Latvia (1.11), Czech Republic (1.17), Belarus (1.23) and Estonia (1.24), as well as Spain (1.15) and Italy (1.22). Council of Europe, *Recent Demographic Developments in Europe 1998* (Strasbourg, Council of Europe Publishing, 1998).

CHART 4.2.1

Shifts in total fertility rate, 1982-1996

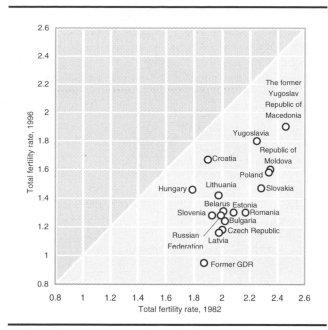

Source: UN/ECE Population Database; Council of Europe, *Recent Demographic Developments in Europe* (Strasbourg), 1998.

pronatalist efforts undertaken since the 1960s in the majority of the former socialist countries. In each of these former Soviet republics the fertility rise ended sometime between 1986 and 1988 and turned into a decline, which, in general, was sharp and uninterrupted. Ten years later, according to the latest available data, the decline was still underway in these seven countries, decelerating, however, in the Baltic states.[584]

Writing at the time when it became known that fertility continued to fall, Darski[585] in 1990 attributed the decline to the deepening social and economic crisis in the former Soviet Union. In his opinion, couples were postponing childbearing until more favourable times by temporarily foregoing second- and third-order births. Contrary to this view, Vishnevsky,[586] writing about Russia a few years later states that: "even if the influence [of social and economic crisis] does exist, it is likely that other factors have contributed to, and are perhaps much more significant determinants of, the phenomenon of fertility decline. The universal trends of demographic transition associated with the modernization of the family and society have played a leading role, and served to

draw the Russian and western models of procreative behaviour in the family closer to one another".

By offering these different views the two authors have opened what is likely to be a protracted debate over the causes of the sharp fertility decline in the former Soviet Union. These competing explanations will be discussed later in this chapter.

In central Europe, the countries belonging to the Visegrad group – the Czech Republic, Hungary, Poland and Slovakia – shared in the sharp decline, but the trajectories were generally different from those of the former Soviet republics (chart 4.2.3). With the exception of Hungary, through the end of the 1980s, they experienced almost uninterrupted declines at varying but moderate speed. In Hungary there was a modest and uneven increase through the beginning of the 1990s from a level that was the lowest in the region. This increase was most probably in response to yet another effort, which started in 1984, at enhancing the already generous support to families with children, which to a certain degree bore comparison with the former Soviet Union. The acceleration of the decline in the Czech Republic and Poland occurred after 1991, in Slovakia after 1993. In Hungary, the turnround occurred after 1991. In sum, in this part of central Europe, the rapid decline set in a few years later than in the former Soviet republics. In contrast to this, the area of the former German Democratic Republic, before and after unification, experienced a fertility decline that has no known parallels.[587]

For south-eastern Europe, the picture is more complex than for central Europe and the former Soviet Union. The fertility decline has been underway in the various former Yugoslav republics since the beginning of the 1980s, which makes the Yugoslav successor states similar to the central European countries. However, unlike in central Europe, the decline in Croatia, Slovenia, The former Yugoslav Republic of Macedonia and Yugoslavia did not turn into a rapid fall as the former SFR of Yugoslavia disintegrated.[588] Bulgaria's and Romania's fertility decline share the feature common to

---

[584] Council of Europe, op. cit.

[585] L. Darski, "Fertility in the USSR. Basic trends", in A. Volkov (ed.), *Population Reproduction and Family Dynamics*, The State Committee of Russian Federation on Statistics (Moscow), 1992.

[586] A. Vishnevsky, "Family, fertility, and demographic dynamics in Russia: analysis and forecast", in J. DaVanzo (ed.), *Russia's Demographic "Crisis"* (Santa Monica, CA, Rand, 1996).

[587] The recorded demographic history provides no evidence of a similar drop in fertility in a sizeable population during peacetime. As the effects of the former GDR's pronatalist policy waned in the first half of the 1980s, the TFR gradually decreased. The decline, similar to that elsewhere in central Europe, accelerated after 1987 and turned into a free fall after 1990. The result was an astonishingly low TFR reached in 1993, 0.76 children per woman. The TFR has rebounded in the last few years but in 1996 was approaching only half of the replacement level.

[588] A comment on the one-time increase in the TFR for The former Yugoslav Republic of Macedonia in 1991 is in order here. This increase, which is spurious, is a result of a change in statistical practices pertaining to the estimation of population followed since independence by the statistical authorities of this country. If it were possible to derive a time series of TFRs since the early 1980s, it would probably show a steady decline in fertility during this decade, although at a level higher than the one shown in chart 4.2.3, and linking up with the trend since 1991.

CHART 4.2.2

Total fertility rate, 1980 and 1996
(Countries with population over one million)

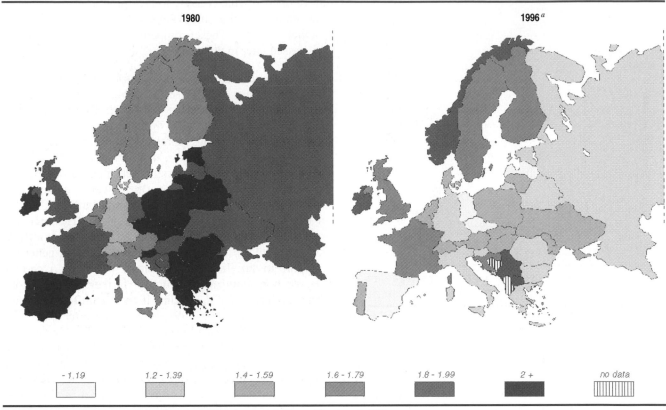

| 1980 | 1996 [a] |

| - 1.19 | 1.2 - 1.39 | 1.4 - 1.59 | 1.6 - 1.79 | 1.8 - 1.99 | 2 + | no data |

Source: Council of Europe, *Recent Demographic Developments in Europe* (Strasbourg), 1998.

a The data for Belgium and Ukraine refer to 1995.

those in central Europe and the former Soviet republics. In Bulgaria there was a gradual decline during the 1980s, which appreciably accelerated after 1988. In Romania, fertility peaked in the middle of the 1980s, most likely as a result of the tightening in 1984 of the highly coercive pronatalist policies practised in the country since the middle of the 1960s. The sharp decline occurred immediately after 1989.

To summarize, there were variations across central and eastern Europe in the paths to sub-replacement fertility during the last decade and a half. The Yugoslav successor states attained those levels without experiencing any major departure from the gradual trends that were underway since the early 1980s. In contrast to this, in all the other countries with transition economies, at one time or another, fertility began to fall at a rapid pace. In some of them, the rapid fall started after a temporary rise, in others after an initial gradual decline. In the majority of countries, the beginning of the new trend occurred during the period 1989-1991. In particular, in Belarus, the Republic of Moldova, Russia and Ukraine, as well as in Estonia, Bulgaria and Romania, it took place earlier than elsewhere – in 1989 or 1990; in eastern Germany and Latvia in 1991. The rapid decline in central Europe started later – in the Czech Republic, Hungary and Poland in 1992, and in Slovakia

in 1994. Lithuania joined in the rapid decline in 1993.[589] In practically all the countries that shared in the rapid decline, TFR fell below 1.5 by 1997. Among the Yugoslav successor states, only Slovenia attained such a level, although it had started from one of the lowest levels in the 1980s.

Once the rapid decline got underway, it generally proceeded almost everywhere without interruption through 1996-1997. (As indicated earlier, eastern Germany was the exception.) The magnitude of the decline by this time, relative to the pre-decline level, was greatest in countries where the decline started relatively early and proceeded at a comparatively rapid pace: thus, in Belarus, Russia, Estonia, Latvia, Bulgaria and Romania, TFRs fell by up to 40 per cent or more. As

---

[589] Establishing the year in which the rapid decline began is not a problem-free task, however, mainly for the former Soviet republics. There, it appears that an early decline after the TFR peaked in the middle of the 1980s was only a downward adjustment that was typically observed in the former socialist countries following a fertility surge produced by fresh pronatalist policy measures. Then, on the coat-tails of the adjustment came the rapid decline, inviting the non-trivial question: when did it begin? In the secretariat's view, in each particular case, this occurred immediately after TFR had reached a level similar to the one that prevailed before the 1981-1983 pronatalist policies were put into effect. In line with this reasoning, for example, for the Republic of Moldova, 1989 was taken as the year when the rapid decline began.

CHART 4.2.3

Trends in total fertility rate in selected transition economies, 1982-1996

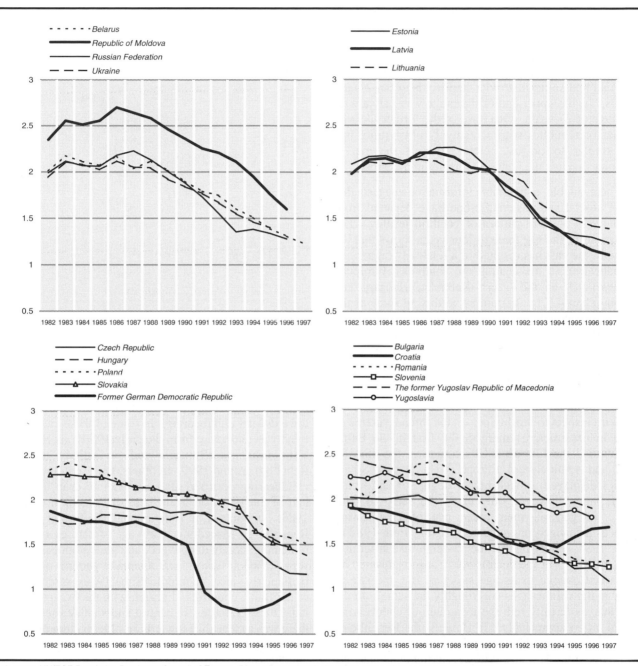

Source: UN/ECE Population Database; Council of Europe, *Recent Demographic Developments in Europe* (Strasbourg), 1998.

these countries had relatively high fertility levels prior to the onset of the rapid decline, they also had the largest absolute losses, approaching one child per woman. The relative losses in transition economies have been generally larger than those in countries with market economies since the middle of the 1960s, a period of rapid postwar fertility reduction in western Europe.[590]

4.3 Shifts in the age structure of fertility

The former socialist countries have been long known for their relatively youthful fertility. The most modern and prosperous among them – the Czech and Slovak Republics, the former German Democratic Republic and Hungary – along with Bulgaria and

[590] The largest proportionate losses in the transition economies during the five-year periods after the rapid decline began were in Estonia and Latvia (just over 38 per cent in both cases) and in the Czech Republic and Romania (close to 36 per cent). The loss in eastern Germany during the

period 1991-1993 approached 50 per cent. The largest comparable declines in countries with market economies were in the Netherlands during 1969-1974 and western Germany in 1968-1973, both being within the 35-36 per cent range.

Romania, have greatly contributed to this image. The women in these countries tended to marry early, have their first child soon after, and go on to complete childbearing before long. As a result, in 1982, mean age of childbearing in these countries was below 25 years and 80-90 per cent of fertility was completed by the age of 30.[591] The other former socialist countries, including the former Soviet republics that later became independent states, had had somewhat older fertility, between 25 and 27 years. At the upper end of the range was Latvia with an average of 27 years. One third of the former socialist countries or republics with a relatively old fertility had levels similar to or just below those of the market economies that had the youngest fertility in this group.

The available, comparable information suggests that parts of central and eastern Europe have departed from this relatively uniform pattern of youthful fertility. The information for the last three to four years shows that the break with the past has resulted in a relatively higher age of childbearing in the central and south-east European countries, such as the Czech Republic, Hungary and Slovenia (chart 4.3.1). In contrast to this, in some of the European CIS countries – Belarus and Russia – as well as Latvia, the age of fertility fell. Over this same period, most of the countries with market economies continued the trend towards ever-older fertility. In spite of data limitations, it is possible to describe the shifts in the age structure of fertility with some accuracy.

With respect to fertility per se, two broad patterns of change in its structure emerged, the first in the Baltic republics and the European CIS countries, the other in central and south-eastern Europe. The former Soviet republics displayed a much higher degree of uniformity than the latter, however, only up to the early- to mid-1990s. In general, their mean age of childbearing remained unchanged or fluctuated slightly from 1982 to 1987 or 1988, signifying that the moderate rise in fertility prior to the onset of the decline was not accompanied by any marked change in its age structure (i.e. the rise in fertility at the various ages was roughly the same). In the late 1980s, as fertility fell, the mean age of childbearing also fell, often appreciably. In Belarus, the Republic of Moldova, Russia and Ukraine, this trend appears to have ended by the middle of the 1990s, resulting in a mean age of childbearing of around 25 years in 1996-1997. In the Baltic states, the decline ended around 1992-1993 and, as recent data appear to suggest, turned into a progressively steeper rise, arriving at a mean age of about 26 years by 1997. In other words, without exception, the rapid drop in fertility up to the early to mid-1990s has been associated with an increasingly younger pattern of childbearing; the fertility rates at higher childbearing ages have fallen relatively more than those at earlier ages.

CHART 4.3.1

Shifts in mean age of childbearing, 1982-1995
(Year of age)

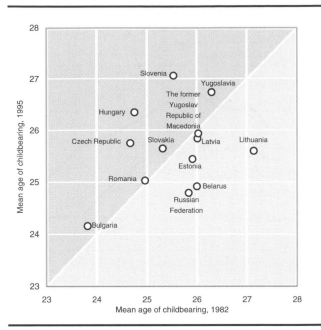

Source: UN/ECE Population Database.

In central Europe and parts of south-eastern Europe – Croatia, Slovenia and Yugoslavia – the trend has been towards later childbearing. In some of these countries the trend was underway from the early 1980s, accelerating in some instances (Slovenia and particularly the Czech Republic) around 1990. In others, the rise in mean age of childbearing occurred after a moderate drop in the first half of the 1980s or, in the case of Poland, after the late 1980s. In contrast, in Bulgaria and The former Yugoslav Republic of Macedonia their age structures of fertility remaining largely unchanged, and grew younger, albeit at very different levels. Romania's pattern of change, particularly since the middle of the 1980s, resembled that of the Baltic countries. In brief, with the exception of the latter three countries, in central and south-eastern Europe there was a clear shift towards an older pattern of fertility, a development that typically signifies a postponement of childbearing.

4.4 The spread of extra-marital fertility

Several former socialist countries had what, by European standards, appears to have been an early and relatively high incidence of extra-marital childbearing.[592] In 1970, it was not unusual in this part of Europe to have more than one out of 10 children born to unwedded mothers, the level that can be considered an upper boundary of relatively low prevalence of out-of-wedlock fertility. The proportion of children born to unmarried

---

[591] The proportion of fertility completed by age 30 is used here as an indicator of the age structure of period fertility. It stands for the percentage of fertility that a hypothetical cohort of women subject to the period age-specific fertility rates would attain by age 30.

[592] The fall in marital fertility, due to delayed or a lower rate of marriages, is usually not offset by the increase in extra-marital fertility, as unmarried couples or single mothers usually opt for fewer children.

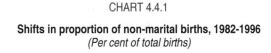

CHART 4.4.1

Shifts in proportion of non-marital births, 1982-1996
(Per cent of total births)

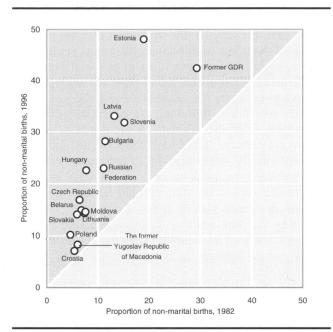

Proportion of non-marital births, 1996

Proportion of non-marital births, 1982

Source: UN/ECE Population Database; Council of Europe, *Recent Demographic Developments in Europe* (Strasbourg), 1998.

mothers was highest in Estonia (14.1 per cent) and the former GDR (13.3 per cent); these were not much behind the proportion in Sweden (18.4 per cent), the highest in Europe. In Latvia, the Russian Federation and Yugoslavia, the proportions have been just above 10 per cent, comparable to Austria and Denmark but not to other European countries. However, when the rise in the prevalence of non-marital childbearing began in earnest in Europe in the 1970s, it was much stronger in the market economies than in the present-day transition economies.

In the early 1980s, almost one third of these former socialist countries had the proportions of extra-marital to total births of over 10 per cent. As had been the case a decade earlier, the former GDR and Estonia were ahead of the others, with, respectively, one third and one fifth of births occurring to unmarried women. The proportions were lower in Slovenia (15 per cent), Latvia (13 per cent), and Bulgaria and Russia (11 per cent) and below 10 per cent elsewhere. However, in the next decade and a half, as out-of-wedlock fertility continued to spread in these societies, other countries crossed the 10 per cent threshold and joined the leaders. In a number of these countries, there was a steady increase during the 1980s, prior to the changes of government in the political and economic systems. In several of them there was a clear acceleration in the 1990s, possibly suggesting that the political and other changes contributed to a more conducive environment for extra-marital childbearing.

The increase in the prevalence of non-marital fertility in the last 15 years was considerably larger in some parts of central and eastern Europe than others

(chart 4.4.1). Estonia and eastern Germany continued to surge ahead, while several other countries – Bulgaria, Latvia and Slovenia as well as Hungary and the Russian Federation – followed behind. At the other end of the spectrum there were a few countries – Croatia, Poland and The former Yugoslav Republic of Macedonia, where non-marital childbearing increased but remained rare. In an intermediate group, the remaining countries with transition economies, the proportion of extra-marital births increased twofold or more, reaching about 15 per cent or above. This group, as well as the low- and high-prevalence groups, includes member countries from all various parts of the region. Unlike the case of fertility and its age structure, there are no discernible subregional patterns in the increase of non-marital childbearing.

4.5 Causes of fertility decline

(i) From one-party rule to democracy

The political changes that swept central and eastern Europe a decade ago were on a scale rarely seen in twentieth century Europe, a period of major political upheavals on the continent. Within a few years, one communist-led regime after another fell, paving the way for multi-party democracies and leading to the dissolution of the former socialist federal states. In the majority of the former eastern European countries, political turbulence preceded the change of government or, in the case of the former Soviet Union and the former Yugoslavia, their breakup. A resurgence of nationalism that pitted one ethnic group against another and threatened or caused violations of minority rights added to political instability in some of the multi-ethnic countries. The turbulence lasted anywhere between a few days and a few years. It ended with a violent clash between opposing forces and a forced change of government in Romania, and a string of wars in the former SFR of Yugoslavia. Elsewhere, the change was by and large peaceful although subject to varying degrees of tension and, in some instances, the threat of violence; the fall of the east German regime occurred in a highly charged political atmosphere. The transition to multi-party democracy has been quick and orderly in several countries, slow in some, and painful and unsettled in the rest. In the latter, democratic institutions and norms are only slowly taking root. In recent years they have continued to experience bouts of political turbulence, leading sometimes to early elections and changes of government.

Decisions that individuals and couples take regarding the forming of a family and the bearing of children – intimate decisions *par excellence* – are invariably influenced by their general condition, including political and economic circumstances that may be perceived as leading to an uncertain future. The survey-based studies coordinated and conducted by Moors and Palomba[593] in

---

[593] H. Moors and R. Palomba (eds.), *Population, Family and Welfare. A Comparative Survey of European Attitudes*, Vol. 1 (Oxford, Clarendon Press, 1995).

nine European countries have, among other things, enquired as to whether individuals in their childbearing years attribute fertility decline, *inter alia*, to "fear of the future", and also, whether the desire not to have a child might be influenced by concerns that individuals may have about the future. The studies showed, more for some countries than for others, that indeed, in the minds of the interviewees, misgivings about the future *are* responsible, among other factors, for the fertility decline as well as for their personal decision to remain childless or not to have another child. In line with this research, it may be hypothesized that confidence in the future might have declined, in some instances abruptly, among the young people in the former socialist countries as they experienced the political and economic transition. With respect to the political changes, it seems plausible that the political transformation and dissolution of countries, especially where they were abrupt and turbulent, led young people to wonder what the future held for their future families and accordingly chose to postpone or altogether forego forming them or having children.

There is unambiguous evidence that the events that led to the fall of the German Democratic Republic and the Romanian regime in December 1989, caused an immediate and massive fertility reaction. The number of births was cut in the former GDR by close to one half within less than a year and, accounting for seasonal variations, by over one fourth within less than six months in Romania (chart 4.5.1).[594] Frightened by political events, couples drastically curtailed births, the number of which did not rebound after the shock. The anxiety about the immediate future persisted.[595]

The link between political events and fertility is less easily demonstrable in other parts of the region. It appears that in the former Soviet Union, couples began opting for fewer children in 1989, a year before the rapid drop in fertility became manifest in the various former republics. By this time, political changes, including the independence movements in the Baltic states that eventually resulted in the dissolution of the Union on 31 December 1991, gained momentum. It may be that the trend in favour of fewer children got underway in response to what could have been perceived as growing

political instability. At this time, there were no signs yet that the economy would go into a major recession; that started to happen only a year or two later.

In central Europe there does not appear to be any link between the political changes and the drop in fertility and this may be due to the fact that the process leading to the abdication of the communist regimes in 1989 was relatively smooth. In Hungary and Poland it was prepared through the round-table discussions that took place between the authorities and the emerging political opposition following its recognition by the government. In the former Czechoslovakia, a stiff resistance to change lasted until 1989 but the end came relatively quickly and peacefully in December 1989. It was followed by a quick succession of radical reforms. As indicated earlier, the turn to rapid fertility reduction occurred in central Europe a few years later, strongly suggesting that the political changes, smooth as they were, did not lead to couples adopting a wait-and-see attitude, which appears to have been the case in the former Soviet Union.

Apart from Romania, south-eastern Europe presents a puzzle. Within a few years of Tito's death in 1981, disagreements and disputes among the former Yugoslav republics set in motion a slow process that eventually led to the breakup of the Federation. It gained a momentum in 1987 with the rise of nationalism, setting the stage for secessionist movements which gained strength during 1989-1991 and resulted in the declaration of independence by Slovenia and Croatia in June 1991. A brief military conflict flared up in Slovenia, then a larger and protracted war engulfed Croatia, as the Yugoslav army sought to prevent the breakup, which was followed by the carnage in Bosnia and Herzegovina. Surprisingly, these events do not seem to have left an imprint on fertility developments in the Yugoslav successor states.[596] Lastly, Bulgaria also offers a puzzle, as it appears that the shift towards fewer births occurred before any of the major political shocks of late 1989, the year when Zhivkov was deposed.

Did the effects on fertility of the sudden change of government, for example in Romania, or the deepening and protracted political crisis, such as that in the former Soviet Union before and soon after its dissolution, persist for some time? The surveys-based results for eastern Germany, referred to above, suggest that this indeed might have been the case. This, however, is not proven, and the present analysis does not attempt to separate the effects of political change from those of other developments, in particular the onset and progression of economic crisis. There is, however, evidence, albeit inconclusive, that the political situation in the former Soviet Union around 1990 did have a more lasting depressing effect on fertility (see below).

---

[594] The abrupt drop in fertility in Romania was made possible by a liberalization of inducted abortion by the new government. The old regime had banned abortion and modern contraceptives in 1966 and reinforced the coercive policy in 1984. As a result, the annual numbers of induced abortions between 1986 and 1989 were below 20 thousand, more than half of the pre-1984 level. Immediately after the liberalization, in 1990, the number skyrocketed to over 90 thousand, a four-and-a-half-fold increase compared to the previous year.

[595] Nearly half of the respondents in eastern Germany, who were interviewed in 1992 in the German Fertility and Family Survey indicated that "fear of the future" was, in their view, a very important reason for the fertility decline in this part of Germany. B. Störtzbach, "Germany: unification in attitudes?", in H. Moors and R. Palomba, op. cit., pp. 122-138. The two other very important reasons, which were more prominent than "fear of the future", were "economic crisis and unemployment" and the "financial burden of raising children".

---

[596] The effects of war on fertility in Bosnia and Herzegovina must have been considerable but could not be analysed as data for the 1990s are unavailable.

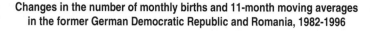

CHART 4.5.1

**Changes in the number of monthly births and 11-month moving averages
in the former German Democratic Republic and Romania, 1982-1996**

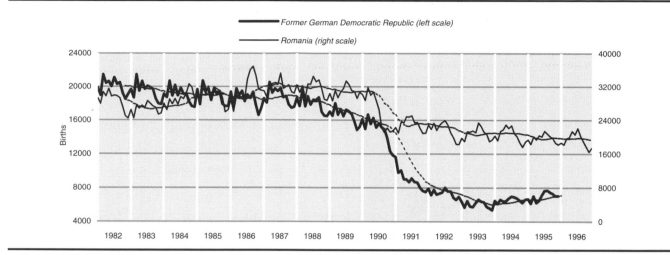

Source: UN/ECE Population Database.

(ii) From slow growth to economic downturn

The 1980s were a period of persistent deepening of structural problems in the former centrally-planned economies. Rates of growth fell to unprecedentedly low levels and the standard of living continued to decline in several of these countries. Perestroika was a response to Soviet economic problems, which eventually contributed to the deepening of the crisis rather than to its resolution. The second half of the decade witnessed a continued sluggish growth in the European part of the former Soviet Union but also in Bulgaria and Poland. Elsewhere, in particular in Romania, the former Czechoslovakia and the former SFR of Yugoslavia, the performance was even worse. As these economies came to a standstill at the end of the decade, the new governments faced the urgent and virtually unprecedented task of reforming them. Economic reforms, accompanied by institutional change were undertaken in many of these countries, with more success in some than in others. Declines in output, employment and trade ensued, accompanied by the emergence (or rise) in unemployment and inflation or hyperinflation. Real wages, social entitlements and services, and living standards declined as well. In some countries the trends have been reversed sooner than in others; in some they still persist. The details have been regularly covered in issues of this *Survey* and need not be discussed here.

The possible relationship between the fertility decline and these economic developments, however, is of paramount interest. The question appears to be not so much as to whether the economic downturn had an effect on fertility but rather; how its strength and duration might have varied in different settings. The question can first be addressed by looking at the bivariate relationship between total fertility rate, on the one hand, and aggregate output, on the other, expressed as the net material product or the gross domestic product relative to its 1989 level (appendix table B.1). Needless to say, bivariate analysis is a primitive tool and GDP is only a crude indicator of the state of the economy and the living standard of the population. Nevertheless, it is used here as a first tentative step towards a more sophisticated study of the relationship between fertility decline and economic change in the transition economies.

The bivariate relationship for all the countries (except eastern Germany, for which the requisite economic information is not available) is presented in chart 4.5.2, where the total fertility rate in any given year, starting in 1985, is paired with NMP/GDP, relative to its 1989 level, lagged by a year. The one-year lag is introduced in order to relate economic conditions at a given time to the reproductive decisions of couples, a decision that affects the number of births about a year later. As with the other various aspects of fertility patterns, there is a high degree of similarity in the relationship in the former European Soviet republics and their successor states. The similarities are less strong in central Europe and almost non-existent in south-eastern Europe.

The relationship between fertility and economic growth in the Baltic states and the European CIS countries is fairly systematic, but only from around the early 1990s. The very early phase of the rapid fertility decline coincided with further, albeit small, improvements in the economy, less so in Russia than in the Baltic republics and the Republic of Moldova. From then on, minor exceptions aside, the decline in TFR went hand in hand with the economic decline. However, the relationship is non-linear: the immediate post-1990 TFR decline is much faster than the decline in output.

CHART 4.5.2

Relationship between total fertility rate and net material product/gross domestic product, 1985-1997
(children per woman and indices 1989=100)

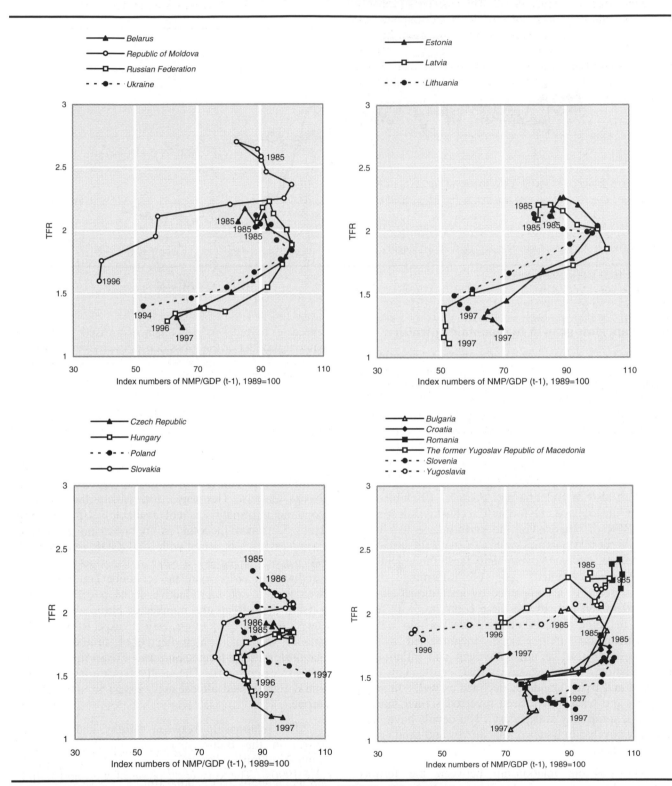

Source: UN/ECE Common Database, derived from national and CIS statistics; UN/ECE Population Database.

Note: Years indicated in the charts above are for total fertility rate (TFR) while the corresponding GDP data are for the prior year.

Could the fertility decline at this early stage have been primarily a result of the unsettled political situation in the former Soviet Union at the time, exacerbated by the failed coup in August 1991? The answer is probably yes. Towards the middle of the 1990s and beyond, the bivariate relationship in these countries suggests that the economic deterioration then became the dominant factor. In Estonia and Lithuania, the relationship has been almost linear since 1990, suggesting the dominant influence of the economic crisis from the outset.

Darski's view[597] that the social and economic crisis has led couples to opt for fewer children, and particularly fewer second- and third-order children appears valid, but perhaps less so for the years around 1990 than the subsequent period. Not only did the total fertility rate fall throughout the Soviet successor states, but this trend was accompanied by a drop in the mean age of childbearing, signifying a likely greater reduction in second- and higher-order births rates than in first-order birth rates.

A broadly positive relationship between the decline in fertility and the economy after around 1990 also holds in central and south-eastern Europe, but only up to a point; the patterns vary substantially, and that for Yugoslavia is a clear outlier (chart 4.5.2).[598] In central Europe the two developments went briefly hand in hand after 1990, while fertility continued to decline after the economy began to improve in the middle of the decade. Clearly, this picture raises difficult questions. Most importantly, why did fertility continue to fall in situations where an economic turnround has occurred or appears to have started? Is it possible that people are still uncertain and awaiting much improved economic circumstances and clear signs of a robust and *persistent* recovery before they commit themselves to having more children than during the early crisis years? Or is it possible that new forms of family and reproductive behaviour favouring smaller families, similar to those seen in western Europe in the last few decades, have been taking root in recent years?

(iii) The spread of western behaviour

In western Europe the middle of the 1960s marked the end of the postwar baby boom and a beginning of a new era of profound, multifaceted fertility change, referred to by some population scholars as Europe's second demographic transition.[599] The postwar generations, coming of age since the 1960s, have increasingly challenged the precepts and norms of their parents in a variety of areas. Among the results were the

---

[597] Darski, op. cit.

[598] The massive and steady economic decline in Yugoslavia has not been accompanied by a significant drop in fertility.

[599] R. Lesthaeghe and D. Van de Kaa (eds.), *Bevolking: Groei en Krimp* (Population: Growth and Decline) (Deventer, Van Loghum Slaterus, 1986); D. Van de Kaa, "Europe's second demographic transition", in *Population Bulletin*, Vol. 40, No. 1, The Population Reference Bureau (Washington, D.C.), March 1987, pp. 1-59.

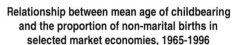

CHART 4.5.3

Relationship between mean age of childbearing and the proportion of non-marital births in selected market economies, 1965-1996

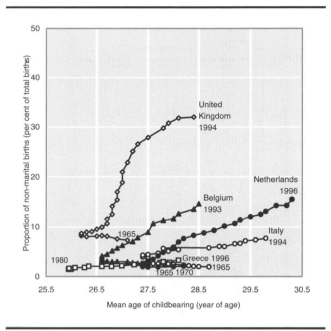

Source: Oxford Population Database (OXPOP); Council of Europe, *Recent Demographic Developments in Europe* (Strasbourg), 1998.

sexual revolution, the anti-war, anti-nuclear and environmental movements, and a revival of the feminist movement ideals.

The norms that for a long time had guided the formation of and the life within families were also brought into question and new forms of family and reproductive behaviour emerged. Cohabitation grew while marriage receded, and having babies in consensual unions became increasingly acceptable. The onset of parenthood, partly in response to longer education of both men and women was gradually pushed towards the late twenties; accordingly, mean age of childbearing increased. Permanent voluntary childlessness spread in some countries, so much so that, for example, 20 per cent of Swiss women now in their late forties are childless. These trends contributed to, and in some instances only accompanied, a rapid reduction in fertility, which in some countries occurred considerably earlier than in others. The rise in cohabitation and non-marital fertility were not, however, the major causes for the postponement of childbearing and fertility reduction; comparisons between the Nordic and Mediterranean countries confirm this. Greece and Italy, the countries that currently have some of the lowest fertility rates in Europe and increasingly later childbearing, also have some of the lowest rates of cohabitation and extra-marital fertility (chart 4.5.3). Growing individualism, changing tastes and expectations, diminishing religiosity, economic independence of women and gender equality seem to be important reasons in many countries for the shift to sub-replacement and late fertility. In the view of some researchers, family policies also play a role.

CHART 4.5.4

Relationship between mean age of childbearing and the proportion of non-marital births in selected transition economies, 1965-1995

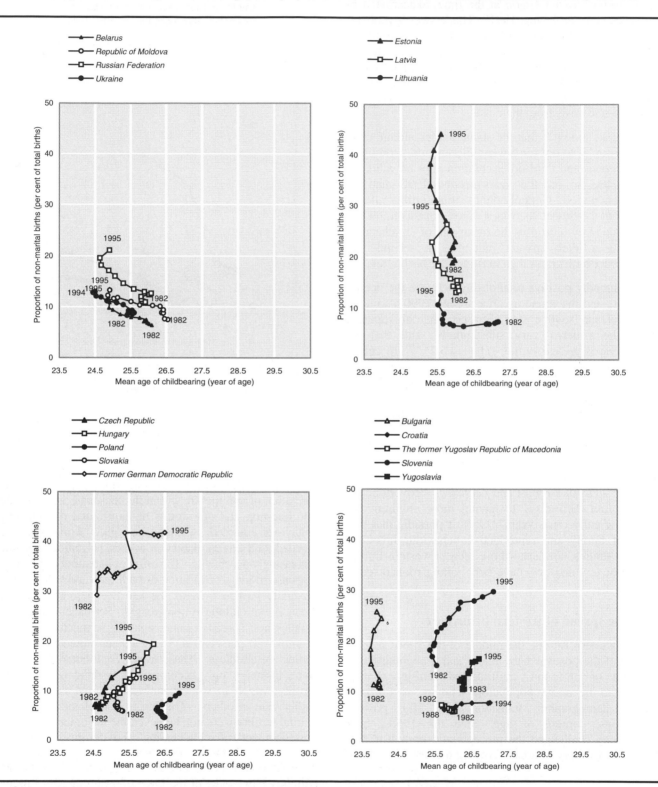

Source: UN/ECE Population Database; Council of Europe, *Recent Demographic Developments in Europe* (Strasbourg), 1998.

In the context of the present analysis, the consideration of these west European developments invites questions pertaining to central and eastern Europe. Has the spread of the new forms of family and reproductive behaviour been confined to the countries with market economies? Or has it made inroads into the former socialist countries since they opened up to the rest of the world, and particularly to their western neighbours? In particular, has the recent fertility change in this part of Europe, including the fertility decline, been a result of the spread of these new forms of behaviour? Evidence, for some central European countries, suggests that this indeed may have been the case. For example, in Slovenia, as noted earlier, there was a steady fertility decline from the beginning of the 1980s. During much of that period fertility grew older and there was increasing incidence of extra-marital fertility (chart 4.5.4), thus bringing it into line with the experience observed in many countries with market economies. With its borders open to the west since the middle of the 1960s, its family and reproductive behaviour was increasingly westernized during the 1980s. It seems most likely that this has been a major force behind its transition to sub-replacement fertility.

Judging by the ageing of fertility and the rising prevalence of non-marital childbearing, it is possible that the new behaviour also spread to the Czech Republic and Hungary and, to a lesser extent, Slovakia and Poland, starting, however, later – in the early 1990s – that is, just about when the rapid fertility decline began in these countries. (The same development may have occurred even earlier in eastern Germany.) Moreover, it is conceivable that the rapid fertility transition to sub-replacement fertility in these countries was initially driven by both political and economic deterioration and the spread of the new patterns of behaviour, but subsequently, after the economic recovery began, the latter factor became increasingly dominant. In other words, it is conceivable that the generations of young people in this part of Europe, as they came of age in the first half of the 1990s, began to embrace life styles and family and reproductive behaviour conducive to sub-replacement fertility.

In the Baltic states, particularly in Estonia, the signs are that young people are also beginning to embrace the new forms of behaviour, particularly as they contribute to late childbearing.[600] If this indeed is true, then the effect would be to reinforce the fertility depressing influence of what appears to have been the dominant factor, namely, economic deterioration. For the European CIS countries, there are no indications suggesting that Europe's second demographic transition

has arrived there; instead and particularly in recent years, the deepening economic crisis has continued to depress fertility. The view of Vishnevsky,[601] namely, that the fall in fertility in Russia is mainly a consequence of the Russian model of procreative behaviour becoming closer to that of the west, does not receive support. In this respect, south-eastern Europe resembles the European CIS countries.

4.6 Conclusions

As this century of unprecedented global demographic change draws to a close, central and eastern Europe has emerged as an area with the lowest fertility in the world. In much of the region, the transition from replacement to low sub-replacement fertility has been accomplished in less than 15 years. For the majority of the region's population, the transition has taken only about a decade. The rapid decline, which, depending on the country, started around 1989 or later, has been generally steeper than elsewhere in postwar Europe. In practically all of the countries, the decline continued through 1997, albeit showing some deceleration in several instances, probably reflecting timidly rising confidence in the reforms.

The fertility decline was accompanied by diverse trends in the age of childbearing and by a systematic spread of extra-marital fertility. In the Baltic states and the European CIS countries, fertility grew younger up to the mid-1990s, while in central Europe and parts of south-eastern Europe it has stopped growing younger since the late 1980s or early 1990s or, in some instances, even earlier. The diffusion of out-of-wedlock fertility throughout the region has been uneven, but its prevalence in some countries is close to that observed in the Nordic countries, where it is most common. It is not yet known, for the majority of the transition economies, whether this is due to an increase of non-marital cohabitation or a growth in the prevalence of childbearing among women without either a spouse or a partner.

Three competing explanations of the recent rapid decline in fertility have been examined – political instability and the attendant "fear of the future", economic decline as a proxy for the drop in living standards, and the spread of western family and reproductive behaviour. The central conclusion is that the developments that seem to explain the transition to low sub-replacement fertility vary greatly across the region; what applies to Slovenia, at one end of the spectrum, does not hold true for Russia and the other CIS members, at the other end. Slovenia appears to have gradually embraced, with some delay, the family and reproductive behaviour of its western neighbours and this has contributed significantly to its fertility

---

[600] Clearly, out-of-wedlock fertility, brought about by non-marital cohabitation, has been present in Estonia and, to a lesser extent, in Latvia for some time, including the period when fertility was around replacement and the mean age of childbearing was close to its postwar low. In these two instances, therefore, it would probably be wrong to attribute the steep rise in non-marital childbearing to a spread of western patterns of family and reproductive behaviour.

[601] A.G. Vishnevsky, op. cit.

decline. In the former Soviet Union, political instability and the attendant social crisis, before and immediately after its dissolution, appear to have triggered the decline. Economic decline, with its many adverse consequences for ordinary people, then reinforced the fertility decline and, in the process, probably became the major driving force. Between these two extremes lie the other countries, where two or all three developments contributed to the fertility decline.

Economic decline has caused erosion of social policies, including family policies, which had often been used by the former socialist governments with the objective of raising fertility. The share of benefits to families with children, such as maternity and child allowances, in family income has generally declined; often this has been achieved by making the benefits income-tested. In some instances, generous child-raising leave has been reduced or completely eliminated. Thus, apart from falling real wages, the once relatively large family benefits have been greatly reduced. Furthermore, the transition to a market economy has involved enormous structural changes, both at the macro and micro levels, which have hit female employment disproportionately.[602] Thus, while those women who remained employed lost their social benefits and part of their wages in real terms, a large proportion of working women lost their jobs and wages altogether. "Feminization of poverty" became widespread in most of these countries. The recovery of output in many economies has mainly led to a reduction in male unemployment while most unemployed women have remained as long-term unemployed and some – in certain countries a large proportion – have left the labour market altogether. This phenomenon, sometimes called the "gender overhang", not only reduced family income but also negatively influenced decision-making against larger families. These economic effects of transition have not yet been fully documented and it is for this reason that the analysis in this chapter has not attempted to explore the link between the decline in fertility and the erosion of family support and the fall in women's participation in economic activity. This is yet another challenge for future research into the causes of the recent fertility decline in central and eastern Europe. When it is successfully met, a body of knowledge on which policies toward fertility and the family can rest may begin to emerge.

Explaining family and reproductive behaviour has, time and again, proven to be an extremely difficult task for social scientists, including population researchers. This is more true of behaviour in modern post-industrial societies than in those undergoing modernization and industrialization. Approaching the subject of the factors behind the rapid fertility decline in the European transition economies requires therefore a measure of humility. In view of this, the above findings on the factors involved, and their relative contributions, should only be taken as tentative (although hopefully plausible) explanations requiring further scrutiny. The competing explanations offered in the case of Russia, particularly as they may also pertain to all of central and eastern Europe, will certainly continue to occupy researchers for years to come.

A major dilemma arising from the transition progress is that the need for social protection has increased considerably while the funds available to support it have been reduced sharply. Thus, fiscal policies need to be re-examined, including consideration of shifting part of these costs of rebuilding social infrastructure to the private sector but with the state still setting the rules and maintaining regulatory oversight. Only then is "reform" likely to mean "progress", not only for the female population but also for families at large.[603]

---

[602] See section 3.5(ii) where the effects of transition on the female labour force and employment are discussed in detail.

[603] For the rebuilding of social infrastructure and roles of different agents in it, see United Nations, *International Expert Meeting on Innovative Employment Initiatives, United Nations-European Regional Follow-Up to the World Summit for Social Development*, papers presented in Vienna (UNOV/VIC), 2-6 February 1998.

STATISTICAL APPENDIX

For the user's convenience, as well as to lighten the text, the *Economic Survey of Europe* includes a set of appendix tables showing time series for the main economic indicators over a longer period. The data are presented in two sections, following the structure of the text: *Appendix A* provides macroeconomic indicators for the market economies of western Europe and North America for 1984-1998, *Appendix B* does the same for the east European countries, the Baltic states and the Commonwealth of Independent States for 1980-1998.

Data for the transition economies are preliminary because re-estimated historical series are not yet available for all countries, and longer time series could in some instances be obtained only by splicing older data with the new statistics (as explained in the notes to the tables).

Data were compiled from international and national statistical sources. Regional aggregations are ECE secretariat estimates based, variously, on 1990-1992 weights. The figures for 1998 are based on data available at mid-March 1999.

APPENDIX TABLE A.1

Real GDP in the ECE market economies, 1984-1998

(Percentage change over preceding year)

	1984	1985	1986	1987	1988	1989	1990	1991	1992	1993	1994	1995	1996	1997	1998
Western Europe	2.5	2.6	3.0	3.1	4.1	3.4	3.4	1.6	1.3	-0.1	2.6	2.5	2.0	2.9	2.7
4 major countries	2.3	2.5	2.9	2.7	4.3	3.3	3.1	1.7	1.1	-0.5	3.0	2.2	1.5	2.3	2.4
France	1.3	1.9	2.5	2.3	4.5	4.3	2.5	0.8	1.2	-1.3	2.8	2.1	1.6	2.3	3.1
Germany [a]	2.8	2.0	2.3	1.5	3.7	3.6	5.7	5.1	2.2	-1.2	2.7	1.2	1.3	2.2	2.8
Italy	2.6	2.8	2.8	3.1	3.9	2.9	2.2	1.1	0.6	-1.2	2.2	2.9	0.9	1.5	1.4
United Kingdom	2.4	3.8	4.2	4.4	5.2	2.1	0.6	-1.5	0.1	2.3	4.4	2.8	2.6	3.5	2.3
17 smaller countries	3.0	2.7	3.2	4.0	3.7	3.6	4.0	1.4	1.6	0.7	1.7	3.3	3.1	3.9	3.3
Austria	0.3	2.2	2.3	1.7	3.2	4.2	4.6	3.4	1.3	0.5	2.4	1.7	2.0	2.5	3.3
Belgium	2.5	1.0	1.5	2.4	4.7	3.6	3.0	1.6	1.5	-1.5	2.4	2.1	1.3	3.0	2.8
Cyprus	8.8	4.7	3.8	7.0	8.5	7.9	7.4	0.6	9.8	0.7	5.9	6.1	2.0	2.5	5.0
Denmark	4.4	4.3	3.6	0.3	1.2	0.3	1.2	1.4	1.3	0.8	5.8	3.0	3.3	3.1	2.4
Finland	3.0	3.4	2.4	4.1	4.9	5.7	–	-6.0	-3.2	-0.6	3.7	4.0	4.1	5.6	4.9
Greece	2.8	3.1	1.6	-0.5	4.5	3.8	–	3.0	0.5	0.2	2.2	2.0	2.4	3.2	3.0
Iceland	4.1	3.3	6.3	8.5	-0.1	0.3	1.2	1.1	-3.4	1.0	3.7	1.0	5.5	5.0	5.6
Ireland	4.4	3.1	-0.4	4.7	5.2	5.8	8.5	2.0	4.2	3.1	7.3	11.1	7.4	9.8	8.5
Israel	2.2	3.6	3.6	6.2	3.4	1.4	6.3	5.7	6.8	3.4	6.9	7.2	4.7	2.7	2.0
Luxembourg	6.2	2.9	7.8	2.3	10.4	9.8	2.2	6.1	4.5	8.7	4.2	3.8	3.0	4.8	4.7
Malta	0.9	2.6	3.9	4.1	8.4	8.2	6.3	6.3	4.7	4.5	5.7	6.2	3.8	4.4	7.6
Netherlands	3.3	3.1	2.8	1.4	2.6	4.7	4.1	2.3	2.0	0.8	3.2	2.3	3.1	3.6	3.7
Norway	5.9	5.2	3.6	2.0	-0.1	0.9	2.0	3.1	3.3	2.7	5.0	4.1	5.5	3.4	2.0
Portugal	-1.9	2.8	4.1	6.4	7.5	5.1	4.4	2.3	2.5	-1.1	2.2	2.9	3.2	3.7	3.5
Spain	1.5	1.7	3.2	5.6	5.2	4.7	3.7	2.3	0.7	-1.2	2.2	2.7	2.4	3.5	3.8
Sweden	4.0	1.9	2.3	3.1	2.3	2.4	1.4	-1.1	-1.4	-2.2	3.3	3.9	1.3	1.8	2.9
Switzerland	3.0	3.4	1.6	0.7	3.1	4.3	3.7	-0.8	-0.1	-0.5	0.5	0.6	–	1.7	2.1
Turkey	6.7	4.2	7.0	9.5	2.1	0.3	9.3	0.9	6.0	8.0	-5.5	7.2	7.0	7.5	2.4
North America	6.7	3.9	3.0	3.0	3.9	3.3	1.2	-1.0	2.6	2.3	3.6	2.3	3.3	3.9	3.8
Canada	5.7	5.4	2.6	4.1	4.9	2.4	0.2	-1.9	0.9	2.5	4.7	2.6	1.2	3.8	3.0
United States	6.8	3.7	3.0	2.9	3.8	3.4	1.3	-1.0	2.7	2.3	3.5	2.3	3.4	3.9	3.9
Total above	4.6	3.2	3.0	3.0	4.0	3.3	2.3	0.3	1.9	1.1	3.1	2.4	2.7	3.4	3.3
Japan	3.9	4.4	2.9	4.2	6.2	4.8	5.1	3.8	1.0	0.3	0.6	1.5	5.0	1.4	-2.9
Total above, *including Japan*	4.5	3.4	3.0	3.2	4.3	3.6	2.7	0.8	1.8	1.0	2.7	2.3	3.0	3.1	2.3
Memorandum item:															
European Union [b]	2.3	2.5	2.8	2.9	4.2	3.5	3.1	1.7	1.1	-0.5	3.0	2.4	1.8	2.6	2.8
Euro area	2.1	2.2	2.6	2.7	4.2	3.9	3.7	2.4	1.3	-1.0	2.6	2.2	1.6	2.5	2.8

Source: National statistics.

Note: All aggregates exclude Israel. Growth rates of regional aggregates have been calculated as weighted averages of growth rates in individual countries. Weights were derived from 1991 GDP data converted from national currency units into dollars using purchasing power parities.

[a] West Germany 1984-1991.

[b] Fifteen countries.

APPENDIX TABLE A.2

Real private consumption expenditure in the ECE market economies, 1984-1998
(Percentage change over preceding year)

	1984	1985	1986	1987	1988	1989	1990	1991	1992	1993	1994	1995	1996	1997	1998
Western Europe	1.8	2.5	4.1	3.6	3.8	3.1	3.4	2.3	1.8	0.1	1.4	1.9	2.3	2.3	2.7
4 major countries	1.8	2.7	4.4	3.9	4.3	3.2	3.1	2.4	1.6	-0.1	1.5	1.7	1.9	1.8	2.4
France	1.1	2.4	3.9	2.9	3.3	3.1	2.7	1.4	1.3	0.2	1.4	1.7	2.0	0.9	3.4
Germany [a]	1.8	1.7	3.5	3.4	2.7	2.8	5.4	5.6	2.8	0.1	1.2	1.8	1.6	0.5	1.9
Italy	2.5	3.1	4.2	4.3	4.6	3.6	2.5	2.7	1.3	-3.4	0.9	1.4	0.8	2.6	1.9
United Kingdom	1.9	3.9	6.6	5.4	7.6	3.3	0.7	-1.7	0.4	2.9	2.9	1.7	3.6	3.9	2.6
17 smaller countries	1.7	2.3	3.6	3.1	2.9	3.1	4.1	2.3	2.0	0.5	1.0	2.3	3.0	3.4	3.2
Austria	-1.3	1.9	2.2	2.9	3.3	3.7	3.8	2.8	3.0	0.7	1.8	2.9	2.0	0.7	1.8
Belgium	0.7	2.0	2.0	2.3	3.2	3.7	2.9	2.9	2.3	-1.4	1.4	1.1	1.8	2.1	2.8
Cyprus	4.5	5.9	1.7	5.5	10.5	6.9	9.0	9.9	3.2	-4.8	4.2	10.6	2.8	2.4	7.0
Denmark	3.4	5.0	5.7	-1.5	-1.0	-0.3	0.3	1.8	2.6	1.4	7.1	3.3	2.7	3.6	3.4
Finland	3.1	3.7	4.0	5.2	5.1	4.3	–	-3.6	-4.5	-3.1	2.6	4.2	3.4	2.2	5.1
Greece	1.7	3.9	0.7	1.2	3.6	6.1	2.6	2.8	1.8	0.1	1.5	1.6	1.9	2.5	1.9
Iceland	3.7	4.2	6.9	16.2	-3.8	-4.2	0.5	4.1	-4.5	-4.5	1.9	4.2	6.4	6.0	10.3
Ireland	2.0	4.6	2.0	3.3	4.5	6.5	1.4	2.1	4.6	2.4	6.3	4.1	6.1	6.3	8.3
Israel	-6.9	0.7	15.1	8.9	4.5	0.4	5.6	7.2	8.0	7.3	9.5	7.2	5.0	4.1	3.3
Luxembourg	1.4	2.7	5.7	4.6	4.6	5.1	5.7	6.3	-0.9	1.7	2.4	2.4	1.9	2.5	2.6
Malta	4.0	5.0	1.4	0.5	9.0	9.2	3.8	3.8	4.3	0.8	2.3	10.5	7.7	2.4	2.9
Netherlands	1.2	2.8	2.6	2.7	0.8	3.5	4.2	3.1	2.5	1.0	2.2	2.0	2.7	3.0	4.4
Norway	3.2	9.4	5.0	-0.8	-2.0	-0.6	0.7	1.5	2.2	2.2	4.1	2.6	4.7	3.4	3.2
Portugal	-2.9	0.7	5.6	5.3	6.9	2.6	5.9	3.7	4.3	1.5	2.2	1.6	2.5	3.0	5.4
Spain	-0.1	2.0	3.3	5.8	4.9	5.7	3.6	2.9	2.2	-2.2	0.9	1.6	1.9	3.1	3.5
Sweden	1.4	2.7	4.4	4.6	2.4	1.2	-0.4	0.9	-1.4	-3.1	1.8	0.8	1.3	2.0	2.7
Switzerland	1.3	1.6	2.3	2.2	1.7	2.3	1.2	1.7	0.1	-0.9	1.0	0.5	0.4	1.7	1.8
Turkey	8.1	-0.6	5.8	-0.3	1.2	-1.0	13.1	1.9	4.0	8.6	-5.4	4.8	8.5	8.4	2.1
North America	5.1	4.7	4.0	3.1	4.0	2.4	1.6	-0.7	2.7	2.8	3.3	2.6	3.1	3.4	4.7
Canada	4.5	5.2	3.9	4.0	4.3	3.4	1.3	-1.4	1.8	1.9	3.1	2.1	2.3	4.1	2.7
United States	5.2	4.7	4.0	3.1	3.9	2.3	1.7	-0.6	2.8	2.9	3.3	2.7	3.2	3.4	4.8
Total above	3.4	3.6	4.0	3.4	3.9	2.8	2.5	0.8	2.2	1.5	2.3	2.3	2.7	2.9	3.7
Japan	2.6	3.3	3.5	4.2	5.3	4.8	4.4	2.5	2.1	1.2	1.9	2.1	2.9	1.0	-1.1
Total above, *including Japan*	3.3	3.6	4.0	3.5	4.1	3.1	2.8	1.1	2.2	1.4	2.3	2.2	2.7	2.6	2.9
Memorandum item:															
European Union [b]	1.5	2.6	4.1	3.9	4.1	3.4	3.1	2.4	1.7	-0.3	1.7	1.7	2.0	2.0	2.7
Euro area	1.3	2.3	3.6	3.7	3.6	3.5	3.7	3.2	2.0	-0.8	1.3	1.8	1.7	1.7	2.7

Source: National statistics.

Note: See appendix table A.1.

[a] West Germany 1984-1991.

[b] Fifteen countries.

APPENDIX TABLE A.3

Real general government consumption expenditure in the ECE market economies, 1984-1998

(Percentage change over preceding year)

	1984	1985	1986	1987	1988	1989	1990	1991	1992	1993	1994	1995	1996	1997	1998
Western Europe	1.7	3.0	2.8	2.8	2.1	1.2	2.8	2.4	2.3	1.2	0.8	1.1	2.0	0.3	1.3
4 major countries	1.8	1.9	2.1	1.9	2.1	–	2.0	1.8	2.5	0.6	1.1	0.7	1.9	-0.1	1.2
France	1.2	2.3	1.7	2.8	3.4	0.4	2.1	2.8	3.4	3.5	1.1	–	2.6	1.2	1.5
Germany *a*	2.5	2.1	2.5	1.5	2.1	-1.6	2.2	0.4	4.1	-0.5	2.1	2.0	2.7	-0.7	0.6
Italy	2.1	3.1	2.5	3.2	2.7	0.9	1.2	1.7	1.2	0.5	-0.6	-1.1	0.3	-0.8	1.4
United Kingdom	1.0	-0.1	1.6	–	–	0.8	2.5	2.9	0.5	-0.8	1.4	1.6	1.7	–	1.5
17 smaller countries	1.5	5.1	4.1	4.5	2.1	3.5	4.2	3.6	1.9	2.5	0.2	1.9	2.2	1.1	1.5
Austria	0.8	1.3	1.8	0.2	1.1	1.4	1.3	2.2	2.0	2.7	2.5	–	0.6	-3.9	1.5
Belgium	0.6	2.5	1.9	0.1	-0.9	-0.9	-0.5	2.0	0.1	1.2	1.6	0.9	1.4	0.8	1.1
Cyprus	3.8	3.7	3.6	5.3	10.5	1.9	17.4	3.9	13.8	-14.3	4.1	2.9	11.9	3.4	7.7
Denmark	-0.4	2.5	0.5	2.5	0.9	-0.8	-0.2	0.7	0.9	4.1	2.9	2.2	3.2	1.1	2.2
Finland	2.7	4.5	3.1	4.3	2.3	2.3	3.8	2.0	-2.3	-4.3	0.3	2.0	2.5	2.9	0.4
Greece	3.0	3.2	-0.8	0.9	5.7	5.5	0.6	-1.5	-3.4	4.8	3.5	1.5	1.0	-0.4	0.8
Iceland	0.6	6.5	7.3	6.5	4.7	3.0	4.4	3.1	-0.8	2.3	3.7	1.3	1.0	1.5	3.0
Ireland	-0.7	1.8	2.6	-4.8	-5.0	-1.3	5.4	2.9	2.4	0.4	5.0	2.6	1.5	4.8	3.0
Israel	5.8	2.9	-9.7	18.3	-2.5	-8.6	7.7	4.1	1.4	4.2	-0.2	0.3	5.7	1.9	2.3
Luxembourg	2.2	2.0	2.7	4.7	4.9	3.9	3.1	3.9	1.5	3.7	2.0	2.2	3.3	1.7	2.8
Malta	-2.5	5.6	4.4	9.1	6.0	12.7	5.7	10.9	8.9	6.0	6.4	8.5	8.4	-1.2	-4.6
Netherlands	–	2.4	3.6	2.6	1.4	1.5	1.6	1.5	1.7	1.5	0.6	0.8	1.2	1.5	2.5
Norway	0.8	2.4	1.9	4.6	-0.1	1.9	4.9	4.3	5.3	2.2	0.7	1.9	3.2	3.0	2.8
Portugal	0.2	6.4	7.2	3.8	8.6	6.6	5.4	10.3	1.1	0.9	2.1	2.2	2.0	2.5	3.6
Spain	2.5	6.0	5.4	8.9	4.0	8.3	6.6	5.6	4.0	2.4	-0.3	1.8	1.0	1.4	1.3
Sweden	2.3	2.4	1.3	1.0	0.6	2.1	2.6	2.8	–	0.2	-0.7	-0.9	-0.2	-2.1	2.0
Switzerland	1.7	3.3	3.3	1.6	4.5	5.3	5.4	3.4	0.8	-0.2	2.1	-0.2	0.6	-0.7	0.6
Turkey	1.9	14.1	9.2	9.4	-1.1	0.8	8.0	4.5	2.8	8.6	-5.5	6.8	8.6	4.1	0.5
North America	1.6	4.8	4.3	2.1	2.2	2.7	2.4	1.1	–	-0.3	0.3	-0.3	0.4	1.1	1.0
Canada	1.2	4.3	1.9	1.4	4.6	2.8	3.7	2.8	1.0	-0.3	-1.2	-0.5	-2.5	-0.8	0.7
United States	1.6	4.8	4.6	2.2	2.0	2.7	2.3	1.0	-0.1	-0.3	0.4	-0.3	0.7	1.3	1.1
Total above	1.6	3.9	3.6	2.4	2.2	1.9	2.6	1.8	1.1	0.5	0.5	0.4	1.2	0.7	1.2
Japan	2.3	0.3	5.1	1.6	2.3	2.0	1.5	2.0	2.0	2.4	2.4	3.3	1.9	1.5	0.6
Total above, *including Japan*	1.8	3.3	3.8	2.3	2.2	1.9	2.4	1.8	1.3	0.8	0.8	0.8	1.3	0.8	1.1
Memorandum item:															
European Union *b*	1.7	2.4	2.5	2.5	2.2	1.1	2.4	2.3	2.2	0.9	1.1	0.8	1.7	0.1	1.3
Euro area	1.8	2.9	2.8	3.0	2.6	1.0	2.4	2.2	2.8	1.2	1.0	0.7	1.8	0.2	1.3

Source: National statistics.

Note: See appendix table A.1.

a West Germany 1984-1991.

b Fifteen countries.

APPENDIX TABLE A.4

Real gross domestic fixed capital formation in the ECE market economies, 1984-1998

(Percentage change over preceding year)

	1984	1985	1986	1987	1988	1989	1990	1991	1992	1993	1994	1995	1996	1997	1998
Western Europe	1.3	2.9	4.2	7.0	8.2	6.7	4.4	–	-0.7	-4.8	1.8	4.1	2.3	3.4	4.7
4 major countries	2.2	1.6	3.1	4.6	8.4	6.2	3.7	0.3	-0.1	-6.1	2.3	2.8	1.0	1.6	4.1
France	-2.6	3.2	4.5	4.8	9.6	7.9	2.8	–	-2.8	-6.7	1.3	2.5	-0.5	0.1	4.6
Germany [a]	0.1	-0.5	3.3	1.8	4.4	6.3	8.5	6.0	3.5	-5.6	3.5	–	-1.2	0.1	1.6
Italy	3.4	0.5	2.0	4.4	6.9	4.4	3.6	0.8	-1.8	-12.8	0.5	7.1	1.9	0.8	3.5
United Kingdom	9.3	4.0	2.1	8.9	14.8	5.9	-2.3	-8.7	-0.7	0.8	3.6	2.9	4.9	6.6	8.0
17 smaller countries	-0.5	5.5	6.3	11.8	7.8	7.7	5.7	-0.6	-2.0	-2.1	0.7	6.7	5.0	6.9	5.8
Austria	0.1	6.9	2.4	4.4	6.8	6.3	6.6	6.3	0.1	-2.0	8.4	1.2	2.5	2.8	4.8
Belgium	2.5	3.9	3.5	6.3	16.4	11.4	9.6	-4.7	1.3	-3.6	-0.1	3.2	0.5	5.4	4.8
Cyprus	21.5	-7.7	-7.1	4.5	10.6	20.0	-2.8	-1.6	16.2	-12.8	-2.5	-1.7	7.8	-8.4	0.6
Denmark	12.9	12.6	17.1	-3.8	-6.6	0.4	-1.0	-2.8	-1.1	-1.9	7.4	12.3	4.9	10.6	5.0
Finland	-2.1	2.2	-0.4	4.9	9.8	14.8	-4.1	-18.8	-16.6	-17.4	-2.8	11.9	8.7	14.2	8.2
Greece	-5.7	5.2	-6.2	-5.1	8.9	7.1	5.0	4.8	-1.0	-1.8	1.2	5.9	8.8	9.6	8.0
Iceland	9.4	1.0	-1.6	18.8	-0.2	-7.9	3.0	2.0	-11.3	-11.4	-1.1	-2.8	26.5	11.2	28.2
Ireland	-2.5	-7.7	-2.8	-1.1	5.2	10.1	13.4	-6.6	-1.9	-3.6	12.2	10.9	13.6	10.9	13.0
Israel	-11.9	-9.2	7.4	6.1	1.6	-2.2	25.3	41.9	5.2	5.3	8.4	6.0	9.3	-2.3	-3.3
Luxembourg	0.1	-9.5	31.0	17.9	15.0	7.0	2.7	31.6	-9.0	28.4	-14.9	3.5	-1.7	14.1	6.5
Malta	-7.0	-4.0	-8.7	30.7	6.1	1.0	17.9	–	-0.2	11.1	8.5	17.8	-3.8	-7.6	-4.1
Netherlands	5.8	7.0	6.9	0.9	4.6	4.9	1.6	0.2	0.6	-2.8	2.2	4.8	5.4	6.8	3.9
Norway	1.0	-4.0	7.6	0.3	-1.8	-6.9	-10.8	-0.4	-3.1	4.3	6.9	1.4	9.6	12.6	6.6
Portugal	-17.4	-3.5	10.9	18.0	14.8	4.4	7.6	3.5	4.8	-6.0	3.4	4.8	5.7	11.3	8.2
Spain	-6.9	6.1	9.9	14.0	13.9	13.6	6.6	1.6	-4.4	-10.5	2.4	7.8	1.8	5.1	8.8
Sweden	6.9	6.3	0.3	8.2	6.6	11.3	1.3	-8.9	-10.8	-17.2	2.0	12.4	3.7	-4.8	10.5
Switzerland	4.7	2.8	5.4	4.0	8.1	5.3	3.8	-2.9	-6.6	-2.7	6.5	1.9	-2.7	1.5	3.8
Turkey	0.9	11.5	8.4	45.1	-1.0	2.2	15.9	1.2	5.5	26.4	-16.0	9.1	14.1	14.8	-2.0
North America	14.6	6.4	2.2	1.2	2.2	2.3	-1.6	-6.4	4.7	4.5	6.6	4.4	7.7	7.5	9.3
Canada	2.5	10.3	5.4	10.7	9.8	5.9	-3.6	-3.5	-1.3	-2.9	7.4	-2.5	6.6	11.1	4.2
United States	15.6	6.1	1.9	0.4	1.5	2.0	-1.4	-6.6	5.2	5.1	6.5	5.0	7.8	7.1	9.7
Total above	7.9	4.6	3.2	4.1	5.2	4.5	1.4	-3.2	2.0	-0.2	4.2	4.3	5.0	5.4	7.0
Japan	4.3	5.0	4.8	9.1	11.5	8.2	8.5	3.3	-1.5	-2.0	-0.8	1.7	11.1	-1.9	-9.0
Total above, *including Japan*	7.3	4.7	3.4	4.9	6.2	5.1	2.5	-2.2	1.4	-0.4	3.4	3.9	6.0	4.3	4.5
Memorandum item:															
European Union [b]	1.2	2.6	3.9	5.4	8.8	7.1	4.1	–	-0.9	-6.4	2.4	4.0	1.8	2.8	5.0
Euro area	-0.6	1.9	4.3	5.0	8.0	7.3	5.5	1.9	-0.6	-7.7	2.1	3.7	0.9	2.0	4.2

Source: National statistics.

Note: See appendix table A.1.

[a] West Germany 1984-1991.

[b] Fifteen countries.

APPENDIX TABLE A.5

Real total domestic demand in the ECE market economies, 1984-1998
(Percentage change over preceding year)

	1984	1985	1986	1987	1988	1989	1990	1991	1992	1993	1994	1995	1996	1997	1998
Western Europe	1.9	2.5	4.1	4.0	4.5	3.6	3.5	1.4	1.3	-1.1	1.9	2.5	1.7	2.6	3.4
4 major countries	2.0	2.2	3.9	3.6	4.8	3.1	2.9	1.5	1.3	-1.7	2.6	1.7	1.1	2.0	3.3
France	0.4	2.5	4.5	3.3	4.7	3.9	2.8	0.6	0.2	-2.2	3.0	1.8	0.9	0.9	3.8
Germany [a]	1.9	1.0	3.3	2.4	3.6	2.9	5.2	4.7	2.8	-1.4	2.7	1.4	0.7	1.4	3.1
Italy	3.0	3.0	3.5	4.3	4.0	3.1	2.6	1.8	0.7	-5.1	1.2	2.0	0.2	2.4	2.6
United Kingdom	2.7	2.9	4.8	4.8	7.8	2.8	-0.3	-2.5	0.8	2.1	3.4	1.8	3.0	3.8	3.5
17 smaller countries	1.7	2.9	4.4	4.7	3.7	4.5	4.8	1.1	1.3	0.1	0.7	4.1	2.8	3.9	3.8
Austria	1.6	1.9	2.1	2.6	3.2	3.0	4.3	3.6	1.4	0.8	3.6	1.9	1.7	1.8	2.8
Belgium	2.2	1.0	2.5	3.3	4.9	4.2	3.4	1.3	1.9	-1.6	1.4	1.4	1.3	2.2	3.0
Cyprus	9.3	2.2	-1.5	5.6	11.3	9.7	6.3	5.1	9.3	-9.5	6.7	7.8	4.5	0.7	5.6
Denmark	5.4	5.4	6.2	-2.3	-1.2	0.3	-0.6	-0.1	1.7	0.5	7.2	4.9	3.3	4.5	3.8
Finland	2.2	2.9	2.2	5.2	6.6	7.6	-1.3	-8.4	-5.9	-5.7	3.6	4.7	2.4	5.4	4.6
Greece	-0.2	5.6	-1.2	-1.5	7.3	5.3	2.8	3.7	0.4	0.4	1.8	3.2	3.0	3.5	3.0
Iceland	6.1	2.9	4.8	15.7	-0.9	-4.3	1.4	5.1	-5.3	-4.1	1.5	3.1	7.5	5.8	12.4
Ireland	1.1	1.2	1.2	-0.2	2.1	7.3	6.4	0.2	0.2	0.8	6.7	7.2	6.9	7.3	7.6
Israel	-1.9	-2.2	5.4	9.0	2.5	-2.8	9.3	12.1	5.3	6.8	5.3	6.9	5.6	1.4	0.9
Luxembourg	2.3	0.7	8.5	5.4	6.7	8.4	3.3	8.6	-1.5	9.4	-0.4	3.1	1.8	4.7	3.7
Malta	0.8	3.5	–	3.5	11.5	8.3	7.6	4.9	0.1	4.8	2.1	13.7	4.5	1.6	5.6
Netherlands	1.8	3.7	3.8	1.4	1.8	4.7	3.5	1.9	1.6	-1.0	3.0	2.3	3.0	3.6	4.0
Norway	4.8	5.6	7.3	-0.8	-3.1	-2.0	-0.3	0.8	1.7	3.1	4.4	3.9	4.7	5.6	4.5
Portugal	-6.5	1.0	8.2	9.9	10.7	3.3	6.1	4.2	5.0	-1.3	3.0	3.0	2.8	5.2	6.8
Spain	-0.9	2.5	5.4	8.1	7.0	7.8	4.8	2.9	1.0	-4.2	1.3	3.2	1.6	2.9	4.4
Sweden	3.2	4.2	2.1	4.3	2.8	3.7	0.9	-2.1	-1.8	-5.2	2.5	2.6	0.1	0.4	4.1
Switzerland	3.2	1.9	4.5	2.0	2.6	4.1	3.9	-0.6	-2.7	-1.0	2.7	1.9	-0.1	1.3	3.8
Turkey	6.4	3.2	7.0	8.9	-1.3	1.5	14.6	-0.9	5.9	14.2	-12.5	11.4	7.6	9.0	1.7
North America	7.5	4.3	3.4	2.9	3.1	2.8	0.8	-1.5	2.7	2.9	3.9	2.0	3.4	4.3	4.8
Canada	4.7	5.8	3.4	4.6	5.3	4.1	-0.1	-1.4	0.9	1.5	3.2	1.6	1.1	5.2	2.2
United States	7.7	4.1	3.4	2.7	2.9	2.7	0.9	-1.6	2.8	3.0	3.9	2.1	3.6	4.2	5.1
Total above	4.7	3.4	3.8	3.4	3.8	3.2	2.2	-0.1	2.0	0.9	2.9	2.3	2.5	3.5	4.1
Japan	3.2	3.8	3.9	5.1	7.4	5.6	5.2	2.9	0.4	0.1	1.0	2.3	5.7	0.1	-3.6
Total above, *including Japan*	4.4	3.4	3.8	3.7	4.3	3.6	2.6	0.4	1.7	0.8	2.6	2.3	3.0	2.9	2.9
Memorandum item:															
European Union [b]	1.6	2.4	3.9	3.8	4.9	3.8	3.0	1.5	1.2	-1.9	2.6	2.1	1.4	2.3	3.5
Euro area	1.3	2.1	3.9	3.8	4.4	4.0	3.8	2.4	1.3	-2.6	2.3	2.0	1.1	2.0	3.4

Source: National statistics.

Note: See appendix table A.1.

[a] West Germany 1984-1991.

[b] Fifteen countries.

APPENDIX TABLE A.6

Real exports of goods and services in the ECE market economies, 1984-1998

(Percentage change over preceding year)

	1984	1985	1986	1987	1988	1989	1990	1991	1992	1993	1994	1995	1996	1997	1998
Western Europe	8.8	4.3	0.9	4.9	6.1	7.4	6.3	4.6	4.3	2.4	9.2	8.2	6.2	10.2	4.8
4 major countries	7.5	4.9	0.6	3.1	5.0	8.5	7.5	5.0	3.5	1.4	8.2	8.4	4.8	9.5	3.9
France	7.0	1.9	-1.4	3.1	8.1	10.2	5.4	4.1	4.9	-0.4	6.0	6.3	5.2	12.6	5.7
Germany [a]	8.2	7.6	-0.6	0.4	5.5	10.2	11.0	12.6	-0.3	-5.0	7.9	6.6	5.1	11.1	5.4
Italy	7.9	3.5	0.8	4.4	5.0	7.7	7.1	0.1	6.8	9.8	10.3	12.0	1.6	5.0	1.3
United Kingdom	6.6	6.0	4.5	5.9	0.6	4.8	4.9	-0.2	4.1	3.9	9.2	9.5	7.5	8.7	2.7
17 smaller countries	11.3	3.1	1.5	8.4	8.4	5.2	4.0	3.8	5.8	4.5	11.2	7.7	8.8	11.5	6.5
Austria	6.3	7.1	-2.3	3.1	10.2	11.3	7.9	5.9	1.7	-1.3	5.6	6.5	6.9	10.1	7.5
Belgium	6.5	0.3	2.7	4.4	9.1	8.2	4.3	3.1	3.5	-0.7	9.5	6.8	2.2	7.1	5.1
Cyprus	15.1	-1.1	-1.7	13.7	13.5	16.8	7.9	-8.4	18.7	-1.3	7.9	4.6	3.7	2.1	-2.0
Denmark	3.5	5.0	–	5.1	7.8	4.3	6.2	7.0	-0.5	0.1	8.2	4.4	3.7	5.5	1.2
Finland	5.0	1.1	1.2	2.7	3.7	1.3	1.4	-7.3	10.4	16.7	13.1	8.7	6.1	14.2	6.6
Greece	16.9	1.3	14.0	16.0	9.0	4.6	-4.0	3.7	8.6	0.5	7.4	2.1	3.0	5.3	5.5
Iceland	2.4	11.1	5.9	3.3	-3.6	2.9	–	-5.9	-1.9	7.1	10.0	-2.2	9.6	5.6	5.7
Ireland	16.6	6.6	2.9	13.7	9.0	10.3	8.7	5.3	13.5	9.7	14.2	19.6	11.7	16.9	19.5
Israel	13.6	10.2	5.6	10.2	-1.5	4.0	2.0	-2.6	14.1	9.9	12.8	8.2	6.8	7.6	6.0
Luxembourg	18.0	9.5	3.3	4.4	11.7	8.1	3.4	6.7	4.8	2.8	4.4	4.4	2.3	6.0	7.5
Malta	4.0	7.4	7.0	12.6	6.1	10.7	13.3	7.5	9.7	5.3	7.1	5.4	-6.7	2.0	5.2
Netherlands	7.5	5.1	1.8	4.0	9.0	6.7	5.3	4.7	2.9	1.5	6.7	6.7	5.2	6.7	5.9
Norway	7.9	7.2	2.2	1.1	6.4	11.0	8.6	6.1	5.2	3.2	8.2	4.1	9.8	5.8	0.5
Portugal	11.6	6.7	6.8	11.2	8.2	13.0	10.0	2.6	4.9	-3.6	8.7	9.1	10.2	8.4	10.1
Spain	11.7	2.7	1.9	6.3	5.1	3.0	3.2	7.9	7.4	8.5	16.7	10.0	10.6	14.8	10.1
Sweden	6.9	1.2	3.7	4.3	2.5	3.1	1.6	-2.3	2.3	7.6	14.0	12.9	6.1	12.8	5.1
Switzerland	7.5	8.0	-0.4	2.3	6.5	6.6	2.1	-2.1	3.0	1.5	1.8	1.6	2.9	9.1	4.1
Turkey	25.4	-1.9	-5.1	26.4	18.4	-0.3	3.1	3.1	11.0	7.7	15.2	8.0	22.0	19.1	3.3
North America	9.1	2.9	7.2	10.4	15.4	10.8	8.2	6.0	6.7	3.7	8.6	11.1	8.3	12.4	2.1
Canada	18.8	5.6	5.3	3.5	9.7	1.1	4.8	2.3	7.9	12.1	13.1	8.8	5.9	8.0	8.1
United States	8.3	2.7	7.4	11.0	15.9	11.7	8.5	6.3	6.6	2.9	8.2	11.3	8.5	12.8	1.5
Total above	8.9	3.6	4.0	7.6	10.7	9.1	7.2	5.3	5.5	3.1	8.9	9.6	7.2	11.3	3.4
Japan	14.8	5.4	-5.7	-0.5	5.9	9.1	6.9	5.2	4.9	1.3	4.6	5.4	6.3	11.6	-2.3
Total above, *including Japan*	9.9	3.9	2.5	6.3	10.0	9.1	7.2	5.3	5.4	2.8	8.2	9.0	7.1	11.3	2.5
Memorandum item:															
European Union [b]	8.0	4.5	1.2	4.0	5.5	7.7	6.5	4.8	4.0	2.2	9.1	8.4	5.5	9.9	5.0
Euro area	8.2	4.4	0.2	3.3	6.4	8.5	7.2	6.0	4.0	1.8	9.0	8.3	5.2	10.2	5.5

Source: National statistics.

Note: See appendix table A.1.

[a] West Germany 1984-1991.

[b] Fifteen countries.

APPENDIX TABLE A.7

Real imports of goods and services in the ECE market economies, 1984-1998

(Percentage change over preceding year)

	1984	1985	1986	1987	1988	1989	1990	1991	1992	1993	1994	1995	1996	1997	1998
Western Europe	6.6	4.3	5.5	9.2	7.8	8.7	7.7	3.9	4.2	-1.7	6.3	8.3	4.8	9.7	7.4
4 major countries	7.2	4.2	5.0	7.6	7.8	8.2	7.0	4.6	4.1	-4.1	6.8	6.9	3.3	8.8	7.1
France	2.7	4.5	7.1	7.7	8.6	8.1	6.1	3.0	1.2	-3.5	6.7	5.1	3.0	8.1	8.2
Germany *a*	5.2	4.5	2.7	4.2	5.1	8.3	10.3	13.1	2.0	-5.9	7.7	7.3	2.9	8.1	6.6
Italy	12.2	5.0	4.3	12.0	6.1	9.0	9.4	3.3	7.4	-8.8	6.8	9.6	-1.1	9.9	6.1
United Kingdom	9.9	2.5	6.9	7.9	12.8	7.4	0.5	-5.0	6.8	3.2	5.4	5.5	9.1	9.5	7.8
17 smaller countries	5.4	4.6	6.3	12.3	7.7	9.7	9.1	2.6	4.5	3.0	5.5	11.2	7.6	11.4	7.8
Austria	10.0	6.2	-2.9	5.4	10.4	8.4	7.3	6.5	1.8	-0.7	8.3	7.0	6.3	8.7	6.8
Belgium	6.3	0.2	4.5	6.1	9.7	9.4	4.9	2.8	4.1	-0.7	8.2	6.1	2.2	6.3	5.5
Cyprus	16.4	-4.5	-11.0	5.5	13.4	20.4	5.8	2.2	18.2	-18.1	8.2	11.5	6.8	1.3	3.6
Denmark	5.5	8.1	6.8	-2.0	1.5	4.2	1.5	3.9	0.2	-1.2	13.2	9.9	3.7	9.8	4.8
Finland	1.6	6.4	2.6	9.2	11.1	8.9	-0.6	-13.5	0.6	1.3	12.8	7.9	6.3	11.4	8.1
Greece	0.2	12.8	3.8	16.6	8.0	10.6	8.7	6.0	4.9	1.0	4.1	6.2	4.9	5.4	4.5
Iceland	9.1	9.4	0.9	23.3	-4.6	-10.3	1.0	5.7	-8.0	-8.6	4.2	3.8	16.6	8.0	25.0
Ireland	9.9	3.2	5.6	6.2	4.9	13.5	5.1	2.3	7.9	7.2	14.8	15.8	12.2	15.6	21.3
Israel	-1.1	-3.7	11.2	19.6	-2.8	-5.0	9.5	16.0	8.8	14.1	10.9	7.2	8.1	2.8	2.1
Luxembourg	13.9	7.0	3.8	7.5	8.2	6.6	4.5	9.0	-0.8	2.8	-0.1	3.8	1.0	6.1	7.0
Malta	3.9	9.2	0.1	12.3	11.1	11.1	15.7	5.4	3.0	5.9	7.5	10.0	-6.3	-2.4	1.6
Netherlands	5.0	6.3	3.5	4.2	7.6	6.7	4.2	4.1	2.1	-2.1	6.7	7.5	5.3	7.1	6.8
Norway	5.8	8.9	11.8	-6.5	-2.4	2.2	2.5	0.2	0.7	4.4	6.9	3.5	8.3	12.3	6.9
Portugal	-4.4	1.4	16.9	23.1	18.0	6.1	14.0	7.3	10.7	-3.3	9.0	7.8	7.5	10.4	15.0
Spain	-1.8	8.0	14.4	20.1	14.4	17.3	7.8	9.0	6.9	-5.2	11.3	11.0	7.4	12.2	11.5
Sweden	5.4	7.8	4.5	7.7	5.3	7.4	0.7	-4.9	1.1	-2.5	13.2	10.2	3.7	11.7	8.9
Switzerland	8.3	3.7	8.1	6.2	5.2	5.9	2.6	-1.6	-4.2	0.1	7.9	5.1	2.7	7.9	8.7
Turkey	19.7	-6.6	-3.5	23.0	-4.5	6.9	33.1	-5.3	10.9	35.8	-21.9	29.6	20.5	22.4	1.8
North America	23.8	6.7	8.4	6.1	4.7	4.1	3.7	-0.3	7.4	9.1	11.6	8.6	8.9	13.8	10.3
Canada	18.2	8.9	8.6	5.7	13.9	6.3	2.3	3.2	6.3	8.1	8.3	6.4	5.4	13.3	6.4
United States	24.3	6.5	8.4	6.1	3.9	3.9	3.9	-0.7	7.5	9.1	11.9	8.8	9.2	13.9	10.6
Total above	15.2	5.5	6.9	7.6	6.3	6.4	5.7	1.8	5.8	3.7	9.0	8.5	6.8	11.8	8.8
Japan	10.5	-1.4	1.9	9.5	20.9	18.6	7.9	-3.1	-0.7	-0.3	8.9	14.2	11.9	0.5	-7.7
Total above, *including Japan*	14.4	4.4	6.2	7.9	8.6	8.3	6.1	1.0	4.8	3.1	8.9	9.4	7.6	10.0	6.2
Memorandum item:															
European Union *b*	5.9	4.8	5.8	8.8	8.5	9.0	6.7	4.5	4.2	-3.6	7.6	7.5	4.0	9.1	7.6
Euro area	5.3	5.0	5.6	9.0	8.0	9.4	8.2	6.7	3.8	-5.1	7.9	7.7	3.0	9.0	7.6

Source: National statistics.

Note: See appendix table A.1.

a West Germany 1984-1991.

b Fifteen countries.

APPENDIX TABLE A.8

Industrial output in the ECE market economies, 1984-1998

(Percentage change over preceding year)

	1984	1985	1986	1987	1988	1989	1990	1991	1992	1993	1994	1995	1996	1997	1998
Western Europe	2.7	3.4	2.7	2.5	4.4	4.1	2.4	-0.2	-0.9	-2.7	4.5	3.8	0.4	3.9	3.3
4 major countries	1.9	3.6	2.2	1.8	4.8	3.8	2.0	-0.3	-1.3	-3.6	4.6	2.6	-0.2	2.8	2.9
France	0.3	2.1	0.6	1.2	4.6	3.7	1.5	-1.2	-1.2	-3.9	4.0	2.1	0.2	3.8	4.5
Germany [a]	3.0	4.8	1.8	0.4	3.6	4.9	5.2	2.4	-2.3	-7.6	3.6	1.2	0.4	3.4	4.6
Italy	3.3	1.4	4.1	2.6	6.9	3.9	-0.5	-0.9	-1.3	-2.1	6.2	6.1	-2.9	2.7	0.8
United Kingdom	–	5.5	2.5	4.0	4.8	2.1	-0.4	-3.4	0.4	2.2	5.4	1.7	1.1	0.8	0.5
13 smaller countries	4.6	2.9	3.7	4.1	3.5	4.7	3.4	–	0.1	-0.7	4.1	6.4	2.0	6.3	4.2
Austria	4.9	4.7	1.2	1.0	4.5	5.8	6.8	1.9	-1.2	-1.5	4.0	4.9	0.8	5.6	3.3
Belgium	2.5	2.5	0.8	2.1	5.8	3.4	3.7	-2.0	–	-5.2	1.9	6.5	0.8	4.4	3.3
Finland	4.8	2.9	1.9	5.0	3.2	3.6	-0.6	-8.7	1.3	5.6	11.3	6.8	3.2	10.0	7.2
Greece	2.3	3.3	-0.3	-1.2	5.0	1.8	-2.4	-1.0	-1.1	-2.9	1.3	1.8	1.2	1.3	7.0
Ireland	9.9	3.4	2.2	8.9	10.7	11.6	4.7	3.3	9.1	5.6	11.9	18.9	8.0	15.3	15.5
Israel	..	..	3.6	4.8	-3.2	-1.6	8.1	6.7	8.2	6.7	7.5	8.4	14.2	16.2	..
Luxembourg	11.7	-1.1	1.9	-0.6	8.7	7.8	2.6	0.3	-0.8	-4.3	5.9	1.4	-1.9	7.2	4.9
Netherlands	5.3	-0.1	–	1.2	–	5.2	2.5	1.7	-0.2	-1.1	4.9	2.9	2.7	1.9	1.2
Norway	6.5	5.7	4.7	6.2	2.8	9.4	2.3	2.6	5.7	3.8	6.9	5.9	5.2	3.5	-0.9
Portugal	2.5	-1.3	7.2	4.4	3.8	6.7	9.0	–	-2.3	-5.2	-0.2	4.7	1.3	2.5	4.0
Spain	0.9	1.8	3.3	4.6	3.1	5.1	-0.3	-0.7	-3.0	-4.7	7.6	4.8	-1.3	6.9	5.5
Sweden	5.6	2.9	0.2	2.8	2.9	2.9	0.3	-5.2	-1.1	0.5	11.9	11.7	2.3	7.4	4.7
Switzerland	2.6	5.6	3.8	1.2	7.8	1.5	4.8	0.5	-1.0	-1.8	4.3	2.0	-0.1	5.4	4.4
Turkey	11.0	5.9	11.7	10.6	1.6	3.6	9.5	2.7	5.0	8.0	-6.2	12.7	7.5	11.5	3.4
North America	9.3	2.0	1.0	4.6	4.7	1.6	-0.4	-2.2	3.0	3.5	5.5	4.9	4.2	6.0	3.5
Canada	12.6	5.4	-0.6	4.4	6.1	-0.4	-2.8	-3.8	1.1	4.5	6.4	4.7	1.3	5.2	2.4
United States	9.0	1.6	1.2	4.6	4.5	1.8	-0.2	-2.0	3.1	3.5	5.4	4.9	4.5	6.0	3.6
Total above	5.6	2.7	1.9	3.5	4.5	3.0	1.1	-1.1	0.8	0.1	4.9	4.3	2.1	4.8	3.4
Japan	9.3	3.7	-0.2	3.5	10.4	4.8	4.2	1.9	-5.8	-4.4	1.3	3.3	2.3	3.5	-6.4
Total above, *including Japan*	6.4	2.9	1.5	3.5	5.7	3.3	1.7	-0.5	-0.5	-0.8	4.2	4.1	2.2	4.6	1.5
Memorandum item:															
European Union [b]	2.2	3.2	2.2	2.1	4.5	4.1	2.0	-0.4	-1.3	-3.3	5.0	3.4	–	3.5	3.3
Euro area	2.6	2.7	2.2	1.8	4.5	4.6	2.5	0.3	-1.6	-4.4	4.8	3.5	-0.2	3.9	3.8

Source: National statistics; OECD, *Main Economic Indicators* (Paris), various issues.

Note: Growth rates of regional aggregates have been calculated as weighted averages of growth rates in individual countries. Weights were derived from GDP originating in industry in 1990. Data were converted from national currency units into dollars using GDP purchasing power parities.

[a] West Germany 1984-1991.

[b] Fourteen countries (excluding Denmark).

APPENDIX TABLE A.9

Total employment in the ECE market economies, 1984-1998
(Percentage change over preceding year)

	1984	1985	1986	1987	1988	1989	1990	1991	1992	1993	1994	1995	1996	1997	1998
Western Europe	0.6	0.9	1.1	1.3	1.6	1.7	1.6	0.4	-1.3	-1.7	0.1	1.0	0.8	0.2	1.2
4 major countries	0.9	0.7	0.7	0.9	1.6	1.6	1.5	–	-1.6	-1.8	-0.4	0.3	0.2	0.1	0.6
France	-0.9	-0.3	0.4	0.3	0.9	1.3	1.0	0.1	-0.7	-1.2	-0.1	1.0	0.2	0.2	1.4
Germany [a]	0.2	0.7	1.4	0.7	0.8	1.5	3.0	2.5	-1.8	-1.7	-0.7	-0.4	-1.3	-1.3	–
Italy [b]	0.4	0.9	0.8	0.4	0.9	0.2	0.9	0.8	-1.0	-2.9	-1.4	-0.3	–	-0.2	0.2
United Kingdom [c]	3.8	1.2	0.2	2.1	3.6	3.2	1.0	-3.2	-2.6	-1.3	0.6	1.1	2.4	1.9	0.9
17 smaller countries	0.1	1.2	1.6	1.8	1.6	1.9	1.7	0.9	-0.9	-1.5	0.7	2.0	1.6	0.3	2.1
Austria	-0.1	0.3	0.3	-0.1	0.3	1.4	1.9	1.6	0.4	-0.5	0.1	0.2	-0.5	0.3	0.9
Belgium [c]	-0.2	0.6	0.6	0.5	1.5	1.6	1.4	0.1	-0.4	-1.1	-1.0	0.5	0.4	0.5	1.2
Cyprus	3.8	3.7	1.1	3.1	4.7	3.9	2.8	0.6	4.1	-0.1	2.8	3.4	1.0	0.2	..
Denmark	1.7	2.5	2.6	0.9	-0.6	-0.7	-0.7	-0.6	-0.8	-1.5	1.4	1.1	0.8	2.0	1.9
Finland	0.4	0.1	-0.4	0.5	0.6	0.7	-0.5	-5.2	-7.0	-6.5	-1.1	1.7	1.0	2.0	2.7
Greece	0.4	1.0	0.3	-0.1	1.7	0.4	1.3	-2.3	1.3	1.0	1.9	0.9	1.2	-0.5	1.4
Iceland [b]	1.5	3.6	3.2	5.7	-3.0	-1.4	-1.0	-0.1	-1.4	-0.7	0.5	0.8	3.0	1.7	2.1
Ireland [d]	-1.9	-2.2	0.2	-0.1	1.0	-0.1	3.3	0.7	1.0	0.6	3.1	5.1	3.9	3.2	6.7
Israel	1.5	0.7	1.4	2.6	3.5	0.5	2.1	6.1	4.2	6.1	6.9	5.2	2.4	1.4	1.8
Luxembourg	0.6	0.9	2.5	2.7	3.0	3.4	4.2	4.1	2.5	1.8	2.5	2.5	2.8	3.2	4.5
Malta [e]	0.6	1.3	2.1	5.9	2.5	0.9	0.8	2.5	1.0	0.5	1.2	3.8	1.0	0.5	0.4
Netherlands [b]	0.1	1.9	2.1	1.7	1.6	1.9	2.3	1.3	1.0	-0.1	-0.4	1.4	2.0	2.6	2.7
Norway	0.6	2.7	3.0	2.1	-0.8	-2.8	-0.8	-0.8	-0.3	0.2	1.3	2.1	2.5	2.9	2.3
Portugal	-1.0	-0.5	2.7	2.3	2.2	1.9	1.7	2.7	-1.7	-2.0	-0.2	-0.7	0.7	1.9	2.8
Spain	-2.7	1.1	2.2	3.1	2.9	4.0	2.6	0.2	-1.9	-4.3	-0.9	2.7	2.9	3.0	3.1
Sweden	0.8	1.0	0.6	0.8	1.4	1.5	0.9	-1.5	-4.4	-5.2	-1.0	1.5	-0.5	-1.0	1.4
Switzerland	1.0	2.0	2.3	2.5	2.6	2.7	3.2	1.8	-1.5	-0.8	-0.1	0.1	0.3	-0.3	1.2
Turkey	1.5	1.7	1.8	2.3	1.5	2.0	1.8	3.1	0.2	0.2	2.8	3.7	2.0	-2.5	1.5
North America	4.6	2.5	1.8	2.9	3.0	2.5	0.6	-0.8	-0.2	1.8	2.5	2.3	1.8	2.5	2.6
Canada	2.7	3.0	3.0	2.7	3.2	2.1	0.6	-1.9	-0.6	1.3	2.1	1.6	1.3	1.9	2.5
United States [f]	4.8	2.4	1.7	2.9	2.9	2.5	0.6	-0.7	-0.1	1.8	2.5	2.4	1.9	2.6	2.6
Total above	2.2	1.5	1.4	1.9	2.2	2.0	1.2	-0.1	-0.8	-0.2	1.1	1.6	1.2	1.2	1.8
Japan	0.3	0.6	0.5	0.4	1.2	1.5	1.7	2.0	1.1	0.4	0.1	0.2	0.5	1.1	-0.6
Total above, *including Japan*	1.9	1.4	1.2	1.7	2.0	1.9	1.3	0.3	-0.5	-0.1	0.9	1.3	1.1	1.2	1.4
Memorandum item:															
European Union [g]	0.4	0.7	0.9	1.1	1.7	1.7	1.6	–	-1.5	-1.9	-0.3	0.6	0.6	0.5	1.1
Euro area	-0.4	0.5	1.1	0.9	1.2	1.4	1.8	1.0	-1.3	-2.1	-0.6	0.5	0.2	0.2	1.1

Source: National statistics; OECD, *National Accounts Detailed Tables*, Vol. II, 1998 and *OECD Economic Outlook,* No. 64, December 1998 (Paris); UN/ECE secretariat estimates.

Note: All aggregates exclude Israel. National accounts statistics, where available; otherwise annual labour force surveys. Unless otherwise indicated, the data refer to the annual average number of persons employed, i.e. no adjustment is made for part-time workers. Comparisons with previous years are limited due to changes in methodology in Denmark (1989), Israel (1986 and 1996), Malta (1995) and Norway (1989).

[a] West Germany 1984-1991.

[b] Full-time equivalent data.

[c] June.

[d] Mid-April estimates.

[e] End of year.

[f] Full-time equivalent employees plus the number of self-employed persons (unpaid family workers are not included).

[g] Fifteen countries.

APPENDIX TABLE A.10

Standardized unemployment rates [a] **in the ECE market economies, 1984-1998**

(Per cent of civilian labour force)

	1984	1985	1986	1987	1988	1989	1990	1991	1992	1993	1994	1995	1996	1997	1998
Western Europe	9.3	9.4	9.4	9.3	8.7	8.1	7.6	8.0	8.9	10.2	10.6	10.1	10.1	9.9	9.2
4 major countries	9.0	9.3	9.3	9.2	8.5	7.9	7.3	7.9	8.8	9.8	10.1	9.8	10.1	10.2	9.7
France	9.7	10.1	10.2	10.4	9.8	9.3	9.0	9.5	10.4	11.7	12.3	11.7	12.4	12.4	11.9
Germany [b]	7.1	7.1	6.4	6.2	6.2	5.6	4.8	5.6	6.6	7.9	8.4	8.2	8.9	9.9	9.4
Italy	8.1	8.5	9.2	9.9	10.0	10.0	9.1	8.8	9.0	10.3	11.4	11.9	12.0	12.1	12.2
United Kingdom	11.1	11.5	11.5	10.6	8.7	7.3	7.1	8.8	10.1	10.5	9.6	8.7	8.2	7.0	6.3
17 smaller countries	9.7	9.6	9.6	9.4	9.0	8.4	7.9	8.2	9.1	10.7	11.2	10.4	10.1	9.5	8.5
Austria	3.8	3.6	3.1	3.8	3.6	3.1	3.2	3.5	3.6	4.0	3.8	3.9	4.4	4.4	4.4
Belgium	11.1	10.4	10.3	10.0	8.9	7.5	6.7	6.6	7.3	8.9	10.0	9.9	9.7	9.2	8.8
Cyprus [c]	3.3	3.3	3.7	3.4	2.8	2.3	1.8	3.0	1.8	2.6	2.7	2.6	3.1	3.4	3.2
Denmark	10.1	9.0	7.8	7.8	6.1	7.4	7.7	8.5	9.2	10.1	8.2	7.3	6.8	5.6	5.1
Finland	5.9	6.1	6.7	4.9	4.4	3.1	3.2	7.1	12.5	16.4	16.8	15.3	14.6	12.7	11.4
Greece	7.2	7.0	6.6	6.7	6.8	6.7	6.4	7.0	7.9	8.6	8.9	9.2	9.6	9.6	9.3
Iceland	1.3	0.9	0.6	0.5	1.2	1.7	1.8	1.5	3.1	4.4	4.8	5.0	4.4	3.9	2.8
Ireland	15.5	16.9	16.8	16.6	16.2	14.7	13.4	14.8	15.4	15.6	14.3	12.3	11.6	9.9	7.8
Israel	5.9	6.7	7.1	6.1	6.4	8.9	9.6	10.6	11.2	10.0	7.8	6.9	6.7	7.7	8.6
Luxembourg	3.1	2.9	2.6	2.5	2.0	1.8	1.7	1.7	2.1	2.7	3.2	2.9	3.0	2.8	2.8
Malta [c]	8.6	8.1	6.9	4.4	4.0	3.7	3.8	3.6	4.0	4.5	4.1	3.8	4.4	5.0	4.9
Netherlands	9.3	8.3	8.3	8.0	7.6	6.9	6.2	5.8	5.6	6.6	7.1	6.9	6.3	5.2	4.0
Norway	3.2	2.6	2.0	2.1	3.3	5.0	5.3	5.6	6.0	6.1	5.5	5.0	4.9	4.1	3.4
Portugal	8.5	8.7	8.4	6.9	5.5	4.9	4.6	4.0	4.2	5.7	7.0	7.3	7.3	6.8	4.9
Spain	20.3	21.7	21.2	20.6	19.5	17.2	16.2	16.4	18.4	22.7	24.1	22.9	22.2	20.8	18.8
Sweden	3.3	2.9	2.7	2.2	1.8	1.6	1.7	3.1	5.6	9.1	9.4	8.8	9.6	9.9	8.2
Switzerland	1.0	0.8	0.7	0.7	0.6	0.5	0.5	1.1	2.5	4.5	4.7	4.2	4.7	5.2	3.8
Turkey	7.6	7.1	7.9	8.3	8.4	8.6	8.0	7.9	8.0	7.7	8.1	6.9	6.0	5.7	5.6
North America	7.9	7.5	7.3	6.5	5.7	5.5	5.9	7.2	7.9	7.4	6.5	6.0	5.8	5.4	4.9
Canada	11.3	10.5	9.6	8.8	7.8	7.5	8.2	10.4	11.3	11.2	10.4	9.5	9.7	9.2	8.3
United States	7.5	7.2	7.0	6.2	5.5	5.3	5.6	6.8	7.5	6.9	6.1	5.6	5.4	4.9	4.5
Total above	8.7	8.6	8.5	8.1	7.4	7.0	6.8	7.7	8.5	9.0	8.8	8.3	8.3	7.9	7.3
Japan	2.7	2.6	2.8	2.8	2.5	2.3	2.1	2.1	2.2	2.5	2.9	3.2	3.4	3.4	4.1
Total above, *including Japan*	7.7	7.6	7.5	7.2	6.6	6.2	6.1	6.8	7.4	7.9	7.9	7.5	7.5	7.2	6.8
Memorandum item:															
European Union [d]	9.8	10.0	9.9	9.7	9.1	8.3	7.7	8.2	9.2	10.7	11.1	10.7	10.8	10.6	9.9
Euro area	9.8	10.1	10.0	10.0	9.6	8.9	8.2	8.3	9.2	10.9	11.6	11.4	11.6	11.6	10.9

Source: National statistics; OECD, *Quarterly Labour Force Statistics*, No. 4, 1998, *Main Economic Indicators*, various issues and *OECD Economic Outlook*, No. 64, December 1998 (Paris); UN/ECE secretariat estimates.

Note: All aggregates exclude Israel. Comparisons with previous years are limited by changes in methodology in Austria (1994), Germany (1984), Israel (1985 and 1995), Italy (1993), Malta (1994), Portugal (1992) and the United States (1990 and 1994).

[a] ILO definition, except for Austria (1984-1992), Cyprus, Denmark (1984-1987), Iceland, Israel, Malta, Switzerland and Turkey.

[b] West Germany 1984-1990.

[c] End of year.

[d] Fifteen countries.

APPENDIX TABLE A.11

Consumer prices in the ECE market economies, 1984-1998
(Percentage change over previous year)

	1984	1985	1986	1987	1988	1989	1990	1991	1992	1993	1994	1995	1996	1997	1998
Western Europe	6.7	5.8	3.5	3.2	3.5	5.0	5.4	5.0	4.3	3.5	2.9	3.0	2.3	1.9	1.6
4 major countries	6.0	5.4	2.7	2.8	3.2	4.9	5.0	4.7	4.2	3.2	2.7	3.0	2.4	1.9	1.6
France	7.4	5.8	2.7	3.1	2.7	3.6	3.3	3.2	2.4	2.1	1.7	1.7	2.0	1.2	0.7
Germany [a]	2.3	2.2	-0.2	0.3	1.2	2.8	2.7	3.6	5.1	4.5	2.7	1.8	1.5	1.8	0.9
Italy	10.6	8.6	6.1	4.6	5.0	6.6	6.1	6.5	5.3	4.2	3.9	5.4	3.9	1.7	1.8
United Kingdom	5.0	6.1	3.4	4.1	4.9	7.8	9.5	5.9	3.7	1.6	2.4	3.5	2.4	3.1	3.4
16 smaller countries	8.4	6.8	5.2	4.0	4.1	5.3	6.2	5.8	4.5	4.0	3.3	3.0	2.3	1.8	1.5
Austria	5.6	3.2	1.7	1.4	2.0	2.5	3.2	3.4	4.0	3.7	3.0	2.2	1.9	1.3	0.9
Belgium	6.4	4.9	1.3	1.5	1.1	3.2	3.4	3.2	2.4	2.8	2.4	1.5	2.0	1.6	1.0
Cyprus	6.0	5.1	1.2	2.8	3.4	3.8	4.5	5.0	6.5	4.9	4.7	2.6	2.9	3.6	2.2
Denmark	6.3	4.7	3.6	4.0	4.6	4.8	2.7	2.4	2.1	1.3	2.0	2.1	2.0	2.2	1.9
Finland	7.1	5.9	2.9	4.1	5.1	6.6	6.2	4.3	3.0	2.1	1.1	1.0	0.5	1.2	1.4
Greece	18.4	19.3	23.0	16.4	13.5	13.7	20.4	19.5	15.9	14.4	10.7	8.8	8.3	5.5	4.8
Iceland	29.2	32.6	22.7	18.8	19.1	20.8	15.4	6.8	3.7	4.1	1.5	1.7	2.3	1.8	1.7
Ireland	8.6	5.5	3.8	3.1	2.1	4.1	3.3	3.2	3.1	1.4	2.3	2.5	1.7	1.4	2.4
Israel	373.8	304.6	48.1	19.9	16.3	20.2	17.2	19.0	12.0	11.0	12.3	10.1	11.3	9.0	5.4
Luxembourg	6.4	4.1	0.3	-0.1	1.4	3.4	3.3	3.1	3.2	3.6	2.2	1.9	1.3	1.4	1.0
Malta	-0.4	-0.3	2.0	0.5	0.9	0.9	3.0	2.5	1.6	4.1	4.1	4.0	2.5	3.2	2.2
Netherlands	3.1	2.3	0.2	-0.8	0.7	1.1	2.5	3.1	3.2	2.6	2.7	2.0	2.0	2.2	2.0
Norway	6.2	5.7	7.2	8.7	6.7	4.6	4.1	3.4	2.3	2.3	1.4	2.4	1.3	2.6	2.3
Portugal	28.9	19.6	11.8	9.4	9.7	12.6	13.4	10.5	9.4	6.7	5.4	4.2	3.1	2.3	2.8
Spain	11.3	8.8	8.8	5.2	4.8	6.9	6.7	5.9	5.9	4.6	4.8	4.6	3.6	2.0	1.8
Sweden	8.0	7.4	4.2	4.2	5.8	6.5	10.4	9.4	2.2	4.7	2.2	2.5	0.5	0.5	-0.1
Switzerland	2.9	3.5	0.8	1.4	1.9	3.1	5.4	5.9	4.0	3.3	0.9	1.8	0.8	0.5	0.1
Turkey	48.3	45.0	34.6	38.8	68.8	63.3	60.3	66.0	70.1	66.1	105.2	88.0	79.8	84.8	86.2
North America	4.3	3.6	2.1	3.7	4.1	4.8	5.4	4.3	2.9	2.9	2.4	2.8	2.8	2.2	1.5
Canada	4.3	4.0	4.1	4.4	4.0	5.0	4.8	5.6	1.5	1.8	0.2	2.2	1.6	1.6	0.9
United States	4.3	3.6	1.9	3.6	4.1	4.8	5.4	4.2	3.0	3.0	2.6	2.8	3.0	2.3	1.6
Total above	5.6	4.7	2.8	3.4	3.8	4.9	5.4	4.7	3.6	3.2	2.6	2.9	2.6	2.1	1.5
Japan	2.3	2.0	0.7	–	0.7	2.4	3.1	3.2	1.7	1.3	0.7	-0.1	0.1	1.8	0.6
Total above, *including Japan*	5.0	4.3	2.4	2.8	3.3	4.5	5.0	4.4	3.3	2.9	2.3	2.4	2.2	2.0	1.4
Memorandum item:															
European Union [b]	6.9	5.9	3.5	3.1	3.5	5.1	5.4	5.0	4.3	3.5	2.9	3.0	2.4	1.9	1.6
Euro area	7.0	5.5	3.1	2.6	2.9	4.4	4.2	4.4	4.4	3.6	2.9	2.9	2.4	1.7	1.3

Source: National statistics.

Note: All aggregates exclude Israel and Turkey.

[a] West Germany 1984-1991.

[b] Fifteen countries.

APPENDIX TABLE B.1

Real GDP/NMP in the ECE transition economies, 1980, 1985-1998

(Indices, 1989=100)

	1980	1985	1986	1987	1988	1989	1990	1991	1992	1993	1994	1995	1996	1997	1998
Eastern Europe	89.4	94.6	97.7	99.2	100.7	100.0	92.5	82.5	78.4	77.9	81.2	86.1	89.6	92.2	94.0
Albania	79.4	88.2	93.1	92.4	91.0	100.0	90.0	64.8	60.1	65.9	71.4	80.9	88.2	82.1	88.6
Bosnia and Herzegovina	..	..	..	..	..	..	..	..	..	..	..	..	..	..	..
Bulgaria	76.2	89.9	93.6	99.3	101.9	100.0	90.9	83.3	77.2	76.1	77.5	79.7	71.6	66.6	68.6
Croatia [a]	99.0	99.8	102.6	102.5	101.6	100.0	92.9	73.3	64.7	59.5	63.0	67.3	71.4	76.0	78.3
Czech Republic	..	91.3	93.2	93.7	95.7	100.0	98.8	87.4	84.6	85.0	87.8	93.4	97.0	98.0	95.4
Hungary	86.3	94.1	95.5	99.4	99.3	100.0	96.5	85.0	82.4	81.9	84.4	85.6	86.8	90.7	95.3
Poland	91.1	90.3	94.1	95.9	99.8	100.0	88.4	82.2	84.4	87.6	92.1	98.6	104.5	111.7	117.1
Romania	88.5	103.4	105.8	106.7	106.2	100.0	94.4	82.2	75.0	76.2	79.2	84.8	88.2	82.1	76.1
Slovakia	..	91.0	94.8	97.1	99.0	100.0	97.5	83.3	77.9	75.1	78.7	84.2	89.7	95.6	99.8
Slovenia	98.9	100.9	104.1	103.5	100.5	100.0	91.9	83.7	79.1	81.4	85.7	89.3	92.4	96.6	100.5
The former Yugoslav Republic of Macedonia	93.3	96.0	102.7	101.4	98.1	100.0	89.8	83.5	76.8	69.9	68.6	67.8	68.3	69.3	71.4
Yugoslavia [a]	95.7	98.7	101.4	100.2	98.8	100.0	92.1	81.4	58.7	40.6	41.7	44.2	46.8	50.3	51.6
Baltic states	68.0	81.6	85.7	89.0	95.9	100.0	97.6	89.7	67.9	58.4	55.4	56.7	59.1	63.6	66.3
Estonia	74.5	85.7	88.2	89.2	93.8	100.0	91.9	82.7	71.0	65.0	63.7	66.4	69.0	76.9	80.1
Latvia	68.5	81.3	85.1	89.0	93.6	100.0	102.9	92.2	60.1	51.1	51.5	51.0	52.7	56.2	58.4
Lithuania	64.7	79.8	84.9	88.9	98.4	100.0	96.7	91.2	71.8	60.2	54.3	56.1	58.7	62.3	65.1
CIS [b c]	77.4	90.2	92.3	93.8	97.9	100.0	96.9	91.2	78.4	70.9	60.8	57.5	55.5	56.2	54.6
Armenia	73.5	95.9	97.7	94.5	92.2	100.0	94.5	83.4	48.6	44.3	46.7	49.9	52.8	54.5	58.4
Azerbaijan	79.6	98.8	100.6	105.1	109.7	100.0	88.3	87.7	67.9	52.2	41.9	37.0	37.4	39.6	43.6
Belarus	65.7	85.2	88.9	91.3	92.4	100.0	98.0	96.8	87.5	80.8	70.6	63.3	65.1	72.5	78.5
Georgia	79.4	100.0	98.8	96.8	103.6	100.0	84.9	67.0	36.9	26.1	23.4	24.0	26.6	29.6	30.5
Kazakhstan	87.0	90.8	92.3	92.1	100.1	100.0	99.0	88.1	83.4	75.8	66.2	60.8	61.1	62.1	60.6
Kyrgyzstan	69.1	82.9	83.6	84.7	95.6	100.0	104.8	96.5	83.2	70.3	56.2	53.1	56.9	62.5	63.7
Republic of Moldova	72.1	82.6	89.2	90.3	91.9	100.0	97.6	80.5	57.2	56.5	39.0	38.3	35.3	35.9	32.8
Russian Federation	78.1	90.7	92.9	94.2	98.4	100.0	97.0	92.2	78.8	71.9	62.8	60.2	58.1	58.6	55.9
Tajikistan	80.8	91.8	95.0	93.9	106.9	100.0	100.2	91.7	62.1	52.0	40.9	35.8	29.8	30.3	32.0
Turkmenistan	80.7	89.5	93.4	97.1	107.5	100.0	101.8	97.0	82.5	83.7	69.2	64.2	68.5	60.7	63.8
Ukraine	75.0	88.7	90.0	93.4	95.2	100.0	96.4	88.0	79.2	68.0	52.4	46.0	41.4	40.1	39.4
Uzbekistan	76.0	88.1	88.0	88.4	97.0	100.0	99.2	98.7	87.7	85.7	81.2	80.5	81.9	86.1	89.9
Total above	80.6	91.2	93.7	95.2	98.7	100.0	95.7	88.6	78.1	72.5	66.6	65.8	65.5	66.8	66.4
Memorandum items:															
CETE-5	89.3	92.0	95.1	97.1	99.6	100.0	92.3	83.7	83.4	85.0	88.9	94.2	98.9	104.3	108.1
SETE-7	89.5	99.1	102.3	102.7	102.3	100.0	93.0	80.5	70.1	66.0	68.3	72.5	74.0	71.7	70.3
Czechoslovakia [b]	84.9	92.7	95.1	97.0	99.3	100.0	98.5	84.4	78.8	..	..	..	..	..	..
Yugoslavia (SFR) [a]	97.7	99.5	103.0	101.0	99.4	100.0	92.4	..	..	..	..	..	..	..	..
Former Soviet Union [b]	77.0	89.9	92.0	93.6	97.8	100.0	96.9	91.1	77.9	70.4	60.6	57.4	55.7	56.5	55.1
Former GDR	..	..	..	..	..	100.0	84.5	68.3	73.6	80.4	88.2	92.0	95.0	96.6	98.5

Source: UN/ECE Common Database, derived from national and CIS statistics (IMF and World Bank data for Albania).

Note: Data for the east European countries are based on a GDP measure, except where otherwise mentioned. For the countries of the former Soviet Union, NMP data for 1980-1990 were chain-linked to GDP data from 1990. Country indices were aggregated with previous year weights (viz., previous year's GDP at 1992 prices).

[a] Gross material product (1980-1989 for Croatia).

[b] Sum of individual country data for former members.

[c] Net material product for 1980-1990 (until 1992 in the case of Turkmenistan).

APPENDIX TABLE B.2

Real total consumption expenditure in the ECE transition economies, 1980, 1985-1998
(Indices, 1989=100 or earliest year available thereafter)

	1980	1985	1986	1987	1988	1989	1990	1991	1992	1993	1994	1995	1996	1997	1998
Bulgaria	..	..	..	..	..	100.0	100.6	92.3	89.4	86.2	82.3	80.7	75.3	64.0	..
Croatia	..	..	..	..	..	..	..	100.0	87.2	85.3	92.0	106.6	109.2	..	..
Czech Republic	..	..	..	91.3	93.1	100.0	104.9	81.0	88.2	90.4	92.6	96.5	102.5	103.2	..
Hungary	92.2	99.2	101.5	104.9	102.0	100.0	97.3	92.2	92.8	97.9	95.6	89.3	86.6	88.4	..
Poland	108.0	105.1	109.3	111.8	114.7	100.0	88.3	94.9	98.2	103.0	106.9	110.4	118.4	125.6	..
Romania	83.9	85.4	85.8	88.7	90.6	100.0	108.9	96.0	90.7	91.8	95.3	105.5	112.9	108.0	104.0
Slovakia	..	81.8	85.4	89.2	92.1	100.0	103.3	76.9	75.6	74.3	71.6	73.9	82.0	85.5	..
Slovenia	..	..	..	..	..	..	100.0	91.6	88.8	99.1	102.6	110.2	113.1	117.2	..
Estonia	..	..	..	..	..	..	..	..	..	100.0	101.2	110.4	116.3	125.7	..
Latvia	..	..	..	..	..	..	100.0	76.7	49.2	46.5	47.4	47.0	50.8	52.7	..
Lithuania	..	..	..	..	..	..	..	..	..	..	..	100.0	105.6	112.2	..
Armenia	..	..	..	..	..	..	100.0	97.4	84.9	66.4	68.9	74.5	76.8	81.5	..
Azerbaijan	..	..	..	..	..	..	..	..	..	100.0	80.3	78.0	84.3	93.2	..
Belarus	..	..	..	..	..	..	100.0	93.4	84.0	82.1	72.1	65.3	67.4	73.8	..
Georgia	..	..	..	..	..	..	100.0	79.2	77.1	45.4	42.4	46.1			..
Kazakhstan	..	..	..	..	..	..	100.0	96.8	96.1	84.9	67.7	55.1	51.2	51.8	..
Kyrgyzstan	..	..	..	..	..	..	..	100.0	87.2	77.1	62.0	52.0	55.3	50.8	50.4
Republic of Moldova	..	..	..	..	..	..	..	..	..	100.0	82.6	90.3	99.8	111.6	105.3
Russian Federation	..	..	..	..	..	..	100.0	93.9	89.0	88.1	85.4	83.1	81.3	82.7	80.6
Ukraine	..	..	..	..	..	..	100.0	94.3	88.6	72.0	65.0	62.6	57.4	59.3	..

Source: UN/ECE Common Database, derived from national and CIS statistics.

APPENDIX TABLE B.3

Real gross fixed capital formation in the ECE transition economies, 1980, 1985-1998
(Indices, 1989=100 or earliest year available thereafter)

	1980	1985	1986	1987	1988	1989	1990	1991	1992	1993	1994	1995	1996	1997	1998
Bulgaria	..	..	..	..	..	100.0	100.0	80.0	74.1	61.2	61.9	71.8	56.6	44.1	..
Croatia	..	..	..	..	..	..	..	100.0	88.5	94.5	93.6	108.2	..	..	..
Czech Republic	..	..	..	93.4	99.4	100.0	97.9	80.5	87.7	81.0	95.0	114.9	124.9	118.8	..
Hungary	114.7	94.6	100.8	110.7	100.6	100.0	92.9	83.1	81.0	82.6	92.9	88.9	94.8	103.2	..
Poland	124.6	111.4	116.4	116.5	126.5	100.0	75.2	71.9	73.6	75.7	82.6	96.2	115.2	140.1	..
Romania	163.7	161.5	163.3	161.0	157.6	100.0	64.4	44.0	48.9	52.9	63.9	68.3	72.2	70.1	57.4
Slovakia	..	..	..	..	..	..	100.0	74.8	71.5	68.5	64.7	64.6	90.3	103.3	..
Slovenia	..	..	..	..	..	..	100.0	88.5	77.1	85.4	97.4	113.8	124.2	138.3	..
Estonia	..	..	..	..	..	..	..	..	..	100.0	106.2	110.5	123.1	138.4	..
Latvia	..	..	..	..	..	..	100.0	36.1	25.7	21.6	21.8	23.7	29.0	32.2	..
Lithuania	..	..	..	..	..	..	..	..	..	..	..	100.0	110.9	137.0	..
Armenia	..	..	..	..	..	..	100.0	67.0	8.6	7.9	11.5	9.5	10.5	11.7	..
Azerbaijan	..	..	..	..	..	..	..	..	100.0	61.0	115.3	94.5	199.8	333.7	..
Belarus	..	..	..	..	..	..	100.0	105.3	85.6	79.1	68.3	48.1	46.6	57.4	..
Georgia	..	..	..	..	..	..	100.0	67.3	49.2	18.5	133.4	219.9	..	..	..
Kazakhstan	..	..	..	..	..	..	100.0	74.2	61.9	44.2	39.2	24.3	18.5	19.1	..
Kyrgyzstan	..	..	..	..	..	..	..	100.0	70.7	55.3	39.3	63.2	54.9	38.7	33.1
Republic of Moldova	..	..	..	..	..	..	..	..	..	100.0	56.5	54.5	68.1	64.9	64.8
Russian Federation	..	..	..	..	..	..	100.0	84.5	49.4	36.7	27.1	25.1	20.9	19.9	18.5
Ukraine	..	..	..	..	..	..	100.0	81.6	69.3	48.2	28.4	19.7	15.2	14.2	..

Source: UN/ECE Common Database, derived from national and CIS statistics.

APPENDIX TABLE B.4

Real gross industrial output in the ECE transition economies, 1980, 1985-1998
(Indices, 1989=100)

	1980	1985	1986	1987	1988	1989	1990	1991	1992	1993	1994	1995	1996	1997	1998
Eastern Europe	83.1	91.6	95.5	98.0	100.6	100.0	83.9	67.7	61.4	60.5	65.1	70.1	74.3	78.5	79.6
Albania	77.0	87.5	91.9	93.3	95.2	100.0	86.7	50.4	35.2	31.7	25.8	23.9	27.2	25.7	28.2
Bosnia and Herzegovina	106.0	104.1	104.1	101.1	98.1	100.0	101.8	76.9	25.5	2.0	1.7	2.8	5.2	7.0	8.7
Bulgaria	71.3	88.3	92.4	98.0	101.1	100.0	83.2	66.4	54.2	48.8	54.0	56.4	58.6	52.6	47.7
Croatia	88.7	95.1	99.4	102.0	100.6	100.0	88.7	63.4	54.2	51.0	49.6	49.7	51.3	54.8	56.8
Czech Republic	81.5	92.0	94.5	96.5	98.5	100.0	96.6	75.7	69.8	66.1	67.4	73.3	74.8	78.1	79.4
Hungary	92.9	102.1	104.0	106.4	105.3	100.0	90.7	74.1	66.9	69.6	76.3	79.8	82.5	91.7	103.2
Poland	86.3	88.5	92.3	95.5	100.5	100.0	75.8	69.7	71.7	76.3	85.5	93.8	101.6	113.3	118.6
Romania	76.9	90.5	96.8	99.2	101.9	100.0	81.9	63.3	49.4	50.1	51.7	56.6	60.1	55.8	46.3
Slovakia	76.7	91.6	95.2	98.6	100.8	100.0	94.0	73.1	66.1	62.5	66.8	72.3	74.1	75.3	78.8
Slovenia	90.3	101.0	102.7	101.6	98.9	100.0	89.5	78.4	68.1	66.1	70.4	71.8	72.5	73.2	75.9
The former Yugoslav Republic of Macedonia	72.1	88.6	95.0	97.3	95.6	100.0	89.4	74.0	62.3	53.7	48.0	42.9	44.3	45.0	47.0
Yugoslavia	80.0	93.6	96.8	97.6	98.4	100.0	88.0	72.5	57.0	35.7	36.2	37.6	40.4	44.2	45.8
Baltic states	72.6	85.5	89.4	93.1	96.9	100.0	99.0	95.7	64.5	44.8	37.6	38.1	39.9	43.6	45.2
Estonia	78.5	90.2	93.5	96.3	99.3	100.0	100.0	92.8	59.8	48.6	47.1	48.0	49.4	56.0	56.5
Latvia	72.5	86.6	89.9	93.7	97.1	100.0	100.8	100.2	65.6	44.6	40.1	38.7	40.8	46.4	47.3
Lithuania	70.0	82.6	87.2	91.2	95.6	100.0	97.4	94.0	65.8	43.2	31.7	33.4	35.0	36.2	38.7
CIS [a]	73.0	87.2	91.0	94.4	98.1	100.0	99.9	93.7	79.1	69.8	54.8	51.6	50.1	51.4	50.2
Armenia	76.3	100.7	105.3	110.3	109.1	100.0	92.5	85.4	44.2	39.7	41.8	42.4	43.0	43.4	42.3
Azerbaijan	76.1	94.5	92.7	96.1	99.3	100.0	93.7	98.2	74.9	69.7	53.9	44.6	41.6	41.7	42.7
Belarus	61.1	79.0	84.3	89.9	95.6	100.0	102.1	101.1	91.6	82.4	68.3	60.3	62.4	74.2	82.3
Georgia	70.6	91.8	93.9	96.2	99.3	100.0	94.3	73.0	39.6	25.0	15.2	13.2	14.1	15.2	14.8
Kazakhstan	72.4	85.8	90.2	94.1	97.6	100.0	99.2	98.3	84.7	72.2	51.9	47.7	47.8	49.7	48.7
Kyrgyzstan	66.7	84.2	87.8	89.0	95.1	100.0	99.4	99.1	72.9	54.5	39.2	32.2	35.1	52.8	55.2
Republic of Moldova [b]	68.7	85.1	87.3	91.6	94.6	100.0	103.2	91.7	66.9	67.1	48.5	46.6	43.6	43.6	38.8
Russian Federation	74.4	87.8	91.8	95.0	98.6	100.0	99.9	91.9	75.4	64.7	51.2	49.5	47.5	48.5	46.0
Tajikistan	72.9	87.1	88.7	93.1	98.2	100.0	101.2	97.6	73.9	68.1	50.8	43.9	33.4	32.7	35.4
Turkmenistan	75.4	86.0	90.1	92.9	96.9	100.0	103.2	108.2	92.0	95.7	72.1	67.5	80.8	54.7	54.8
Ukraine	72.6	86.4	90.0	93.4	97.3	100.0	99.9	95.1	89.0	81.9	59.5	52.4	49.7	49.6	48.8
Uzbekistan	68.5	86.0	91.2	93.4	96.5	100.0	101.8	103.3	96.4	99.9	101.5	101.6	104.2	108.5	114.8
Total above	75.7	88.3	92.2	95.3	98.7	100.0	95.7	86.9	74.0	66.6	57.0	56.1	56.1	58.3	57.8
Memorandum items:															
CETE-5	85.8	91.5	94.8	97.4	100.6	100.0	83.4	72.1	70.2	72.2	79.1	85.9	91.2	99.7	104.7
SETE-7	79.3	91.8	96.6	98.9	100.5	100.0	84.5	61.4	48.9	43.9	45.1	47.8	50.5	48.5	44.1
Czechoslovakia	80.5	91.9	94.8	97.2	99.2	100.0	96.5	75.2	67.6	..	..	..	..	..	..
Yugoslavia (SFR) [a]	86.9	96.4	99.3	99.7	98.7	100.0	88.3	71.7	..	..	..	..	..	..	..
Former Soviet Union	73.0	87.1	91.0	94.4	98.1	100.0	99.9	93.7	78.5	68.8	54.1	51.1	49.7	51.1	50.0
Former GDR	75.2	89.5	92.5	94.7	97.7	100.0	72.7	37.0	34.8	36.8	42.0	44.4	45.9	48.5	52.2

Source: UN/ECE Common Database, derived from national and CIS statistics (IMF and World Bank data for Albania).

Note: Data for former Czechoslovakia and the SFR of Yugoslavia for 1980 to the breakup obtained as sum of individual country data for former members. For the countries of the former Soviet Union, data for 1980-1990 were chain-linked to national or CIS data from 1990. Country indices were aggregated with previous year gross industrial output weights.

[a] Generated from components.

[b] Excluding Transdniestria since 1993.

APPENDIX TABLE B.5

Total employment in the ECE transition economies, 1980, 1985-1998

(Indices, 1989=100)

	1980	1985	1986	1987	1988	1989	1990	1991	1992	1993	1994	1995	1996	1997	1998
Eastern Europe	94.7	96.6	97.4	98.0	97.9	100.0	97.0	91.3	85.0	82.3	82.3	81.9	82.5	82.4	..
Albania	77.9	90.1	93.1	95.9	97.6	100.0	99.2	97.5	76.0	72.7	80.7	79.0	77.5	76.9	76.6
Bosnia and Herzegovina						100.0	94.6	87.5	22.1	9.9	9.1	10.1	22.5	31.2	..
Bulgaria	100.0	102.2	102.5	102.8	102.4	100.0	93.9	81.6	75.0	73.8	74.3	75.2	75.3	73.3	..
Croatia	87.4	95.9	98.6	100.6	100.4	100.0	96.9	88.5	77.9	76.5	74.8	73.9	73.9	73.4	..
Czech Republic	95.3	97.5	98.5	98.9	99.4	100.0	99.1	93.6	91.2	89.7	90.4	92.8	93.4	92.4	..
Hungary [a]	104.2	102.6	102.6	101.7	100.7	100.0	96.7	86.8	77.0	72.1	70.6	69.3	69.0	69.1	70.3
Poland	102.0	100.8	101.1	100.8	100.1	100.0	95.8	90.1	86.3	84.3	85.1	86.7	88.3	90.8	..
Romania [b]	94.6	96.7	97.5	97.9	98.7	100.0	99.0	98.5	95.5	91.9	91.5	86.7	85.7	82.4	..
Slovakia [a]	91.3	96.8	98.4	99.4	100.2	100.0	98.2	85.9	80.4	80.4	78.9	80.7	81.3	81.0	..
Slovenia [c]	84.0	88.9	90.4	101.9	101.3	100.0	96.1	88.7	83.8	81.3	79.3	79.1	78.7	78.6	78.7
The former Yugoslav Republic of Macedonia	79.1	92.7	96.0	100.5	100.1	100.0	98.5	95.6	91.2	86.2	81.7	73.9	70.6	66.8	..
Yugoslavia	83.4	93.7	96.5	99.0	99.8	100.0	97.0	94.1	90.9	88.3	86.5	85.3	84.8	83.6	..
Baltic states [d]	94.9	98.0	98.8	99.4	99.6	100.0	98.5	98.9	94.4	89.0	83.2	80.6	80.1	80.9	..
Estonia		96.7	97.9	97.6	97.6	100.0	98.6	96.4	91.4	84.5	82.7	78.3	77.0	77.4	..
Latvia	97.0	99.1	99.8	100.4	100.5	100.0	100.1	99.3	92.0	85.6	77.0	74.3	72.3	73.7	..
Lithuania	93.4	97.7	98.5	99.5	99.8	100.0	97.3	99.7	97.5	93.4	88.0	86.4	87.2	87.7	..
CIS	94.3	97.8	98.3	98.9	99.3	100.0	100.2	98.9	96.5	94.1	91.3	90.4	89.6	88.3	..
Armenia	86.6	97.2	98.6	99.5	101.4	100.0	102.4	105.0	99.2	97.0	93.5	92.8	90.2	86.2	84.9
Azerbaijan	79.8	90.9	92.7	95.2	95.8	100.0	100.9	105.8	101.4	101.2	99.0	98.5	100.5	100.7	101.1
Belarus	95.4	98.4	98.8	99.0	99.5	100.0	99.1	96.6	94.1	92.9	90.4	84.8	84.0	84.1	84.5
Georgia	92.7	98.8	100.1	101.0	101.1	100.0	102.3	93.3	73.5	66.4	64.8	79.0	79.1	82.7	83.3
Kazakhstan	86.2	92.6	93.5	94.7	96.0	100.0	101.3	100.1	98.3	89.9	85.4	85.0	84.6	84.0	81.8
Kyrgyzstan	81.9	92.8	95.0	97.9	98.7	100.0	100.5	99.6	105.6	96.6	94.6	94.4	95.0	97.1	97.5
Republic of Moldova [e]	97.3	99.5	99.6	99.7	98.9	100.0	99.1	99.0	98.0	80.7	80.4	80.0	79.4	78.7	77.7
Russian Federation	96.9	99.1	99.5	99.7	99.9	100.0	99.6	97.7	95.3	93.7	90.6	87.9	87.2	85.5	85.1
Tajikistan	76.7	89.5	91.2	94.5	96.9	100.0	103.2	104.9	101.6	98.8	98.8	98.7	92.2	95.3	95.8
Turkmenistan	76.4	89.7	91.7	94.3	96.8	100.0	103.4	105.3	105.4	110.0	111.6	112.1	111.7	112.3	..
Ukraine	99.6	100.6	100.5	100.3	99.9	100.0	99.9	98.3	96.3	94.1	90.5	93.3	91.3	88.8	87.7
Uzbekistan	75.4	86.8	88.9	93.2	95.9	100.0	104.2	109.2	108.7	108.5	109.9	110.8	112.3	113.8	115.4
Memorandum items:															
CETE-5	99.8	99.9	100.4	100.6	100.1	100.0	96.7	89.8	85.1	82.8	82.9	84.1	85.1	86.3	14.2
SETE-7	87.8	92.2	93.4	94.4	94.9	100.0	97.4	93.4	85.0	81.7	81.5	79.0	78.9	77.0	..
Former Soviet Union	93.7	97.8	98.3	98.9	99.3	100.0	100.2	98.9	96.4	94.0	91.1	90.1	89.3	88.1	..

Source: UN/ECE Common Database, derived from national and CIS statistics.

[a] End of year, up to 1992, since 1992 onwards annual average.

[b] End of year.

[c] Self-employed excluded until 1987.

[d] Excluding Estonia until 1985.

[e] Excluding Transdniestria since 1993.

APPENDIX TABLE B.6

Registered unemployment in the ECE transition economies, 1990, 1994-1998
(Thousands and per cent of labour force, end of period)

	Thousands						Per cent of labour force					
	1990	*1994*	*1995*	*1996*	*1997*	*1998*	*1990*	*1994*	*1995*	*1996*	*1997*	*1998*
Eastern Europe	2 773	7 190	6 583	6 300	6 196	..	..	13.6	12.5	11.7	11.9	12.6
Albania	150	262	171	158	194	235	9.5	18.0	12.9	12.3	14.9	17.6
Bosnia and Herzegovina	..	..	..	185	222	257	..	..	..	..	39*	38*
Bulgaria	72	488	424	478	524	465	1.8	12.8	11.1	12.5	13.7	12.2
Croatia	196	248	249	269	287	303	..	17.3	17.6	15.9	17.6	18.6
Czech Republic	39	167	153	186	269	387	0.7	3.2	2.9	3.5	5.2	7.5
Hungary	101	520	496	479	464	404	1.7	10.9	10.4	10.5	10.4	9.1
Poland	1 126	2 838	2 629	2 360	1 826	1 831	6.5	16.0	14.9	13.2	10.3	10.4
Romania	150	1 224	998	658	881	1025	1.3	10.9	9.5	6.6	8.8	10.3
Slovakia	40	372	330	330	348	427	1.6	14.8	13.1	12.8	12.5	15.6
Slovenia	55	124	127	125	129	127	..	14.2	14.5	14.4	14.8	14.6
The former Yugoslav Republic of Macedonia [a]	156	196	229	245	258	..	..	33.2	37.2	39.8	42.5	..
Yugoslavia [a]	688	751	777	827	794	849	..	23.9	24.7	26.1	25.6	27.2
Baltic states	..	197	245	237	236	269	..	5.3	6.6	6.4	6.3	7.3
Estonia [b]	..	35	34	37	31	35	..	5.1	5.0	5.6	4.6	5.1
Latvia	..	84	83	91	85	111	..	6.5	6.6	7.2	6.7	9.2
Lithuania	..	78	128	109	120	123	..	4.5	7.3	6.2	6.7	6.9
CIS	..	6 011	7 185	8 519	9 673	10 741	..	4.4	5.8	6.6	7.6	8.5
Armenia	..	92	132	159	174	134	..	6.0	8.1	9.7	11.0	8.9
Azerbaijan	..	24	28	32	38	42	..	0.9	1.1	1.1	1.3	1.4
Belarus	..	101	131	183	126	106	..	2.1	2.7	4	2.8	2.3
Georgia	..	76	61	58	143	99	..	3.8	3.4	3.2	8.0	4.2
Kazakhstan	..	70	140	282	259	252	..	1.0	2.1	4.1	3.9	3.7
Kyrgyzstan	..	13	50	77	55	56	..	0.8	3.0	4.5	3.1	3.1
Republic of Moldova	..	21	25	23	28	32	..	1.0	1.4	1.5	1.7	1.9
Russian Federation [c]	..	5 478	6 431	7280	8 133	8 930	..	7.5	8.9	10.0	11.2	12.4
Tajikistan	..	32	35	46	51	54	..	1.8	1.8	2.4	2.8	2.9
Turkmenistan	..	..	..	..	..	..	..	..	..	..	..	..
Ukraine	..	82	127	351	637	1 003	..	0.3	0.6	1.5	2.8	4.3
Uzbekistan	..	22	25	28	29	33	..	0.3	0.3	0.3	0.3	0.4
Total above	..	13 398	14 013	15 056	16 105	..	..	6.9	7.8	8.1	8.8	9.6
Memorandum items:												
CETE-5	1 361	4 021	3 735	3 480	3 036	3 176	..	12.9	12.0	11.2	9.8	10.2
SETE-7	1 412	3 169	2 848	2 635	2 936	..	..	14.6	13.7	12.5	14.3	15.4
Russian Federation [d]	..	1 637	2 327	2 506	1 999	1 929	..	2.1	3.2	3.4	2.8	2.7

Source: National statistics and direct communications from national statistical offices to UN/ECE secretariat.

[a] The data reported on employment cover only the social sector in agriculture, hence unemployment rates are biased upwards. In Yugoslavia, according to the labour force survey, the unemployment rate was 13.8 per cent in October 1997, instead of the officially reported rate of some 26 per cent. Also, in The former Yugoslav Republic of Macedonia, according to the labour force survey, the unemployment rate was 34.5 per cent in April 1998 instead of reported estimates of some 40 per cent.

[b] Job seekers.

[c] Based on Russian Federation Goskomstat's monthly estimates according to the ILO definition, i.e. including all persons not having employment but actively seeking work.

[d] Registered unemployment.

APPENDIX TABLE B.7

Consumer prices in the ECE transition economies, 1989-1998

(Annual average, percentage change over preceding year)

	1989	1990	1991	1992	1993	1994	1995	1996	1997	1998
Albania	..	..	35.5	193.1	85.0	21.5	8.0	12.7	33.1	20.3
Bosnia and Herzegovina	36.8	594.0	116.2	64 218.3	38 825.1	553.5	-12.1	-21.2	11.8	4.9
Bulgaria	6.4	23.8	338.5	91.3	72.9	96.2	62.1	123.1	1 082.6	22.2
Croatia *a*	1 200.0	609.5	123.0	663.6	1 516.6	97.5	2.0	3.6	3.7	5.9
Czech Republic	1.4	9.9	56.7	11.1	20.8	10.0	9.1	8.9	8.4	10.6
Hungary	17.0	28.9	35.0	23.0	22.6	19.1	28.5	23.6	18.4	14.2
Poland	264.3	585.8	70.3	45.3	36.9	33.2	28.1	19.8	15.1	11.7
Romania	1.1	5.1	170.2	210.7	256.2	137.1	32.2	38.8	154.9	59.3
Slovakia	1.3	10.4	61.2	10.2	23.1	13.4	10.0	6.0	6.2	6.7
Slovenia	1 285.3	551.6	115.0	207.3	31.7	21.0	13.5	9.9	8.4	7.9
The former Yugoslav Republic of Macedonia *a*	1 246.0	608.4	114.9	1 505.5	353.1	121.0	16.9	4.1	3.6	1.0
Yugoslavia	1 265.0	580.0	122.0	8 926.0	2.2E+14	7.9E+10	71.8	90.5	23.2	30.4
Estonia	4.0	18.0	202.0	1 078.2	89.6	47.9	28.9	23.1	11.1	10.6
Latvia	5.2	10.9	172.2	951.2	109.1	35.7	25.0	17.7	8.5	4.7
Lithuania	2.1	9.1	216.4	1 020.5	410.1	72.0	39.5	24.7	8.8	5.1
Armenia	0.8	6.9	174.1	728.7	3 731.8	4 964.0	175.5	18.7	13.8	8.7
Azerbaijan	0.5	6.1	106.6	912.6	1 129.7	1 663.9	411.5	19.8	3.6	-0.8
Belarus	1.7	5.5	98.6	971.2	1 190.9	2 219.6	709.3	52.7	63.9	73.2
Georgia	0.9	4.2	78.7	1 176.9	4 084.9	22 470.6	177.6	39.4	6.9	3.6
Kazakhstan	1.8	5.6	114.5	1 504.3	1 662.7	1 879.5	175.9	39.1	17.4	7.3
Kyrgyzstan	1.6	5.5	113.9	854.6	1 208.7	278.1	42.9	30.3	25.5	12.1
Republic of Moldova	1.1	5.7	114.4	1 308.0	1 751.0	486.4	29.9	23.5	11.8	7.7
Russian Federation	2.5	5.3	100.3	1 528.7	875.0	309.0	197.4	47.8	14.7	27.8
Tajikistan	1.7	5.9	112.9	822.0	2 884.8	350.3	682.1	422.4	85.4	43.1
Turkmenistan	2.5	5.7	88.5	483.2	3 128.4	2 562.1	1 105.3	714.0	83.7	16.8
Ukraine	2.0	5.4	94.0	1 209.6	4 734.9	891.2	376.7	80.2	15.9	10.6
Uzbekistan	0.7	5.8	97.3	414.5	1 231.8	1 550.0	315.5	56.3	73.2	..

Source: UN/ECE Common Database, derived from national statistics.

Note: From 1992 onwards indices derived from monthly data. Retail prices for Bulgaria and CIS countries for 1989.

a Retail prices.

APPENDIX TABLE B.8

Producer price indices in the ECE transition economies, 1989-1998

(Annual average, percentage change over preceding year)

	1989	1990	1991	1992	1993	1994	1995	1996	1997	1998
Albania	..	..	..	..	..	..	..	..	..	..
Bosnia and Herzegovina	..	..	129.5	70 374.7	10 967.6	1 184.8	68.7	-4.8	3.2	3.6
Bulgaria	2.8	14.7	296.4	56.1	28.3	59.1	48.9	129.7	888.1	22.8
Croatia	1 346.7	455.3	146.3	826.0	1 510.4	77.7	0.8	1.3	3.7	-1.5
Czech Republic	0.1	2.5	70.3	10.8	9.3	5.4	7.8	4.9	5.1	4.9
Hungary	15.4	22.0	32.6	12.3	14.1	12.3	28.5	22.3	20.9	11.4
Poland	212.8	622.4	40.9	28.0	32.6	31.0	26.0	13.4	12.2	7.2
Romania	..	26.9	220.1	184.8	165.0	140.7	35.3	50.0	150.5	33.6
Slovakia	0.0	5.2	68.9	5.3	17.2	10.0	9.1	4.0	4.6	3.3
Slovenia	1 413.3	390.4	124.1	215.7	23.3	17.8	12.4	6.7	6.1	6.0
The former Yugoslav Republic of Macedonia	1 357.0	393.8	112.0	2 193.5	258.6	88.7	4.7	-0.1	4.2	4.2
Yugoslavia	1 301.0	468.0	124.0	8 993.0	1.4E+13	7.9E+10	75.7	88.8	20.6	25.9
Estonia	..	19.3	208.4	1 208.0	75.2	36.1	25.5	14.7	8.8	3.8
Latvia	..	..	192.0	1 310.0	117.1	17.0	12.0	13.8	4.3	2.0
Lithuania	..	..	148.2	1 510.0	391.7	44.7	28.7	16.5	6.0	-3.8
Armenia	..	..	120.0	947.0	892.0	4 394.4	187.8	36.3	21.7	4.7
Azerbaijan	..	..	135.0	1 303.0	1 040.7	3 971.6	1 340.1	70.6	11.4	-5.5
Belarus	..	..	150.0	2 326.7	1 536.3	3 362.1	538.6	35.7	89.4	70.4
Georgia	..	..	..	..	..	..	..	..	..	..
Kazakhstan	..	..	193.0	2 369.0	1 342.0	2 952.2	173.6	24.8	15.6	1.0
Kyrgyzstan	..	..	..	..	..	223.6	34.0	31.0	27.0	9.4
Republic of Moldova	..	..	130.0	1 210.9	1 078.5	711.7	52.2	30.2	14.9	9.7
Russian Federation	..	..	138.0	1 949.0	887.0	340.0	237.6	50.7	15.0	7.3
Tajikistan	..	..	163.0	1 316.5	1 080.0	665.5	351.7	342.2	107.2	28.4
Turkmenistan	..	..	211.0	994.0	1 610.0	911.0	296.5	2 974.9	260.6	-30.5
Ukraine	..	..	122.0	2 668.8	4 698.3	901.2	450.8	54.6	15.1	13.2
Uzbekistan	..	..	147.0	1 296.0	1 119.0	2 162.6	792.5	128.5	53.9	40.5

Source: UN/ECE Common Database, derived from national statistics.

Note: Indices generally derived from monthly data from 1992 onwards for east European countries and from 1994 for Baltic and CIS countries.

APPENDIX TABLE B.9

Nominal gross wages in industry in the ECE transition economies, 1990-1998

(Annual average, percentage change over preceding year) [a]

	1990	1991	1992	1993	1994	1995	1996	1997	1998
Albania [b]	..	..	..	69.5	34.5	29.3	..	..	..
Bosnia and Herzegovina [c]	..	..	..	..	..	..	249.4	50.8	31.1
Bulgaria	20.8	175.5	132.8	55.1	53.9	57.7	95.0	909.3	..
Croatia [c]	453.7	40.7	466.7	1 444.1	130.5	44.0	11.8	16.3	..
Czech Republic	3.0	16.5	21.0	22.6	16.9	18.3	17.7	12.1	10.7
Hungary [b]	27.2	33.4	24.3	24.9	21.4	21.0	21.7	21.8	16.6
Poland [c]	365.5	64.0	39.4	37.8	39.8	30.1	25.8	22.1	..
Romania [c]	9.7	125.0	173.5	210.7	139.4	55.3	56.7	99.5	53.1
Slovakia [b]	4.4	15.0	16.9	23.1	17.7	15.2	14.6	9.3	8.6
Slovenia	361.5	68.4	196.7	45.1	27.1	17.1	14.0	12.1	10.5
The former Yugoslav Republic of Macedonia [c]	433.6	79.2	1 083.7	454.0	105.8	11.1	3.6	2.3	3.1
Yugoslavia [c]	400.0	100.6	4 886.4	-62.5	229.6	74.1	74.5	41.7	..
Estonia [d]	..	122.2	570.3	93.3	71.3	34.6	23.8	19.7	..
Latvia	..	104.5	599.1	111.7	62.7	24.1	14.9	21.6	..
Lithuania	15.2	183.9	632.5	231.6	59.3	48.8	34.9	24.2	..
Armenia	6.0	46.9	341.1	737.3	3 345.9	203.9	78.8	31.6	..
Azerbaijan	4.4	82.9	870.4	700.8	575.7	354.8	53.0	36.8	..
Belarus	13.4	113.3	910.9	1 073.8	69.6	618.7	58.5	96.8	112.1
Georgia	6.0	33.9	457.3	2 114.7	23 327.5	87.5	145.4	12.7	..
Kazakhstan	11.0	91.5	1 056.0	1 008.6	1 422.8	178.2	30.9	22.5	..
Kyrgyzstan	0.5	62.1	638.3	745.6	176.3	54.8	29.1	60.3	-1.4
Republic of Moldova	14.2	90.1	815.0	773.0	284.4	37.1	38.7	24.9	..
Russian Federation	13.0	94.9	1 065.7	798.2	260.2	131.4	64.3	21.6	23.9
Tajikistan	8.0	76.2	550.2	917.5	142.2	139.2	418.3	85.4	..
Turkmenistan	..	83.8	1 010.1	1 467.7	622.2	686.2	915.3	121.5	25.4
Ukraine	..	107.6	1 421.7	2 296.2	747.0	403.5	107.1	17.0	..
Uzbekistan	..	82.3	706.1	1 159.3	806.8	278.4	99.8	76.3	..

Source: UN/ECE Common Database, derived from national statistics.

[a] Calculated from reported annual average wages.

[b] Gross wages in total economy. For Hungary for 1990-1992; for Slovakia for 1990-1991.

[c] Net wages in industry. For Poland and Romania for 1990-1992.

[d] Manufacturing for 1991-1993.

APPENDIX TABLE B.10

Merchandise exports of the ECE transition economies, 1980, 1986-1998

(Billion dollars)

	1980	1986	1987	1988	1989	1990	1991	1992	1993	1994	1995	1996	1997	1998
Eastern Europe	56.367	60.117	63.550	65.020	63.850	61.733	57.241	59.333	62.675	72.937	94.777	100.206	106.963	117.060*
Albania	0.320	0.230	0.230	0.230	0.302	0.231	0.101	0.072	0.123	0.139	0.202	0.213	0.141	0.190*
Bulgaria	7.160	7.599	7.841	7.554	6.651	5.232	3.433	3.992	3.769	3.935	5.345	4.890	4.914	4.298*
Czechoslovakia	10.475	12.160	12.355	12.381	11.988	10.728	11.319	..	..	..	..	..	..	..
Czech Republic	..	..	..	..	..	..	..	8.767	14.463	15.882	21.273	22.180	22.779	26.358
Slovakia	..	..	..	..	..	..	..	3.500	5.458	6.714	8.585	8.822	9.639	10.667
Hungary	8.609	9.170	9.584	9.999	9.673	9.731	10.226	10.681	8.921	10.701	12.867	15.704	19.100	23.010
Poland	13.071	13.130	14.095	14.573	14.665	18.291	14.912	13.187	14.202	17.240	22.887	24.440	25.751	26.313*
Romania	9.217	8.159	8.580	8.971	8.076	4.570	4.266	4.363	4.892	6.151	7.910	8.085	8.431	8.296*
Yugoslavia (SFR)	7.514	9.669	10.866	11.311	12.496	12.950	12.984	14.772	..	..	..	..	..	..
Bosnia and Herzegovina	..	..	..	1.550	2.100	1.850	..	..	..	..	0.024	0.058	0.109	0.171*
Croatia	..	..	..	2.300	2.600	4.020	3.310	4.353	3.709	4.260	4.633	4.512	4.171	4.541
Slovenia	1.836	2.567	2.757	3.278	3.408	4.118	3.874	6.681	6.083	6.828	8.316	8.310	8.372	9.049
The former Yugoslav Republic of Macedonia	..	..	..	..	0.654	1.113	1.095	1.199	1.055	1.086	1.204	1.147	1.180	1.310*
Yugoslavia	..	3.974	4.063	4.298	4.461	4.651	4.704	2.539	..	..	1.531	1.846	2.376	2.858
Baltic states	..	..	..	..	..	..	..	2.139	4.197	4.324	5.844	6.877	8.461	8.738
Estonia	..	..	..	..	..	..	..	0.444	0.802	1.305	1.838	2.079	2.929	3.214
Latvia	..	..	..	..	..	..	..	0.843	1.401	0.988	1.304	1.443	1.672	1.812
Lithuania	..	..	..	..	..	..	..	0.852	1.994	2.031	2.705	3.355	3.860	3.712
CIS	..	..	..	..	..	..	..	51.110	52.516	62.654	80.007	87.839	89.177	75.146*
Armenia	..	..	..	..	..	..	..	0.026	0.030	0.058	0.101	0.157	0.138	0.142
Azerbaijan	..	..	..	..	..	..	..	0.754	0.351	0.378	0.352	0.341	0.403	0.320
Belarus	..	..	..	..	..	..	1.860	1.061	0.758	1.032	1.776	1.888	1.922	1.900
Georgia	..	..	..	..	..	..	..	0.068	0.069	0.039	0.057	0.070	0.102	0.089
Kazakhstan	..	..	..	..	..	..	..	1.398	1.501	1.357	2.367	2.738	3.515	3.200
Kyrgyzstan	..	..	..	..	..	..	..	0.077	0.112	0.117	0.140	0.112	0.285	0.288
Republic of Moldova	..	..	..	..	..	..	..	0.167	0.178	0.160	0.279	0.252	0.267	0.190
Russian Federation [a]	..	..	..	..	..	..	47.266	42.376	44.297	53.001	65.607	70.975	69.954	57.700
Tajikistan	..	..	..	..	..	..	..	0.108	0.227	0.399	0.497	0.439	0.473	0.394
Turkmenistan	..	..	..	..	..	..	..	0.908	1.049	0.494	0.951	0.551	0.300	0.202*
Ukraine	..	..	..	..	..	..	..	3.297	3.223	4.653	6.168	6.995	8.643	8.200
Uzbekistan	..	..	..	..	..	..	..	0.869	0.721	0.966	1.712	3.321	3.175	2.521*
Former Soviet Union	57.942	60.043	63.406	62.016	62.286	59.056	46.660	53.733	56.713	66.978	85.851	94.716	97.638	83.884*
Total	114.310	120.161	126.957	127.035	126.136	120.788	103.901	113.066	119.389	139.915	180.628	194.922	204.602	200.944*

Source: UN/ECE secretariat, based on national statistical publications and direct communications from national statistical offices.

Note: Data exclude intra-CIS trade, but now include the "new trade" among members of other recently dissolved federal states: former Czechoslovakia (from 1993), the former SFR of Yugoslavia (from 1992), and the trade of the Baltic states with the former USSR (from 1992). Data excluding the "new trade" were shown in earlier issues of this publication. Changes in the method of recording trade are reflected from 1993 in data for the Czech Republic (inclusion of OPT transactions, etc), from 1995 in Latvia (imports registered c.i.f.) and Lithuania (change from special to general system), from 1996 in Hungary (inclusion of trade flows of free trade zones) and from 1997 in Slovakia (inclusion of OPT transactions, etc.).

All trade values for the years 1991-1998 are expressed in dollars at prevailing market exchange rates. For earlier years, values reported in national currencies were adjusted by the UN/ECE secretariat to remove distortions stemming from mutually inconsistent national rouble/dollar cross-rates in the valuation of the then important intra-CMEA trade flows. For details on the revaluation, see the note to table 2.1.3 and the discussion in box 2.1.1 in UN/ECE, *Economic Bulletin for Europe*, Vol. 43 (1991).

[a] Data not adjusted for non-registered flows. Through 1997, GosTamkom data revised by the Russian Goskomstat and include off board sales of fish and other sea products as well as natural gas deliveries under debt repayment agreements with former CMEA countries.

APPENDIX TABLE B.11

Merchandise imports of the ECE transition economies, 1980, 1986-1998

(Billion dollars)

	1980	1986	1987	1988	1989	1990	1991	1992	1993	1994	1995	1996	1997	1998
Eastern Europe	65.443	59.532	62.033	60.158	61.185	63.408	61.610	68.388	76.285	86.128	117.026	135.886	146.134	157.609*
Albania	0.320	0.230	0.230	0.280	0.385	0.381	0.409	0.524	0.421	0.549	0.650	0.913	0.620	0.780*
Bulgaria	6.321	8.679	8.222	8.131	7.325	5.584	2.700	4.530	5.120	4.272	5.638	5.074	4.886	4.838*
Czechoslovakia	10.619	10.277	12.503	12.180	11.772	11.808	10.962	..	..	..	..	..	..	..
Czech Republic	..	..	..	..	..	..	..	10.368	14.617	17.427	25.265	27.919	27.563	28.822
Slovakia	..	..	..	..	..	..	..	3.889	6.332	6.634	8.777	11.112	11.672	12.959
Hungary	9.188	9.594	9.859	9.372	8.863	8.797	11.449	11.123	12.648	14.554	15.466	18.144	21.234	25.700
Poland	14.705	12.315	12.686	12.987	12.941	12.619	15.531	16.141	18.758	21.566	29.043	37.137	42.308	47.487*
Romania	11.061	6.411	6.355	5.361	5.834	6.889	5.793	6.260	6.522	7.109	10.278	11.435	11.280	10.732*
Yugoslavia (SFR)	13.229	12.026	12.178	11.847	14.064	17.330	14.765	..	..	..	..	..	..	..
Bosnia and Herzegovina	..	..	..	1.300	1.850	1.750	..	..	..	..	0.524	1.204	1.555	1.050*
Croatia	..	..	..	2.900	3.750	5.133	3.811	4.346	4.166	5.229	7.510	7.788	9.104	8.383
Slovenia	2.463	2.740	2.722	2.914	3.216	4.727	4.131	6.141	6.501	7.304	9.492	9.421	9.358	10.098
The former Yugoslav Republic of Macedonia	..	..	..	..	0.934	1.531	1.274	1.206	1.199	1.484	1.719	1.627	1.754	1.912*
Yugoslavia	..	4.753	4.851	4.915	5.383	6.701	5.548	3.859	..	..	2.665	4.113	4.801	4.848
Baltic states	..	..	..	..	..	..	..	1.802	4.101	5.251	8.006	10.110	12.812	13.744
Estonia	..	..	..	..	..	..	..	0.406	0.896	1.659	2.540	3.231	4.444	4.759
Latvia	..	..	..	..	..	..	..	0.794	0.961	1.240	1.818	2.320	2.724	3.189
Lithuania	..	..	..	..	..	..	..	0.602	2.244	2.352	3.649	4.559	5.644	5.796
CIS	..	..	..	..	..	..	..	42.203	33.354	36.745	45.680	49.670	57.977	50.259*
Armenia	..	..	..	..	..	..	..	0.050	0.086	0.188	0.340	0.568	0.593	0.675
Azerbaijan	..	..	..	..	..	..	..	0.333	0.241	0.292	0.439	0.621	0.443	0.660
Belarus	..	..	..	..	..	..	..	0.751	0.779	0.975	1.887	2.369	2.872	3.000
Georgia	..	..	..	..	..	..	..	0.227	0.167	0.065	0.233	0.416	0.600	0.680
Kazakhstan	..	..	..	..	..	..	..	0.469	0.494	1.384	1.154	1.296	1.969	2.200
Kyrgyzstan	..	..	..	..	..	..	..	0.071	0.112	0.108	0.169	0.351	0.274	0.393
Republic of Moldova	..	..	..	..	..	..	..	0.179	0.184	0.183	0.272	0.420	0.567	0.600
Russian Federation [a]	..	..	..	..	..	..	39.294	36.984	26.807	28.344	33.117	32.798	39.363	32.400
Tajikistan	..	..	..	..	..	..	..	0.132	0.374	0.314	0.332	0.286	0.268	0.265
Turkmenistan	..	..	..	..	..	..	..	0.030	0.501	0.782	0.619	0.924	0.531	0.471*
Ukraine	..	..	..	..	..	..	..	2.049	2.651	2.908	5.488	6.427	7.242	6.600
Uzbekistan	..	..	..	..	..	..	..	0.929	0.958	1.202	1.630	3.195	3.255	2.315*
Former Soviet Union	52.218	55.016	53.794	58.044	64.983	64.963	45.405	44.166	37.455	41.997	53.686	59.780	70.788	64.003*
Total	117.661	114.548	115.827	118.202	126.168	128.371	106.901	112.554	113.740	128.124	170.712	195.667	216.923	221.612*

Source: UN/ECE secretariat, based on national statistical publications and direct communications from national statistical offices.

Note: See appendix table B.10.

a Data not adjusted for non-registered flows. Through 1997, GosTamkom data revised by the Russian Goskomstat and include off board sales of fish and other sea products as well as natural gas deliveries under debt repayment agreements with former CMEA countries.

APPENDIX TABLE B.12

Balance of merchandise trade of the ECE transition economies, 1980, 1986-1998

(Billion dollars)

	1980	1986	1987	1988	1989	1990	1991	1992	1993	1994	1995	1996	1997	1998
Eastern Europe	-9.076	0.585	1.517	4.861	2.665	-1.675	-4.369	-9.055	-13.610	-13.190	-22.250	-35.681	-39.171	-40.548*
Albania	–	–	–	-0.050	-0.083	-0.150	-0.308	-0.452	-0.298	-0.410	-0.448	-0.701	-0.479	-0.590*
Bulgaria	0.839	-1.080	-0.381	-0.577	-0.674	-0.352	0.732	-0.538	-1.352	-0.336	-0.293	-0.184	0.028	-0.540*
Czechoslovakia	-0.144	1.882	-0.147	0.201	0.216	-1.080	0.356	..	..	..	..	..	..	..
Czech Republic	..	..	..	..	..	..	..	-1.601		-0.154	-1.545	-3.992	-5.739	-4.784	-2.464
Slovakia	..	..	..	..	..	..	..	-0.389	-0.874	0.080	-0.192	-2.290		-2.033	-2.292
Hungary	-0.579	-0.423	-0.276	0.627	0.810	0.934	-1.223	-0.442	-3.727	-3.853	-2.599		-2.440	-2.134	-2.690
Poland	-1.634	0.815	1.409	1.586	1.724	5.672	-0.619	-2.955	-4.555	-4.326	-6.156	-12.697	-16.556	-21.174*
Romania	-1.844	1.748	2.225	3.610	2.242	-2.320	-1.528	-1.897	-1.630	-0.958	-2.368	-3.351	-2.849	-2.436*
Yugoslavia (SFR)	-5.715	-2.357	-1.312	-0.536	-1.568	-4.380	-1.780	14.772	..	..	..	..	..	..
Bosnia and Herzegovina	..	..	..	0.250	0.250	0.100	..	..	..	..	-0.500	-1.146	-1.446	-0.879*
Croatia	..	..	..	-0.600	-1.150	-1.113	-0.501	0.007	-0.457	-0.969	-2.877	-3.276	-4.933	-3.842
Slovenia	-0.626	-0.173	0.035	0.365	0.192	-0.609	-0.257	0.540	-0.418	-0.476	-1.176	-1.111	-0.986	-1.049
The former Yugoslav Republic of Macedonia	..	..	..	..	-0.280	-0.418	-0.179	-0.007	-0.144	-0.398	-0.515	-0.480	-0.574	-0.602*
Yugoslavia	..	-0.779	-0.788	-0.617	-0.922	-2.050	-0.844	-1.320	..	..	-1.134	-2.267	-2.425	-1.990
Baltic states	..	..	..	..	..	..	..	0.337	0.096	-0.927	-2.162	-3.232	-4.350	-5.006
Estonia	..	..	..	..	..	..	..	0.038	-0.094	-0.353	-0.702	-1.152	-1.515	-1.545
Latvia	..	..	..	..	..	..	..	0.049	0.440	-0.252		-0.514	-0.877	-1.052	-1.377
Lithuania	..	..	..	..	..	..	..	0.250	-0.250	-0.322		-0.944	-1.204	-1.784	-2.084
CIS	..	..	..	..	..	..	..	8.907	19.163	25.909	34.328	38.168	31.200	24.887*
Armenia	..	..	..	..	..	..	..	-0.024	-0.056	-0.130	-0.239	-0.411	-0.456	-0.533
Azerbaijan	..	..	..	..	..	..	..	0.422	0.110	0.086	-0.087	-0.280	-0.040	-0.340
Belarus	..	..	..	..	..	..	1.860	0.310	-0.021	0.057	-0.111	-0.481	-0.950	-1.100
Georgia	..	..	..	..	..	..	..	-0.159	-0.098	-0.026	-0.176	-0.346	-0.498	-0.591
Kazakhstan	..	..	..	..	..	..	..	0.930	1.007	-0.027	1.213	1.442	1.547	1.000
Kyrgyzstan	..	..	..	..	..	..	..	0.006	–	0.009	-0.029	-0.239	0.011	-0.105
Republic of Moldova	..	..	..	..	..	..	..	-0.012	-0.006	-0.023	0.007	-0.168	-0.300	-0.410
Russian Federation [a]	..	..	..	..	..	..	7.972	5.392	17.491	24.657	32.490	38.177	30.591	25.300
Tajikistan	..	..	..	..	..	..	..	-0.024	-0.147	0.086	0.165	0.154	0.205	0.129
Turkmenistan	..	..	..	..	..	..	..	0.879	0.548	-0.288	0.332	-0.374	-0.231	-0.269*
Ukraine	..	..	..	..	..	..	..	1.248	0.572	1.745	0.680	0.568	1.401	1.600
Uzbekistan	..	..	..	..	..	..	..	-0.060	-0.237	-0.236	0.082	0.126	-0.080	0.206*
Former Soviet Union	5.724	5.027	9.612	3.972	-2.697	-5.907	1.255	9.567	19.259	24.982	32.165	34.936	26.850	19.881*
Total	-3.351	5.613	11.130	8.833	-0.032	-7.583	-3.000	0.512	5.649	11.791	9.916	-0.745	-12.321	-20.667*

Source: UN/ECE secretariat, based on national statistical publications and direct communications from national statistical offices.

Note: See appendix table B.10.

[a] Data not adjusted for non-registered flows. Through 1997, GosTamkom data revised by the Russian Goskomstat and include off board sales of fish and other sea products as well as natural gas deliveries under debt repayment agreements with former CMEA countries.

APPENDIX TABLE B.13

Merchandise trade of the ECE transition economies by direction, 1980, 1986-1998

(Shares in total trade, per cent)

	1980	1986	1987	1988	1989	1990	1991	1992	1993	1994	1995	1996	1997	1998[a]
Eastern Europe, *to and from:*														
Exports														
World	100.0	100.0	100.0	100.0	100.0	100.0	100.0	100.0	100.0	100.0	100.0	100.0	100.0	100.0
ECE transition economies	48.5	52.5	50.2	46.5	44.4	38.1	28.5	23.0	28.2	26.3	25.8	26.1	26.0	23.6
Former Soviet Union	27.1	31.0	29.7	27.2	25.5	22.3	17.9	12.4	9.8	9.0	8.9	9.4	10.4	8.5
Eastern Europe	21.4	21.5	20.5	19.3	18.9	15.8	10.7	10.7	18.5	17.4	16.9	16.7	15.6	15.1
Developed market economies	35.7	32.3	35.2	38.7	42.6	49.5	59.8	63.0	58.0	62.5	64.5	65.0	66.3	70.5
Developing economies	15.8	15.2	14.6	14.8	13.0	12.4	11.7	14.0	13.8	11.2	9.7	8.9	7.7	5.9
Imports														
World	100.0	100.0	100.0	100.0	100.0	100.0	100.0	100.0	100.0	100.0	100.0	100.0	100.0	100.0
ECE transition economies	42.0	50.3	45.6	40.5	36.4	26.6	25.5	24.7	29.3	26.1	25.3	23.8	22.2	19.7
Former Soviet Union	26.8	34.5	30.7	26.3	23.5	18.3	20.2	17.9	16.5	14.1	13.2	12.7	11.4	19.7
Eastern Europe	18.8	21.2	20.5	19.6	18.7	14.3	8.1	6.8	12.8	12.0	12.1	11.1	10.8	8.9
Developed market economies	38.7	32.3	36.1	41.1	44.0	53.3	58.3	64.4	61.5	65.0	65.8	66.6	68.0	70.4
Developing economies	19.3	17.4	18.3	18.4	19.5	20.1	16.1	10.9	9.2	9.0	8.9	9.6	9.8	9.8
Former Soviet Union/Russian Federation, *to and from:*														
Exports														
World	100.0	100.0	100.0	100.0	100.0	100.0	100.0	100.0	100.0	100.0	100.0	100.0	100.0	100.0
ECE transition economies	34.5	38.5	33.5	29.4	26.6	21.8	25.9	22.3	18.1	15.1	16.8	18.2	19.5	18.7
Eastern Europe	34.5	38.5	33.5	29.4	26.6	21.8	25.9	20.7	16.8	11.7	13.2	14.3	14.9	14.8
Developed market economies	42.2	31.0	35.3	38.9	41.8	49.5	56.5	57.9	59.7	66.6	60.6	58.1	58.6	59.9
Developing economies	23.3	30.5	31.2	31.7	31.6	28.7	17.6	19.9	22.2	18.3	22.6	23.8	21.9	21.4
Imports														
World	100.0	100.0	100.0	100.0	100.0	100.0	100.0	100.0	100.0	100.0	100.0	100.0	100.0	100.0
ECE transition economies	31.5	38.6	38.2	32.4	27.6	24.7	26.0	15.9	10.6	14.1	15.5	12.6	13.7	12.6
Eastern Europe	31.5	38.6	38.2	32.4	27.6	24.7	26.0	15.0	10.0	11.7	12.4	10.6	11.1	10.4
Developed market economies	46.4	40.9	40.7	46.3	50.1	52.9	58.1	62.4	60.6	70.3	69.5	67.8	68.2	67.5
Developing economies	22.1	20.5	21.1	21.3	22.3	22.4	15.9	21.7	28.8	15.6	15.0	19.6	18.1	19.9

Source: UN/ECE Common Database, derived from national statistics.

Note: Data for 1980-1990 refer to the east European CMEA countries (Bulgaria, Czechoslovakia, German Democratic Republic, Hungary, Poland and Romania) and to the former Soviet Union. Trade data in national currencies were revalued at consistent rouble/dollar cross-rates (see the note to appendix table B.10). For 1991-1997, eastern Europe covers Bulgaria, former Czechoslovakia (from 1993, Czech Republic and Slovakia including their mutual trade), Hungary, Poland and Romania, and the second panel reflects non-CIS trade of the Russian Federation only.

Partner-country grouping has been recently revised with subsequent revisions back to 1980. Thus, the earlier reported "Transition economies" group is now replaced by "ECE transition economies", which covers the Baltic states, CIS and the east European countries including the successor states of the former SFR of Yugoslavia. The "Eastern Europe" partner-group now covers Albania, Bulgaria, the Czech Republic, Hungary, Poland, Romania, Slovakia and the successor states of the former SFR of Yugoslavia, which earlier were in the "Other socialist countries" subgroup. The rest of subgroup "Other socialist countries", which in previous series covered China, Cuba, Democratic People's Republic of Korea, Mongolia and Viet Nam, is now included in the "Developing countries" group.

a January-September.

APPENDIX TABLE B.14

Exchange rates of the ECE transition economies, 1980, 1986-1998

(Annual averages, national currency units per dollar)

	Unit [a]	1980	1986	1987	1988	1989	1990	1991	1992	1993	1994	1995	1996	1997	1998
Albania	lek	..	..	..	..	..	8.90	24.20	75.03	102.06	94.62	93.14	104.33	148.93	150.63
Bulgaria	lev	0.86	0.94	0.87	0.83	0.84	0.79	17.45	23.42	27.85	54.13	67.08	177.88	1 681.87	1 760.37
Czechoslovakia	koruna	5.37	16.20	14.79	14.37	15.06	18.56	29.56	28.30	..	..	..	..	..	..
Czech Republic	koruna	..	..	..	..	..	..	..	..	29.15	28.79	26.54	27.14	31.70	32.29
Slovakia	koruna	..	..	..	..	..	..	..	..	30.80	31.93	29.71	30.68	33.62	35.15
Hungary	forint	32.64	45.83	46.97	50.41	59.07	63.21	74.73	78.98	91.91	105.11	125.69	152.65	186.79	214.40
Poland	zloty [b]	3.05	175.28	265.08	430.64	1 439	9 500	10 576	13 627	18 136	22 723	2.42	2.70	3.28	3.49
Romania	leu	4.47	16.80	16.00	16.00	16.00	22.43	71.84	307.98	760.12	1 654	2 033	3 085	7 183	8 876
Yugoslavia (SFR)	dinar [c]	24.64	379.22	737.00	25 239	28 760	11.32	19.64	..	..	..	..	..	..	..
Bosnia and Herzegovina	dinar	..	..	..	..	..	..	..	..	..	..	..	..	..	..
Croatia	kuna [d]	..	..	..	..	..	..	18.80	264.30	3 577.63	6.00	5.23	5.43	6.10	6.36
Slovenia	tolar	..	..	..	..	..	..	27.57	81.29	113.24	128.81	118.52	135.37	159.69	166.13
The former Yugoslav Republic of Macedonia	denar [e]	..	..	..	..	..	..	19.69	508.07	23.26	43.25	38.05	39.92	50.40	54.48
Yugoslavia	dinar [f]	..	..	..	..	..	..	19.64	508.07	..	..	4.74	4.96	5.72	5.99
Estonia	kroon [g]	..	..	..	..	..	..	..	12.11	13.22	12.98	11.46	12.03	13.88	14.08
Latvia	lats [h]	..	..	..	..	..	..	..	..	0.67	0.56	0.53	0.55	0.58	0.59
Lithuania	litas [i]	..	..	..	..	..	..	..	..	4.37	3.98	4.00	4.00	4.00	4.00
Armenia	dram	..	..	..	..	..	..	..	..	8.66	288.35	405.93	413.47	490.70	504.86
Azerbaijan	manat	..	..	..	..	..	..	..	..	..	1 169	4 417	4 295	3 987	3 869
Belarus	rouble [j]	..	..	..	..	..	..	..	..	2177	4 017	11 538	13 472	26 729	48 650
Georgia	lari [k]	..	..	..	..	..	..	..	..	..	1.10	1.29	1.26	1.30	1.39
Kazakhstan	tenge	..	..	..	..	..	..	..	..	..	35.54	60.95	67.30	75.43	78.26
Kyrgyzstan	som	..	..	..	..	..	..	..	..	..	10.86	10.83	12.81	17.37	21.37
Republic of Moldova	leu	..	..	..	..	..	..	..	..	..	4.07	4.50	4.60	4.62	5.36
Russian Federation	rouble [l]	0.65	0.70	0.63	0.61	0.63	0.59	1.74	192.75	927.46	2204	4 559	5 121	5 785	9.71
Tajikistan	rouble	..	..	..	..	..	..	..	..	..	..	107.59	292.89	560.64	778.30
Turkmenistan	manat	..	..	..	..	..	..	..	..	..	19.50	110.42	3 509	4 143	4 941
Ukraine	hryvnia [m]	..	..	..	..	..	..	..	..	4 796	31 700	147 314	1.83	1.86	2.51
Uzbekistan	sum [n]	..	..	..	..	..	..	..	..	932.15	9.96	29.81	40.15	66.43	94.79
Memorandum item:															
Former GDR	mark [o]	3.30	8.14	8.14	8.14	8.14	8.14	1.66	1.56	1.65	1.62	1.43	1.50	1.73	1.76

Source: UN/ECE Common Database, derived from national, IMF and CIS statistics. Annual averages are unweighted arithmetic averages of monthly values. Change or redenomination of currency is indicated by a vertical bar.

Note: Under the central planning system with its state foreign trade monopoly, exchange rates served primarily statistical and accounting purposes (notably the conversion of foreign trade values for statistics expressed in domestic currency), without direct impact on domestic price formation. Market-based exchange rates and a meaningful link to domestic currency values emerged only with the transformations from 1989 onward. The official exchange rates of the earlier period are therefore not suitable for the conversion to dollars of macroeconomic and other data of these countries expressed in domestic currency. These strictures should be kept in mind in the interpretation and use of the data for the 1980s shown above.

[a] Currency unit of the last period shown. For prior periods, see footnotes.

[b] The zloty was redenominated at 1:10,000 from 1 January 1995.

[c] The dinar was redenominated at 1:10,000 from 1 January 1990.

[d] The kuna replaced the Croat dinar on 3 May 1994 at 1:1,000; the 1994 average is shown in kuna terms.

[e] The denar (which had replaced the Yugoslav dinar 1:1 on 26 April 1992) was redenominated 1:100 on 1 May 1993; the 1993 average is shown in terms of that unit.

[f] The dinar was further redenominated on 1 July 1992 (1:10), 1 October 1993 (1:1 million), 1 January 1994 (1:1 trillion) and 24 January 1994 (1:13 million). Average annual exchange rates not available for 1993-1994.

[g] The kroon replaced the Soviet rouble in June 1992 with a peg to the deutsche mark (8:1); the average shown for 1992 refers to June-December.

[h] The lats replaced an earlier Latvian rouble at 1:200 on 18 October 1993; the 1993 average is shown in lat terms.

[i] The litas replaced the earlier talonas at 1:100 on 1 June 1993; the 1993 average is shown in litas terms.

[j] The Belarus rouble was redenominated 1:10 on 10 August 1994; the 1994 average here assumes this applied to the entire year. Annual averages were calculated from end-of-period monthly rates.

[k] The lari replaced the lari-kupon on 25 September 1995; the annual average for 1994 is shown in million lari-kupon, and that for 1995 in lari.

[l] 1980-1991: Soviet rouble/dollar rate used in the conversion of foreign trade data for statistical purposes. The rouble was redenominated at 1:1,000 from 1 January 1998.

[m] The hryvnia replaced the former karbovanets on 2 September 1996 at 1:100,000; the average for 1996 is shown in hryvnia terms.

[n] Sum-kupon in 1993.

[o] German Democratic Republic mark through 1990, deutsche mark thereafter.

APPENDIX TABLE B.15

Current account balances of the ECE transition economies, 1990-1998
(Million dollars)

	1990	1991	1992	1993	1994	1995	1996	1997	1998 [a]
Eastern Europe	-3 914	-2 502	-862	-7 338	-4 197	-1 090	-13 189	-14 662	-16 974
Albania	-118	-168	-51	15	-43	-15	-107	-271	-50*
Bulgaria	-1 710	-77	-360	-1 098	-25	-26	16	427	-273
Croatia [b c]	-500	-589	329	600	786	-1 284	-858	-2 434	-1 554
Czech Republic	-122	1 709	-456	456	-787	-1 369	-4 292	-3 211	-800*
Hungary [d]	127	267	324	-3 455	-3 911	-2 480	-1 678	-981	-2 298
Poland [d e]	716	-1 359	-269	-2 329	-944	5 455	-1 352	-4 268	-6 810
Romania [d]	-1 650	-1 369	-1 460	-1 174	-428	-1 774	-2 571	-2 338	-2 633
Slovakia	-767	-786	173	-559	712	646	-2 098	-1 347	-2 300*
Slovenia [b]	518	129	926	192	600	-23	39	37	-6
The former Yugoslav Republic of Macedonia	-409	-259	-19	15	-158	-222	-288	-275	-250*
Baltic states	..	..	681	371	-71	-816	-1 425	-1 889	-1 854
Estonia	..	..	153	40	-178	-185	-423	-563	-370
Latvia	..	..	207	417	201	-16	-279	-345	-456
Lithuania	..	..	322	-86	-94	-614	-723	-981	-1 028
CIS	-6 608	2 947	-4 881	1 360	6 977	4 421	6 522	-2 914	-11 366
Armenia	..	..	..	-67	-106	-279	-291	-305	-297*
Azerbaijan	..	..	..	..	-121	-401	-931	-916	-945*
Belarus	..	..	131	-404	-506	-567	-516	-799	-797
Georgia	..	..	..	..	-278	-218	-277	-347	-258*
Kazakhstan	..	..	..	..	..	-518	-750	-912	-689
Kyrgyzstan	..	..	..	-88	-84	-235	-425	-138	-228
Republic of Moldova	..	..	..	-155	-82	-95	-188	-267	-280
Russian Federation [f]	-6 300	2 500	-5 700	2 700	9 284	7 938	12 096	3 335	-5 625
Tajikistan	..	..	..	-208	-170	-54	-74	-50	-45*
Turkmenistan	-308	447	926	776	84	24	43	-596	-525*
Ukraine	..	..	..	-765	-1 163	-1 152	-1 185	-1 335	-1 310
Uzbekistan	..	..	-238	-429	119	-21	-980	-584	-368*
Total	-10 522	445	-5 062	-5 606	2 709	2 515	-8 093	-19 466	..

Source: National balance of payments statistics; IMF for Tajikistan, Turkmenistan and Uzbekistan.

[a] Full year except for Baltic states and CIS which are January-September.

[b] Excludes transactions with the republics of the former SFR of Yugoslavia: Croatia (1990-1992), Slovenia (1990-1991) and The former Yugoslav Republic of Macedonia (1990-1992).

[c] Data for 1993-1997 were revised in 1998 according to a new methodology.

[d] Convertible currencies. Hungary until 1995; Romania until 1992 and Poland until 1997.

[e] As of 1995 the current account of Poland includes non-classified current account transactions. Excluding this item the current account balance was a $2,299 million deficit in 1995.

[f] 1990-1993 excluding transactions with the Baltic and CIS countries.

APPENDIX TABLE B.16

Inflows of foreign direct investment [a] in selected ECE transition economies, 1990-1998
(Million dollars)

	1990	1991	1992	1993	1994	1995	1996	1997	1998 [b]
Eastern Europe	605	2 329	3 120	4 107	3 491	9 172	7 577	9 116	13 155
Albania [c]	–	–	20	58	53	70	90	48	36
Bulgaria [c]	4	56	42	40	105	90	109	505	141
Croatia	–	–	16	96	113	101	533	388	854
Czech Republic	180	513	1 004	654	869	2 562	1 428	1 300	1 617
Hungary	311	1 459	1 471	2 339	1 146	4 453	1 983	2 085	1 935
Poland [c]	88	117	284	580	542	1 134	2 768	3 077	6 326
Romania	–	37	73	94	341	419	263	1 215	1 598
Slovakia	18	82	100	134	170	157	206	161	401
Slovenia	4	65	111	113	128	176	186	321	165
The former Yugoslav Republic of Macedonia [c]	–	–	–	–	24	9	11	16	83
Baltic states	–	–	111	236	471	457	684	1 142	1 828
Estonia	–	–	58	160	225	205	150	267	485
Latvia	–	–	43	45	214	180	382	521	286
Lithuania	–	–	10	30	31	73	152	355	1 057
European CIS	–	100	1 678	1 626	820	2 365	3 096	7 128	2 939
Belarus	–	–	7	10	9	15	73	192	118
Republic of Moldova	–	–	17	14	12	67	24	72	69
Russian Federation [c]	–	100	1 454	1 404	640	2 016	2 479	6 241	1 977
Ukraine	–	–	200	198	159	267	521	623	775
Total	605	2 429	4 909	5 969	4 782	11 994	11 358	17 386	17 922

Source: National balance of payments statistics; IMF for Tajikistan, Turkmenistan and Uzbekistan.

[a] Inflows into the reporting country.

[b] Full year data except for Albania, the Czech Republic, Slovakia, The former Yugoslav Republic of Macedonia, the Baltic states and the European CIS for which extrapolations of January-September rates were used.

[c] Net of residents' investments abroad. Bulgaria, 1990-1994; Poland, 1990-1995; and Russian Federation, 1990-1992.

OTHER RECENT PUBLICATIONS IN ECONOMIC ANALYSIS FROM
THE UNITED NATIONS ECONOMIC COMMISSION FOR EUROPE

- *Economic Survey of Europe, 1998 No. 3*, Sales No. E.98.II.E.25 (November)

  This issue brings the survey of economic developments in the ECE region up to November 1998 and pays special attention to the aftermath of the Russian crisis, both in Russia itself and in other transition economies. A special study looks at the difficulties of reaching production sharing agreements in Russia while emphasizing their potential role in attracting foreign investment in the country.

- *Economic Survey of Europe, 1998 No. 2,* Sales No. E.98.II.E.18 (July)

  This issue contains in Part One an overview of the economic situation and outlook in the ECE region at mid-year and, *inter alia*, discusses the emergence of financial declines in Russia prior to the August crisis. Part Two contains a selection of papers presented to the UN/ECE Spring Seminar in April 1998 which was devoted to the problems of restructuring the banking and enterprise sectors of the transition economies.

- *Economic Survey of Europe, 1998 No. 1,* Sales No. E.98.II.E.1 (April)

  This publication contains an extensive review of economic developments over the previous year and the outlook for 1998 in western Europe and North America, central and eastern Europe, Russia and the other members of the CIS; the implications of the Asian crisis are discussed at length with special emphasis on the transition economies; also included is a special study of economic developments in the three Caucasian economies from 1991 to 1997; and finally, a large number of statistical tables including an appendix with historical time series.

- International Migration in Central and Eastern Europe and the Commonwealth of Independent States, *Economic Studies No. 8*, Sales No. GV.E.96.0.22

  An analysis of international migration within and from central and eastern Europe and the CIS. An overview of the migration flows and issues is followed by 11 country studies plus one on the countries of the former Soviet Union.

- The Role of Agriculture in the Transition Process Towards a Market Economy, *Economic Studies No. 9*, Sales No. GV.E.97.0.12

  Proceedings of a Symposium conducted in association with the Südost Institute, Munich, and the Thyssen Foundation. Eleven case studies by national experts of agricultural adjustment in eastern Europe, the CIS and China, plus a comparative overview in an analytical framework and a summary of the discussions.

* * * * *

More details about other publications and activities of the United Nations Economic Commission for Europe, which pay special attention to issues concerning the transition economies, can be found at the secretariat's website: http://www.unece.org

* * * * *

To obtain copies of publications contact:

Publications des Nations Unies
Section de Vente et Marketing
Organisation des Nations Unies
CH-1211 Genève 10
Suisse

Tele: (4122) 917 2612 / 917 2606 / 917 2613
Fax: (4122) 917 0027
E-mail: unpubli@unog.ch

United Nations Publications
2 United Nations Plaza
Room DC2-853
New York, NY 10017
USA

Tele: (1212) 963 8302 / (1800) 253 9646
Fax: (1212) 963 3489
E-mail: publications@un.org